PUBLIC BUDGETING AND FINANCE

PUBLIC ADMINISTRATION AND PUBLIC POLICY

A Comprehensive Publication Program

Executive Editor

JACK RABIN

Graduate Program for Administrators

Rider College

Lawrenceville, New Jersey

Other volumes in preparation

PUBLIC BUDGETING AND FINANCE

BEHAVIORAL, THEORETICAL, AND
TECHNICAL PERSPECTIVES

Revised and Expanded Third Edition

Edited by

ROBERT T. GOLEMBIEWSKI
University of Georgia
Athens, Georgia

JACK RABIN
Rider College
Lawrenceville, New Jersey

MARCEL DEKKER, INC.   New York and Basel

350.722
P96

Library of Congress Cataloging in Publication Data

Main entry under title:

Public budgeting and finance.

(Public administration and public policy)
Includes index.
1. Budget—United States—Addresses, essays, lectures.
2. Budget—Addresses, essays, lectures. I. Golembiewski,
Robert T. II. Rabin, Jack, [date]. III. Series.
HJ2051.P795   1982   350.72'2   83-1826
ISBN 0-8247-1668-X

MARCEL DEKKER, INC.
270 Madison Avenue, New York, New York 10016

Current printing (last digit):
10 9 8 7 6 5 4 3 2 1

PRINTED IN THE UNITED STATES OF AMERICA

PREFACE TO THE THIRD EDITION

The 13 years intervening between this edition and its first predecessor make this series seem a very good prophet indeed. Work in public administration has burgeoned; no other area has experienced more need for teaching/learning resources than public budgeting and finance. All three editions rest on those two basic propositions, and this edition does so even more than the others.

This Third Edition also seeks to change with the times in at least four significant ways. First and paramount, this edition does not have to do the job that faced the First Edition. Fortunately so. An almost total lack of teaching/learning resources characterized those early days—few texts, no readers, no workbooks. Today those elemental deficiencies no longer exist.

So this Third Edition need not be—indeed, cannot be—that which the times required of the First Edition. What did those times require? The First Edition sought to be all and do all, for all users, and unattractive challenges, failures, and egregious compromises could not be avoided.

The Third Edition can count on other resources—especially the now numerous introductory texts—as a takeoff point. Those sources do many things well. Thus, they describe the various institutions relevant in budgetary processes, such sources document well historical changes in concepts of budgeting and approaches to it. They also tend to do an especially thorough job—even verging on overkill, at times

—of sensitizing their readers to the political nature of budgetary processes, and so on. These constitute valuable components toward a reasonable working knowledge of public budgeting and finance.

Second, given these new riches, important questions come to mind. What remains undone for this Third Edition? And why not simply allow the Second Edition to go quietly out of print? Well, plenty still needs to be done. Specifically, the Third Edition seeks to complement and reinforce the available resources in three broad areas:

- *Behavioral,* via a focus on how and why individuals or groups respond in budgeting and financial settings;

- *Theoretical,* by enriching the operating models relevant to budgeting and finance, so that readers will have better "handles" for describing reality and can work toward more specific predictions about what is likely to happen under specific circumstances; and,

- *Technical,* by emphasis on both systemic and subsystemic approaches to the "how to" of budgeting and finance.

In this sense, then, this Third Edition is at once much less *broad* than its predecessors and yet very much *deeper.*

How do the other available teaching/learning resources fare in these three critical areas? Judgments will vary concerning one resource or another. However, approximate judgments safely can be made. Let us summarize.

- On *behavioral* materials, the other resources typically do little, sometimes even nothing.

- On *theoretical* materials, the record is better, but only a little, except for selected foci such as "incrementalism," concerning which we have talk, in general, and too much of it.

- On *technical* materials, the other resources no doubt provide the best coverage of the three broad areas considered here, but that "best" typically still falls far short of what is practically necessary, not to mention ideally desirable.

Third, over 75 percent of the selections reprinted here were published after the publication date carried by the Second Edition. That obviously reflects a major change in the contents of successive editions.

Fourth, this Third Edition seeks to preserve a substantial sense of the introductory sections of earlier editions. Readers of earlier editions seemed to profit from those introductions. Despite major changes in their substance, the present introductory notes retain much of the flavor of their predecessors.

Let us make one final note. Again, special thanks go to Mrs. Sandra Daniel who contributed much of the detailed work on which this volume rests.

Robert T. Golembiewski
Jack Rabin

CONTENTS

I

SOME CONCEPTUAL CONTEXTS: What Is "It?" How Does "It" Get Done?

Public budgeting and finance patently encompass a wide range of phenomena, the breadth and diversity of which can only be suggested here. However inadequate the attempt must be, we cannot avoid trying to indicate in conceptual (theoretical) terms part of what is meant by the term "public finance and budgeting." The two focal questions in this attempt are: What is it? How do we do what is required? The perspective here is intentionally broad. Subsequent chapters will add much detail.

TWO INTRODUCTORY PERSPECTIVES

The "what" of public budgeting and finance can be given some initial content by focusing in two ways on the possible uses of financial data. First, consider budgets as an instrument of control as well as a plan of action. Stedry provides a useful discussion in a piece not reprinted here (1). He focuses on "standards" and "standard costs" because to "plan" and "control" requires an estimate of how much of which resources are required for specific objectives. Thus budgets require commitment to some total figure as well as to their component standards. Standards or standard costs imply what can be generated for a certain sum of dollars in a certain period of time. For example, a department in a university may have a large budget for salaries, but if the faculty-to-student ratio is also low, this implies a standard that many professors may find unattractive even though their salaries are quite pleasing.

Directly, budgeting and finance must motivate individuals to strive to meet a total budget as well as induce them to accept its component standards. Even such brief allusions establish that the "what" of public budgeting and finance encompasses many phenomena at the heart of the management of people and the coordination of cooperative behavior. Only a little interpretation will make the matter clearer. The "plan" aspects of budgeting and finance require that their processes lean toward the future and embody some sense of things as they might be improved or even as they would be at their best. The plan, however, cannot command total attention. The "control" aspects imply that the processes of public budgeting and finance also must rest on a strong sense of things as they are or even as they might be at their worst. Avoiding the worst while attempting to permit the best—this is a human challenge of heroic dimensions. Precisely this challenge rests at the heart of public budgeting and finance.

Second, from a related perspective, Simon and his associates (2) provide useful introductory conceptual detail about the "what" of public budgeting by classifying the ways in which management uses figures. Basically, they argue that three types of questions must be considered by any comprehensive program of the "internal reporting" of financial data. According to Simon, these three types of questions are (1) *score card questions,* i.e., questions such as, "Am I doing well or badly?" (2) *attention-directing questions,* such as, "What problems should I look into?" and (3) *problem-solving questions,* or questions such as, "Of the several ways of doing the job, which is the best?" These questions relate to both the planning and control aspects of financial reporting stressed by Stedry.

In their own way, the three types of questions isolated by Simon and his collaborators sharply indicate the centrality of the phenomena associated with public budgeting and finance. Score card questions patently must play a crucial role in every organization, i.e., organizations have as their basic purpose the effective utilization of resources. "Are we doing well or badly?" consequently must be of central organizational concern. Providing appropriate answers to score card questions is, however, not the only central need. Perhaps more important, the processes of providing those answers are very delicate ones indeed. Directly, budgeting and finance personnel could easily come to be seen as punitive because of their basic and traditional role. These personnel provide answers to score card questions, and thereby enable top management to control those at lower levels. This policing role can make life difficult for budgeting and finance personnel.

Hence the importance of giving extensive and successful attention to attention-directing questions and problem-solving questions. At least three features contribute to this importance and answers to these two types of questions can be helpful at many levels of organization. In providing such answers, and particularly in providing them directly to lower levels of organization, finance and budgeting officials can help compensate for the punitiveness inherent in some of their other activities, such as providing answers to score card questions.

Financial and budgeting officials apparently are less active in seeking answers to the latter two types of questions, particularly problem-solving questions. No doubt the traditional concern with score card questions helps explain this common inactivity, implying as it does that internal financial reporters are less equipped and motivated to handle the other types of questions. In addition, answering problem-solving questions requires working closely with officials at all levels, while budgeting and finance personnel typically identify more closely with top management. Finally, officials at various management levels who had been disciplined via answers to score card questions would be reticent to accept or ask for help, because to do so risks providing "inside information" to budgeting and finance officials, which in turn might be used against the manager. That is, budgeting and finance officials can be seen to play this game with others: "Tell me enough about your operations so that I can determine whether or not we should fire you." Such a perception seems well designed to elicit caution, if not absolute silence! An emphasis on attention-directing and problem-solving questions can help counterbalance this punitiveness.

The three types of questions involving financial data highlight the breadth and diversity of public budgeting and finance. That significance extends from providing data about the effectiveness of performance all the way to providing yardstick data in helpful and humane ways that motivate those at multiple levels of organization.

INTRODUCING FIVE DETAILED PERSPECTIVES

These brief orienting comments receive detailed and variegated elaboration in this volume, specifically from five selections reprinted below that are introduced here. These selections add rich conceptual and theoretical detail to the "what" of public budgeting and finance. In summary, all of us interested in public budgeting or finance must "sink or swim" in terms of the concepts or theories we carry in our heads.

That is, weak concepts and theories lead to halting and ineffective applications. And the five selections below seek to enhance or enrich the concepts or theories in the minds of readers. The selections sharpen insight as well as increase the comprehensiveness of concepts and theories underlying public budgeting and finance in these five crucial and related particulars:

- By detailing the manifold forms in which the "budget idea" developed and then spread, with its leading orientations being at once a lifeline and a tether for today's students and practitioners

- By acknowledging the several dysfunctions associated with budgeting and finance, as well as specifying ways and means concerning how those dysfunctions might be alleviated

- By enlarging the theoretical base of what may be called "management accounting" to build a more comprehensive and useful model of the relevant world from which helpful predictions may be made

- By questioning the adequacy of macrolevel models of budgeting and financial behavior, about which the quantity of thought far surpasses the quality

- By specifying the features of the various environmental contexts within which budgeting and finance activities take place, again for the purpose of increasing the comprehensiveness of our working models so as to enlarge understanding

The Spread of the "Budget Idea"

Edward A. Lehan sketches the historical context out of which modern practices evolved in his "Public Budgeting." From one engaging perspective, Lehan sees public budgeting as having moved along this continuum: from a basic responsibility-oriented concept to a goal-fulfilling orientation. The latter is far more demanding than the former, patently. For example, a responsibility-oriented concept basically asks only this kind of question: Was an expenditure made in accordance with law and regular procedures?

We do not demean the significance of the question. But one fact remains. A goal-fulfilling orientation asks very much broader questions, e.g., was an expenditure the best of several possible alternative uses of resources? And was an expenditure made in ways that suitably motivated the appropriate people, as well as having been made in accordance with accepted procedures?

Lehan sketches several specific senses in which budgeting made this journey from responsibility to a goal-fulfilling orientation, but two basic factors characterize all developmental stages encompassed by his conceptual end-points. First, all decisions involve the allocation of scarce resources among alternative uses; hence budgeting is a critical activity in decision making because it can help explicitly in the choice between alternative uses, especially if the focus is on programs rather than individual activities.

Second, the structures and procedures of large organizations do not necessarily all trend in the same direction. Fragmentation of effort may be *the* basic mode, in fact; and it clearly represents an elemental fact in all organizational life. Here again, budgeting and finance can be critical linkages. Specifically, the budget process can be critical in integrating the fragmented parts of a large organization by providing a sense of common thrust and direction to parts that have a tendency to go off in different directions.

Lehan's contribution leads to an easy conclusion. Given the scope of the phenomena relevant to public budgeting and finance, and given the tendency of the parts of government to go their diverse ways, the underlying theory and its associated arts will get a real test, at the very least. Control over public expenditures constitutes an issue of enormous significance—perhaps only formidable but maybe even overwhelming. In fact, if Northcote Parkinson's jaunty argument (3) has even an approximate validity, concern about the level of expenditures is more or less pointless. Expenditures will rise at least as fast as income does, goes the central core or Parkinson's argument. Some would add that public expenditures may rise even faster than income. The common point has a simple form. In effect, what goes up in this case is not likely to come down. Wars encourage sharp rises in the level of public expenditures, and recent relative peacetimes never seem quite capable of reversing the trend toward massive spending. Expenditures still chase after income, even if they do not surpass it. Individuals become accustomed to large public outlays and perhaps to the inevitable wastefulness associated with massive expenditures.

Parkinson is a determined skeptic, then. Two parkinsonian "laws" underly his skepticism: (1) work expands to fill the time available and (2) one multiples subordinates but not superiors. Parkinson does acknowledge boundary conditions that can curb the reinforcing inevitabilities that balloon public expenditures, but he sees these boundary conditions only as "danger points" that presage "international disaster." Therefore, his boundary conditions offer little hope this side of calamity.

Toward Reducing Dysfunctions in Budget Systems

W. Bruce Irvine's "Budgeting: Functional Analysis and Behavioral Implications" takes a more optimistic approach than Parkinson's contribution, even as Irvine sees problems aplenty. Irvine acknowledges that budgeting/finance can set in motion vicious cross-currents. Practices and techniques can help control expenditures, to illustrate; but budgeting/finance also can induce threat and hence resistance or evasion. So the intellectual task of providing a useful theory for guiding the practice and techniques of budgeting/finance has a simply profound character: increase the functional consequences and decrease the dysfunctional ones.

Irvine does not shrink from the task he sets for the concepts and theories guiding budgeting and analysis. Indeed, with emphasis on the business sector, Irvine deals subtly with the interplay of intended and unintended effects, of the functions and dysfunctions of budgeting and finance. And he seeks ways out of what can be deep dilemmas. Let us illustrate. Budgeting and finance personnel can often be viewed as keeping a watch on chicken houses, to oversimplify, and the habits and attitudes associated with such a role—suspicion, secretiveness, and so on—often will not be endearing to others. What does Irvine prescribe as a way out of this sticky situation? He suggests that budgeters look closely at "participative" techniques, among other things. In effect, such techniques can reduce the problems of patrolling the public chicken coops, even though a few potential wolves may now and again end up on patrol! This may appear a contradiction to some and a subtle balance to others.

Admitting Behavioral Assumptions

Edwin H. Caplan's "Behavioral Assumptions of Management Accounting" adds depth to an understanding of why Irvine saw dysfunctional as well as useful consequences in common budgeting/financial practices and concepts. Directly, Caplan proposes, those practices and concepts commonly rest on inadequate or even fallacious assumptions. No wonder, then, that reliance on them can lead to unexpected effects, often *unattractive* unexpected effects.

Caplan's analysis can only be sketched here. In simplified terms, he does two things. He isolates a number of behavioral assumptions underlying what he calls the "traditional" theory of the firm, which he finds lacking in important senses. In a complementary way, Caplan suggests a new set of assumptions on which to build budgeting and financial practices. These alternative assumptions he derives from "modern organization theory."

Caplan's argument thus amounts to a kind of point, counterpoint model. He contrasts and compares "traditional" and "modern" assumptions. And he sees some very distinct advantages in the latter assumptions, on balance, which typically get short shrift in budgeting/finance concepts and theories.

Testing Macrolevel Assumptions

Paralleling Caplan's argument, but at a macrolevel of analysis, Lance T. LeLoup also challenges a commonly accepted set of assumptions related to budgeting behavior. The title of LeLoup's contribution highlights his important target: "The Myth of Incrementalism: Analytical Choices in Budgetary Theory." LeLoup hunts big game. "Incrementalism" more or less reflects the prevailing sense of what budgeting typically *is,* and many propose that incrementalism also prescribes how budgeting *ought to be.*

LeLoup writes a heavyweight piece, and he can be left to make his own case in detail. But the reader need not remain in the dark about his basic conclusion. "Incrementalism was developed as a fully articulated theory," he writes, "on the basis of a number of implicit analytical choices appearing so obvious as to preclude the consideration of alternatives; however, they were costly [implicit choices] providing a misleading view of budgeting."

From whence came the beguiling simplifications of incrementalism? Perhaps basically, the notion derives from a basic contrast in ways of thinking that this volume will illustrate more than once. Let us briefly chart that contrast.

Economists once made life simple for themselves; they let assumptions take the place of descriptions. Thus classical economists assumed widespread consumer knowledge, more or less perfect competition between producers, and rational decision making by both producer and consumer. Under such conditions, even in the relatively short run, people reflected what they valued by the prices they were willing to pay for any array of goods. There was little need for strategy in all this, little need for long-range planning. Economic man got what he could while he could, basically. This is an elemental strategy.

Similarly, public finance and budgeting would be simple indeed if some cousinly assumptions are made. Classical budgeting man could spring from a small handful of assumptions. The assumptions include:

1. Relatively complete and comparable knowledge by both voters and policy makers about what individuals and groups want and how to get it.

2. Meaningful comparisons between alternative programs or agencies so that scarce budget dollars can be assigned in terms of such criteria as the relative efficiency of attaining social ends of various orders of preference.

3. Rational decision making by both voters and policy makers.

Much evidence suggests that the assumptions of the classical economist must be modified or rejected, as can be illustrated in terms of two models of decision making that are relevant to all types of administration. Table 1 sketches the properties of these two models, which derive from the insightful contribution of Charles E. Lindblom. Basically, the rational comprehensive model of decision making is consistent with the ideal assumptions detailed above for economic man and budgeting man. Classical economic man, for example, has the knowledge of values and reality demanded by the rational comprehensive model. In addition, because all consumers and producers are assumed to have small and relatively equal shares of influence in the model's marketplace, everyone's knowledge and desires are afforded full and equal but minor play. There is no special need for alternative strategies under these conditions.

The successive limited approximations (SLA) model of decision making stands in sharp opposition. Economic man and budgeting man would not find the SLA model congenial. Indeed, they would be immobilized by conditions like those assumed by the SLA model. Thus the SLA model implies incomplete knowledge of what is desired and how it may be obtained. Here alternative strategies take on considerable significance, and chance and insight play major roles. Under the SLA model, Lindblom advises, the premium is definitely on "muddling through."

The two models can be generalized as comprehensive or incremental, respectively, and this is no mere play on words. For many purposes, the theoretical and practical differences are substantial. Consider only two points. First, the two views differ because their proponents are looking at somewhat different things in

Table 1 Two Models of Decision Making

Rational comprehensive model	Successive limited approximations model
1a. Values or objectives are determined and clarified separately, and usually before considering alternative policies.	1a. Objectives and action alternatives are considered to be intertwined.
1b. Policy formation is approached through ends-means analysis, with agreed upon ends generating a search for appropriate ways of attaining them.	1b. Means-end analysis is often inappropriate because means and ends are not distinct.
1c. A "good" policy is therefore one providing the most appropriate means to some desired end.	1c. A "good" policy is one about which various analysts agree, without their agreeing that it is the most appropriate means for some objective.
1d. Every important relevant factor is taken into account.	1d. Analysis is limited in that important possible outcomes and important values are neglected.
1e. Theory often is heavily relied on.	1e. Successive comparisons greatly reduce the need for theory.

Source: Modified from C. E. Lindblom, The science of muddling through, *Public Administration Review 19*:79–88, Spring 1959.

somewhat different ways. Incrementalists tend to stress how things actually are; in contrast, comprehensive budgeters are given to emphasizing how they ought to be. Matters do not improve when incrementalism is prescribed as *an ought*. Comprehensive budgeters will get even more apoplectic at that.

Consequently, budgeters of the two persuasions, are liable to find themselves at odds on a wide range of issues. Emphases on the "is" and the "ought," in short, reflect different habits of mind and analytic approaches. Indeed, the predisposition to emphasize one or the other may reflect basic and unyielding personality differences.

Second, political strategy and maneuvering are all important to the incrementalist view, whereas they are distinctly secondary in any comprehensive approach to budgeting. The comprehensive approach strongly tends to seek support for a program in terms of its consistency with national objectives. Its bias thus is toward articulating those objectives, and perhaps complaining if movement toward them is sluggish. Although this view admits of some exaggeration, the incrementalist seeks strategies that are acceptable even if agreement about objectives has not been achieved or is in fact unlikely or impossible. Illustratively, even if no agreement exists about "national objectives," life must go on regardless. Of course, agreement about objectives probably always is desirable. Failing that, the question is, Is there some program we can agree is good enough, lack of agreement about objectives notwithstanding?

Thus proponents of the two views about budgeting and financial decisions will find themselves leaning in opposite directions. The contrast is not absolute; strategies are relevant in the comprehensive approach, and objectives cannot be neglected by the incrementalist. Usually, however, the emphases are so opposed that the contrasts are sharp and pervasive.

Third, deep philosophical differences may underlie the two approaches to budgeting and financial decisions. The incrementalist position is more at home with a pluralist concept of what the basic form of government is or ought to be. The comprehensive approach inclines more toward some form of elitism as a descriptive or prescriptive guide for governance. Again the point must not be pushed to extremes, for pluralism and elitism may have developmental ties. For example, "too much" pluralism may in practice lead to social and political chaos. In such a case, overexuberant pluralism may then lead to elitism.

In any case, the theoretical differences between the two approaches to budgeting decisions may reflect or be strongly reinforced by the philosophies or world views of the individuals espousing them. The differences in approach in such a case may rightly be called ultimate.

Specifying Budgetary Contexts

The preceding four senses in which concepts and theories relevant to budgeting/ finance need greater precision do not do the full job. Jeffrey D. Straussman provides important reinforcement and amplification of the fact that greater specificity is needed. Basically, he indicates that our theories relevant to budgeting and finance must be specific in a crucial regard. Oversimply, perhaps, a "what" is always applied "somewhere"; and "where" often will determine which "what" will work.

Basically, then, Straussman provides one approach to distinguishing the multiple "where" in which specific budgeting/finance techniques or approaches can be applied. This may oversimplify Straussman's important message in "A Typology of Budgetary Environments: Notes on the Prospects for Reform." But oversimplified or not, his contribution helps budgeting/finance move in the right direction to deepen understanding and to expand comprehensiveness of our theoretical and conceptual networks.

How does Straussman approach this critical integration of "what" and "where?" Straussman essentially distinguishes four sets of conditions, or scenarios, which rest on a twofold rating of two features. Thus Straussman is concerned about whether the "fiscal climate" is relatively "tight" or "unrestrained." And he distinguishes whether the budget process is "reformed" or "unreformed."

What happens to a budget innovation? Straussman argues reasonably that it depends on which of the four composite scenarios holds. Thus even a world-beating budgeting innovation might well have rough sailing where the budgeting process is unreformed. Moreover, if the fiscal climate is favorable, you might have to place your bets and take your chances. Innovations would be easier to finance, for example, but there might well be less motivation to try for improvement. Where the fiscal climate is tight, alternatively, motivation for innovation might be high but the threat level also might be higher among any potential "losers."

REFERENCES

1. Stedry, Andrew C. *Budget Control and Cost Behavior.* Englewood Cliffs, N. J., Prentice-Hall, 1960, pp. 3-12.
2. Simon, Herbert, Kozmetsky, George, and Guetzkow, Harold. *Centralization vs. Decentralization in Organizing the Controller's Department.* New York, Controllership Foundation, 1954, esp. pp. 1-33.
3. Parkinson, Northcote. *The Law and the Profits.* Boston, Houghton Mifflin, 1960, esp. pp. 5-8, 150-153, and 218-222.

1

PUBLIC BUDGETING*

Edward A. Lehan

THE BUDGET IDEA

American experience with public budgeting now spans three-quarters of a century. In the beginning, the "budget idea," as it was called, was part and parcel of the reform ideal of "responsible government." To turn-of-the-century reformers, budgeting procedures enhanced the popular control of government in two ways: (1) by concentrating financial authority in the chief executive and (2) by providing formal, open procedures for the exercise of that authority. As a consequence, budgeting was justified primarily on politicoadministrative grounds. About four decades were to pass before this original emphasis on the coordination and control features of budgeting was seriously questioned and the broader, policy-making and economic potentials of the budget idea debated and explored.

It all started when New York City embraced the budgeting idea in 1907. Thence, riding on the reform tide, the idea spread rapidly to other local govern-

*From *Essays in Public Finance and Financial Management: State and Local Perspectives,* ed. John E. Petersen and Catherine Lavigne Spain. Chatham, New Jersey: Chatham House, 1980. Copyright © 1978 and 1980 by the Municipal Finance Officers Association of the United States and Canada. Reprinted by permission of the publisher.

ments, and to the states. The crest of this remarkable movement came 14 years later with the passage of the Federal Budget and Accounting Act of 1921, which one commentator, C. F. Willoughby, said "made the President the working head of the administration in fact as well as in name."[1] Willoughby's remark may be regarded as quintessential, as it reflected the reformer's faith in the coordinating and control values of budgeting.

The phenomenal spread of the budget idea during the early decades of the twentieth century was due far more to its intimate connection with the dominant "responsibility ethos" of the reform movement than to any widespread appreciation of its possible utility in the determination of public policy.[2]

To be sure, the coordination and control features of budgeting were defined in economic as well as political terms by many of the early advocates of public budgeting, particularly by the business allies of the reform movement, who saw budgeting as cost cutting, pure and simple. Naturally, all this emphasis on budgeting as a negative force meant that the positive, or goal-fulfilling, potential of the budget idea as a device for rational decision making was pretty much dormant during the first four decades of the twentieth century. As a result, the commodity, or line-item, form of budgeting (LIB) became entrenched throughout the American governmental system. It was not until 1940, when V. O. Key published his trail-blazing critique, "The Lack of a Budgetary Theory," that the latent potential of the budget idea became the principal focus of interest.[3]

THE FORMAT ISSUE

What might be called the format issue was also largely dormant during the first four decades of American experience with budgeting, despite two significant efforts to call attention to the advantages of a functional approach to expenditure classification.

In 1912, the Taft Commission on Economy and Efficiency submitted its famous report recommending that the national government adopt budget procedures. The commission counseled against adopting an itemized commodity approach, suggesting instead that expenditures be classified by type of work, organizational unit, source of funding, and the character, rather than the item, of expense.[4]

In 1917, the New York Bureau of Municipal Research also attacked the utility of the itemized commodity format in the New York City budget. Instead of a detailed itemization of commodities, the bureau recommended that the city's budget be designed to facilitate policy planning and decision making, a concept which would command much attention from budgeteers 50 years later, in the 1960s.[5] In addition to foreshadowing the planning/programming/budgeting system (PPBS) approach of the 1960s, the bureau report is also noteworthy as the first systematic inquiry into the operational consequences of budgeting procedures. One might say that this report marked the beginning of the critical literature on budgeting, as the bureau's researchers tried empirically to assess the impact of budget format and procedures on city decisions and operations.

Although neither the Taft Commission nor the Bureau of Municipal Research effort had any noticeable effect on the spreading use of commodity formats, both reports reflect a lively appreciation for the power of procedures. The authors of these reports frankly acknowledge that procedures are not neutral, that the *means* of budgeting somehow affect the *ends* of budgeting. This powerful and complex idea was well stated by Jesse Burkhead in the preface to his classic, *Government Budgeting:* "The way in which revenues and expenditures are grouped for decision-making is the most important aspect of budgeting."[6]

The possibility that different formats and/or procedures might produce different budgetary outcomes also fascinated other distinguished students of budgeting—Wildavsky, Mosher, and Barber, to name but three who have competently explored the impact of formats and procedures on decision making.[7] Aaron Wildavsky, for example, placed great emphasis on the format issue in *The Politics of the Budgetary Process.* This influential work provided a defense of commodity budgeting, suggesting that factions found it easier to compromise differences by bargaining over items of expense rather than by open struggling over the underlying policy issues. He pointed out that programmatic formats and the accompanying tendency toward comprehensive annual reviews of all programs would simultaneously threaten many interests, burdening the budget process with unmanageable political tension and conflict.

Formats are important. People tend to think about what is put in front of them. Budget classifications, as F. C. Mosher pointed out, define reality for budget makers and reviewers, and thus channel their attention and thought. As a case in point, study Exhibit One, which shows a code enforcement budget in a commodity format.

There is little question that this commodity format invites (almost compels) discussion about things to be bought, rather than stimulating concern with policy

Exhibit One

Code enforcement	Budget
Personal services	$60,238
Contractual services	7,863
Supplies	1,376
Outlay	235
	$69,712

Exhibit Two

Code enforcement	Budget
Leadership	$15,526
Plan examination	12,331
Inspection	40,339
Innovation	850
Education	666
	$69,712

and procedural issues. Furthermore, a display of commodities often tempts reviewing officials to alter the expenditure pattern in ways which are unrelated to
policy issues and/or service levels. Often, such changes (usually reductions) are
not accompanied by explanations or expressions of legislative intent. Now, study
Exhibit Two. It reclassifies the code enforcement budget of Exhibit One along
programmatic lines.

The expenditure titles of Exhibit Two invite questions about work routines,
and focus the attention of budget makers and reviewers on such important issues
as code revision, improved inspection procedures, and the effort put into the
"education" of personnel, the regulated interests and the general public, as a code
compliance technique.

As already indicated, the format issue was raised by the Taft Commission
and by the New York Municipal Research Bureau without success. The issue lay
dormant until 1949, when another presidential commission, appointed by President Truman and chaired by former President Hoover, again turned a spotlight
on format reform. This time, the message sank in. The commission recommended
that

> the whole budgetary concept of the federal government should be re-
> fashioned by the adoption of a budget based upon functions, activities,
> and projects; this we designate a performance budget.[8]

This call for "performance" budgeting excited and inspired a whole generation of
budgeteers, and initiated the contemporary era of experimentation in format and
procedure.

On the whole, however, despite the enthusiasm engendered by the Hoover
Report, the performance budgeting idea found only partial lodgment in American budgetary practice. Today, a quarter century after its introduction, one can
find only selected use of unit costs, the key technique of performance budgeting,

Exhibit Three

Fire prevention	Last year	This year	Next year
Expenditures	$24,085	$27,875	$29,295
Inspections	9,634	10,000	10,500
Unit costs	$ 2.50	$ 2.76	$ 2.79

in many jurisdictions. See Exhibit Three for an example of a budget display using unit costs to relate expenditures to work load. Budgeteers found the performance budgeting concept of practical use in only those activities for which measurable work units, such as inspections, were easily available. It must also be noted that performance budgeting requires sophisticated accounting support, a grave deficiency in almost every American jurisdiction.

GOAL-ORIENTED APPROACHES

Performance budgeting using unit cost calculations and comparisons is the best way to relate expenditures to work loads. Relating expenditures to work loads may help in rationalizing expenditures in a jurisdiction, but the performance budget approach does not in itself help budget makers and reviewers solve *the* fundamental problem of budgeting, which is determining the relative worth of the various purposes supported by budget allocations.

It was V. O. Key who first went to the heart of the budgetary problem in his 1940 essay. Key noted that much energy had been absorbed in the tasks of establishing the mechanical foundations of budgeting, but little attention had been given to the basic budgeting problem on the expenditure side—deciding on what basis funds should be allocated to one activity as opposed to another.[9]

Curiously, Key was pessimistic about the practical value of applied economics in budget making, particularly the application of the doctrine of marginal utility, even though his article defined budgeting as a problem of economic theory. Despite this pessimistic appraisal, his idea that budget making should be examined from the perspective of economic theory proved seminal.

Verne Lewis, for example, carefully examined the potential use of the theory of marginal utility in an influential article in 1952. Lewis proposed the idea of alternative budgets: a basic budget accompanied by alternatives which might be set at 80, 90, 110, and 120 percent of the basic amount.[10] According to Lewis, this structure of incremental alternatives would assist budgeteers in exploring the marginal benefits of different spending plans. This idea was popularized in 1973 under the rather misleading rubric "zero-base budgeting" (ZBB).[11]

Serious criticism of budgetary practices mounted during the 1950s, with economists in the van. This stream of criticism stimulated widespread experimentation with program budgeting (ProB) and its evolutionary successors, PPBS and ZBB. Each of these approaches involves budgeting formats and procedures organized around goals to be achieved with public funds, rather than things to be bought (the line-item approach), or things to be done (the performance approach). These goal-oriented approaches represent attempts to work allocation criteria into the budget process by asking budgeteers to weigh the costs and benefits of alternative ways of achieving public ends. A noble vision, but what is the contemporary reality? Have budgeteers found an answer to Key's fundamental question? Recent studies reveal that the concepts of desirable practice have outrun the apparent capacity for application.

BUDGETARY BEHAVIOR

Allen Schick, in a comprehensive study of state budget innovations, found techniques of performance budgeting (PerB) and PPBS only partially incorporated in the budgetary practice of the states by the late 1960s.[12] He blamed the weight of the control and management tradition and bureaucratic inertia for the failure of the states to swing more completely to the goal-oriented approaches, but remained hopeful for the future. Aaron Wildavsky, already noted as a critic of programmatic approaches, was not as optimistic, concluding in his latest work on budgeting that the goal-oriented approaches have failed, and will continue to fail, because no one knows how to do them.[13]

In 1975, Lewis Friedman reported on the results of an 88-city survey, noting that only 10 cities of this sample seemed to be heavily engaged with the techniques of goal-oriented budgeting, such as benefit/cost studies, multiyear forecasting, etc.[14] Friedman's report also shed some light on the validity of Allen Schick's hypothesis that budget reform is an evolutionary process involving stages of control, management, and planning, each providing the foundation for the next. He found some evidence to support Schick's thesis that governments probably must build up their capability in budgeting generally before they are ripe for tackling the new techniques. Cities without a heavy commitment to control forms of budgeting were not heavily engaged in performance budgeting, for example. Further, cities without a commitment to performance budgeting were not found to be heavily engaged with goal-oriented budgeting.

In a widely noted 1973 article reviewing the state of the art as revealed in the literature, Don Axelrod reflected the exasperation of many practitioners and students of budgeting. Axelrod warned against "new acronyms" and the "packaged panacea," pointing out that budgeting techniques were not mutually exclusive procedures or stages, and that governments were using—and would continue to use—a variety of techniques to solve allocation and efficiency problems.[15]

Since Don Axelrod's review in 1973, things have gotten worse. A new acronym, ZBB, has invaded the field. This newest "packaged panacea" (fervently endorsed by President Jimmy Carter) requires that budget proposals be presented in priority order at each level of decision making, thus focusing attention on the criteria of allocation. At the time of this writing, a large number of jurisdictions appear to be experimenting with this latest attempt to find answers for V. O. Key's fundamental question: "On what basis shall it be decided to allocate x dollars to activity A instead of activity B?"

The jury is still out on the practical results of the ZBB approach. However, its onset has underscored the schizophrenia of the budgetary world, a world already marked by a wide rift between the realities of budget preparation and control (firmly anchored in itemized, incremental decision making) and the ideal, goal-oriented models (PerB, ProB, and PPBS) featured in the literature and classroom.

EMPIRICAL STUDIES OF BUDGETARY BEHAVIOR

Much research has been devoted to explaining how—budget formats and official prounouncements aside—decisions are, in fact, made among the competing sources and uses of funds. The analyst must be forever wary in this respect, because how public officials act in allocating may vary greatly from what they report they are doing, perhaps even from what some believe they are doing.

An important example of this divergence is found in the reporting of uses of funds, such as is required under various federal grant programs. In the use of general revenue sharing, for example, researchers kept coming up with the results that actual fiscal impacts varied from those reported by the recipients.[16] The problem, of course, is embedded in the fungibility of dollars: a dollar received from a particular source becomes submerged in the flood of other dollars and may be put to any of a great number of uses. A variety of effects can be generated by the added dollar, including its substitution for other funds in the budget (that once freed are spent on other items), a reduction in other revenues (substituting among revenue sources), building up assets (increasing revenues but not expenditures), or even stimulating more than a dollar of expenditures and revenues (because of matching requirements or expenditure complementarity).

Tracing how marginal changes in funds affect the budget thus becomes a complex analysis of patterns of behavior, capturing "fiscal effects," as funds are added to or, conversely, taken away from the budget. The thrust here is a positive analysis of how governments behave in their budgetary outcomes. Perhaps the most active area of surveillance has been that of the designs of various intergovernmental assistance programs. Results of empirical studies indicate that governmental budgetary reactions will vary depending on program design (such as the matching nature of the formula).[17] Responses will also be conditioned by the degree of fiscal pressure that recipients are under and the presence that local budgeteers ascribe to the assistance program.[18]

Another branch of research that has blossomed to assist in the "what is" analysis of budgetary behavior relies on the approach of organization theory. In this discipline, public budgeting is viewed as a large, complex process. In carrying out the process, officials operate with limited information and analytic skills and under sundry constraints. To conquer the maze, they adopt problem-solving routines—a series of "rules-of-thumb"—by which they bring the budget into balance.[19]

Computer simulations of government budgetary behavior incorporating such decision rules have been created and tested. While handicapped by lack of data and inherent simplicity of their rendering of the process, they nonetheless present some hope of sorting out the maze of decision relationships. Their policy implications are clear; behavioral models that have some explanatory and predictive power will be useful in projecting the consequences of additions or subtractions of dollars into municipal budgets.[20] A word of caution: the mathematical relationships hold only so long as the behavior repeats itself. In the real world, that is likely to be the very short run.

BUDGETARY LITERATURE

Is it far from the mark to say that most practitioners regard the budgetary literature as a lush growth of description and prescription without firm roots in the procedural reality of government? Able students of budgeting, including Aaron Wildavsky, point out that goal-oriented approaches to public budgeting confront, and go beyond, the limits of politics. Surely these rationalistic approaches require intellectual capabilities which the actors in the budgetary drama most likely do not possess.

What is "good" budgeting? This is a normative question which even experienced budgeteers have trouble answering. The field is marked by semantic and procedural confusion, torn by conflicts of professional perspective and political interest, and lacks accepted criteria for judging "good" from "bad." For example:

- To an economist, a good budget produces equivalent benefits at the margin of expenditure, i.e., the last dollar spent on public safety, let us say, yields a benefit equal to that produced by the last dollar spent on other functions.

- To a student of politics, a good budget promotes civic morale by incorporating the interests of "interests" within the expenditure and revenue scheme.

- To an elected chief executive, a good budget redeems the promises of the last campaign and consolidates support for the next.

- To a finance director, a good budget reflects accurate, balanced estimates, useful in financial planning and control.

In addition to coping with the variations in criteria that flow naturally from such differences in perspective and/or interest, a conception of good budgeting must cut through the semantic and procedural confusion introduced into the field by the four alternatives to LIB, i.e., PerB, ProB, PPBS, and ZBB.

Empirical research on the subject of optimal budgeting should be directed toward two objectives: (1) the reconciliation of a voluminous and growing theoretical literature with actual practice and (2) the establishment of an authoritative factual and normative basis for improvement of public budgeting.

It is hypothesized that the practice of public budgeting has not been significantly affected by the literature advocating the so-called output or goal-oriented approaches.[21] This hypothesis, and a number of derivative researchable issues,[22] could form the core of a research agenda designed to probe the basic reification and relationship problems of public budgeting, such as

- Ambiguous terminology
- Impact of different formats and procedures on budgetary outcomes
- Relative costs (in time, talent, accuracy, money, etc.) of different approaches
- Impact of different procedures on informational needs of user groups, and
- Accounting, data base, and other institutional and pedagogical requirements of different approaches

EDUCATION OF BUDGETEERS

One important point remains. It concerns the educational foundations of budget work. Apparently, most budgeteers are trained on the job and thus are dependent on the quality of supervision found in their budget units—a most unsatisfactory state of affairs from a pedagogic point of view. Further, the literature of budgeting is silent on the pedagogy of budgeting. Given the strategic placement of budgeteers in the decision-making process and the profusion of budgeting models which provoke broad and deep thinking about society and its problems, this "pedagogic deficit" should alarm the academic and training community—and stir it into action.

NOTES

1. C. F. Willoughby, The budget, *Encyclopedia of the Social Sciences,* Vol. 3, New York, Macmillan, 1930, p. 40.
2. For a sample of the literature on the "budget idea" at the high tide of the

reform movement, see an excellent collection of essays on budgeting in the *Annals of the American Academy of Political and Social Science,* Nov. 1915.
3. V. O. Key, The lack of a budgetary theory, *American Political Science Review, 34* December 1940, p. 1138.
4. U.S. President's Commission on Economy and Efficiency, The Need for a National Budget, H. Doc. 854, 62nd Cong., 2nd sess., 1912.
5. New York Bureau of Municipal Research, Some results and limitations of central financial control in New York City, *Municipal Research, 81* (1917).
6. Jesse Burkhead, *Government Budgeting,* New York, Wiley, 1956, p. viii.
7. Aaron Wildavsky, *The Politics of the Budgetary Process.* Boston, Little, Brown, 1964; F. C. Mosher, *Program Budgeting,* Chicago, Public Administration Service, 1954; and J. D. Barber, The Intellectual Work of the Board of Finance, Storrs, Conn., Institute of Public Service, University of Connecticut, 1973.
8. U.S. Commission on Organization of the Executive Branch of Government, Budgeting and Accounting. Washington, D.C., Government Printing Office, 1949, p. 8.
9. Key, The lack of a budgetary theory.
10. Verne B. Lewis, Toward a theory of budgeting, *Public Administration Review, 12* 1952, pp. 42-54.
11. Peter A. Pyhrr, *Zero-Base Budgeting: A Practical Management Tool for Evaluating Expenses,* New York, Wiley, 1973.
12. Allen Schick, *Budget Innovation in the States,* Washington, D.C., Brookings Institution, 1971.
13. Aaron Wildavsky, *Budgeting,* Boston, Little, Brown, 1975.
14. Lewis C. Friedman, Control, management and planning: An empirical examination, *Public Administration Review,* Nov.-Dec. 1975, pp. 625-628.
15. Donald Axelrod, Post Burkhead—The state of the art or science of budgeting, *Public Administration Review, 33* Nov.-Dec. 1973, pp. 576-584.
16. See Richard Nathan, Allen Manvel, and Susannah Calkins, *Monitoring Revenue Sharing.* Washington, D.C., Brookings Institution, 1975.
17. See, for example, Edward M. Gramlich and Harvey Galper, State and local fiscal behavior and federal grant policy, *Brookings Papers on Economic Activity,* 1973.
18. General revenue sharing research provided a wealth of information on the differential impacts of a widespread, broad-scale block program of assistance. See F. Thomas Juster, ed., *The Economic and Political Impact of General Revenue Sharing,* Ann Arbor, Institute of Social Science Research, University of Michigan, 1976.
19. The field was pioneered by John P. Crecine, *Governmental Problem Solving: A Computer Simulation of Municipal Budgeting,* Chicago, Rand McNally, 1969.

20. Thomas Anton, Understanding the fiscal impact of general revenue sharing, *General Revenue Sharing,* Vol. 2, *Summaries of Impact and Process Research,* Washington, D.C., National Science Foundation, 1975.
21. For an illuminating insight into the state of the art, see Municipal Finance Officers Association, "Budget Committee Questionnaire," Chicago, Municipal Finance Officers Association, 1977. In response to this poll, over 1,100 local finance officers identified the most pressing information and training needs of local government budgeteers as (1) revenue forecasting, (2) budget planning and priority selection, and (3) budget execution and control.
22. For an example of an empirical evaluation of budget hypotheses along the lines here suggested, see Lewis Friedman, *Budgeting Municipal Expenditures.* New York, Praeger, 1975.

2

BUDGETING: Functional Analysis and Behavioral Implications*

V. Bruce Irvine

Many of those who have written about budgets have emphasized the problems resulting from typical budgeting systems. Little enthusiasm has been voiced for the practical effectiveness of budgets as a means of obtaining the optimal benefits of which such a device is capable.

A more positive approach might result from a consideration of the control and motivational effects of budgets on the behavior of people. But an analysis of the reactions of these people (supervisors, foremen, laborers) to control devices (such as budgets) has received little attention as a specific subject in the literature of the past decade. The studies reported have usually concentrated attention on improving the usefulness of budgets from a top management viewpoint and have deemphasized the subordinate positions. Also, many of the studies have been conducted by behavioral scientists and have not been incorporated into accounting and management thought and teaching. Consequently, although accountants and management are aware that their actions have behavioral implica-

---

*Condensation of a thesis submitted for R.I.A. qualification to the Society of Industrial Accountants of Saskatchewan. Reprinted from an article appearing in *Cost and Management* (vol. 44, no. 2) by V. Bruce Irvine, by permission of The Society of Management Accountants of Canada.

tions, they have not thoroughly understood what these are. The result is uncertainty, confusion, and indecision when human problems do arise.

The purpose of this chapter is to make a functional analysis of budgeting toward the goal of maximizing long-run profits (considered to be the present value of the owner's net worth). An analysis of reactions of the employees on whom budgets are primarily exercised rather than a purely management viewpoint analysis will be used to develop basic propositions. Human behavioral aspects of budgets, therefore, become a very relevant factor in this approach. After investigation of why employees react as they do, the usefulness of budgets in view of such reactions and the implications of suggestions for making budgets more successful and acceptable can be considered within particular situations facing modern day business.

DEFINITIONAL AND TECHNICAL CONSIDERATIONS

A functional analysis considers the various consequences of a particular activity and determines whether or not these consequences aid in the achievement of the organization's objective. According to Merton,[1] the consequences of an activity are functional if they increase the ability of a given system to achieve a desired goal. A consequence is dysfunctional if it hinders the achievement of the goal. Consequences of an activity may also be classified as manifest (recognized and intended by the participants in the system) or latent (neither intended nor recognized). Decisions based only on manifest consequences may often be incorrect because of latent consequences.

A budget is a device intended to provide greater effectiveness in achieving organizational efficiency. To be effective, however, the functional aspects must outweigh the dysfunctional aspects. Whether or not this will be true depends on many factors, which will be discussed and summarized in a model of the elements of budgeting.

First it is necessary to understand what a budget is. Although formal definitions of a budget exist, a definition is not always the most relevant aspect of a concept.

Amitai Etzioni distinguishes between two types of models in organizational analysis.[2] The survival system consists of activities which, if fulfilled, allow a system to exist. Budgets are not part of such a system. Organizations in the past have functioned and in the future will function without the help of budgets. Budgets can be classified within an effectiveness system. These "define a pattern of interactions among the elements of the system which would make it more effective in the service of a given goal."[3]

A budget, as a formal set of figures written on a piece of paper, is in itself, merely a quantified plan for future activities. However, when budgets are used for control, planning, and motivation, they become instruments which cause functional and dysfunctional consequences, both manifest and latent, which determine how successful the tool will be.

Budgets mean different things to different people according to their different points of view. Accountants see them from the preparation aspect, managers from the implementation aspect, and behavioral scientists from the human implication aspect. All of these viewpoints must be melded together if budgets are to obtain the best functional results.

There are many types of budgets. The major purpose of having budgets, the type of organization using a budget, the personalities of people handling the budget, the personal characteristics of people subject to budget direction, the leadership style of the organization, and the method of preparing a budget are all factors accounting for budget type and style.

The technical procedures involved in the preparation and use of budget figures are similar for most organizations. People make estimates (standards) of what they expect should reflect future events. These estimates are then compared to what actually happened and the differences (variances) are studied.

THE FUNCTIONAL ASPECTS OF BUDGET SYSTEMS

In what specific way do budgets make management action more efficient and effective in maximizing the present value of the owners' worth?

Basically, a budget system enables management to more effectively plan, coorginate, control, and evaluate the activities of the business. These are functional, manifest consequences in terms of their desirability.

Planning means establishing objectives in advance so that members of the organization will have specific, activity-directed goals to guide their actions. Budgets are quantitative plans for action. As such, they force management to examine the available resources and to determine how these can be used efficiently.

The point that budgets require this clarification and concrete quantification of ideas is not usually recognized directly by budgeting people as a benefit. As such, it could be considered functional and latent.

The planning aspect of budgeting has other latent functions. Planning requires that the plans be communicated to those involved in carrying them out. Communication is enhanced by distributing the budget to those responsible for various parts of it.

A budget makes lower level managers more aware of where they fit into an organization. Their budget indicates what is expected of them and that they have a goal towards which their activities are to be directed.

With a budget, junior (new) members of an organization have a better idea of where the company is going and are made to feel that the business is concerned about their future. This can affect both their own future plans and the company's recruitment policy and turnover problems.

When a person is given an objective, he is more likely to feel that he is part of the organization and that the upper echelons are interested in his work. Conversely, top management is likely to become more interested in, and aware of, the activities of lower level employees.

These latent, functional consequences of budgets create interest and, possibly, enthusiasm, which increases morale and could result in greater efficiency and initiative.

Planning of departmental activities must be coordinated so that bottlenecks do not occur and interdepartmental strife can be limited. A budget system can assist in this coordination. By basing organizational activity on the limiting factor (such as sales, production, working capital), a comprehensive budget coordinating all of the firm's activities can be approved by top management and the controller. Such a budget permits these people to bring together their overall knowledge of the firm's abilities and limitations. By using budgets to coordinate activities, the organization is more likely to operate at an optimal level, given the constraints on its resources.

The control consequences are among the more important aspects of budgeting. Because a budget plan exists, decisions are not merely spontaneous reactions to stimuli in an environment of unclarified goals. The budget provides relevant information to a decision maker at the time he must choose between alternatives. Therefore, a budget implicitly incorporates control at the point of the decision. However, provision for taking advantage of unforeseen situations should certainly be allowed even though a budget is violated.

A second type of control can be derived from budgets. A comparison of actual with budgeted performance after decisions have been made reveals to management the performance of the organization as a whole and of the individual responsible members.

A comparison merely reveals discrepancies. The action which is taken as a result of variances is in the hands of management. But the investigation of why there are variances, whether or not they are controllable, and the resulting control procedures is stimulated by the budgeting process. The result is the discovery of methods to save costs, improvement in the firm's efficiency, and better future planning.

Control of both types is important to top management because it cannot maintain personal contact with those in the lower management ranks. Devices such as budgets, employment contracts, job descriptions, and rules are therefore necessary to direct subordinate behavior. In general, control is based on the assumption that individuals are motivated by their own security needs to fulfil the plans and obey the rules. To the extent that this is true, the benefits to be derived from the control aspects of budgeting can be deemed functional and manifest.

These benefits could be obtained only in the ideal situation where budgets work as they are intended to work. The theoretical benefits make budgets very appealing devices, but the practical problems of implementing and using them greatly affect their usefulness. Most of the problems arise from the difficulty of convincing people to accept and use a budget. Mechanical problems also exist. These difficulties create many possibilities for dysfunctional consequences to occur with the result that some functional consequences become difficult, if not impossible, to attain.

DYSFUNCTIONAL ASPECTS OF BUDGET SYSTEMS

Any system which involves motivation and control of individuals has dysfunctional aspects, simply because human behavior cannot be predicted or controlled with certainty. Frequently, activities by management to obtain desired functional results will actually lead to dysfunctional consequences. Management must understand why such a reversal can occur so that existing problems can be solved or an environment created which prevents problems arising.

This section will indicate how results of a budget system can be dysfunctional in nature. The basic approach will be to analyze the deterrents to achieving particular functional results. Within a particular organization, the dysfunctional aspects must be considered in relation to the functional aspects in order to evaluate the worthiness of a budget system. Obviously, if the dysfunctional consequences of an action outweigh the functional aspects, management should delete the activity. Because each business is unique, no attempt can be made to state that certain activities will be dysfunctional or functional in every situation.

Because factors which can lead to dysfunctional consequences are complex, each will be analyzed separately although it is realized that they are usually interrelated.

The Term "Budget"

The first dysfunctional consequence of a budget system results from the name itself. Traditionally, budgets have carried a negative connotation for many:

> Some of the words historically associated with the term budget are: imposed, dictated by the top, authorized. And what are the original purposes of control—to reduce, to eliminate, to increase productivity, to secure conformance, to assure compliance, to inform about deviation. An historical meaning of budget is to husband resources—to be niggardly, tight, Scrooge-like.[4]

If attitudes expressing such beliefs are not eliminated at the start, the budget will never get off the ground. One method of eliminating this problem is to refrain from calling the activity "budgeting."

Organizational Arrangements of Authority and Responsibility

If a budget system is to be used to control and evaluate personnel, the persons involved must possess responsibility and authority over what is being assigned to them. Consequently a large and/or decentralized organization would probably have a greater potential use for budgeting than a small, highly centralized business.

Centralized organizations may simply use budgets to plan and coordinate future activities. Because responsibility, control, and authority rest with the top executives in such a business, any attempt to reward, punish, or hold lower level employees responsible for variances would achieve nothing beneficial and would probably cause resentment. Any negative feelings on the part of those who follow directives in carrying out operations would likely lead to less than optimal achievement of organizational objectives. Therefore, even though budgets can be used to improve planning and coordination, assignment of control responsibilities where there is no power to carry out those responsibilities could easily create dysfunctional, latent consequences.

On the other hand, overemphasis on departmentalization can also have dysfunctional, latent effects:

> Budget records, as administered, foster a narrow viewpoint on the part
> of the user. The budget records serve as a constant reminder that the
> important aspect to consider is one's own department and not one's own
> plant.[5]

Overemphasis on one's own department can lead to considerable cost in workhours, money, and interpersonal relations when responsibility for variances, particularly large ones, is being determined. The result is a weakening of cooperation and coordination between departments.

Role Conflict Aspects of Budgeting

Status differences or, more accurately, role conflict between staff and line personnel is an important source of dysfunctional consequences. The problems created affect budget usefulness directly and also indirectly through their effect on communication, motivation, and participation. The basic difficulties arise because of differences in the way budget staff people and line personnel understand the budgeting system and each other.

From Table 1[6] it can be seen how important budgets and the budget staff are in the supervisors' or foremen's working world. Ninety-nine percent of the supervisors and foremen questioned in four companies stated that the budget department was either first or second in importance of impact on the performance of their activity.

Table 1 Responses to the Request "Name the departments affecting your actions most" Asked of Supervisors and Foremen Individually in Four Firms[6]

	Most affect	2nd Most affect	Total
Production Control	55%		
Budget Department	45%	54%	99%

From the supervisors' and foremen's follow-up comments, it was readily apparent that the budget department's influence was not only significant, it was usually considered troublesome as well. Why should this be so? Some suggested reasons are:

1. Line employees see budgets as providing results only and not the reasons for those results. Any explanations of variances by the financial staff, such as failure to meet expected production or inadequate use of materials, prove grossly insufficient. Causes behind these explanations still have to be determined before the supervisors and foremen could consider budget reports as being useful to them or presenting a fair appraisal of their activities to top management.

2. Budgets are seen as emphasizing past performance and as a device for predicting the future. Supervisors and foremen are basically concerned with the present and with handling immediate problems. Budget figures would often be ignored in order to solve present difficulties.

3. Supervisors and foremen apparently see budgets as being too rigid. In some cases, budget standards have not been changed for 2 or 3 years. Even if they now meet such a budget, they often would not be performing efficiently. Budget people would then adjust the budget. In such cases, those working under a budget would not really know what was expected of them until after they had submitted their cost reports and had received a control report.

4. Supervisors and foremen would also resent the opposite treatment of constantly changing a budget in the belief that increased efficiency would result. Such a procedure would lead them to believe, and often justly so, that budgets were unrealistically set. Budget men would be seen as individuals who could never be satisfied as they would raise the budget if a person made or came close to his previous budget. This would only result in frustration for the supervisor or foreman. The feeling that the

company executives did not believe in the supervisor's own desire to do a good job could easily be implied when budgets are continually changing.

5. Thoughts about budgets are further aggravated when foremen and supervisors receive budget reports on their performance in a complicated format with an analysis that is incomprehensible to them. Supervisors felt that the job of budget people was to be critical and that the use of jargon and specialized formats enabled them to justify their criticism of others without too much debate.

Whether or not these criticisms are logical and rational is not important. The point is that such feelings can and do exist. If the budget is regarded as merely emphasizing history, being too rigid, unrealistic, unattainable, and unclear and if budget people are seen as overconcerned with figures, unconcerned with line problems, and cut off by a language of their own, there can be no doubt that the effectiveness of a budget system would deteriorate.

The problems are compounded if the budget personnel's attitude is unconducive to overcoming these opinions. Budget people should see thier jobs as examining, analyzing, and looking for new ways to improve plant efficiency. They should also think of a budget as an objective that should fairly challenge factory personnel. Since it cannot be assumed that line personnel subscribe to or even recognize these ideas, the ideas should be impressed upon them directly through adequate budget introduction and education. Moreover, the effective use of budgets cannot be forced on supervisors and foremen; it must be accepted by them. This can only be accomplished if budget people try to work constructively with line people as compatriots rather than commanders. This accord is usually very difficult to bring about. Often budget people will not even attempt it or simply give up on it because of lack of success. They conclude, correctly or incorrectly, that the line personnel's unsatisfactory use of budgets is due to their lack of education, understanding, and interest.

Given this unwillingness to buck line opposition by the budget personnel and the line's viewpoint of budgeting as a hindrance to their performance, a classic role conflict is created. The optimal benefits possible from budgeting cannot be obtained in such an environment.

Argyris also determined how foremen and supervisors felt the potential dysfunctional results of budgeting could be overcome. Suggestions dealt mainly with improving the outlook of budget men. According to the line personnel, budgeting people should be taught that budgets are merely opinions, not the "be-all and end-all." They should also be taught, it was felt, that line employees are not inherently lazy, that budget men should learn to look at a problem from another's point of view, and that they are not superior to supervisory people. Also suggested were the use of timely and understandable reports to foremen and supervisors, the practice of conferring with people who have variances so that the budget report indicates the real cause to top management, and the setting of realistic budgets.

The problems arising are not, however, entirely the fault of the budget staff. Supervisors and foremen must put more effort into understanding the budget figures, they must not be continually suspicious of budgets, and they should use budgets in performing their duties. Most important, they should alter their outlook toward budgeting. Budgets must be realistic and fair, but also foremen and supervisors should realize that the budget is designed to help them achieve the standards management expects of them.

How can these requirements be achieved? An educational program involving foremen, supervisors, middle and upper management, and budget personnel could help to clarify the different viewpoints and promote understanding of each other's objectives and difficulties. Such a program should precede the introduction of a budgeting system and continue after the system has been introduced.

Budgets and Nonmanagement People

The involvement of laborers (nonmanagement personnel) in the budgeting process presents both functional and dysfunctional possibilities. Often, front-line supervisors who have a budget to meet do not use it as a device to spur their subordinates. According to the comments reported by Argyris, they fear that workers would look upon such action unfavorably and that no benefit would be received.

The proposition that workers would not respond to budgetary pressures is challenged by W. F. Whyte:

> How do workers see budgets? They often recognize that management people are worried about costs, but with the foremen afraid to put the cost situation to them, they remain uninvolved in the struggle.[7]

Since workers generally have not been directly involved in budgetary systems, the question of whether or not such involvement would be functional is unresolved.

Motivational Aspects of Budgeting

The most controversial area of budgeting concerns its motivational implications.

The budget makes available information for comparison of expected with actual performance. When such an evaluation of performance is known to result in rewards and punishments, people are expected to be motivated to do their best. Let us examine this assumption and its possible functional or dysfunctional consequences.

Argyris states that budgets are principal instruments for creating pressure which motivates individuals.[8] Budgets can also be seen as creating more pressure than they actually do. This pressure illusion is due to the fact that the budget is a concrete, quantitative instrument and managers and supervisors, feeling pressure from more abstract sources, place the blame for it on the concrete budget.

Factors directly related to budget pressures are budget "pep" talks (A), red circles around poor showings (B), production and sales drives using budgets (C), threats of reprimand (D), and feelings of failure if budgets are not met (E). These can all be considered as functional and manifest in terms of their motivational intent.

There are, however, counteracting effects which can be dysfunctional and latent in terms of budget effectiveness. These factors include informal agreements among managers and/or supervisors (V), fear of loss of job if efficiency increases but cannot be maintained (W), union agreements against speed-ups (X), performance abilities of individual employees (Y), and abilities of work teams as a whole (Z).

Equilibrium is attained when:

$$A + B + C + D + E = V + W + X + Y + Z$$

Management, by increasing one or more of the components on the left hand side of the relationship or by adding additional ones, can increase productivity. This increase is matched by an increase in tension, uneasiness, resentment, and suspicion on the part of the employees. This pressure increase is absorbed by joining groups which are strongly cohesive against top management and budget people. Again equilibrium is attained but each time pressures are increased by top management, they must become more intense as resistance is higher.

When and if management feels that the pressures are detrimental to the organization, it may attempt to reduce the causes on the left hand side of the equation. This does not result in decreased antimanagement feeling because the groups have developed into relatively permanent social units and the individuals feel the pressures may occur again. Therefore, in the long run, increasing pressures may be very dysfunctional because of these latent features.

The rational way for management to approach this problem would be to concentrate its activities on reducing the forces that decrease efficiency rather than on increasing the factors that tend to increase efficiency.

Other dysfunctional ways of relieving motivational pressure could easily exist:

1. Interdepartmental strife could occur. A manager, supervisor, or foreman could try to blame the variances on someone else. This would result in concentrated effort by individuals to promote only the cause of their own departments. The personal rivalries thus caused and the lack of cooperation among departments could mean decreased efficiency for the company in achieving its overall goals.

2. Another type of strife develops when the line employees blame the staff employees for their predicaments and absolve themselves of the responsibility for the variances. Budget people become scapegoats for problems and salesmen are blamed for incorrect predictions of orders that make the production process unstable.

3. An individual may internalize the personal pressure he feels. By not outwardly showing his problems, he would build up tension within himself. Eventually, frustration would develop and he would perform less efficiently in the long run.

4. If internal means of relieving pressure are used, manipulation of activities may result. Reporting sizable variances when one knows he will be over his budget may allow him to shift his costs so that he will easily make his budget in the next period. Saving easy jobs until just before the end of a budget period may enable a person to achieve the stipulated goal.

The point is that in the short run increasing motivational pressure through budgets may be functional, but in the long run it may also be very dysfunctional.

Andrew C. Stedry postulates additional concepts concerning motivation through budgeting.[9] Through experiment, Stedry developed the findings shown in Figure 1.

The level of costs for which a person will strive (aspired costs) will be conceived by the individual in relation to past experience, confidence in personal skills, expectation of future difficulties, and feelings about the budget costs. Aspired and budget costs do not necessarily (or usually) coincide. The aspired costs are what the individual sets for himself. The budget costs are set by top

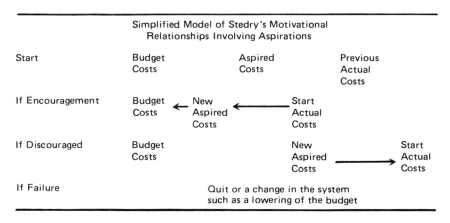

Figure 1 Simplified model of Stedry's motivational relationships involving aspirations.

management. When actual costs are compared to these two costs, the reaction of the employees depends on the discrepancies involved:

1. Other things being equal, aspiration levels will move relative to the actual costs depending on the degree of discrepancy.

2. A person will be encouraged if the discrepancy between actual costs and aspired costs is not greater than an amount known as the discouragement point. Aspirations would be set higher on the next period of performance measurement.

3. A person will be discouraged if the discrepancy is greater than the discouragement point but less than a failure point. In this case, aspirations would move downward.

4. If the discrepancy is greater than the failure point, the system would cease to exist or a new one would be needed. Otherwise the individual concerned would resign.

Stedry concludes that management should set high, unattainable budgets to motivate individuals to achieve the greatest efficiency. "Unattainable" would have to mean that the discrepancy between aspired costs, formulated after the high budget was presented, and actual costs could not exceed the discouragement point. Such a policy would mean that individuals receiving separate budgets would be manipulated in accordance with the variances in the size of their discouragement points.

This may sound all right in theory but in practice the reactions of employees could make this a dangerous proposition for long-run efficiency. If individuals found out that they were the subjects of outright manipulation, they could become rebellious and ignore future budgets whether they were fair or not. Other management control devices would probably be considered with unwarranted suspicion. Moreover, how is management going to determine the aspiration level and discouragement point of each individual, a necessary requirement for setting "personal" budgets? The use of individual budget standards would also have to be kept confidential. Otherwise, the resentment that employees would feel might lead them to resist all budgeting attempts and even to leave the organization.

Stedry's study suggests that participation in budget preparation is not as beneficial as having management set the budget. He points out, however, that participation may be desirable where low budgets are given as managers, supervisors, and foremen would likely feel that they are capable of achieving greater efficiency and would say so.

Stedry's study is limited in that long-run results were not extensively examined. Also, the nature of his "laboratory" data leads to serious questions as to whether real business world conditions were reproduced.[10] However, his research on the reactions of lower level management to budgets does help to explain the behavior of these people. The study also indicates how management can improve a budgeting process where budgets are being ignored or causing personnel problems because it shows why such situations exist.

Another consequence of budgetary motivation which has received little emphasis involves "a fear of failure" on the part of the individual. The failure to meet a budget or at least come close to it when it is accepted and fairly determined and when other members of a person's reference group are successful represents a potential loss of status within both the group and the organization. A person's self-concept is also deflated in such circumstances.

The fear of such a loss may be a stronger motivating factor for a person to achieve his budget than any of the other pressures mentioned. "Fear of failure, then, is a very powerful functional consequence of budgeting systems and, quite likely, is latent."

One of the major benefits of budgeting is motivation, explicitly incorporated in the use of standards. Budgets should reflect a goal which people can strive for and achieve. To provide maximum motivation for employees, management should judge failure to achieve an objective in the context of the situation causing failure and not merely in terms of a figure circled in red. All members of the organization must be aware of this basic principle.

Participation in Budgeting

In a participatory system of budgeting, preparation of budget schedules would start at the lower levels of the hierarchy and move upward. As it moved upward, various people would make additional suggestions and some eliminations until the schedules reached the controller and top management. These people would analyze it and see that it was a coordinated plan in accordance with organizational goals before final approval would be given. Movement up and down the hierarchy could be made if drastic changes were necessary. By reciprocal communications, people would know why changes were justified and could constructively criticize them if they desired.

Behavioral scientists and accountants generally believe that such a system would be an improvement on imposed budgets. The functional, manifest results claimed for this system are:

1. It would have a healthful effect on interest, initiative, morale, and enthusiasm.

2. It would result in a better plan because the knowledge of many individuals is combined.

3. It would make all levels of management more aware of how their particular functions fit into the total operational picture.

4. It would increase interdepartmental cooperation.

5. As a result of their direct involvement in the planning function, it would make junior management more aware of the future with respect to objectives, problems, and other considerations.

It is possible to achieve these benefits through successful participation. There are, however, factors that have a significant impact on whether or not participation can lead to successful results.

One essential requirement is that participation be legitimate. If participation is allowed but top management continually changes the budgeted figures resulting from participation, legitimate participation does not exist. This might better be described as a form of "pseudoparticipation." The supposed "participants" would likely resent such a policy and the consequences would be dysfunctional. This is borne out by the studies of V. H. Vroom, who found that productivity was higher when participation was viewed as legitimate, but lower when it was viewed as not legitimate.[11]

Other factors limiting the usefulness of budget participation are:

1. Personality differences of managers as reflected in their leadership style are important. Aggressive managers can put forth their demands more strongly than meek ones. Subordinates would view the latter as not looking out for their interests and antagonism between subordinates and their superiors, and managers themselves, could easily develop.

2. An autocratic, centralized organization would have little use for a participation policy whereas a democratic, decentralized organization would likely benefit from, and almost require, a participation policy.

3. Those allowed participation rights must be positively oriented toward the objectives of the firm. Only if the group is cohesive in thought and desire toward, and understands, the plan can participation policy be functional.

4. The cultural setting of an organization and the background of employees should be considered. People in rural areas or with a rural background are more inclined to accept assigned tasks. In such an atmosphere, a participation policy would probably meet with little response.

Studies have been carried out showing that participation in any situation is not necessarily useful for increasing efficiency.[12] Other studies have reported that when a nonparticipative group became participative and was compared with an existing nonparticipative or participative group, the former never caught up in terms of performance with the latter two groups. These studies imply that the introduction of a participation policy for a formerly nonparticipative group would not likely lead to increased efficiency and may even result in decreased efficiency. If this conclusion is accepted, a group should be endowed with the right to participate only when the group is created or the budget system is being implemented and not after either has previously been directed through decisions made by superiors.

The most severe criticism offered against participation is that the increased morale which supposedly results does not necessarily result in increased efficiency. Is high morale a cause of increased efficiency or is greater efficiency a cause of high morale, or is there some intervening variable which must be present if a true causal relationship is to exist? Group cohesiveness seems to be the most significant of possible variables that have been examined although other variables are obviously involved. Figure 2 shows postulated relationships that could develop using group cohesiveness with regard to subordinate thoughts toward management.

As those participating in a budget (foremen and up) would be management-oriented, at least to some extent, they would probably have a positive approach to management activities and objectives. The previous discussion on role conflict situations shows, however, that negative attitudes toward budgeting are quite possible.

If the group is antimanagement or antibudget, a participation policy would be of little use. Supervisors may even propose ridiculously low standards and upper management would be forced to revise them. Pseudoparticipation would exist and likely result in the increase of negative attitudes toward management or budgeting.

If the atmosphere is favorable for allowing participation, group cohesiveness

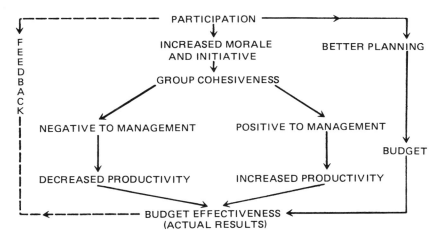

Figure 2 Participation and budgets.

toward management and budgeting should be maintained and enhanced if possible. Group discussions led by an able management person to inform *and* listen to supervisors, foremen, and other management people could probably aid in implementing the budget. By listening to and taking action on suggestions made by the group, he would be able to indicate his and top management's sincerity in gaining successful participation in the budgeting system.

Undoubtedly, the evidence on the effectiveness of participation in budgeting is mixed. Supporters of participation readily admit that it is by no means a panacea for achieving the full motivational potential of the budget. The fact is that participation is not a segregated aspect of management but embraces several technical and behavioral concepts which make it more or less useful in different organizations. The organization's particular situation with regard to the development of these concepts must be recognized and thoughtfully considered when contemplating or evaluating a participation policy.

It should be noted that even if productivity does not increase directly through participation, better planning and increased morale and initiative may of themselves justify such a policy.

Communication Aspects of Budgeting

Researchers on control and motivation generally agree that information on planned and actual results should be communicated to the employee whose performance is being measured.

Nevertheless, many budget departments merely communicate the results to management with the result that the employee does not know how he has done until he is called up to discuss his performance report. Consequently, the individual may ignore the budget and perform without a guide, hoping for the best.

When results are communicated as rapidly as possible, an employee's mistakes can be associated with his recent actions and he is likely to learn more from the experience than if reports are received long after the action has been taken. This learning would likely result in improved performance on future budgets.

When reports given to management employees are timely, reasonably accurate, and understandable, functional consequences are more likely to occur than if the opposite exists. Figure 3 summarizes the effect of the communication system on the behavior of line people.

Employee Group Behavior and Its Effects on Budgeting

Peter Blau's study on the use of statistical measures in evaluating employee performance has implications for evaluating and understanding budgeting.[13] The study examined the effect of group cohesiveness, in the sense of willingness to cooperate among members, and the resulting productivity in different situations.

His findings showed that the group which cooperated was more productive

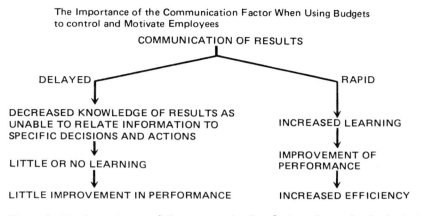

Figure 3 The importance of the communication factor when using budgets to control and motivate employees.

than the group which did not cooperate but competed individually among themselves. He also discovered that highly competitive individuals in the latter group were more productive than any individual in the cooperative group. Blau's hypothesis was that a paradox existed:

> The resulting paradox is that competitiveness and productivity are inversely related for groups but directly related for individuals in the competitive group.[14]

In terms of the achievement of organizational objectives, the implication is that cooperative cohesiveness among group members assigned a particular task is most desirable. When this is achieved, cooperation will result in each member helping others in the group, even though it may result in a decrease in the performance record of the assisting individual.

Applying this to budgeting, the suggestion is that individual performance should not be the ultimate objective in the eyes of top management or employees. Rewards and punishments should not be based entirely on an individual's performance as compared to the plan. The budget reports should be only one of many factors used for evaluation and superiors should recognize this fact. The result would be a decline in individual competition and greater cooperation toward the achievement of a goal. This environment could eliminate possible dysfunctional consequences. Group cohesiveness will be greatly affected by the leadership style of the group's superior. Whether he believes in rigidity or flexibility, whether he is authoritative or democratic, and the freedom granted him by the organizational structure and policies, will influence the way he controls his subordinates.

Mechanical Considerations of Budgeting

Dysfunctional consequences can arise from the mechanical aspects of budgeting.

Budgeting systems cost money to install and continue. These costs must always be considered when evaluating the worthiness of a system.

It must also be remembered that budgets are merely estimates or predictions. As such, they could be incorrect or inappropriate because of economic, technical, and environmental changes. The estimating procedure itself may be inappropriate. If budgets are thought of as a goal rather than a means of reaching the goal, the emphasis on budgets cannot help but carry dysfunctional consequences, particularly when the estimates have been incorrectly computed.

A final mechanical problem involves the assignment of costs to the person deemed responsible for them. There is always a strong possibility that costs assigned to one person may have been caused by another. The subsequent bickering and ill-feeling would obviously be dysfunctional.

Budgets must be capable of flexibility. This is fundamentally the result of management attitudes and not inherent in the budget itself. Management must recognize that forced adherence to a plan could cause decisions to be made that are not in the long-run interest of the business. Unforeseen opportunities may arise which were not planned. A decision resulting in a significant, unfavorable variance on the short-range plan may be the best alternative in terms of long-range profitability. Failure to take advantage of such situations may result in adherence to the budget but also in dysfunctional consequences in terms of achieving the objectives of budgeting.

Alternatively, failure to adhere to budget figures when they are correct, merely to protect the individuals involved or their superiors, must also be avoided. Such an attitude would destroy one of the cornerstones of a successful budgeting system.

GENERAL MODEL OF THE CONSEQUENCES OF A BUDGETING SYSTEM

Figure 4 summarizes the factors which must be considered when determining the functional and dysfunctional consequences possible from a budgeting system.

The square immediately outside the budget square indicates the potential benefits to be derived from a successful budgeting system. These benefits are functional to the more efficient achievement of an organization's goal of making profit. The next surrounding square indicates many of the factors which can aid or prevent the achievement of the desired benefits. The descriptive model is arranged so that the effects of various environmental circumstances and managerial policies (participation, motivational intentions, organization structure, etc.) can be immediately related to a particular benefit (planning). The square at the top

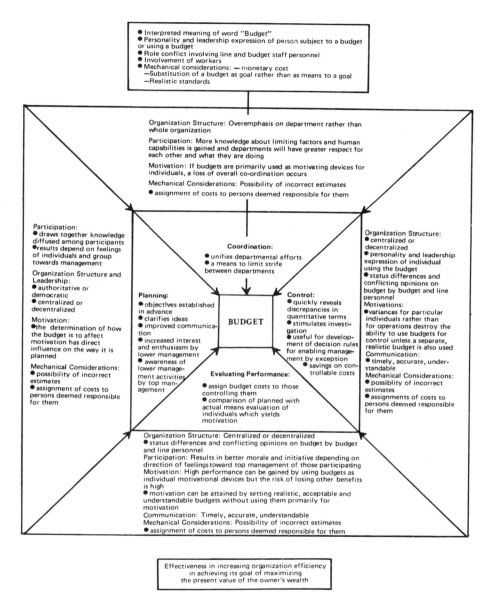

Figure 4 General model of the factors to consider when determining the functional and dysfunctional aspects of introducing and using a budgeting system.

of the diagram includes factors which are not specifically related to any one particular benefit but which have an important influence on the success or failure of the overall budget system.

The points mentioned in the peripheral square and the top square cannot be clearly identified as either functional or dysfunctional. The relationship of these points to the benefits of budgeting depends on the particular circumstances.

CONCLUSION

The model which has been developed to point out the functional possibilities of budgeting and to identify the sources of possible dysfunctional consequences represents a summary of relevant findings and statements by behavioral scientists, accountants, and managers.

Budgeting is only one type of control technique used by top management. Many of the propositions developed are equally applicable to other types of quantitatively oriented control techniques.

The points developed in this chapter should be considered by any organization using or contemplating the introduction of a budgeting process. The importance of each point will vary, however, according to the particular organization, its strategy, history, organizational structure, reasons for using the system, the personalities involved, the leadership style of individuals in responsible positions, the general attitudes of employees toward the organization and control devices, the cohesiveness of reference groups working on and with the budget, and the personal attitudes of employees regarding the justification of, and methods of achieving, organizational goals.

The major proposition suggested is that a budgeting system designed to accomplish the designated benefits is something more than a series of figures. Its origination, implementation, and degree of success are significantly related to the behaviorally oriented problems that can easily arise. Management methods for solving these problems cannot be generalized into a specific set of rules. Definite rules can seldom cover the particular developments of unique situations. Therefore, only general aspects of budgeting systems with emphasis on behavioral topics have been considered.

The only absolute conclusion that can be proposed is that the human factors involved are generally more difficult to identify and deal with and more serious in nature than the development of quantifying and figure determination techniques. Accountants and managers must recognize this fact if they expect to perform their functions adequately.

NOTES

1. R. Merton, A paradigm for functional analysis in sociology, in *Sociological Theory: A Book of Readings,* L. Coser and B. Rosenberg, (eds.), New York, Macmillan, 1957, pp. 458-467.
2. Amitai Etzioni, Two approaches to organizational analysis: A critique and a suggestion, in Bobbs-Merrill Reprint Series in the Social Sciences 8-80. Reprinted by permission of *Administrative Science Quarterly, 5,* Sept. 1960, pp. 257-278.
3. Ibid., p. 272.
4. David Green, Jr., Budgeting and accounting: The inseparable siamese twins, *Budgeting, Nov. 1965,* p. 11.
5. Chris Argyris, *The Impact of Budgets on People,* Ithaca, N.Y. Prepared for the Controllership Foundation at Cornell University, 1952, p. 23.
6. The source of this figure and study is Argyris, *The Impact of Budgets on People,* a summary of comments and statements, pp. 10-12.
7. W. F. Whyte, *Men at Work,* Irwin and Dorsey Press, Homewood, Ill., 1961, p. 495.
8. Argyris, *The Impact of Budgets on People.*
9. Andrew C. Stedry, *Budget Control and Cost Behavior,* Englewood Cliffs, N.J., Prentice-Hall, 1960.
10. Selwyn Becker and David Green, Jr. Budgeting and employee behavior, in *Journal of Business, 35,* 1962. These are among the authors who debate the practical application of Stedry's conclusions.
11. Andrew C. Stedry, Budgeting and employee behavior: A reply, in *Journal of Business, 37,* April 1964, p. 198.
12. See ibid., p. 196; also Nancy Morse and E. Reimer, The experimental change of a major organizational variable, in *Journal of Abnormal and Social Psychology, 52,* 1956, pp. 120-129; and J. R. P. French, Jr., E. Kay, and H. H. Meyer, *A Study of Threat and Participation in a Performance Appraisal Situation,* New York, General Electric Co., 1962.
13. Peter M. Blau, Cooperation and competition in a bureaucracy, in Bobbs-Merrill Reprint Series in the Social Sciences, S-28. Reprinted by the permission of the *American Journal of Sociology, 59,* May 1964.
14. Ibid., p. 530.

3

BEHAVIORAL ASSUMPTIONS OF MANAGEMENT ACCOUNTING*

Edwin H. Caplan

Accounting has been closely associated with the development of the modern business organization. Thus, we might expect accountants to show a strong interest in recent contributions to organization theory which increase our understanding of the business firm and how it functions. An examination of accounting literature, however, suggests that (despite the steadily increasing flow of accounting articles and texts incorporating the words "management" and "decisions" in their titles) accountants have been relatively unconcerned with current research in organization theory. Although the past few years have witnessed the beginnings of an effort to bridge this gap, much still remains to be done.[1] This chapter attempts to demonstrate that an understanding of behavioral theory is relevant to the development of management accounting theory and practice.

The discussion to be presented here may be summarized as follows:

1. The management accounting function is essentially a behavioral function and the nature and scope of management accounting systems is materially

---

*Reprinted from *The Accounting Review,* vol. 41, no. 3 (July 1966), pp. 496-509. References have been renumbered.

influenced by the view of human behavior which is held by the accountants who design and operate these systems.

2. It is possible to identify a "traditional" management accounting model of the firm and to associate with this model certain fundamental assumptions about human behavior. These assumptions are presented in Table 1.

3. It is also possible to postulate behavioral assumptions based on modern organization theory and to relate them to the objectives of management accounting. A tentative set of such assumptions appears in Table 2.

4. Research directed at testing the nature and validity of accounting assumptions with respect to human behavior in business organizations can be useful in evaluating and perhaps improving the effectiveness of management accounting systems.

Table 1 Behavioral Assumptions of "Traditional" Management Accounting Model of the Firm

Assumptions with Respect to Organization Goals

A. The principal objective of business activity is profit maximization (economic theory).

B. This principal objective can be segmented into subgoals to be distributed throughout the organization (principles of management).

C. Goals are additive—what is good for the parts of the business is also good for the whole (principles of management).

Assumptions with Respect to the Behavior of Participants

A. Organization participants are motivated primarily by economic forces (economic theory).

B. Work is essentially an unpleasant task which people will avoid whenever possible (economic theory).

C. Human beings are ordinarily inefficient and wasteful (scientific management).

Assumptions with Respect to the Behavior of Management

A. The role of the business manager is to maximize the profits of the firm (economic theory).

B. In order to perform this role, management must control the tendencies of employees to be lazy, wasteful, and inefficient (scientific management).

C. The essence of management control is authority. The ultimate authority of management stems from its ability to affect the economic reward structure (scientific management).

(continued)

Table 1 (continued)

D. There must be a balance between the authority a person has and his responsibility for performance (principles of management).

Assumptions with Respect to the Role of Management Accounting

A. The primary function of management accounting is to aid management in the process of profit maximization (scientific management).

B. The accounting system is a "goal allocation" device which permits management to select its operating objectives and to divide and distribute them throughout the firm, i.e., assign responsibilities for performance. This is commonly referred to as "planning" (principles of management).

C. The accounting system is a control device which permits management to identify and correct undesirable performance (scientific management).

D. There is sufficient certainty, rationality, and knowledge within the system to permit an accurate comparison of responsibility for performance and the ultimate benefits and costs of that performance (principles of management).

E. The accounting system is "neutral" in its evaluations—personal bias is eliminated by the objectivity of the system (principles of management).

Table 2 Some Behavioral Assumptions from Modern Organization Theory

Assumptions with Respect to Organization Goals

A. Organizations are coalitions of individual participants. Strictly speaking, the organization itself, which is "mindless," cannot have goals—only the individuals can have goals.

B. Those objectives which are usually viewed as organizational goals are, in fact, the objectives of the dominant members of the coalition, subject to whatever constraints are imposed by the other participants and by the external environment of the organization.

C. Organization objectives tend to change in response to (1) changes in the goals of the dominant participants, (2) changes in the relationships within the coalition, and (3) changes in the external environment of the organization.

D. In the modern complex business enterprise, there is no single universal organization goal such as profit maximization. To the extent that any truly overall objective might be identified, that objective is probably organization survival.

E. Facing a highly complex and uncertain world and equipped with only limited rationality, members of an organization tend to focus on "local" (i.e., individual and departmental) goals. These local goals are often in conflict with each other. In addition, there appears to be no valid basis for the assumption that they are homogeneous and thus additive—what is good for the parts of the organization is not necessarily good for the whole.

Table 2 (continued)

Assumptions with Respect to the Behavior of Participants

A. Human behavior within an organization is essentially an adaptive, problem-solving, decision-making process.

B. Organization participants are motivated by a wide variety of psychological, social, and economic needs and drives. The relative strength of these diverse needs differs between individuals and within the same individual over time.

C. The decision of an individual to join an organization, and the separate decision to contribute his productive efforts once a member, are based on the individual's perception of the extent to which such action will further the achievement of his personal goals.

D. The efficiency and effectiveness of human behavior and decision making within organizations is constrained by (1) the inability to concentrate on more than a few things at a time, (2) limited awareness of the environment, (3) limited knowledge of alternative courses of action and the consequences of such alternatives, (4) limited reasoning ability, and (5) incomplete and inconsistent preference systems. As a result of these limits on human rationality, individual and organizational behavior is usually directed at attempts to find satisfactory—rather than optimal—solutions.

Assumptions with Respect to Behavior of Management

A. The primary role of the business manager is to maintain a favorable balance between (1) the contributions required from the participants and (2) the inducement (i.e., perceived need satisfactions) which must be offered to secure these contributions.

B. The management role is essentially a decision-making process subject to the limitations on human rationality and cognitive ability. The manager must make decisions himself and must effectively influence the decision premises of others so that their decisions will be favorable for the organization.

C. The essence of management control is the willingness of other participants to *accept* the authority of management. This willingness appears to be a non-stable function of the inducement-contribution balance.

D. Responsibility is assigned from "above" and authority is accepted from "below." It is, therefore, meaningless to speak of the balance between responsibility and authority as if both of these were "given" to the manager.

Assumptions with Respect to the Role of Accounting

A. The management accounting process is an information system whose major purposes are (1) to provide the various levels of management with data which will facilitate the decision-making functions of planning and control and (2) to serve as a communications medium within the organization.

Table 2 (continued)

B. The effective use of budgets and other accounting control techniques requires an understanding of the interaction between these techniques and the motivations and aspiration levels of the individuals to be controlled.

C. The objectivity of the management accounting process is largely a myth. Accountants have wide areas of discretion in the selection, processing, and reporting of data.

D. In performing their function within an organization, accountants can be expected to be influenced by their own personal and departmental goals in the same way other participants are influenced.

MANAGEMENT ACCOUNTING AS A BEHAVIORAL PROCESS

The management of a business enterprise is faced with an environment—both internal and external to the firm—that is in a perpetual state of change. Not only is this environment constantly changing, but it is changing in many dimensions. These include physical changes (climate, availability of raw materials, etc.), technological changes (new products and processes, etc.), social changes (attitudes of employees, customers, competitors, etc.), and financial changes (asset composition, availability of funds, etc.).

An important characteristic of "good" management is the ability to evaluate past changes, to react to current changes, and to predict future changes. This is consistent with the view that management is essentially a decision-making process and the view that accounting is an information system which acts as an integral part of this decision-making process. It is inconceivable, however, that any workable information system could provide data relative to all, or even a substantial portion, of the changes occurring inside and outside of the organization. There are several reasons for this. Many changes—particularly those that occur in the external environment—are simply not available to the information system of the firm. These changes represent "external unknowns" in a world of uncertainty and limited knowledge. Further, a substantial number of changes that occur within the firm itself may not be perceived by the information system. Thus, there exist internal as well as external unknowns.

Even if accountants were aware of all the changes which are taking place—or if they could be made aware of them—they still would not be able to reflect them all within their information system. There must be a selection process, explicit or implicit, which permits the gathering and processing of only the most critical information and facilitates the screening out of all other data. In the first place, many items of information would cost more to gather and process than the value of the benefits they would provide. Also, an excessive flow of data would "clog" the system and prevent the timely and efficient passage and evaluation of more important information.[2] Therefore, only a certain, very limited, set of data (i.e., observations about changes) can be selected for admission into the system. The essential point to be noted here is that decisions regarding what information is the most critical, how it should be processed, and who should receive it are almost always made by accountants. In addition, they are often directly involved, as participants, in the management decision-making process itself.

In carrying out these activities, accountants utilize a frame of reference that is, in effect, their view of the nature of the firm and its participation. The operation of their system requires them to be constantly abstracting a selected flow of information from the complex real world and using this selected data as the variables in their "model" of the firm. It seems clear that accountants exercise choice in the design of their systems and the selection of data for admission into them. It also seems clear that the entire management accounting process can be viewed from the standpoint of attempting to influence the behavior of others. It follows, therefore, that they must perform these functions with certain expectations with respect to the reactions of others to what they do. In other words, their model of the firm must involve some set of explicit or implicit assumptions about human behavior in organizations.

THE "TRADITIONAL" VIEW OF BEHAVIOR

Once it has been demonstrated that the management accounting function does by necessity involve assumptions about behavior, the next task is to identify these assumptions. Our investigation is complicated by the fact that nowhere in the literature of accounting is there a formal statement of the behavioral assumptions of the management accounting model of the firm. It is necessary, therefore, to attempt to construct such a statement. We begin with the premise that present day management accounting theory and practice is the product of three related conceptual forces, namely, industrial engineering technology, classical organization theory, and the economic "theory of the firm." An examination of the literature of management accounting suggests that accountants may have avoided the necessity of developing a behavioral model of their own by borrowing a set of assumptions from these other areas. If this thesis is valid, an appropriate point to begin the search for such assumptions is by an examination of the assumptions of these related models. Since much of the engineering view appears to be incorporated in the classical organization theory model,[3] it can probably be eliminated from this analysis without significant loss. Further, it appears that classical organization theory and economics do not represent two completely different views of human behavior, but rather that they essentially share a single view.

The following paragraphs will attempt to demonstrate that—with the exception of the modern organization theory concepts of recent years—there has been a single view of human behavior in business organizations from the period of the industrial revolution to the present and that management accounting has adopted this view without significant modification or serious question as to its validity.

The Economic Theory of the Firm

It has been suggested that, from the beginnings of recorded history, the traditional determinant of human behavior in organizations has been either custom or physical force.[4] As long as this was the case, there was no real need for an organization theory or economic theory to explain how and why human beings worked together cooperatively to accomplish common goals. However, the changing structure of society, which accompanied—and to an extent caused—the industrial revolution, destroyed much of the force of these traditional determinants of behavior. The new entrepreneurial class of the eighteenth century sought not only a social philosophy to rationalize its actions, it also sought practical solutions to the immediate problems of motivating, coordinating, and controlling the members of its organizations. The second of these needs resulted in the development of the classical organization theories which will be discussed in the following section. The first need, i.e., the quest for a rationalization, ultimately led to the incorporation of the economic theory of the firm into the logic of the industrial society.

The economic theory of the firm can be summarized as follows. The entrepreneur is faced with a series of behavior alternatives. These alternatives are limited by the economic constraints of the market and the technological constraints of the production function. Within these constraints he will act in such a way as to maximize his economic profit. This behavior is facilitated by the personality characteristic of complete rationality and the information system characteristic of perfect knowledge. Finally, the individual so described is one who is entirely motivated by economic forces. A more subtle elaboration of this last point is the view that leisure has value and that a person will not work except in response to sufficient economic incentives. Thus, the classical economist specifically assumed that man was essentially "lazy" and preferred to minimize his work effort.[5]

Most modern economists would agree that the classical theory of the firm is based on several rather severe abstractions from the real world of business enterprise.[6] Nevertheless, despite these criticisms, there can be little doubt that it has had a substantial influence on the development of management philosophy and practice. The explanation of human behavior offered by economists, i.e., economic motivation and profit maximization, was incorporated into the patterns of thought of the merging industrial community, where it not only became established in its own right but also provided the philosophical and psychological foundations of the scientific management movement.

Classical Organization Theory

At the turn of the century, Frederick W. Taylor began a major investigation into the functioning of business organizations which became known as the scientific management movement. Taylor's approach combined the basic behavioral assumptions of the economic theory of the firm with the viewpoint of the engineer seeking the most effective utilization of the physical resources at his disposal. He was concerned with people primarily as "adjuncts to machines" and was interested in maximizing the productivity of the worker through increased efficiency and reduced costs. Implicit in this approach was the belief that if men who might otherwise be wasteful and inefficient could be instructed in methods of achieving increased productivity and at the same time be provided with adequate economic incentives and proper working conditions, they could be motivated to adopt the improvements, and the organization would benefit accordingly.[7]

March and Simon have noted that the ideas of the scientific management movement are based predominantly on a model of human behavior which assumes that "organization members, and particularly employees, are primarily *passive instruments,* capable of performing work and accepting directions, but not initiating action or exerting influence in any significant way."[8]

The scientific management movement flourished and rapidly became an important part of the business enterprise scene; in fact, for many years it virtually dominated this scene. Furthermore, even a brief glance at current management literature and practices should satisfy the reader that most of Taylor's views are still widely accepted today. Newer theories of management may have supplemented but they have never entirely replaced the scientific management approach.

The work of Taylor and his scientific management successors led them into detailed studies of factory costs and provided an important stimulus for the development of modern cost and management accounting. Administrative management theory further contributed to this development through its emphasis on control and departmental responsibility and accountability. Finally, all of this occurred within the overall setting provided by the economic theory of the firm. In summary, it seems clear that with respect to both its philosophy and techniques, much of contemporary management accounting is a product of, and is geared to, these classical theories. This is what is referred to here as the traditional management accounting model of the firm.

A Tentative Statement of the Behavioral Assumptions
Underlying Present Day Management Accounting

It should now be possible to draw together the several strands of the preceding discussion and attempt to postulate some of the fundamental behavioral assumptions that appear to underlie the traditional management accounting model.

These assumptions were presented in Table 1. The parenthetical notations note the major conceptual sources of the assumptions. In some cases, there appears to be a considerable overlapping of sources; however, since this is not crucial to the present investigation, the notations have been limited to the primary or most significant area.

SOME BEHAVIORAL CONCEPTS OF MODERN ORGANIZATION THEORY

The preceding paragraphs were concerned with an effort to identify a set of behavioral assumptions which could be associated with current theory and practice in management accounting. We will now attempt to develop an alternative set of behavioral assumptions for management accounting—one that is based on concepts from modern organization theory.

Of the several different modern organization theory approaches, the "decision-making model" of the firm has been selected for use here. The basis for this choice is the close relationship which appears to exist between the decision-making model and the information system concept of management accounting discussed earlier. The decision-making approach to organization theory effectively began with the writings of Chester I. Barnard, particularly in *The Functions of the Executive*, and was further developed by Simon and others.[9] The model is primarily concerned with the organizational processes of communication and decision making. While drawing heavily on sociology and psychology, it is distinguished from these organization theory approaches by its emphasis on the decision as the basic element of organization.

Organizations are viewed as cooperative efforts or coalitions entered into by individuals in order to achieve personal objectives which cannot be realized without such cooperation. These individuals are motivated to join the organization and contribute to the accomplishment of its objectives because they believe that in this way they can satisfy their personal goals. It is important to note that these personal goals include social and psychological, as well as economic, considerations. Thus, the survival and success of the organization depends on the maintenance of a favorable balance between the contributions required of each participant and the opportunities to satisfy personal goals which must be offered as inducements to secure effective participation.

It is common practice to speak of organization goals; however, to be completely precise, it is the participants who have goals. The organization itself is mindless and therefore can have no goals. In the sense that it is used here, the term "organization goals" is intended to mean the goals of the dominant members of the coalition subject to those constraints which are imposed by other participants and by the external environment. This view implies an organizational goal structure which is in a constant state of change as the environment and the balances and relationships among the participants change. Under such circumstances, it seems meaningless to talk of a single universal goal such as profit maximization. To the extent that any long-run overall objective might be identified, it appears that this objective would have to be stated in very broad and general terms, such as the goal of organization survival.

The decision-making process is usually described as a sequence of three steps: (1) the evoking of alternative courses of action, (2) a consideration of the consequences of the evoked alternatives, and (3) the assignement of values to the various consequences.[10]

It has been suggested that any behavioral theory of rational choice must consider certain limits on the decision maker.[11] These include his (1) limited knowledge with respect to all possible alternatives and consequences, (2) limited cognitive ability, (3) constantly changing value structure, and (4) tendency to "satisfice" rather than maximize. Rational behavior, therefore, consists of searching among limited alternatives for a reasonable solution under conditions in which the consequences of action are uncertain.

The behavioral concepts which flow from the decision-making model have a number of interesting implications. For example, authority is viewed as something which is accepted from "below" rather than imposed from "above"[12]; in other words, there must be a *decision to accept* authority before such authority can become effective. Further, human activity is considered to be essentially a process of problem-solving and adaptive behavior—a process in which goals, perception, and abilities are all interrelated and all continually changing.

To summarize the decision-making model, the basic element of organization study is the decision. The objective of managerial decision making is to secure and coordinate effectively the contributions of other participants. This is accomplished by influencing, to the extent possible, their perception of alternatives and consequences of choice and their value structures, so that the resulting decisions are consistent with the current objectives of the dominant members of the organization.

While the theorists of the decision-making school have paid substantial attention to behavioral concepts, the literature does not appear to contain a detailed and complete statement of their underlying behavioral assumptions. Accordingly, it becomes necessary, as it was with the traditional accounting model, to abstract and formulate a set of assumptions. The modern organization theory assumptions presented in Table 2 represent an attempt by the present writer to identify and extend the behavioral assumptions of the decision-making model in terms of the management accounting function.

BASIC CONFLICTS BETWEEN THE BEHAVIORAL ASSUMPTIONS OF TRADITIONAL MANAGEMENT ACCOUNTING AND MODERN ORGANIZATION THEORY

An examination of the two sets of behavioral assumptions developed above suggests a number of interesting questions. Answers to these questions, however, can only be found through extended empirical analysis. Thus, whatever value attaches to the foregoing discussion appears to relate to its possible contribution in providing a theoretical framework for future empirical research. This research might be designed to explore such questions as the following:

1. What behavioral model provides the most realistic view of human behavior in business organizations? (Accountants should, perhaps, be willing to accept the research findings of organization theorists regarding this question.)

2. Is it possible to draw any general conclusions about the view of behavior actually held by accountants (and managers) in practice?

3. What, if any, are the major differences in the behavioral assumptions of the views in 1 and 2 above?

4. What, if any, are the consequences for the organization and its participants of the differences in the behavioral assumptions of the views in 1 and 2?

5. Is it possible to design management accounting systems which are based on a more realistic view of behavior, and would such systems produce better results than present systems?

Lacking empirical evidence, any attempt to investigate the implications of the differences between the two views of behavior discussed in this chapter must be considered highly speculative. We might, however, examine briefly a few of the major differences in order to illustrate the nature of the problem. Let us assume for the moment that the decision-making model represents a more realistic view of human behavior than the traditional management accounting model. Let us further assume that the traditional model is a reasonably accurate summary of actual management accounting views in practice. Under these circumstances, what are some of the consequences for business organizations of the use of accounting systems based on the traditional management accounting model of behavior?

Assumptions with Respect to Organization Goals

In comparing these two sets of assumptions, the most immediately apparent difference concerns the relative simplicity and brevity of the traditional accounting assumptions as contrasted to those of the organization theory model. This should not be particularly surprising since such a difference seems to be consistent with the general philosophies of the two models. There can be little doubt that the view of human behavior associated with the scientific management movement and classical economics is much less complicated than the behavioral outlooks of modern organization theory. In fact, the principal conflict between modern and classical organization theories appears to rest precisely on this issue. Since traditional management accounting is closely related to the classical models, it seems reasonable to expect that it will also tend toward a relatively simple and uncomplicated view of behavior. For example, with respect to organization goals, the behavioral assumptions of the accounting model focus on a single universal objective of business activity. The organization theory assumptions, on the other hand, suggest a much broader and rather imprecise structure of goals.

The traditional management accounting view of organization goals, which appears to be directly related to the theory of the firm of classical economics, may be summarized as follows: The principal objective of business activity is the maximization of the economic profits of the enterprise; the total responsibility for the accomplishment of that objective can be divided into smaller portions and distributed to subunits throughout the organization; the maximization by each subunit of its particular portion of the profit responsibility will result in maximization of the total profits of the enterprise.

The entire structure of traditional management accounting appears to be built around this concept of profit maximization and the related (but quite different) idea of cost minimization. Management accountants have, for the most part, limited the scope of their systems to the selection, processing, and reporting of data concerning certain economic events, the effects of which can be reduced—without too many complications—to monetary terms. This approach is justifiable only if the particular class of events under consideration can be viewed as *the* critical variables affecting the organization. Thus, accountants have been able to rationalize the importance of the data flowing through their systems by relating these data and their use directly to the assumed goal of profit maximization. However, the classical economic view of profits as the universal motivating force of business enterprises has come under substantial attack in recent years. This attack has been based on two general issues. First, questions have been raised concerning the adequacy of economic profits as the sole significant explanation for what takes place within an organization. Second, it has been suggested that limitations on the decision-making process result in behavior which is best described as satisficing rather than maximizing.

It should be particularly emphasized that the recognition of a more complex goal structure does not mean that economic profits can be ignored. Obviously, business firms cannot survive for any extended period of time without some minimum level of profits.

What is the practical implication of these observations? How would management accounting change if accountants did not concentrate exculsively on profit maximation?

The traditional accounting assumption with respect to the divisibility and additivity of the responsibility for the accomplishment of organization goals seems to warrant some additional comment. Research in organization theory has indicated that individual members of an organization tend to identify with their immediate group rather than with the organization itself. This tendency appears to encourage the development of strong subunit loyalties and a concentration on the goals of the subunit even when these goals are in conflict with the interests of the organization. The usual departmental budgeting and accounting techniques, by which management accountants endeavor to measure the success of the various subunits within an organization in achieving certain goals, are based on the assumption that profit maximization or cost minimization at the departmental level will lead to a similar result for the firm as a whole. Thus, accounting reports tend to highlight supposed departmental efficiencies and inefficiencies. Reports of this type seem to encourage departmental activities aimed at "making a good showing" regardless of the effect on the entire organization. It appears to be common for departments within an organization to be in a state of competition with each other for funds, recognition, authority, and so forth. Under such circumstances, it is not very likely that the cooperative efforts necessary to the efficient functioning of the organization as a whole will be furthered by an accounting system which emphasizes and, perhaps, even fosters interdepartmental conflicts.

The tendency for intraorganizational conflict appears to be further compounded by some of the common management accounting techniques for the allocation and control of costs. For example, in some organizations with relatively rigid budgeting procedures, it appears to be a normal practice for departments to deliberately attempt to use up their entire budget for a given period in order to avoid a reduction in the budgets of succeeding periods. Another example is the emphasis often placed on the desirability of keeping costs below some predetermined amount. In such cases, it is likely that, even though a departmental expenditure would be extremely beneficial to an organization, it will not be undertaken if such action would cause the costs of that department to exceed the predetermined limit.

CONCLUSIONS

This chapter has attempted to postulate a set of behavioral assumptions which could be associated with the theory and practice of "traditional" management accounting. The resulting set of 15 assumptions represents an accounting adaptation of what might be termed the classical view of human behavior in business organizations. This view emphasizes such concepts as profit maximization, economic incentives, and the inherent laziness and inefficiency of organization participants. It is a model which is structured primarily in terms of the classical ideas of departmentalization, authority, responsibility, and control. The accounting process which has emerged in response to the needs presented by this classical model appears to treat human behavior and goals essentially as given. Further, the generally accepted measure of "good" accounting seems to be one of relevance and usefulness in the maximization of the money profits of the enterprise.

In addition, we have examined a set of behavioral assumptions based on research in modern organization theory. It seems clear that a management accounting system structured around this second set of behavioral assumptions would differ in many respects from the accounting systems found in practice and described in the literature.

One should not infer that the traditional assumptions considered here are completely invalid. The very fact that they have endured for so long suggests that this is not the case. It should at least be recognized, however, that in many respects the extent of their validity may be subject to question. Also, it is not argued that all accountants limit themselves at all times to this traditional view. Rather, the two sets of behavioral assumptions discussed might be considered as extreme points on a scale of many possible views. The significance of the traditional point on such a scale appears to be twofold: (1) it is likely that the traditional model represents a view of behavior which is relatively common in practice and (2) this view seems to underlie much of what is written and taught about accounting.

If the modern organization theory model does ultimately prove to be a more realistic view of human behavior in business organizations, there is little doubt that the scope of management accounting theory and practice will need to be expanded and broadened. In particular, accountants will have to develop an increased awareness and understanding of the complex social and psychological motivations and limitations of organization participants. What is urgently needed, and what we have had very little of in the past, is solid empirical research designed to measure the effectiveness with which management accounting systems do, in fact, perform their functions of motivating, explaining, and predicting human behavior.

NOTES

1. See, for example: Robert T. Golembiewski, "Accountancy as a Function of Organization Theory," The Accounting Review, April 1964, pp. 333-341; and John J. Willingham, "The Accounting Entity: A Conceptual Model," The Accounting Review, July 1964, pp. 543-552.
2. This is the "capacity problem" discussed by Anton. See Hector R. Anton,

Some Aspects of Measurement and Accounting, Working Paper No. 84, Berkeley, Cal., Center for Research in Management Science, University of California, 1963.

3. One of the earliest, and perhaps the best, example of this consolidation can be found in the work of Taylor. See Frederick W. Taylor, *Scientific Management,* New York, Harper & Brothers, 1911.

4. Robert L. Heilbroner, *The Worldly Philosophers,* ed. rev.; New York, Simon and Schuster, 1961, pp. 7-8.

5. This assumption is the basis for the "backward bending" labor supply curve found in the literature of economics.

6. See, for example, Andreas G. Papandreou, Some basic problems in the theory of the firm, *A Survey of Contemporary Economics,* Vol. 2, Bernard F. Haley (ed.), Homewood, Ill., Irwin, 1952, pp. 183-219.

7. James G. March and Herbert A. Simon, *Organizations,* New York, Wiley, 1958, pp. 12ff.

8. Ibid., p. 6.

9. Chester I. Bernard, *The Functions of the Executive,* Cambridge, Harvard University Press, 1938; Herbert A. Simon, *Administrative Behavior,* New York, Wiley, 1947; March and Simon, *Organizations;* and Richard M. Cyert and James G. March, *A Behavioral Theory of the Firm,* Englewood Cliffs, N.J., Prentice-Hall, 1963. The preceding works represent the principal theoretical sources for the decision-making model discussed here.

10. March and Simon, p. 82.

11. Simon, pp. xxv-xxvi.

12. Douglas McGregor, *The Human Side of Enterprise,* New York, McGraw-Hill, 1960, pp. 158-160.

4

THE MYTH OF INCREMENTALISM: Analytic Choices in Budgetary Theory *

Lance T. LeLoup

INTRODUCTION

Of all the subfields of political science, budgeting is most dominated by one theory to the exclusion of competing theories. For over a decade, *incrementalism* has dominated conceptualization, analysis, and description of the budgetary process. This chapter attempts to show that this dominance has been detrimental to an overall understanding of the dynamics and processes of budgeting. Incrementalism was developed as a fully articulated theory on the basis of a number of implicit analytic choices appearing so obvious as to preclude the consideration of alternatives; however, they were costly in that they provided a misleading view of budgeting.[1]

A growing number of studies challenge the incremental theory of budgeting. The coherent integration of previously isolated challenges in terms of analytic and interpretive choices in the development of budgetary theory will be attempted here. This will not only help to clarify incrementalism but also suggest a number of alternative approaches and explanations. New directions refocusing budgetary

*Reprinted from *Polity,* vol. 10, no. 4 (Summer 1978), pp. 488–509.

theory on annual budgeting and multiyear budgetary decisions will be proposed as more promising for theoretical development. Finally, the conclusion will review the persistence of incrementalism and its relevance to budgeting.

INCREMENTALISM AS BUDGETARY THEORY

When V. O. Key lamented the lack of a budgetary theory, he was referring to the lack of normative theory to guide allocative decisions under conditions of scarcity.[2] Subsequently attempts were made, perhaps in response to Key, to specify a normative theory of budgeting,[3] and the literature supporting planning/programming/ budgeting (PPB) can be seen as a recent extension of such efforts.[4] While incrementalism has a normative foundation in pluralism,[5] our analysis seeks to avoid the explicitly normative dimensions and instead concentrates on explanatory and descriptive aspects of budgetary theory.

The "incrementalists" are the authors of the most influential works on budgeting in the last two decades: Lindblom, Wildavsky, Fenno, Davis et al., and Sharkansky. In "The Science of Muddling Through," Lindblom suggests that in governmental decision making, successive limited comparison of policies is more feasible and rational than comprehensive analysis.[6] Limited, noncomprehensive, incremental change, representing mutual adjustment of participant groups, is portrayed as the most common method of policy formulation.[7] Muddling through is not only what *is* done, it is what *should* be done.

Incorporating Lindblom's thesis, the fully devloped and most influential statement of incremental budgeting is found in Wildavsky's *The Politics of the Budgetary Process,* where he examines the interaction of agencies and Congress and the resulting appropriations decisions.[8]

> Budgeting is incremental, not comprehensive. The beginning of wisdom about an agency budget is that it is almost never actively reviewed as a whole every year in the sense of reconsidering the value of all existing programs as compared to all possible alternatives. Instead, it is based on last year's budget with special attention given to a narrow range of increases or decreases.[9]

Incrementalism explains the strategies and behavior of participants as well as the observed patterns of budgetary stability. The incremental process of mutual adjustment is built around the reinforcing roles and expectations of the participants; agencies attempt to establish a base and then gradually expand it. Their strategy is to ask for an increase, but a modest increase. While they expect to be cut back and take this into account in their calculations, too large a request might result in severe cutbacks. Congress, through the appropriations committee and subcommittees, makes incremental cuts in agency requests because it expects the agencies to request more than they need.

Focusing on the appropriations process in Congress, Richard Fenno detailed the roles assumed by the appropriations committees.[10] As "guardians of the public purse," subcommittees normalize their decision making by routinely making cuts in request.[11] As political subsystems, they develop stable relationships over time with the agencies. Looking at annual changes in agency appropriations, Fenno concludes:

> Committee decisions are primarily incremental ones. These kinds of decisions represent the logical outcome of incrementalism which appears in the agency's expectations about committee action and in the committee's perception of agency budgets.[12]

It is apparent that incrementalism is used in at least two different senses: (a) to characterize the decision-making process of mutual adjustment and bargaining, and (2) to describe the budgetary outcomes that result from that process.[13] Using Fenno's data, Wildavsky interprets budgetary outcomes as incremental because in a majority of cases the final appropriation varies within a range of ± 10 percent of the previous year's appropriation. This is the closest one gets to a firm definition of an incremental income. Fenno's conclusion that committee decisions reveal a basic incrementalism is similarly made without establishing the necessary criteria.

The work of Lindblom, Wildavsky, and Fenno was essentially descriptive of the process of calculation, decision, and the budgetary outcomes. The most important explanatory variable is the budget base, specifically, last year's appropriation.

From descriptive incrementalism, the theory was elevated to what Moreland has called "analytic incrementalism," that is, mathematical representation of the process using regression equations.[14] The empirical models of agency appropriations by Davis, Dempster, and Wildavsky are the most influential tests of the theory.[15] In the initial model (1966), eight equations were hypothesized to explain the decision rules used by the participants. The dependent variable was the final appropriation voted by Congress. Using data from 56 domestic agencies from 1946 to 1963, Davis et al. found they could account for 86 percent of the appropriation decisions. One model each for Congress and the agencies best represented the decisions. The dominant agency decision rule in calculating requests was to take a fixed percentage increase over last year's appropriation. The dominant congressional decision rule in voting appropriations was to make a fixed percentage cut in the agency's request. These two simple calculations summarize the process and the results of incrementalism: the "striking regularities of the budgetary process" that are indicative of the stable decision rules employed by the participants.[16] Change in appropriation patterns are defined as "random shocks in an otherwise deterministic system," the result of "disturbances" and "special circumstances."[17] The causes of disturbances, special circumstances, shift points, or changes in decision rules are left largely unexplained.

   The final elevation of incrementalism was to a predictive theory using econometric modeling techniques.[18] This represented an effort to explain what were previously assumed to be random shift points. These shifts had been detected in years of partisan political change; added to this factor were a number of social, economic, administrative, and political explanatory variables. The inclusion of these environmental variables increased the explanatory power of the models, but since the R^2 were so high under the initial model, the improvement was only marginal.[19] Environmental factors were included as binary variables, "to model the abrupt changes in behavior in response to exogenous forces."[20] Agencies performing services to the administration and population and in the natural resources areas were found to be most susceptible to environmental influences. The impact of the political, social, economic, and administrative variables was found to be evenly distributed among the categories.[21] The latest refinement, although recognizing for the first time the potential impact of external factors, is based on the same theoretical assumptions and reinforced the conclusions of earlier work.

   The theory of budgetary incrementalism is not limited in application to the United States federal budget; subsequent studies have applied it to virtually every level of United States government as well as to other nations and international organizations. Separate studies by Sharkansky and Anton concluded that incrementalism explained budgeting in the American states.[22] John Crecine extended the focus to municipal budgeting with the important caveat that incremental calculations are constrained by revenue projections.[23] Gerwin found incrementalism in school district budgeting.[24] Cowart et al. extended the theory to Norway,[25] and Hoole et al. found incremental decision rules in the United Nations, the World Health Organization, and the International Labor Organization.[26] Wildavsky's latest work, developing a comparative theory of budgeting, makes some important distinctions between governments on the basis of wealth and predictability.[27] The common basis of budgeting in his comparative theory, however, revolves around the concepts of incrementalism. Because of the tremendous scope of these studies, they cannot be examined here, and we shall therefore limit ourselves to United States federal budgeting. A final testament to the pervasive dominance of incrementalism, however, is found in secondary works. Incrementalism has filtered down and is heavily relied on in a range of basic texts on American government, state and local, Congress, the bureaucracy, public policy, etc.[28] The range of different meanings applied to the term and to the theory has further confused the issue.

   In spite of its widespread acceptance, some scholars have been critical of the theory. Some of the criticism is on the normative level; as an outgrowth of pluralism it is said to dignify an irrational, biased process with rational status.[29]

More general criticism has objected to the view of budgeting it provided, producing as it does a uniform set of results in the face of political bargaining. The upshot is an almost apolitical, deterministic, mechanistic explanation of budgeting. Some have attacked the failure to account for the most important points: the bases from which incrementalism proceeds.[30] The present critique of incrementalism will focus on interpretative questions and the analytic framework itself.

INTERPRETIVE QUESTIONS

Are budgetary outcomes clearly incremental as Wildavsky, Fenno, and others have stated? Some suggest that the incrementalists did not interpret their descriptive data correctly. Bailey and O'Connor claim that this misinterpretation is a result of the confusion between incrementalism in the process and incrementalism in outcomes.[31]

> When incremental is thus defined as bargaining, we are aware of no empirical case of a budgetary process which is nonincremental. Further, the working assumption has been that the products of bargaining are incremental outputs. If this is accepted as true by definition, then incrementalism as a descriptive concept is simply not useful. Indeed, the interesting question concerns the range of outputs from bargaining processes and the linkages between nonincremental outputs and the processes which generate them.[32]

Reexamination of Fenno's data reveals a surprising amount of change, greater than 10 percent. Additional budgetary data reveal a similar diversity in budgetary outcomes. Looking at state, federal, and comparative foreign budgetary data, Bailey and O'Connor conclude that all reveal a broad range of results.[33] From 1960 to 1971 the Army Corps of Engineers had nine of eleven annual changes (82 percent) in the ±10 percent range; during the same period the United States Office of Education had only one of eleven changes (9 percent) in that range.[34] While there may be some question as to the exact definition of an incremental outcome, it seems clear that there exists a broader range of budgetary outcomes than the incrementalists have described.

A second major question concerns the interpretation of the regression equations. Both Moreland and Gist suggest that the high correlations found by Davis et al. are the direct result of not controlling for secular trends in the data.[35] Controlling for collinearity, Gist found that at least 50 percent of the variance in requests and appropriations is explained by the secular trend alone.[36] Examining the impact of administrative maturity on budget outcomes while controlling for collinearity, Moreland concluded that agencies in the Department of Agriculture could only count on receiving 44 cents of each dollar appropriated in the previous year.[37] Both found that when serial correlation is accounted for, the impact or existence of incrementalism is dramatically reduced.

A related criticism was made by John Wanat.[38] Using sensitivity analysis, he concluded that strategic interpretations of budgetary incrementalism are not warranted on the basis of the correlation analysis of Davis et al. He found that the magnitude of correlations in randomly generated data approximates those found by Davis et al. Therefore, one cannot validly support the existence of budgetary decision rules on the basis of high correlation coefficients.

Based on their request/appropriation figures the incrementalists concluded that there is a basic similarity in agency strategies, i.e., requesting a moderate (incremental) increase. One of the first critics of this interpretation was Ira Sharkansky (who nonetheless remained supportive of the theory). He complained that this conclusion was reached without a comparison of individual agency strategies.[39] He suggested that some agencies are more assertive than others in that they ask for larger increases and concluded that different strategies exist in the form of varying degrees of assertiveness affecting budgetary outcomes. To get more, agencies need to ask for more. Examining the same phenomena, Sharkansky's interpretation ran counter to Wildavsky, Fenno, and Davis et al., who had argued that agencies asking for large increases are cut back more severely.

Changing requests in the president's budget for eight agencies revealed that agencies requesting larger increases tended to have significantly greater budget growth.[40] A recent study found a great deal of variation in agency strategies and outcomes.[41] The incrementalists make the assumption that agency requests contained in the president's budget reflect the goals and desires of agencies. In the study of agencies in the Department of Agriculture (DOA), data on initial agency estimates, department requests, and Office of Management and Budget (OMB) recommendations were all included in the analysis. The results indicated a much greater variation in agency behavior and demonstrated the error of assuming that requests in the president's budget are indicative of agency strategies. In two out of three cases the agencies requested an increase of more than 10 percent, and in one-quarter of the cases the agencies requested increases of more than 50 percent.[42]

Additional findings in this study call in question the incremental dichotomy of "spenders" vs. "savers." The budgetary roles assumed by the DOA and the OMB appeared to be significantly different. The DOA assumed what might be called a balancing role, tending to increase requests for agencies which requested a cut in funding while, concomitantly, severely cutting back agencies which requested the largest increases. The OMB, on the other hand, tended to make across-the-board cuts in agency requests regardless of the size of the increase asked for. The findings confirmed the existence of alternative strategies to the single incremental strategy of moderation and showed that assertiveness has an important impact on budgetary results and that further differentiation among roles is necessary.

Much of the theory of incremental budgeting rests on Wildavsky's and Fenno's interpretation of their extensive descriptive data and on empirical tests. Their work contains a great deal of interesting information on the appropriations process. It appears, however, that incremental assumptions structured their analysis and conclusions. Reanalyzed and reinterpreted, their empirical data could support a more differentiated set of conclusions.

ANALYTIC CHOICES AND ALTERNATIVES

In addition to its questionable interpretation of results, incrementalism as a theory of budgeting is built on a number of analytic choices that affect its forms of empirical validation and applicability. No attempt is made to delimit the application of incrementalism to only certain budgetary decisions; the clear implication is that it applies to the full range of phenomena. Their choices were not necessarily the wrong choices but strictly limit the applicability of the theory.

This section attempts to specify a number of interrelated analytic choices, their implications, critical responses, and some alternatives. Three main areas of analytic choice are (1) level of aggregation, (2) time and object of analysis, (3) dependent and independent variables.

Level of Aggregation

The incrementalists chose to focus on domestic budget items aggregated at the agency level. This was an obvious choice for analysis; totals are available, agency officials and members of Congress are certainly concerned with the final appropriation, and it is commonly a visible figure. A number of recent studies have shown, however, the negative consequences of using this level of aggregation.

Aggregating at the agency level treats all components of an agency's request and appropriation as equal; the highest common denominator is dollars. But agency budgets can be disaggregated into different components. Gist asserts that agency budgets must be divided into mandatory and controllable components.[43] He suggests that mandatory spending items preclude any strategic manipulation in incremental strategies. If these decisions are previously determined, incrementalism cannot explain budget stability in such categories.[44] Gist further refines this point in a subsequent study. Becuase of the increase in uncontrollable spending, the budget base is not only reviewed but has become a fairly regular target for reductions.[45]

> The contention of incrementalism that the budget base is not reviewed cannot be sustained. While attention to the annual increment may be

the normal state of affairs . . . , it has not characterized congressional budget behavior over the past decade or so . . . , Congressional budgeting has become as often "basal" as "incremental."[46]

Wanat also differentiates between components of appropriations. Agency budgets consist of three parts: the base, mandatory needs, and programmatic desires.[47] Wanat's mandatory component has a different meaning from the conventional use of mandatory or uncontrollable spending.[48] It refers to the new costs required to keep the agency operating at the same level as last year: an inflation factor. The program component represents the desire for new programs or expansion of old ones. Examining the Department of Labor budget, he found that agencies differentiate between these components in their presentations to Congress. Results, according to Wanat, can be empirically explained on the basis of an agency's mandatory needs. His study makes the important point that agencies conceptualize components differently and that budgetary decisions are subject to external constraints (this theme will be pursued later).

Another alternative level of budget aggregation is the intraagency program level. Several studies have concluded that the agency level of aggregation used by the incrementalists leads to erroneous conclusions about policy stability. Natchez and Bupp argue that a stable appropriation pattern may belie substantial program shifts occurring at lower levels.[49] Looking at the Atomic Energy Commission, the authors show patterns of growth, decay, and fluctuation among AEC programs in nuclear rockets, high-energy physics, thermonuclear research, and nuclear weapons, all within the context of stable, apparently incremental budget totals.[50] They conclude that significant policy change is missed by the incremental perspective; the most interesting questions of social and political change require more extensive probing into the lower levels of the administrative process where key decisions are made:

> In this regard, Davis, Dempster and Wildavsky's stochastic models perpetuate a fundamental error about the way the government operates. . . .
> We have seen that real change does occur within this "massive stability,"
> reflecting real conflicts over purpose and priority.[51]

Arnold Kanter makes a similar observation by uncovering significant program variation in the Department of Defense.[52] The risk of a higher level of aggregation is that variation is often masked, gains and losses by competing programs cancel each other out in the totals, and that it has a tendency to bias results toward incremental interpretations. Gist also breaks down the defense sector budgets into their major program components. Both Kanter and Gist find that after disaggregating totals, nonincremental patterns actually dominate. The rate of growth in procurement and research and development were significantly greater than growth in the overall defense budget.[53] Gist includes a similar dissaggregation of the budgets of the National Aeronautics and Space Administration (NASA), the AEC, and the State Department. While the incremental model still predicts accurately in some cases (more frequently for Congress than the agencies), nonincremental decisions are evident in every budget item analyzed.[54]

In choosing total agency budgets as the level of aggregation, the incrementalists made the assumption that all dollars in the budget were the same. Such a choice and concomitant assumptions helped to ensure finding incremental results. The alternative analytic choices discussed above facilitate a fuller understanding of underlying processes and policy changes in the budgetary process.

Time and Object of Analysis

Related to the choice of level of aggregation is time and object of analysis. Incremental theorists focus on annual appropriation decisions. This, too, is an apparently obvious choice since the yearly submission and review of appropriation requests are perhaps the most salient feature of the budgetary process. But annual appropriations are not the only important budgetary decisions and may not even be the most important.

The annual budget consists of a revenue as well as an expenditure side. Of critical importance ot appropriation decisions are revenue estimates, taxation decisions, and decisions on the approximate size of the deficit (or surplus) and, most recently, expenditure ceilings. Based on these decisions, there is a certain maximum amount of change that can occur in a given year. While the tax structure in the United States is not reviewed in an orderly yearly fashion and has been relatively stable, some major changes have occurred in the past decade in the sources and nature of federal revenues.[55] Decisions on revenues, deficit, and outlays constrain the appropriations process. With the implementation of new budget procedures in Congress, decisions on these totals are made consciously, and they create tighter parameters for subsequent decisions.[56] Using appropirations as the sole object of analysis eliminates the possibility of detecting relationships between decisions on the whole and decisions on parts.

Along with annual decisions are a host of multiyear spending decisions that affect the budget. These include a number of substantive legislative and administrative decisions on the so-called uncontrollable spending items that are not reviewed every year.[57] The previous consideration of level aggregation referred to the need to separate out mandatory spending items. Yet the resolution of this problem by excluding these categories, estimated to be approximately 75 percent of the budget for fiscal year (FY) 1978,[58] from analysis is unsatisfactory. This is a point that has been ignored by the critics of incrementalism as well as by the incrementalists themselves. The analytic choice of single years as the time frame precludes theoretical explanation of three-quarters of the budget. The impact of long-term spending decisions has become so great that one cannot hope to understand budgeting without considering them. The next section discusses in more detail some suggestions for a nonannual perspective; it is important to recognize here that selection of annual appropriations represents an analytic choice that virtually excludes these other important budgetary decisions.

Dependent and Independent Variables

A third set of related analytic choices concerns specific dependent and independent variables. The selection of final appropriations as the variable to be explained has led the incrementalists to specify single important explanatory variables: last year's appropriation for agencies; this year's request for Congress. Certainly these are key variables in budgetary decision making. Alternative measures of budgetary results are available, however, and suggest a broader range of relevant independent variables. Changing the dependent variable from final appropriations to the percentage change in appropriations may suggest a new set of theoretical variables.[59] In one study, the level of presidential support for an agency was shown to relate to changes in requests and appropriation growth.[60] Priorities expressed in the public statements of the president affect changes in the rate and amount of change in agency budgets. At the same time, change in appropriations in the previous year had virtually no impact on percentage changes in agency requests or appropriations. This dependent variable does not preclude finding stability; if rates of change were constant, this would be reflected in the results. Davis, Dempster, and Wildavsky's 1974 study including a variety of environmental variables represents a substantial improvement. Their inclusion as binary variables in the model, however, only begins to suggest the potential impact of political, social, and economic factors on budgetary change. Shull has found that coalitions in Congress and the executive branch affect appropriation outcomes.[61] The partisan makeup of Congress and the presidency, the degree of congressional support for the president, and the level of conflict in Congress all have an impact on agency budgets.[62]

As described earlier, Sharkansky, and LeLoup and Moreland found that variation in agency strategies affects budget results. Variations in the level of support from departments and the Budget Office also affect success and growth.[63] Moreland indicated that agency size and administrative experience of the agency staff correlate with greater appropriations. An additional analytic alternative is to use annual appropriation data with secular trends removed and examine the residuals.[64] As Gist has shown, analysis of residuals can confirm incremental conclusions, but it also reveals evidence of nonincremental decision rules.

THE VALIDITY AND APPLICABILITY OF INCREMENTALISM

It would be a simple task to debunk a theory if disconfirming evidence were obtained from a "straightforward" test. But with incrementalism, where empirical validation of the highest order continues to result, the nature of the tests themselves ensures something close to incremental results. There are several critical problems in dealing with the theory. Beyond the confusion between incremental decision making (mutual adjustment) and incremental results (small annual changes), there is a general confusion surrounding the term: it has taken on a host of nontheoretical meanings. In most secondary, casual treatments (introductory texts, for example), it simply refers to the truism that budgets (or governments) do not change radically from year to year. But why? Because most spending commitments are for periods of longer than a year, and in any given year there are externally determined parameters to the amount of change that can occur. Incrementalism takes no account of these critical factors, which must be included in budgetary theory. More serious than the general confusion associated with the term is the tautological nature of the theory itself and the self-confirming nature of the empirical tests. Wildavsky's barb at critics is suggestive:

> The huge increase in the size of the budget . . . should end the vacuous debate over the importance of making decisions in small increments as opposed to large proportions of the total. For one of the secrets of incrementalism is that the base is as important as the rate of increase.
> Another secret of incrementalism is that one can get a long way by rapid movements, if they continue long enough.[65]

When a theory applies to all situations at all times without the possibility of disconfirming evidence, it is no longer a theory and little use for explanation or even description.

An additional problem related to the dominance of incrementalism is the tendency to characterize budgetary studies in either/or terms. A nonincremental approach does not necessarily have to assume that budgeting is unstable, that all components of the budget are reviewed from the ground up every year, or that budgeting conforms to the rational-comprehensive model.

In spite of this, it would not be accurate to say that incrementalism is totally wrong. It correctly describes some aspects of annual budgetary decision making in some agencies and some congressional subcommittees. However, its applicability is limited to a subset of annual appropriations decisions; it provides a misleading view and explanation of the overall budgetary process. To be sure, some of the underlying concepts of incremental budgeting are relevant, but they are in need of modification:

1. *Complexity:* Budgeting is complex, and participants employ aids to calculation. Yet some participants deal with the budget as a whole (president, OMB, budget committees) and are generalists, using aids in calculation required by the complexity of the process which are not mentioned by the incrementalists. Other participants may use nonincremental aids in making calculations at the agency level.

2. *Budget base:* Last year's appropriation may not be the only base for agency calculations, and the multiple components of the base itself are treated differently by the actors. Changes are made by reviewing bodies in the controllable base and the increment.[66] For those responsible for budget totals, last year's budget may be of less value than current policy estimates of a "standpat" budget.[67]

3. *Roles:* The roles adopted by participants are more complex than the simple advocate/guardian dichotomy. Within the executive branch, agencies, departments, and the OMB differ in their behavior and may adopt multiple or mixed roles. In Congress, differing roles adopted by authorization, appropriations, and budget committees are apparent. For example, the authorization committees behave like advocates to the budget committee, but as guardians to the agencies.

4. *Bargaining:* The incrementalists correctly claim that budgeting is political; allocations cannot be and are not made "rationally" on the basis of a total view of the public interest. Yet some actors do bargain over the totals. The scope, object, and intensity of bargaining differs across policies, decision-making levels, and time. Conflict and its resolution shifts dramatically depending on the actors involved, partisan control of the presidency, economic conditions, and other external factors.

5. *Outcomes:* Bargaining matters; it does not always result in a deterministic pattern of stability. Change cannot be assessed without defining the time frame. Over the long run, significant reallocation can occur and has occurred. But even in the short run, budgeting produces a set of results that cannot simply be described as "incremental." Within the budget, at lower levels of aggregation, significant changes can occur within a pattern of overall stability.

The incremental theory of budgeting was formulated on the basis of a number of interrelated analytic choices. As has been shown, these choices played a critical role in determining what was found and what conclusions were drawn. Focusing on striking regularities, crucial changes were obscured; in a relatively simple explanation of budgetary decision making, complex alternatives were ignored. The history of incrementalism presents a dramatic example of the pitfalls of social science theory. What appeared to be an obvious and self-evident analytic approach actually involved numerous choices and excluded alternatives. The consequences of these choices are a set of findings highly skewed toward a single interpretation.

DEVELOPING BUDGETARY THEORY

Significant changes have occurred in the composition of the federal budget in the past 30 years. Income security increased its share of the budget 700 percent, health 2000 percent, and social services 2100 percent between 1946 and 1976. At the same time the defense share of the budget fell from 64 to 27 percent of the total. The most dramatic changes in the budget have occurred within the last decade. The growth in uncontrollable spending has aroused concern over the amount of annual discretion for decision makers. Changes have also taken place in the budgetary process. The Bureau of the Budget became the OMB in 1970 and, more significantly, Congress overhauled its procedures in 1974. The relevance of budgetary theory depends on its ability to comprehend the changing composition of the budget within the context of a set of external and internal constraints on the actions of key actors in the budgetary process.

In attempting to suggest new directions in developing budgetary theory, several key factors must be included. The shortcomings of incrementalism can be as instructive to the scholar as the observations and alternatives suggested in the many studies cited. Five key considerations should be recognized in attempting to advance our theoretical understanding of budgeting:

1. Perhaps the most important step is to expand the definition of relevant decisions. Besides the agencies and appropriations committees, many actors make decisions that affect the levels of revenues and expenditures. The authorization committees have become particularly important but are often excluded since their main function is not budgeting.

2. Time is essential in the reformulation. Most decisions are nonannual, having a duration of more or less than one year.

3. Budgetary decisions are made at different levels from different perspectives. Some actors are responsible for the whole budget, most for just a part of the budget. Budgetary decision making differs considerably depending on how general or specific the decisions themselves are.

4. Annual budgeting is not simply a one-way process, aggregating from small parts to the whole. One of the weaknesses of incrementalism is that budgeting is portrayed only as building increments on a base. This ignores the existence of external parameters, decisions on totals, that constrain the process. Budgeting can be seen as both an upward and downward process, with relevant theoretical questions focusing on the existence of parameters, their determination, and their impact.

5. Finally, budgetary theory must analyze discretion. How much flexibility do decision makers have in the shortrun? Even the distinction between controllable and uncontrollable spending does not provide an accurate determination of the actual range of discretion for decision makers.

Based on these key points, we are suggesting below a tentative framework for the analysis of national budgeting in the United States. While incrementalism has had a much wider application, our critique has focused on its application at this level. With appropriate modifications, some of the proposals may suggest new directions in other applications of budgetary theory.

"Levels" of Decisions

Budgetary decisions range from the broad and the general to the narrow and the specific. Decisions can be classified in terms of three categories:

- *Priority decisions:* These are a set of choices on budget totals for expenditures, revenues, deficit, and spending subtotals in functions such as defense, health, agriculture, etc. Priority decisions are macrobudgeting actions representing priorities in economic and fiscal policy. Such decisions are made annually and are the most general type of budgetary actions.

- *Program decisions:* These concern program authorizations, agency appropriations, entitlement programs, construction projects, and a variety of decisions concerning agencies and programs. Decisions made at the program level review the legal basis of programs, fund existing programs, and may initiate new programs. Decisions at this level may be annual, multiyear, or open ended.

- *Operations decisions:* These allocate and obligate funds to specific purposes. Included are decisions on the timing of spending, the amount of spending, carrying over balances, future funding, reprogramming, and transferring funds between accounts. Operations decisions are continual, occurring daily, weekly, monthly, quarterly, etc., and are the most specific type of budgetary actions.

Key Actors

Different sets of actors are most prominent in the decision-making processes on the three levels. Priority decision makers include the president and his advisors, Congress (the budget committees), and the OMB. Implementation of the Budget Control and Impoundment Act has made the decisions on totals more explicit in Congress and the bargaining between the president and Congress more visible. Program decisions involve the largest group of actors, and participants may vary depending on whether decisions are annual or multiyear. Appropriation decisions center on the familiar relationship between agencies and appropriations subcommittees. Key actors making authorization decisions (annual, multiyear, permanent) include agencies, standing committees, interest groups, and occasionally the president, OMB, and Congress. Specific entitlement programs and long-term construction projects involve combinations of these actors. Operations decisions are dominated by agencies, and include periodic interactions with appropriations committees and subcommittees and the OMB.

Key Relationships

Decisions at different levels are highly interrelated and interdependent. The most important limiting factors are the spending commitments made in previous years. Within the parameters imposed by these continuing commitments, it is possible to identify interrelationships between the general (higher level) and the specific (lower level) decisions. Higher level decisions establish *constraints* for lower level decisions, i.e., priority decisions set boundaries for program and operations decisions. At the same time, budgeting involves combining smaller items into larger ones; *aggregation* may be defined as the process of successive combinations of lower level into higher level decisions. For example, priority decisions on totals may represent the aggregation of various program level decisions. Budgeting, then, is an interactive process combining constraint and aggregation. At any given time, one set of relationships may be ascendant. For example, prior to 1975, congressional budgeting was closer to an aggregative process, although presidential totals were sometimes used as reference points. The implementation of budget reform has increased the constraints imposed on authorization and appropriation decisions by totals agreed to in the concurrent budget resolutions.

Environmental Factors

Finally, decisions at all levels are affected by external factors, such as economic, social, and political trends. Economic changes may have the most significant direct impact. Rising unemployment, under existing statutory requirements, decreases tax collections and increases expenditures for unemployment, welfare, etc. Cost of living escalators translate general increases in price levels into larger expenditures for Social Security, federal retirement, etc. Other political and social trends have a less direct impact, but often affect changes in budgetary directions.

Figure 1 summarizes the concepts and relationships discussed above and suggests a variety of hypotheses. For example, one may speculate on the degree of constraint, the relative dominance of Congress or the executive at different levels, or the impact of external changes in the environment. Specific policies and actors may predominantly occupy a certain level; others cut across levels.

Discretion

It is not enough just to recognize that a large proportion of the budget is uncontrollable because controllability, as officially defined, does not translate into discretion.[68] Expenditures classified as "uncontrollable" are not equally uncontrollable. Fixed costs (such as interest on the national debt) constitute firmer commitments than long-term construction of weapons, dams, etc. These projects, in turn, offer less possibility for control than entitlement programs. Efforts

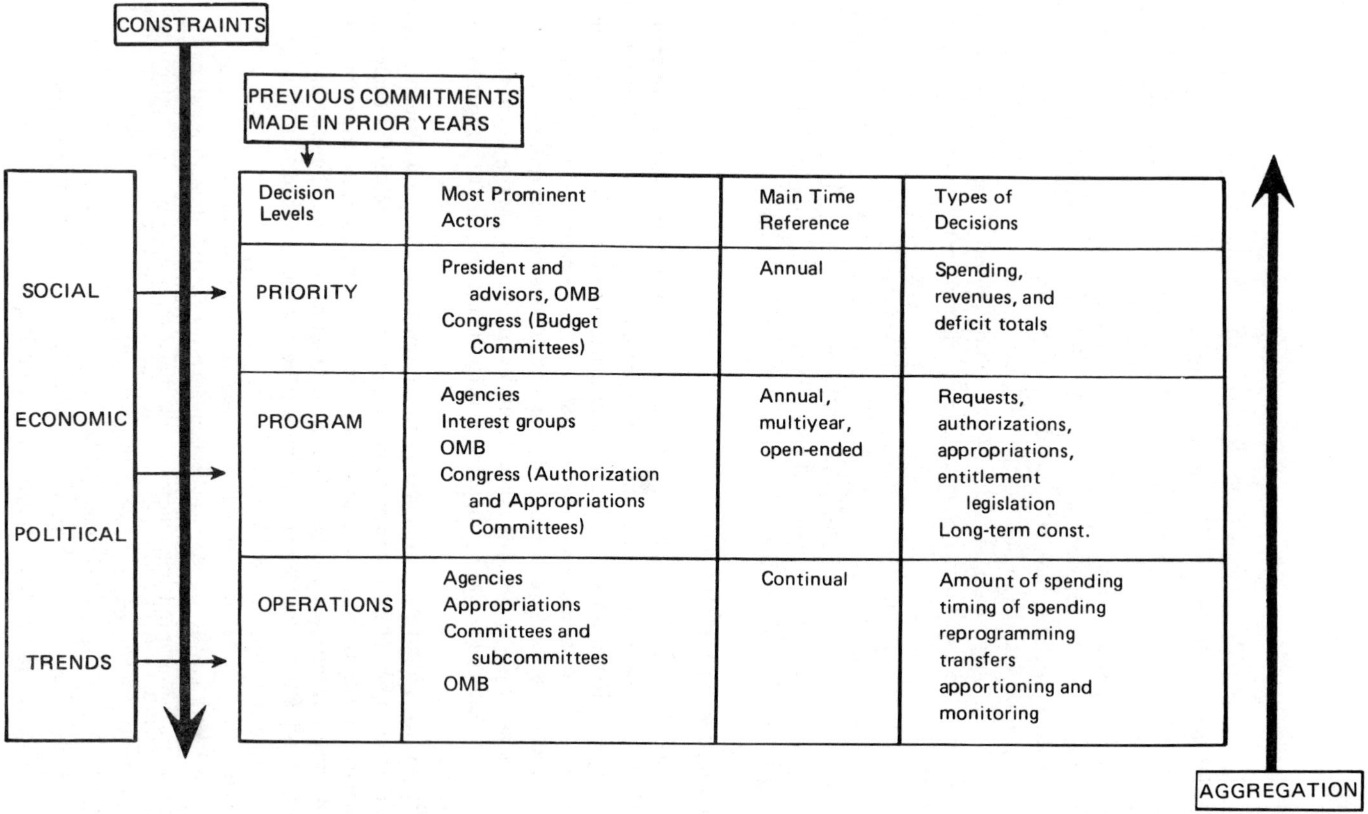

AGGREGATION

CONSTRAINTS

PREVIOUS COMMITMENTS MADE IN PRIOR YEARS

SOCIAL
ECONOMIC
POLITICAL
TRENDS

Decision Levels	Most Prominent Actors		Main Time Reference	Types of Decisions
PRIORITY	President and advisors, OMB Congress (Budget Committees)		Annual	Spending, revenues, and deficit totals
PROGRAM	Agencies Interest groups OMB Congress (Authorization and Appropriations Committees)		Annual, multiyear, open-ended	Requests, authorizations, appropriations, entitlement legislation Long-term const.
OPERATIONS	Agencies Appropriations Committees and subcommittees OMB		Continual	Amount of spending timing of spending reprogramming transfers apportioning and monitoring

Figure 1 A framework for budgetary analysis.

made in 1975 and 1976 to tighten eligibility for food stamps, to restrict cost of living escalators, and to hold back mandated federal pay increases demonstrate that some potential for control exists. While the percentage that may change in a given year is small, the fact that these expenditures constitute just under half of the total budget allows more discretion than many "controllable" expenditures that make up only a small portion of the total.

Similarly, all expenditures categorized as controllable are not equally controllable. Since most of the controllable portion of the budget consists of personnel costs, civil service rules concerning severance pay, sick leave accumulation, etc., making large-scale changes is very difficult. It has been estimated that in 1976 only $5 to 7 billion could be cut from the controllable portion; this is approximately the same amount that could be cut from the uncontrollable portion.[69]

The official controllable/uncontrollable dichotomy can be misleading; a continuum from most to least controllable expenditures would provide a more useful notion of discretion. The limits of annual discretion and the importance of multi-year decisions show that budgeting is a much more dynamic process than the correlation of consecutive appropriations patterns would indicate.

SUMMARY AND CONCLUSIONS

In all probability incrementalism will remain in prevalent use regardless of findings to the contrary; it is a truism that government changes only marginally from year to year. Even though the precise descriptive validity of the term has been challenged, many devotees of incrementalism will persist in the belief that government and budgeting will remain "incremental." Unfortunately, its self-fulfilling nature renders incrementalism nearly useless for social science theory. If it retains any validity after process is distinguished from outcomes, it is only in relation to a relatively narrow range of annual appropriations decisions.

This study has attempted to clarify the meaning of incrementalism as a theory of budgeting and integrate recent studies which challenge the theory. From the perspective of the social scientist, incrementalism appears predicated on a number of implicit analytical choices. Specification of these choices and alternatives clarifies the biases of incrementalism and suggests some of the difficulties encountered in the construction of theory.

The main bias of incrementalism is towards stability and against change. Analytical alternatives and the general suggestions for the development of budget theory presented here undoubtedly have their own biases. But in light of the experience of the previous decade, these alternatives may have greater promise for developing a balanced set of budget theories relevant to both the stability of budgeting and the mechanisms of change.

NOTES

1. This theme could logically be discussed in terms of paradigm dominance and change as suggested by Thomas Kuhn in *The Structure of Scientific Revolutions* (Chicago: University of Chicago Press, 1970). However, because of the controversy among philosophers of science and some highly problemmatic applications of Kuhn's ideas by political scientists, this approach is avoided. Also see Imre Lakatos and Alan Musgrave, *Criticism and the Growth of Knowledge* (Cambridge: Cambridge University Press, 1970).
2. V. O. Key, The lack of a budgetary theory, *American Political Science Review* 34 (December 1940), pp. 1137-1144.
3. Verne B. Lewis, Toward a theory of budgeting, *Public Administration Review* 12 (Winter 1952), pp. 42-54. Arthur Smithies, *The Budgetary Process in the United States* (New York: McGraw-Hill, 1955).
4. Fremont J. Lyden and Ernest G. Miller (eds.), *Planning Programming Budgeting* (Chicago: Markham, 1972). Charles Schultz, *The Politics and Economics of Public Spending* (Washington, D.C.: Brookings, 1968). David Novick (ed.), *Program Budgeting* (Cambridge, Mass.: Harvard University Press, 1965).
5. Allen Schick, Systems politics and systems budgeting, *Public Administration Review* 29 (March-April 1969), pp. 137-151.
6. Charles Lindblom, The science of muddling through, *Public Administration Review* 19 (Spring 1959), pp. 79-88.
7. Lindblom, The science of muddling through, p. 88.
8. Aaron Wildavsky, *The Politics of the Budgetary Process* (Boston: Little, Brown, 1964, 1974).
9. Wildavsky, *The Politics of the Budgetary Process,* p. 15.
10. Richard Fenno, *The Power of the Purse* (Boston: Little, Brown, 1966), p. 15.
11. Richard Fenno, *Congressmen in Committee* (Boston: Little, Brown, 1973), pp. 47-51.
12. Fenno, *The Power of the Purse,* p. 354.
13. John Bailey and Robert O'Connor, Operationalizing incrementalism: Measuring the muddles, *Public Administration Review* 35 (January-February 1975), pp. 60-66.
14. William Moreland, A nonincremental perspective on budgetary policy actions, in R. Ripley and G. Franklin (eds.), *Policy Making in the Federal Executive Branch* (New York: Free Press, 1975), Chap. 3.
15. Michael Davis, Michael Dempster, and Aaron Wildavsky, A theory of the budgetary process, *American Political Science Review* 60 (Sept.: 1966), p. 529. Idem., On the process of budgeting II: An empirical study of congressional appropriations, in Byrne et al. (eds.), *Studies in Budgeting* (Amsterdam and London: North-Holland, 1971). Idem., Toward a predictive theory of the Federal Budgetary Process (Paper delivered at the Annual Meeting of the

American Political Science Association, New Orleans, Sept. 1973). Idem., Towards a predictive theory of government expenditure: U.S. domestic appropriations, *British Journal of Political Science* 4 (October 1974), pp. 419-452.

16. Davis et al., A theory of the budgetary process, p. 529.
17. Ibid., p. 531.
18. Davis et al., Towards a predictive theory of government expenditure.
19. Aaron Wildavsky, *Budgeting: A Comparative Theory of Budgetary Processes* (Boston: Little, Brown, 1975), table 3-2, p. 52.
20. Ibid., p. 51.
21. Ibid., pp. 65-68.
22. Ira Sharkansky, Four agencies and an appropriations subcommittee: A comparative study of budget strategies, *Midwest Journal of Political Science* (August 1965), pp. 254-281. Idem., Agency requests, gubernatorial support and budget success in state legislatures, *American Political Science Review* 62 (Dec.: 1968), p. 1222. Thomas Anton, *The Politics of State Expenditure in Illinois* (Urbana: University of Illinois Press, 1966).
23. John Crecine, A computer simulation model of municipal budgeting, *Management Science* (July 1967), pp. 786-815. Idem., *Government Problem Solving, A Computer Simulation of Municipal Budgeting* (Chicago: Rand McNally, 1969).
24. Donald A. Gerwin, *Budgeting Public Funds: The Decision Process in an Urban School District* (Madison: University of Wisconsin Press, 1969).
25. Andrew Cowart, Tore Hansen, and Karl-Erik Brofoss, Budgetary strategies and success at multiple decision levels in the Norwegian urban setting," *American Political Science Review* 69 (June 1975), pp. 543-558.
26. Francis Hoole, Brian Job, and Harvey Tucker, Incremental budgeting and international organizations, *American Journal of Political Science* 20 (May 1976), pp. 273-301.
27. Wildavsky, *Budgeting.*
28. Without undertaking a thorough survey of texts, readers are referred to familiar books used in classes.
29. Schick, Systems politics and systems budgeting, p. 95.
30. B. L. R. Smith, Letters to the editor, *American Political Science Review* 61 (March 1967), pp. 150-152.
31. Bailey and O'Connor, Operationalizing incrementalism, p. 60.
32. Ibid., p. 65.
33. Ibid., p. 65.
34. Lance T. LeLoup, Agency policy actions: Determinants of nonincremental change, in Ripley and Franklin (eds.), *Policy Making,* Chap. 5, p. 76.
35. John R. Gist, Mandatory expenditures and the defense sector: Theory of budgetary incrementalism, *Sage Professional Papers in American Politics,*

Vol. 2, series 04-020 (Beverly Hills and London: Sage): pp. 13-14. More-land, A nonincremental perspective, p. 49.

36. Gist, Mandatory expenditures, p. 31.
37. Moreland, A nonincremental perspective, p. 61.
38. John Wanat, The bases of budgetary incrementalism, *American Political Science Review* 68 (Sept.: 1974), pp. 1221-1228.
39. Sharkansky, Four agencies. Idem., Agency requests.
40. Lance T. LeLoup, *Explaining Agency Appropriations Change, Success and Legislative Support: A Comparative Study of Agency Budget Determination* (Ph.D. diss., Ohio State University, 1973).
41. Lance T. LeLoup and William Moreland, Agency strategies and executive review: The hidden politics of budgeting, *Public Administration Review* (forthcoming).
42. Ibid.
43. Gist, Mandatory expenditures, p. 15.
44. Ibid., p. 10.
45. John Gist, "Increment" and "base" in the congressional appropriations process, *American Journal of Political Science* 21 (May 1977), pp. 341-352.
46. Ibid., pp. 350-351.
47. Wanat, The bases of budgetary incrementalism, p. 1225.
48. Barry M. Blechman, Edward M. Gramlich, and Robert W. Hartman, *Setting National Priorities, the 1976 Budget* (Washington, D.C.: Brookings, 1975), pp. 191-192.
49. P. B. Natchez and I. C. Bupp, Policy and priority in the budgetary process, *American Political Science Review* 67 (Sept.: 1973), pp. 951-963.
50. Ibid., p. 960.
51. Ibid., p. 963.
52. Arnold Kanter, Congress and the defense budget: 1960-1970, *American Political Science Review* 66 (March 1972), pp. 129-143.
53. Gist, Mandatory expenditures, p. 18. Kanter, Congress and the defense budget, p. 133.
54. Gist, Mandatory expenditures, p. 36.
55. Blechman et al., *Setting National Priorities,* Chap. 6.
56. Budget and Impoundment Control Act, 1974, Public Law 93-344.
57. Murray Weidenbaum, Institutional obstacles to relocating government expenditures, in R. Haveman and J. Margolis (eds.), *Public Expenditures and Policy Analysis* (Chicago: Markham, 1970), pp. 232-245.
58. U.S. Office of Management and Budget, *Budget of the United State Government, Fiscal Year 1978* (Washington, D.C.: U.S. Government Printing Office, 1977).
59. Ripley and Franklin (eds.), *Policy Making in the Federal Executive Branch* (New York: Free Press, 1976). Selections in this volume suggest several different sets of relevant variables.

60. LeLoup, Agency policy actions, p. 83.
61. Steven A. Shull, Coalitions and Budgeting. Paper presented at Annual Meeting of Midwest Political Science Association, Chicago, May 1975.
62. LeLoup, Agency policy actions. Shull, Coalitions and budgeting.
63. LeLoup and Moreland, Agency strategies and executive review.
64. Gist, Mandatory expenditures, pp. 30-36.
65. Wildavsky, *The Politics of the Budgetary Process,* Preface to the Second Edition (1974), pp. xix, xx.
66. John Crecine et al., Controllability of "Uncontrollable" Expenditures: Manipulation of Ambiguity in Budgetary Decision Making. Paper presented at Midwest Political Science Association, April 21, 1977, Chicago. Preliminary findings suggest that uncontrollables are manipulated within the executive branch as are controllables.
67. Current policy estimates (Congressional Budget Office) and current services estimates (OMB) are projections of outlays in the next fiscal years if no programs are changed and services maintained a constant real level.
68. Lance T. LeLoup, Discretion in national budgeting: Controlling the controllables, *Policy Analysis* (Fall 1978); see this for a detailed attempt to estimate discretion.
69. Blechman et al., *Setting National Priorities,* pp. 192-194. See also Weidenbaum, Institutional obstacles, pp. 234-238; Joel Havemann, Ford, Congress seek handle on "uncontrollable" spending. *National Journal* 6(48) (Nov. 29, 1975).

5

A TYPOLOGY OF BUDGETARY ENVIRONMENTS:
Notes on the Prospects for Reform*

Jeffrey D. Straussman

> So, even though zero-base budgeting is a fraud, and even though the
> good parts of it are not new, experienced budget people should not let
> the phrase make them nauseous. They should disregard the rhetoric and
> latch onto the term as a way of accomplishing what really needs to be
> accomplished anyway (1).

The "new" federal budget process has not been unanimously praised by bureaucratic veterans in Washington. Of course, resistance to zero-base budgeting, Carter style, is to be expected, for budget reforms always have had difficulty gaining
acceptance. Why does a budget reform like ZBB surface shortly after an earlier
one (program budgeting) has died? Robert Anthony, former Comptroller in the
Department of Defense during McNamara's tenure, is surely correct in the quota-
tion above when he implies that the efforts to improve agency performance by
reforming the budget process have been widely accepted as a laudable goal. Why

---

*Reprinted from: A Typology of Budgetary Environments: Notes on the Prospects for
Reform by Jeffrey D. Straussman, in *Administration and Society,* vol. 11, no. 2 (August
1979), pp. 216-226, with permission of the Publisher, Sage Publications, Beverly Hills.

then should one be so skeptical about current proposals for budget reform if the basic goal is generally regarded as desirable?

The following paragraphs point out the characteristics of budgetary politics that provide major stumbling blocks for advocates of budget reform. If reformers are to be successful in the perennial quest for rationality in budgeting, then reform objectives must be linked to the roles and strategies of the major participants in the process. The four budgetary environments illustrate that when reform objectives include incompatible objectives, such a link is difficult to make. Consequently, the proposal is prone to failure at the outset and the goal of rationality in budgeting remains as elusive as ever.

ENVIRONMENT ONE: THE UNREFORMED BUDGET PROCESS IN A RELATIVELY UNRESTRAINED FISCAL CLIMATE

The "traditional" budget-process best summarizes this first budgetary environment and has the following characteristics:

- Agencies generally request larger budgets than they expect to receive based on the assumption that a relatively fixed portion of the difference between last year's appropriation and this year's budget request is cut at successive stages in the budget process.
- The Budget Bureau, anticipating such "padding," fairly routinely cuts these agency requests. These Budget Bureau cuts tend to reflect the "control" orientation of the Budget Bureau and therefore often have few policy implications. Budget cutting at this stage is more severe for agencies that try to maximize their budgets beyond the "fair share" increases that agencies can really expect to receive. The Budget Bureau, in other words, distinguishes between acquisitive and nonacquisitive agencies, and "punishes" acquisitiveness by cutting agency budget requests.
- *Acquisitive agencies* recognize differential treatment by the Budget Bureau, but adopt the risky strategy because
  a. they anticipate some restoration of their request by the legislature
  b. they can count on client or citizen support, or
  c. they assume that a shift in policy priorities by the executive and/or a change in administrations might provide a budget recommendation beyond the expected "base" and "fair share" calculation leading to *long-term* budget expansion.
- Legislative scrutiny of the budget focuses on line-item appropriations. "Control" is therefore exercised through budget cutting which, however, is smaller than budget cutting by the Budget Bureau (i.e., the legislature tends to support the executive budget). In addition, the legislature serves as an "appeals board" for agencies that incur excessively large cuts by the Budget Bureau.

Fiscal roles are performed by the central budget office and the legislature. Both are primarily concerned with controlling budget growth through line-item budget cutting. Programmatic concerns are centered in agencies; they (programs) are used to justify budget expansion.

This budget scenario ignores V. O. Key's (2:1138) classic question: "On what basis shall it be decided to allocate tax dollars to activity A instead of activity B?" In particular, reformers have often shown that in a traditional budget process as outlined above there are no obvious connections between agency performance and budget expansion, or performance and fiscal restraint. But in the past reformers tended to focus on the first dimension—the relationship between performance and budget expansion—which leads to the second budgetary environment.

ENVIRONMENT TWO: BUDGET REFORM IN A FAIRLY UNRESTRAINED FISCAL CLIMATE

What tends to happen in a budget environment without a stringent fiscal climate and yet one that attempts to improve agency performance? In such an environment a reformed budget process may improve the way the Budget Bureau or the legislature identifies "whose ox should be fattened." Observe this situation in the following exchange from a congressional hearing several years ago concerning the implementation of program budgeting at the federal level:

> Senator Jordan: Has it [PPBS] enabled your agency to identify the project of low priority that you might otherwise have thought excellent?
> Mr Ross [Deputy Undersecretary for Policy Analysis and Evaluation, HUD]: We take the positive approach, Senator. We have identified projects of higher priority (3:76).

If performance is supposed to be the major concern of budget reform, one might suppose that agencies will try to demonstrate that superior performance should be "rewarded" in the form of a budget appropriation *beyond* the base and anticipated increment. Yet, the incentive for self-evaluation as a part of budget reform is minimal, since in a generally favorable fiscal environment the agency will receive its base and increment anyway. Such was the experience with zero-base budgeting in New Mexico, according to John D. LaFaver, staff member of the Legislative Finance Committee. In his words (4:109),

> Since the state's fiscal outlook was optimistic, there was little impetus to cut budgets or eliminate marginal programs. Thus, a budget system designed to locate duplication and thus reduce budgets was out of phase in a period of increasing revenues.

The comments by Ross and LaFaver suggest that a budget reform aimed at improving agency performance will not succeed in a favorable fiscal environment. To put it another way, the "traditional" budget process of Environment One will remain sufficiently intact insofar as there is no immediate need to curtain expenditure growth beyond the routine budget-cutting practices of the Budget Bureau and the legislature. If this is indeed the case, it simply means that if a budget reform requires a performance review, such a review will not likely penetrate budget routines; consequently, many inefficient and ineffective programs continue to be funded when the fiscal climate is favorable. Improvements in agency performance are unlikely for some agencies unless they are not accompanied by fiscal constraints, since they can still expect to receive at least their "fair share" in the upcoming fiscal year. In other words, *the objective of improving agency performance is not a sufficient condition for the success of a budget reform in a fairly unrestrained fiscal climate.*

ENVIRONMENT THREE: AN UNREFORMED BUDGET PROCESS IN A DETERIORATING FISCAL CLIMATE

As the level of scarcity increases in this third type of budgetary environment, fiscal actors (the Budget Bureau and the legislature) cut more sharply into agency requests as a way to enforce fiscal discipline. Budgetary theory and practice suggest, however, that agencies will not initially respond by curtailing acquisitiveness, since budget cutting is such a well-established expectation in the budget game. But should the fiscal environment continue to worsen, techniques such as budget freezes, ceilings, and across-the-board cuts are likely to be used to control expenditure growth. These tactics really signify the admission that agency behavior does not automatically respond to changes in the level of fiscal scarcity; consequently, traditional roles, such as "purse string" control by the legislature, must be reasserted. Notice that the traditional budget process of Environment One is once again still very much intact. Fiscal scarcity *by itself* does not alter agency and legislative behavior.

At this point, reformers will surely surface to claim that the legislative tactics mentioned above are not rational because they do not distinguish among levels of agency performance. The fact that high-performance and low-performance agencies are cut equally is clearly undesirable from a reform perspective. Reformers would like to replace this nonrational approach with one that permits *planned fiscal retrenchment.* In other words, while everyone's ox typically gets gored in a period of fiscal decline, budget reformers are now saying that some oxen should get gored more than others.

The adoption of zero-base budgeting in New Jersey followed this pattern. Faced with rising expenditures and declining revenues, Governor Byrne said, "it must be clear to all that for some activity or programs, appropriations in FY [fiscal year] 1976 may have to be eliminated entirely or reduced below the FY 1975 level" (5:174). It was assumed that ZBB would be an appropriate device to accomplish this goal. According to Michael J. Scheiring, program analyst in the New Jersey Bureau of the Budget, one "aim of ZBB is to provide budget decision-makers with a rational way to reduce and control budget growth" (5:176). Thus, the environment for budget reform—ZBB in this case—is very different from the New Mexico example cited above. What should agency and legislative behavior look like under conditions of increasing fiscal scarcity *combined* with a reformed budget process?

ENVIRONMENT FOUR: A REFORMED BUDGET PROCESS IN A WORSENING FISCAL CLIMATE

This last combination represents the budgetary environment in many states and cities in the United States today. Specifically, several state and local governments have experienced a decline in the tax base as residents and industry have located elsewhere. To compound the problem, inflation has put upward pressure on expenditures at the same time that voters pressure elected officials to limit tax increases.

While the present political atmosphere mainly focuses on fiscal restraint, the other objective—improving agency performance—is also very much alive. For example, productivity is often a major issue in current public sector collective bargaining, particularly in municipalities that want to join performance with fiscal restraint. Similarly, many state and local governments now require agency heads to identify *and* justify the anticipated programmatic effects of alternative funding levels when submitting initial budget requests. At a more extreme level, "sunset" legislation is expected to terminate the life of agencies that do not perform effectively. Environment Four, in other words, is all around us. The problem for proponents of budget reform who operate in this environment is to establish conditions whereby *both* goals are compatible. Unfortunately, creating such conditions is extremely difficult.

Consider, for example, a hypothetical reform that requires agencies to reveal their actual costs of producing public goods and services when preparing budget requests. The rationale for this type of procedure is twofold. First, according to some critics of bureaucracy, the monopoly position of most public agencies allows the bureaucrat to obfuscate the bureau's production process (6). At the aggregate level, this obfuscation creates upward pressure on the size of the public budget. Therefore, if agency heads were required by the legislature to reveal the actual costs of producing a level of output (or, to put it another way, their real budgetary needs), fiscal restraint would be exercised by those agencies.

Second, by shifting attention to agency output, there is an assumption that agencies will adjust their level of output in accordance with the programmatic intent of the legislature. Once appropriations are linked to what agencies produce, theoretically it should be possible to reduce the total size of the budget. Traditional agency "padding" presumably will be removed from budget submissions. Surely, this is one reason for the current popularity of zero-base budgeting, expecially among fiscally strained state and local governments.

But the problem with this argument is that even if the link can be made between appropriations and desired output levels, there is no reason to assume that both programmatic and fiscal goals should *necessarily* be achieved. The output of agencies may be reduced to conform to the need for economy. Whether or not the programmatic intent of the legislature is realized depends on the *outcomes* of agency activities—a subject that is conceptually and empirically separate from the level of output. This is nothing more than the classic distinction between efficiency and effectiveness. Yet, the political conditions of Environment Four require that efficiency and effectiveness be connected.

The major difficulty in joining the two objectives lies in implementation. While it may be possible to improve agency performance and at the same time exercise fiscal restraint, the two goals place demands on the legislature that may be excessive—for both analytic and political reasons. If a legislature wants to maximize both goals, then desired agency outputs (assuming that they are translated into "desirable" performance) must be capable of being altered to accommodate changes in the fiscal environment. Given the nature of the appropriation cycle, this requires that fairly accurate forecasts of the fiscal environment be used in budgetary decision making so that desired agency funding levels can be attained. If the fiscal environment worsens during the budget cycle, the legislature should then recalculate the level of goods and services needed in the new fiscal environment so that appropriations mirror fiscal changes. Even when appropriations are sequential, this rather detailed and "rational" procedure is simply not feasible for a legislative body. When appropriations are made at the same time the budget as a whole is adopted, as is the case for many state and local governments, the analytic and decision-making problems are compounded.

What is one hypothetical outcome in the above budgetary scenario? Some agencies are likely to get "too much." Our knowledge of agency behavior suggests that agencies in this situation will have an incentive to expand their activities either by starting up new programs or by increasing the funding level for existing programs. In either case the fiscal objective of the legislature is thwarted.

Since some agencies receive too much, other agencies necessarily must receive "too little." Given that the legislature anticipated agency activity and performance that was based on the *prior* fiscal environment, we might infer that agencies falling into the second category will not receive the level of funding sufficient to perform as anticipated. Given reduced funding, some program objectives may not be achieved. Logically, this latter condition can be eliminated if the legislature simply changes its expectations of agency performance (for those agencies which received too little) to reflect the changes in the fiscal environment. For example, the range of agency activity should be expected to narrow to conform to reduced funding. But here, again, the analytic and political requirements appear quite complex. The legislature may continue to anticipate performance outcomes from the first fiscal environment, thereby placing unrealistic demands on the agency. To the extent that this budgetary scenario sheds light on Environment four, *neither* the goal of fiscal restraint nor the goal of improving agency performance will be realized.

CONCLUSION

The above picture seems overly cumbersome from a decision-making perspective. A legislature is unlikely to adopt the calculations just discussed because of the analytic complexity—even if the information is available. Generally, we would like to think that analysis improves the rational bases of budgetary decision making. If rationality is taken to mean better and more widely agreed upon criteria for making choices, then it is doubtful that budget reforms will readily succeed in being more rational.

This typology of budgetary environments does more than point out conflicting objectives behind reform proposals. From the standpoint of research, it suggests how we might investigate the ways participants in the budget process accommodate roles and strategies to changes in the budgetary environment. But there is also a practical dimension here. The typology of budgetary environments highlights the dilemmas encountered when an existing complex process is made even more complex by incompatible purposes. This is not meant as another justification of incrementalism. Yet it does alert one to the potential problems of piling up unrealistic demands on participants in the budget process in the guise of reform. The history of budget reform has demonstrated that the search for rational criteria for budgetary decision making has been an elusive one. The typology of budgetary environments is one "cognitive map" to focus that theoretical and practical search.

REFERENCES

1. Anthony, R. N. Zero-base budgeting is a fraud. *Wall Street Journal,* April 27, 1977, *22.*
2. Key, V. O., Jr. The lack of a budgetary theory. *American Political Science Review,* 940, *34,* 1138-1144.
3. U.S. Congress, Joint Economic Committee. *Planning-Programming Budgeting System: Progress and Potentials, Hearings.* Washington, D.C., U.S. Government Printing Office, 1967.

4. LaFaver, J. S. Zero-base budgeting in New Mexico. *State Government,* 1974, *47,* 108-112.
5. Scheiring, M. J. Zero-base budgeting in New Jersey. *State Government,* 1976, *49,* 174-179.
6. Niskanen, W., Jr. *Bureaucracy and Representative Government.* Chicago, Aldine, 1971.
7. Vanderbilt, D. H. Budgeting in local government: Where are we now? *Public Administration Review,* 1977, *37,* 538-542.

II

SOME BEHAVIORAL CONTEXTS: Differences and Similarities Between People in Organizations

The study of human behavior wrestles with two apparently contradictory strains. For genetic reasons, as well as philosophical ones in the Western civilizations, the uniqueness of the individual must be stressed. However, if people do differ in many significant ways, they also can be similar in equally significant ways. Perhaps more precisely, many people in fact behave similarly enough under similar conditions that one would be foolish to insist in practice on the unmodified uniqueness of the individual. Such behavioral similarities in no way deny significant individual uniqueness and certainly acknowledge ultimate uniqueness.

There is no resolving the tension between uniqueness and similarity. Behavioral sciences must continually seek generalizations that respect individual uniqueness. At the same time, however, behavioral scientists must frame their concept of human uniqueness in ways that acknowledge substantial similarities.

Public finance and budgeting is in the differences/similarities business. The chapters reprinted in this part establish the point in diverse ways. By way of introductory support, note only that budgets set goals. Immediately, then, the budget maker is involved in balancing the differences and similarities of those persons subject to the budget. Will any thousand individuals respond best to a "tight" budget and work resolutely even though the budget is unrealistic and unattainable? Or does Sam work best when he experiences the success of "bringing a project in under budget," and the more so the better, as far as he is concerned? Setting a "loose" budget is appropriate in such a case, even though that budget is also "unrealistic."

The practical difficulty, of course, is that budget makers can seldom have it both ways. They must be acutely conscious of that point where enough people will respond similarly and positively enough to the standards that all budgets imply. Budget makers must see the thousands and also the individuals who constitute the thousands, in sum.

This chapter takes three kinds of steps toward highlighting differences/similarities related to budgeting and finance. First, some summary attention will be given to differences/similarities as they operate within organizations. Second, brief attention will be given to the *context* of institutions and traditions within which public organizations exist because these contextual variables often impact significantly on similarities/differences in behavior. Third, and more specific, four selections will be introduced that variously sharpen our understanding of differences and similarities between persons in organizations that affect public budgeting and finance.

SOME INTRAORGANIZATION DIFFERENCES/SIMILARITIES

We take a convenient approach to suggesting the interplay of differences and similarities within organizations, relying on a classic work by Chris Argyris (1). He goes right to the heart of important differences that characterize relations with budgeting and finance personnel in organizations. He finds that those specially charged with responsibility for budgeting or finance are likely to see their activity differently from those performing other activities of which budgeting and finance constitute only a part (line supervisors). And all likely will agree that very real differences often exist. Hence a common similarity in perceiving basic differences often characterizes those in organizations who are "financial" and those who are "nonfinancial."

The differences between the perceptions of those in budgeting and those in line supervision often are sharp, as Argyris develops them. For example, he compares the perceptions of the two types of organization members concerning this theme: What are the uses of budgets? As might be expected, budgeting personnel see their activity as crucial and strategic. Budgeting is the "watchdog" of the firm. Consequently, budgeting and finance personnel tend to identify with top management, to whom they supply some of the data required for overhead control. Line supervisors have a different view. In sharp contrast, budgets can complicate the line supervisor's job of dealing freely with individual cases, and budgeting personnel can be seen as uninformed and pretentious, sometimes even malicious.

These differences in perceptions suggest the delicacy of relations of budgeting and finance personnel with other organization members, especially because perceptual differences get reinforced in many ways. Argyris develops a list of major bones of contention between budgeting and line supervisors. Some of these complaints clearly are "objective dilemmas" because they are inherent in differences in tasks, i.e., some personnel specialize in "getting the work out" and others specialize in seeing that the work gets done within prespecified financial and time constraints. Undue emphasis on one specialization can complicate the other. The problems of handling objective dilemmas, whether more or less acute, will exist. Other difficulties may derive from "standard practices," i.e., from established ways of doing things. Standard practices may be changed, of course. Thus this second class of difficulties may be sharply reduced if organization members are willing and able.

There are no easy ways to solve the many issues faced by budgeting and finance personnel. Inherent issues will remain, of course. Their severity can be reduced, but only by getting mutual cooperation, and the sharp differences in perceptions identified by Argyris suggest that getting cooperation often will be difficult. Usual practices can be changed, but again only if free and open communication is possible. Sharp differences in perceptions close channels of communication, however, and perceptions are difficult to change. The magnitude of the challenge is plain.

In summary, given the sometimes extreme differences in perceptions of budgeting people and those of line supervisors, the most reasonable prediction calls for considerable stress and inefficiency in coping with problems, whether they derive from objective dilemmas or from usual practices. The summary might have to be softened as the organization, level, and job are varied. What Argyris saw in four factories does not necessarily apply universally to all organizations. Even with such qualifications, however, striking commonalities exist between Argyris's description and the relationships that exist in many organizations.

Note that this conclusion puts us firmly back in the differences/similarities business. The point can be made explicit in many ways. Consider only one such way here: students and practitioners can neglect only at their own peril the differences in perceptions that Argyris isolates. But neither can they neglect the marked similarities between other organizations and those described by Argyris.

PUBLIC SECTOR ENVIRONMENTS AND DIFFERENCES/SIMILARITIES

The basic institutional settings and practices of the public sector also serve to induce major differences and similarities in behavior. Given that this generalization variously applies in specific cases at the several levels of American governance, the conclusion still holds rather more than less. A contrast between two basic types of political systems helps develop the significant point at issue here.

An old European saying has it that wise persons put all their eggs in one basket, and then *watch that basket.* Given due attention and strength or lack of thieves, these persons can conveniently protect all their eggs. If attention wavers or strength is inadequate, however, all of the eggs may be lost in one fell swoop. The underlying strategy thus minimizes the risk of a small loss. Alas, the strategy also implies the risk of a total loss.

The men who helped shape our political institutions followed an opposed strategy. They advised, in effect, that we distribute our political eggs among several baskets. The negative root belief is that the electorate cannot be expected to be either vigilant or broadly informed at all times. The positive root belief is that the interests of the electorate can, will, and should be engaged in enough significant cases to make their impact felt, if the mass electorate gets some help from appropriate structural arrangements that seek to lower the probability of drastic mistakes or losses.

The working accommodation in America has been the despair of doctrinnaire thinkers, having as it does dual goals: the control of necessary (but also dangerous) political elites and the involvement of vital (but often lethargic) mass electorates. The native cunning of those who designed our basic political system, therefore, provided that political institutions be set against one another so that some degree of mutual surveillance gets built into the political system without rigidfying it. As a result, our political eggs are scattered, with dual expectations, in several institutional baskets. Thus the chances are increased that no faction can steal all our political eggs. Relatedly, any really active egg snatchers probably will get multidirectional attention that sooner or later will motivate the electorate to turn the rascals out. The underlying strategy minimizes the chance of maximum loss and is prepared to absorb smaller losses as a major cost.

How American political institutions put their eggs in several baskets may be suggested via the late Morton Grodzins' image of a political layer cake (2). Grodzins described the "vertical" sharing of power in our federal system—between the central government, the states, and local governments—as the several multicolored strata of a layer cake. The differing widths of the various strata of the cake reflect the differing powers of the several levels of government in various issue areas. The analogy permits multiple comparisons with life. The thicknesses of the several strata in a layer cake vary from point to point, for example, just as the power of various levels of government varies in different areas. Further, the several strata also blend subtly into one another in some places while standing boldly distinct at others. Just so is public power usually shared, although at times one level or another may exercise a virtual monopoly.

Grodzins' image can be extended to the "horizontal" sharing of powers at the federal level between the legislative, executive, and judicial branches, which is commonly referred to as the "separation of powers" plus "checks and balances." The analogy also applies to state and local governments in much the same ways.

Putting our political eggs in several baskets has profound effects on public finance and budgeting. Indeed, perhaps the central issue of all public administration today concerns the basic redefinition of the scope of the power of various governments. The nature of this power has been a recurring problem, and observers agree increasingly that the issue is as central today as it was, for example, during the 1860s.

Disagreement begins beyond this point, of course. Some observers thank their lucky stars for the welter of countervailing governmental powers which operate vertically between national, state, and local levels, as well as horizontally between the several branches at each level of government. Basically, in this view, the tangle of countervailing and shared powers provides the major bulwark against using public policy as a vehicle for drastic or premature social experimentation. In this view, the country tends to get into serious trouble only when too many eggs get transferred into too few baskets. Then some rascals—a wicked or inept president, a few covetous legislators, some well-placed and insulated bureaucrats, or whoever—can make a killing.

Oppositely, the dominant opinion seems to be that the pattern of pervasive countervailing and shared powers is at the heart of the crisis of contemporary governance. In short, the multiple-basket pattern impedes, and probably prevents, needed adaptations to new conditions. The orthodox criticisms of national expenditure and taxation decisions, for example, clearly imply that (at best) too much has been made of countervailing and shared powers. The results are massively untidy, goes this argument. Specifically, Charles E. Lindblom (3) details the characteristics of expenditure and taxation decisions that most economists criticize, with an obvious emphasis on the federal level:

1. The lack of specific policies and procedures for coordinating revenues and expenditures.

2. The conflict between the President and Congress, between the two houses of Congress, and the multiple subcommittees within each house.

3. The committees of Congress that authorize programs typically do so in relative independence of the committees that make appropriations.

4. The appropriations committees tend to review segments of the budget, not the entire package, so many meaningful cost/benefit comparisons are not even attempted, or may even be deliberately avoided.

5. Many budgetary results are outcomes of unrelated decisions, as opposed to decisions deriving from some comprehensive review.

This brief analysis suggests diverse sets of similarities and differences. Consider only one basic set: most observers see the same features in our broad political institutions and practices, but those same observers may differ profoundly as to whether they see disease or remedy. To illustrate, legislative-executive relations at the federal level are not simply an inevitable outgrowth of the separation of powers, but Congress and its electoral system do foster localism and also provide multiple points of access for diverse organized interests who seek to get their concept of public or private advantage embodied in legal principle or in actual practice. These "organized interests" include both executive agencies and multifarious associations representing industries, the professions, veterans, and so on. In Freeman's view, the special flavor of the legislative product comes from the semiautonomy of three sets of critical actors (4):

1. The legislative committees and subcommittees that are often more meaningful and impactful than that collective abstraction, "the Congress"

2. The bureaus of federal agencies, which sometimes go substantially their own way because of vagaries of political control and the concentration of long-tenured specialists in the bureaus

3. The "interests" or "associations" whose focus is understandably particularistic rather than comprehensive

Much the same characterization applies to legislative bodies at all levels of government, as does this probable hypothesis. Perhaps our "mixed" institutions do not, on the overall, do as well as they might. But perhaps also they are therefore unlikely to do as poorly as more "pure" institutions might.

INTRODUCING FOUR SELECTIONS RELEVANT TO DIFFERENCES/SIMILARITIES

More specifically, the four chapters reprinted below provide diverse content for the two themes that preoccupy this part: similarities and differences between persons in organizations. To preview those chapters they deal with

*   The impact of one general context on budgeting and financial behavior, that context being state government

*   The differences in characteristics or needs of individuals, which will influence how specific persons respond to various stimuli or techniques

*   A detailed development of the different kinds of budget processes that might be tailored to differences in what motivates individuals

*   The description of the diverse impacts of four different models of how organizations do and/or should function, which description has major implications for budgeting and financial processes

Characteristics of State Budgeting

We start with a macroview. All budget and finance personnel are different in that they have different genetic endowments, their own sets of values or preferences, their own biases or prejudices. Although unique in such senses, similar environments or contexts will nonetheless encourage many people toward some central tendencies or similarities in attitudes and behaviors. That, in sum, is the argument of S. Kenneth Howard in "The Real World of State Budgeting."

Howard details a number of specific senses in which his basic theme holds. He writes of powerful forces, more or less omnipresent. As he notes: "It is not surprising that the state budgeting process reflects the environment from which it emerges." Basically, Howard argues, the budgeter faces an environment that is complex, uncertain, fragmented, and typically poor in resources relative to the problems that need resolution. So the budgeting or financial administrator usually resorts to a search for ways of simplifying the reality that otherwise would be overwhelming. Thus officials may develop guidelines for making "fair" decisions; and they may very well abandon loftier aims and scale down their aspirations to do well enough to survive.

This hurly-burly emphasized by Howard departs substantially from the view of the cool and detached decision maker, but so much the worse for that image. When all is said and done, Howard likes his product. He concludes:

> This generalized description of the state administrator's milieu is not totally satisfying, nor totally accurate or comprehensive. But it is a far more nearly accurate model than the rational one, or any other that we have, of the administrative world that surrounds state budgeting.

Characteristics or Needs of Individuals

Roger N. Blakeney shifts the focus of attention concerning similarities/differences to the level of the individual in his "motivation theories." He provides a catalog of the several ways in which the behavioral sciences have tried to distinguish what individuals need and hence what stimuli they will respond to. In McClelland's system, for example, individuals are seen as desiring some blend of three "needs"—for achievement, for affiliation, and for power. The most effective motivational system, by extension, will be that one which best relates to an individual's particular profile on such needs and which best permits meeting those needs. What motivational system would be next best? Well, the one that relates to the needs of most relevant actors. And one could go down the line in a similar way, moving through motivational systems that get more or less completely imposed on individuals by threat or intimidation.

These differences between people have profound implications for public budgeting and finance, which says an important mouthful because such differences typically do not get the explicit attention they deserve. That is, the very stimulus that motivates one individual may be neutral or even counterproductive to another individual. And several readings in this volume join Blakeney in emphasizing that the tasks of budgeting and finance, rightly conceived, extend not only to planning and control but to motivation as well. Indeed, planning and control are empty except for appropriate motivation.

Blakeney's emphases fit quite nicely with another useful elaboration of the differences/similarities theme by Andrew C. Stedry (5), which can be usefully sketched here. Stedry focused on the crucial role of "levels of aspiration" in budgeting. He surveyed the applicable literature and found it wanting for his purposes. Consequently, he designed a laboratory experiment to test the validity of a variety of hypotheses about levels of aspiration, performance, and kinds of budgets.

The issues confronted by Stedry can be put in skeletal form. Basically, all people tend to develop "levels of aspiration," internalized standards of performance toward which they are committed to strive. "Estimates of performance" must be distinguished from levels of aspiration. For example, consider a Major Leaguer who could realistically be a .400 hitter in baseball. If he is motivated to extend himself only when he is below .350, however, his aspiration level in this case would be below a realistic estimate of performance. Of course, estimates of performance may coincide with levels of aspiration, and they can even surpass them.

Raising the issue of levels of aspiration immediately calls forth a host of important questions which beg for attention. What happens to his performance if any individual settles on a level that is easy to achieve? Or simply impossible? And do some people habitually overestimate or underestimate their actual performance? With what consequences in each case? Such questions imply great challenges to the behavioral sciences and far outstrip the available answers in theory or practice, but such are the questions which daily confront budgeters and financial officers.

Fortunately, some useful behavioral benchmarks exist. For example, an individual will tend to decrease his level of aspiration in response to consistent failure. That generalization does not hold for all individuals under all conditions, but the generalization constitutes a reasonable bet. The practical implications seem direct. Budgets ought not be so demanding that they preclude success, for example. If budgets are impossibly high, individuals will tend to reject them because those budgets unavoidably require that an individual will fail psychologically even if that person does a great job. As a consequence, levels of aspiration may be lowered by an approach that seeks to raise them too much.

Despite our existing knowledge, much remains to be learned about the interaction of estimates of performance, levels of aspiration, and externally imposed budgets. Consider only that in typical budgeting an external demand is more or less imposed on the individual to accept a specific level of aspiration. The situation is complex, because the individual may estimate that the required performance is unattainable under any conditions. In addition, even if the subject (S) estimates he could attain the budget goal, S's own level of aspiration may be such that he is unwilling to do all that might be necessary to attain the external goal. And much evidence suggests that people will often reject or resist an imposed standard for the very reason that it is imposed, reasonable or not.

Of course, S could accept the external goal as his own internal level of aspiration. Sometimes that acceptance will just occur—because an individual does not care one way or the other, needs the job too much to raise an issue, or whatever. More generally, the probability of acceptance will be a direct function of the specific management practices used in formulating and administering the budget as well as of the individual's trust in authority figures or reliance on them.

Matters could be further complicated but, if nothing else, this brief review can trigger a useful airing of differing points of view. Stedry notes that the experimental subjects who performed best in his experiment were individuals who first received their high-performance budget from the experimenter (E) and then set their own aspiration levels. The worst performers were those S's who first set their own aspirations and then were given E's high-performance budget. Stedry's high performers had policy set for them by an authority figure and then participated in implementing decisions. Stedry's low performers, oppositely, participated initially in setting low aspiration levels, which were later seen as in conflict with the E's tougher standards. Stedry explains:

> An hypothesis which might satisfactorily explain this phenomenon is as follows: The high performing group formed its aspirations with the high budget levels in mind, while the low performing group rejected the high budget after forming aspirations with relation to their last performance . . . [Alternatively,] the stress, at least for some subjects, was so high that they may have been "discouraged" and may have ceased to try to improve performance.

Others can explain similar effects in other ways, to which later attention will be given.

"An Expectancy Theory Approach to the Motivational Impacts of Budgets" begins to provide some answers to these central questions suggested above. Ronen and Livingstone describe the expectancy theory of motivation in some detail. For present purposes, expectancy theory can be simplified to dual concerns: the probability that effort will be reflected in performance at work and the probability that effective performance will be rewarded in ways that the individual values. This done, Ronen and Livingstone essentially focus on *the* new question: what kinds of budgeting processes will lead to which kinds of effects, given expectancy theory with what the research literature seems to say about five major assumptions that accountants often have made about the budgeting process:

- The budget should be set at a reasonably attainable level.

- Managers should participate in the development of budgets for their own functions in the organization.
- Managers should operate on the principle of management by exception.
- Personnel should be charged or credited only for items within their control.
- Dimensions of performance that cannot be conveniently measured in monetary terms are outside the budget domain.

Of course, previous discussion already has been concerned with some of these assumptions, as in the description of Stedry's experiment.

The contribution of Ronen and Livingstone can be extended explicitly to this earlier discussion. Consider the emphasis at several points above on "participation." Thus Becker and Green (6) in an article not reprinted here observe that "participation" in the making of budgets "can lead to better morale and increased initiative." Their analysis usefully covers much ground, starting with the basic belief that participation is no panacea but that it can produce beneficial results under specified circumstances. Roughly, participation is one way of increasing the chances that an employee's level of aspiration will be more or less consistent with the demands and standards inherent in an organization's budget. Without participation, individual aspirations will tend to differ widely and, hence, conflict with organizational goals will be more likely.

Care must govern any conclusions about the efficacy of participation because the associated phenomena are complex. Becker and Green argue that sufficient employees respond similarly enough to participation opportunities that under specified conditions the student for many practical purposes can devote less attention to the differences that patently exist between individuals. Directly, opportunities for participation often can increase the likelihood that all employees will accept a budget as embodying their own internal level of aspiration.

But Ronen and Livingstone suggest that such effects are not inevitable. Indeed, "participation" might even be counterproductive. Where the conditions of expectancy theory do not hold, Ronen and Livingstone remind us, participative techniques also could generate resistance to management's budget, as by permitting group forces to mobilize when employees come to feel that management is employing pseudoparticipation, the results of which are only accepted when they coincide with management's desires. Employees might be led to reject that game in various ways, as by great reluctance to "participate" or by more overt ways of resisting.

Characteristics of Organizations

Having begun above at the broad level of the state government environments to develop the point, the next chapter in this section deals with aspects of the individual level of analysis. Richard F. Elmore closes an important analytic loop for us in his "Organizational Models of Social Program Implementation." And El-more raises our conceptual sights again—this time to the level of the larger organization.

Elmore's work starts from a reasonable place, i.e., different models might guide the management of specific organizations. He selects four types for detailed description:

- *A systems management model,* which represents the mainstream view of policy analysis
- *A bureaucratic process model,* which is common in most organizations
- *An organizational development model,* which assumes the possibility of a substantial commonality of interests reflected in a substantial meshing of individual needs and organization demands
- *A conflict-and-bargaining model,* which focuses on how individuals "with divergent interests coalesce around a common task" by higgling and piggling

Elmore's work does not draw specific implications for budgeting and finance, but his illustrative emphasis on the implementation of social programs can without violence be extended to numerous considerations raised in the selections introduced above. Thus the organization development model seems best suited to the earlier emphasis on employee involvement and participation, as well as to the meeting of individual needs. No doubt, also, the bureaucratic model probably would rank lowest of the four in those regards. Looked at from another vantage point, the bureaucratic model would provide a relatively comfortable home for concepts and theories of budgeting and finance that derive from the traditional theory of the firm, examples of which get cited at several points in these first two chapters.

But Elmore does not extend his argument in such directions. Each model has its strengths and advantages, he notes, and some of them differ significantly in core ideas—such as the radically different degree of mutuality or commonality of purpose on which some models are based—while others ineluctably blend into one another.

REFERENCES

1. Argyris, Chris. *What Budgets Mean to People.* New York, Controllership Foundation, 1954, esp. pp. 2-14.
2. Grodzins, Morton. *The American System.* Chicago, Rand McNally, 1966, pp. 156-171.
3. See Lindblom, Charles E. Decision-making in taxation and expenditures. In National Bureau of Economic Research, *Public Finances.* Princeton, N.J., Princeton University Press, 1961, esp. pp. 295-298.

4. Freeman, J. Leiper. *The Political Process.* New York, Random House, 1965.
5. Stedry, Andrew C. *Budget Control and Cost Behavior.* Englewood Cliffs, N.J., Prentice-Hall, 1960, esp. pp. 17-91.
6. Becker, Selwyn W., and Green, David Jr., Budgeting and employee behavior. *Journal of Business,* October 1962, *35,* 392-402.

6

THE REAL WORLD OF STATE BUDGETING[*]

S. Kenneth Howard

THE ADMINISTRATOR IN NATIVE HABITAT[1]

A state administrator, as a human being, has his own value system, his own capacities, his own biases and prejudices, and his own perceptions of the world—in short, the set of characteristics that make him peculiarly who he is. He is not the totally rational creature postulated in classical economic theory. His goals are not clear; he cannot manage the tremendous number of calculations required in evaluating comprehensively every consequence of every alternative before him; and as a processor of information and data, he can scarcely rival machines in speed or accuracy. Clearly he has an irrational as well as a rational side. His rationality is bounded on all sides:

> He is limited by his unconscious skills, habits and reflexes; he is limited by his values and conceptions of purpose, which may diverge from the organization goals; he is limited by the extent of his knowledge and information.[2]

---

*From *Changing State Budgeting* (Lexington, Kentucky: The Council of State Governments, 1973), Chapter 2, pp. 27-33, 43-67. Copyright ©1973 the Council of State Governments. References have been renumbered.

Over time, all of these limitations can be altered, more or less, but at any given time they provide the personal environment within which the administrator must make a decision. The best we can say for administrative man, assuming that his personal psychological makeup is normal, is that he intends to be rational.[3] He does not intentionally make wrong decisions; when he makes them, he believes they are correct.

Other people are a part of the environment in which the administrator must carry on decision making. He should recognize that these individuals, as humans, are subject to the same limitations on their rationality as he is. It comes as no real surprise to him, then, that others viewing a given problem may not perceive it exactly as he does (i.e., that not all participants have the same definition of the situation). From the multitudinous objective facts that might relate to a certain situation, the administrator must decide which "facts" are to be recognized in defining both the problem and the decision required. Others with different value systems and perceptions may not accept that these are indeed the "facts," or that they are relevant. Even if men can agree on the facts, they may not agree on the meaning or weight that ought to be assigned to them. For example, economists may agree on what has happened over a period of time to wholesale prices and to the value of unfilled orders in durable-goods industries, but they may disagree on the importance to be assigned to these facts and about the relation that these factors have to changes in total productive output.

This discussion leads to another characteristic of the administrator's environment—it has more tension and conflict than peace and tranquility. The amount of potential conflict an administrator faces or has to evaluate will vary in part with his level in the organizational hierarchy. The higher he is, the broader the perspective and the wider the variety of interests (and potential sources of disagreement) he will need to consider.[4] A number of other factors (age of the organization, its size, its prestige, the nature of its program) will also affect the amount of conflict perceived in the environment. In public life, where control and influence over general social policy are highly sought commodities, conflict situations are daily fare for many state administrators.

Conflicts are sometimes rooted in basic value differences among the participants. As a result, it is often difficult to get agreement on the goals that are being pursued in any particular situation. In fact, in state government, explicitly identifying goals can often be the most divisive course of action an administrator can adopt; it may open value breaches that an organization cannot successfully bridge.

Administrators have another objection to the explicit definition of goals: such statements tend to reduce their flexibility. This tendency is heightened if the goals are made public. Despite the frustrations that a lack of goal clarity may entail, most state administrators appear to prefer broad and ambiguous objectives so that they can adapt their actions and decisions to the specific situations they face. Whether or not we prefer a system of laws rather than of men, the ability to be flexible will remain jealously guarded among state administrators.

Another important characteristic of the administrator now emerges—he is action-oriented. He wants to get things done.

> Disciplined, orderly thought is the characterization given to analysis, but disciplined orderly thought suggests certain traits: reflectiveness, self-criticism, and the willingness to reconsider past commitments without self-justification. However rarely or frequently encountered in the general human population, these are not traits characteristic of the action-oriented, incisive individuals who reach policy making positions. Questioning and self-doubt lead to Hamlet-like decisionmakers.[5]

In order to get action, a state administrator is more likely to "muddle through" than to proceed in accordance with the model of rationality. He will not seek to know all consequences of all alternatives before him right now. He will concentrate on those marginal values and marginal differences that separate present from proposed policies. He will seek agreement on policies rather than on values or goals, recognizing that different men can support the same policy because each foresees its fulfilling his goal, which may be quite different from and sometimes incompatible with the goals of other policy supporters. The state administrator's idea of a good decision or policy tends to be one that achieves satisfice, i.e., sufficient agreement among the concerned individuals or organizations that continued progress (as he defines it) is possible. He will perhaps seek a decision that maximizes, but he will usually settle and more often obtain one that achieves satisfice. In general, he will proceed by making incremental changes rather than sweeping, comprehensive ones.[6] He is less uncertain about the consequences that will flow from incremental or less drastic changes because past experience with similar policy provides some guidance. Also, sweeping changes, particularly in public life, may generate a level of conflict that is intolerable to the survival of the organization. There may indeed be organizations that should be swept aside, but the administrator can surely be forgiven if he considers the survival of his own organization rather vital and if, over his career, he has developed a capacity to equate the work of his organization with the public interest.

A high order of judgment is required as the administrator tries to estimate how others will respond to certain actions on his part. There is some hope that computers will help reduce uncertainty by making information more readily available, but the ability of a computer to apply that information to a specific problem seems far off, if ever to be reached at all. It is not enough to know the pattern of responses given in certain situations by middle-aged, white, Anglo-Saxon, Protestant males with college educations at Ivy League schools. The administrator must evaluate how a specific individual who fits into these categories will respond in this particular environment. Undoubtedly, things now considered unquantifiable will be subject to quantified analysis in the future but the role of judgment is not likely to diminish appreciably in decision making.

As the administrator tries to deal with the complexity and uncertainty he faces, he seeks ways of simplifying his problem. Such simplifications are imperative because there is an enormous discrepancy between his cognitive abilities, even if they are abetted by electronic computers and other devices, and the complexity of the problems he is attempting to solve. Often more information will help, but getting it takes time and money, and these two resources are often not abundant in state government.[7] In reducing the burden of his calculations, the administrator may break a problem into smaller parts, may deliberately ignore parts of it in the hope that others will look after what he ignores, may develop decision criteria (such as satisfice) that will accelerate his way through the maze despite the fact that increased speed contains obvious risks, and may develop practices (such as proceeding incrementally rather than sweepingly, except under the most dire circumstances) that enable him to comprehend more readily the business he is about. The world of state budget administrators and budget staffs may be rendered more poignant than that of other state administrators by its nearness to the governor and the responsibility these officials have for assuming a view that tries to encompass all of state government. Governors' time is very limited, and consequently issues are often determined faster and with less patience for considerations of fact and analytic background than this discussion has suggested thus far. Furthermore, at this level, partisan political considerations may have a much more important bearing on decisions than they do in functional agencies.[8]

This generalized description of the state administrator's milieu is not totally satisfying, nor totally accurate or comprehensive. But it is a far more nearly accurate model than the rational one, or any other that we have, of the administrative world that surrounds state budgeting.

CHARACTERISTICS OF STATE BUDGETING

It is not surprising that the state budgeting process reflects the environment from which it emerges. In addition to the general factors described thus far, other specific state requirements keenly affect state budgeting. The most obvious of these is the requirement, frequently constitutional, that state budgets balance. The states thus lack both the fiscal resources and the fiscal flexibility of the national government—budgetary deficits are simply not allowed at the state level or as readily obscured as at the national level.

State budgeting employs a number of devices and procedures to simplify making the calculations and judgments that are required. It also is fragmented, reveals a number of different strategies, and lacks flexibility because of mandatory requirements.

Simplifying Calculations

The most critical calculations in budgeting entail judgment, not mathematics, in allocating scarce resources across a variety of possible expenditures, the permutations, combinations, and implications become interrelated, immensely complex, and virtually unfathomable. These difficulties are real and continuing; they cannot be easily brushed aside. Of necessity, state budgeting has developed a number of devices that make the calculations more manageable.[8]

Roles. Participants in the state budgeting process are expected to play certain roles. If there is general agreement on the role each participant is playing, mutual expectations can be developed. Each participant is expected to play his role to the best of his ability, but his individual calculations are simplified because he needs to consider only those aspects of the problem required by his particular role. He can assume that participants playing different roles will bring out considerations he is not expected to recognize. Since these roles are not the same, differences and disagreements arise, and it is hoped that from the ensuing debate and bargaining, desirable public policy and expenditure decisions will evolve.

Units outside the central budget agency are normally expected to initiate budget requests. The power of initiation almost always lies with line agencies. Since people working in a given endeavor usually feel some loyalty to that work and deem it important, they are expected to maintain that more money should be devoted to it.

As a matter of practical strategy, agencies usually try to spend all appropriations made in the last fiscal period. In some instances it is harder to justify why the money was *not* spent than to spend it. Agencies tend to assume that getting more money during the next fiscal period is unnecessarily complicated if they have not spent virtually all of an even smaller appropriation previously granted. Of course, spending shortages and overages do not always arise as *planned* strategies.

Agency requests cannot include every conceivable thing that might be wished. Normally agencies will top off or cap their total requests by seeking support for programs they want badly but can do without—desirable but not mandatory or top-priority items. In deciding what to ask for, officials must have some feel for the political situation—some sense of "what will go."

> The word "pad" may be too crass to describe what goes on; administrators realize that in predicting needs there is a reasonable range within which a decision can fall and they just follow ordinary prudence in coming out with an estimate near the top. "If you do not do this," an official told me rather vehemently, "you get cut and you'll soon find that you are up to your ass in alligators.[10]

A central budget staff is supposed to possess a more comprehensive and co-ordinated viewpoint, usually compatible with that of the governor, than can be expected of the line agencies acting individually. The budget staff is far more sensitive than the line agencies to the requirement for total budgetary balance. Since total requests typically exceed what is considered feasible politically, budget staffs are placed in the position of having to cut requests, often substantially. Central budget staffs lack line agency expertise in determining what ought to be done in particular substantive fields, but they maintain the imposing responsibility of making comparisons among different values to different people so that the budget has both fiscal and political balance. There is no completely objective method for establishing priorities among programs at this level. To reduce the burden of their calculations, central budget staffs have often focused on short-range fiscal management and expenditure control objectives without enough appreciation for the implications that decisions reached on these bases may have for the effectiveness of various state programs. When this occurs, the agencies with their focus on "needs" and the central budget staffs tend to talk past each other: "Agencies press for expansion using programmatic criteria while budget review officers attempt to negate expansion using financial criteria."[11] The negative aspects of agency-budget staff exchanges are diminishing as the budget staffs give increasing attention to program effectiveness and to programmatic implications in evaluating agency requests.

State legislatures ultimately hold the power of the purse. They see themselves as the guardians of the treasury. This viewpoint usually stresses a more restrictive than expansive posture, cutting proposals rather than initiating ideas. This is not really a criticism because legislatures are better structured and equipped to play the role of evaluator and reactor than of initiator and creator. It is understandable that legislators try to impose cuts that will not significantly affect their own constituencies. To meet the enormous complexity of the calculations they must make, legislatures divide up the task. Members can more or less specialize in certain types of policies and substantive fields. The committee system itself is a reflection of the need to specialize and to break the total task into smaller and more manageable parts.

The state budgetary process with its various roles can perhaps be characterized as involving "contained specialization."[12] This phrase suggests that specialists or key individuals are assigned within the legislative and executive branches to formulate taxing and spending proposals, that they can reach decisions on controversial issues with minimal partisan bickering, and that other members of the executive and legislative establishments tend to accept their recommendations. Thus the conflict inherent in resource allocations gets contained in institutions whose members are partly selected for their ability to represent various viewpoints in the controversy but who have yet not become so attached to those perspectives that they cannot compromise.

Agreement on the roles that various participants are to play and consistent execution of those roles allows mutual expectations to evolve. Those expectations simplify the calculations that all participants must make. If it can be assumed that others will play their role in the prescribed manner and with the assigned perspectives, then each participant can adopt a more limited perspective with some assurance that competition among participants will allow conflicting values and questions of intrinsic worth to be raised and given consideration. These assumptions provide the basis for the workings of state budgeting today.

Repetitiveness. State budgeting takes place again and again on an annual or biennial cycle, and this repetitiveness, like roles, can be a device for making budgeting more manageable. Calculations are simplified, and the decisions that are made at any one time become less psychologically agonizing if they are not seen as "all or nothing" finalities. Most new endeavors are seen as experimental, and decisions are deemed tentative and subject to change at a future time. In this way problems tend to be worn down rather than solved outright.

Incrementalism. Incrementalism tries to simplify decision making and the complexity of calculations by narrowing the range of decisions to be made. Specifically, attention is focused on the differences, margins, or increments that exist between what is presently being done and what is proposed. Consideration is limited to the increment of change, and decisions are made through a series of successive limited comparisons.[13] Concentration on the changes or differences means that total programmatic evaluations are not made and what is already present is generally accepted without serious consideration or review as the proper base on which to make changes.

> Budgetary calculations are incremental, using a historical base as the point of departure. The existing level of expenditures is largely taken for granted and, for the most part, only small changes are seriously considered.[14]

Satisfice. A great difficulty in decision making is determining when a good decision has been uncovered. What constitutes a good decision? By what criteria is "goodness" determined? In state budgeting, a primary test of goodness is whether the proposal achieves satisfice, i.e., sufficient agreement among various concerned parties that action can be taken. A policy may obtain agreement even if it is not the one that achieves some goals most effectively or has the most substantial impact on some target area or group. Differences over goals and target areas or groups are played down in an attempt to get agreement on more specific policies and actions. Satisficing is a very real and vital part of state budgeting.

Fair Share and Base. It is easier to proceed in an incremental and satisficing manner if there is agreement about the base from which the differences or increments will be measured. Most state budgeting decisions are premised on some sense of a base figure. Normally this base is very close either to the last appropriation or to the most recent estimate of total current spending for the activity involved. The various subparts comprised in the base are generally not reviewed in detail because there is not enough time to go about "rediscovering the wheel" each budget period. Calculations are simplified if most items contained in existing programs (the base) are simply not reconsidered. Perhaps nowhere in the Union were "base" and incremental budgeting more fully institutionalized than in North Carolina. For years three different budget documents were prepared in that state. The A budget covered appropriations necessary to keep current operations at their present or future mandatory levels, the B budget included appropriations desirable for program expansions, and the C budget covered capital outlays.[15] The separation of capital outlays from operating expenditures, a common practice in many states, is another reflection of efforts to simplify the burden of calculations.

The notion of fair share suggests that when more resources are made available, they should be divided "fairly" among various competing state activities. Although certain agencies and programs increase their spending more rapidly than others, there is a general upward trend throughout all agencies (if only because salaries for all employees are steadily rising). If any new resources become available, they are usually allocated among many agencies and programs rather than concentrated on those few deemed of highest priority. In short:

> Budgeting turns out to be an incremental process, proceeding from a historical base, guided by accepted notions of fair shares, in which decisions are fragmented, made in sequence by specialized bodies, and coordinated through repeated attacks on problems and through multiple feedback mechanisms. The role of the participants, and their perceptions of each other's powers and desires, fit together to provide a reasonably stable set of criteria on which to base calculations.[16]

State reliance upon some of the methods for simplifying calculations (such as roles, incrementalism, fair share, and base) may diminish as more and more emphasis is given to program as contrasted with organizational considerations and more analytic approaches to decision making are used.

Fragmentation

State budgeting is a highly fragmented process. Compartmentalization and specialization become necessary in any large organization. This natural fragmentation has been abetted in state governments by two factors that grant certain agencies a degree of financial independence from central control. The first is federal grant programs. Many agencies rely heavily on federal support and have become more responsive to federal regional and national offices than to gubernatorial offices. The second factor is the earmarking of particular revenues to specific activities or agencies.[17] This fragmentation enormously complicates achieving the coordinated and sound priority setting for which state budgeting strives.[18]

Normally budget preparation and presentation is recognized as one of the most vital executive powers, but not all states have given this responsibility to the executive branch.[19] Arkansas uses a legislative budget, and Mississippi and South Carolina use a budget prepared by a joint legislative-executive body. Although the Texas governor submits a budget, a legislative budget board submits its own complete budget as well.

Although the power to propose a budget in the remaining states lies in executive hands, the governors' formal powers are not necessarily total in this field. In at least four states—Idaho, Indiana, Louisiana, and North Carolina—budget-making authority is vested in the governor but another agency has certain advisory powers. The membership of these bodies is usually dominated by legislators, and their effective power is often far greater than their formal advisory status would suggest.[20]

The fragmentation that the legislature imposes on budgeting is obvious. All states but one have bicameral legislatures, and most of them use separate committees for revenue and spending matters. Fragmentation is further present in those states that follow the federal legislative practice of separating substantive program legislation from appropriations. Substantive committees make authorizations, but appropriations committees consider what portion of the authorized amounts will be funded.

Perhaps the most important fragmentation occurs within the budget process itself.[21] Operating agencies have little administrative and virtually no political responsibility for raising revenues. They are pressured by programmatic considerations and politics to emphasize expenditures, not revenues. Central budget staffs are often equally one-sided in their internal structuring because revenue matters are usually the chore of the revenue administrators or budgeting personnel, who are not concerned with the detailed examination of spending requests. Revenue pressures come to focus on governors and budget directors, but their ability to withstand the pressures for spending that have been generated by the one-sided nature of the process up to that point is clearly circumscribed.

Strategies

State budgeting is a competitive process in which the stakes are very important to the participants. Not surprisingly, the contestants employ a variety of strategies in this combat. Perhaps the most widespread device is to find (establish if necessary) and nurture a clientele. Such "outside" support can be extremely valuable in bringing a governor or a legislative committee around to an agency's point of view. Of course, this approach is not one-sided. Typically, the clientele does not allow itself simply to be used by the agency. It may make demands on the agency on its own and seek to take over the agency entirely. Many times agency officials curry several clienteles to avoid being captured by any one of them and to give the agency itself some flexibility by playing off the demands of one client group against the pressures from another. In fact, state budgeting procedures may stimulate interest group competition if they involve identifying target or clientele groups—the "have-nots" will have a factual basis on which to lay their claims of relative deprivation.

Agencies also try to have their competence recognized by all other participants. This competence entails knowing not only their substantive field but how to play in the political arena as well. Agencies try to conduct and present themselves so that others, particularly governors and key legislators, have confidence in their judgment and recommendations.

The fragmentation of the entire state budgeting process offers innumerable opportunities to play off one fragment against another—whether individuals, client groups, branches of government, legislative committees, legislative chambers, or other possible sources of division.

If cuts must be made, they can sometimes be made where an agency's most effective client group is most seriously affected, thus forcing the group to put its weight behind efforts to restore the cuts. At other times it may be argued that even a small cut will cause an entire program to die or be rendered almost totally ineffective.

If increases are sought, it is desirable that they appear to be small and to arise from "natural" or mandatory causes. Sometimes the existence of a backlog of work can be used to justify increases.

At all times agencies strive to move rapidly and forcefully if certain events, such as natural disasters or prison riots, afford a sudden upsurge in public awareness and concern that can be parlayed into an expansion of programs and services.

Agency survival and continued growth are usually important considerations in designing agency strategy.

> Since neither dramatic expansion nor dramatic reduction takes place
> very often, programmatic and financial justifications are used less as
> criteria for decisions than as symbolic shields, behind which agency
> administrators and budget officials both play a game of organizational
> status maintenance.[22]

Clearly, state budgeting includes not only budgetary procedures, techniques, and strategies, but also all the political power struggles and bargaining activities in which participants must engage to survive and obtain the allocations they deem desirable.

Mandatories

Incoming governors are often dismayed to learn how little discretion they have in the resource allocations they must make. These constraints are summarized by the word "mandatories." Included in this category are contributions to retirement systems, funds required to match current federal grants-in-aid and other support programs, and funds that must be provided under the various formulas governing aid to local governments. A governor could free some resources by simply dropping or sharply reducing some of these programs or levels of aid, but such actions are rarely feasible politically. Mandatories constitute a substantial portion of most state budgets. When this limitation is combined with the lack of any significant control over the receipt and expenditure of a variety of earmarked revenues (some of which may not even be included in the budget) and with other political restraints (particularly the necessity to maintain existing programs), the governor finds his choices far more limited than he would like and his vital budgetary powers less compelling than he would wish.

In summary, the executive budget has been viewed as a principal instrument for providing executive leadership and responsibility in state government. But the budgeting process itself is fragmented, and gubernatorial flexibility is limited by mandatory expenditures, political realities, and the roles and strategies that other participants adopt. Furthermore, the decision-making authority of governors in budgeting remains divided within, between, and among individuals, administrative agencies, boards, legislators and their committees, private interest groups, and others, including a phalanx of separately elected officials within the governor's own executive hierarchy.[23]

DETERMINANTS OF STATE EXPENDITURES

Despite the apparent chaos and lack of objective rationality that attend state budgeting, attempts have been made to find out what factors explain or determine the level and nature of the expenditure decisions that emerge from the budgeting process.[24] These efforts have revealed some obvious characteristics about state spending. For example, states with larger populations tend to have greater total expenditures. More significantly, studies have also shown that spending per capita by states tends to vary positively with a state's wealth (as measured by per capita personal income), in other words, the rich states spend more per resident in absolute terms. While this is not automatically true in all cases or fields of activity, it certainly holds true in the largest single domestic program area—education.[25] Furthermore, residents in wealthy states may actually be able, because of their greater resources, to devote a smaller proportion of their higher income to public activities than citizens in less prosperous states. In short, citizens in the wealthier states pay more but may feel it less; they get an equivalent or a greater level of public spending while devoting a smaller proportion of their resources to these activities.

Four other points that emerge from these efforts to establish the determinants of state expenditures deserve more thorough discussion. First, current levels of spending are highly correlated with previous levels of spending. Second, there is disagreement over the relative impact of economic and political factors on state spending. Third, there is no necessary correlation between the levels of spending and the quality of services. Fourth, regional patterns of spending are present, but their causes are unclear.

Impact of Previous Year's Spending

No experienced state budget official will find startling or new the suggestion that expenditures this year are very similar to those of last year or that this factor in a statistical sense explains more variance from one year to the next than any other factor thus far uncovered.[26] He might be surprised at just how high correlations between present and past spending remain even when carried back over periods of more than 60 years.[27] The stability of this relationship creates a strong conservative bias in state budgeting and reflects the force of incremental budgeting practices.

> Budget processes that respect the past may have a peculiar appeal in the midst of ongoing, pluralistic struggles for change that surround state and local authorities. The budgetary process is one predictable element of stability. As a conservative bulwark, the budget may permit legislators, administrators, and private interests to tolerate competition for change because no radical change is likely to survive the funding process. If a new program does win approval in the state or local legislatures, it can be disciplined by a budgetary process that puts a premium on incremental growth.[28]

Although the relationship between present and past spending seems to show a good deal in a statistical sense it is far less satisfactory as an explanation. This relationship can be very useful in predicting future levels of spending, but it does not indicate why differences in spending patterns between states arose or why a given state has a particular spending pattern. To say that this year's spending is "explained" by last year's, which is explained by the previous year's, which is explained . . . , and so on reveals nothing about what caused the differences originally somewhere between here and the Garden of Eden. High correlations within each state as a unit and similar consistency within all states year after year in no way explain the differences in resource allocations that exist *between* the states.[29]

Second, although these findings support, the view that state budgeting is a highly incremental process, the existence or use of incrementalism does not really explain the results encountered. Even if the incremental process is used, might similar results be obtained with a different style of budgeting? Furthermore, if many states are actually employing incremental decision making, how does that fact in any way explain the differences in budgetary allocations that exist among those using the same process.[30]

Economic vs. Political Factors

Researchers in this field are divided over the relative importance of economic rather than political factors in explaining the differences that exist in state spending patterns. Economic forces are usually represented in quantitative analyses by statistics on per capita personal income, the extent of industrialization, and the degree of urbanization. Political factors include measures of partly competition, voter turnout, and the extent of state legislative apportionment in accordance with population patterns.

Economic factors have been found more significant than political factors in explaining differences in state policy outcomes generally,[31] and specifically differences in educational policies and levels of expenditure,[32] civil rights policies,[33] and the distribution of spending responsibilities between state and local governments.[34]

Naturally, those who believe in the importance of the political process have not been overly pleased with the economic determinism that these findings tend to present. It would appear that economic factors shape both the political process and the policy results that emerge from it and that the political process has no substantial independent impact on policy outcomes. If this is true, differences in the nature of the states' politics—such as the extent of party competition, the extent of fragmentation within state government, and similar considerations—are of little importance in explaining policy differences that exist between states. The findings call into question concepts of representation and theories of party and group conflict that have been the foundation of much American political thinking.[35]

In response to these challenges, it has been suggested that the political process be viewed as a system—having an environment carrying on certain internal processes, and producing various results.[36] In these terms, economic variables form part of the environment within which political activities such as party competition operate to produce outputs—government expenditures, in this example. To be sure, environmental factors have an impact on the political process, not only in terms of its structure but also in terms of the demands, supports, and communications with which it must deal. But there is no obvious and direct linkage between economic characteristics in the environment and policy outcomes. Part of the required linkage is provided by the political process, including budgeting, that is filled with value considerations. It is thus contended that political factors play a linking role between social characteristics and policy outcomes. The political process is affected by social characteristics, but it also has its own independent impact on policy outcomes.[37]

Since political characteristics such as voter turnout, party strength, interparty competition, and features of state legislatures have not explained much of the expenditure variation between states, attempts have been made to reconcile the apparent differences in beliefs about the importance of economic factors. With the linkage ideas discussed above as a basis, it has been contended that political influences are not missing—the measures chosen have simply not revealed them.[38]

A second line of reasoning holds that the impact of economic characteristics varies with the structure or policy field under consideration. For example, economic factors correlate more highly with differences in combined state and local spending than with differences in state spending considered alone, but state spending of itself is very much affected by the variations that exist between the states in the division of programs and responsibilities between the state and local levels.[39] It has also been suggested that socioeconomic factors are more important for policies in the highway-natural resource area, while political factors are slightly more important in the welfare-education field.[40] But this finding tends to ignore the facts that highway-natural resource expenditures and their benefits may be more obvious to taxpayers than those in the welfare-education area and that the former expenditures tend to be financed from segregated user funds, so that less central policy control may be exercised over them.

> Our findings show that different social and economic characteristics have different relevance for policies, and their relevance varies between substantive areas of policy. . . .
> There is no single answer to the question: "Is it politics or economics that has the greatest impact on policy?" The answer (contrary to the thrust of much recent research) varies with the dimensions of each phenomena that are at issue.[41]

It has also been suggested that political factors, even though they may not be major determinants of the level of state spending, may be important determinants of how the burdens and benefits of that spending are distributed in the states.[42] Furthermore, expenditure is only one measure and dimension of policy decisions and perhaps the very one most subject to influence by economic factors.[43] Analysis of decisions outside the budgetary field might reveal that political factors have substantial impact on policy matters. It has been found that the speed with which states adopt new ideas in a wide range of policy fields relates to both economic and political factors.[44]

It may also be that the importance that political factors such as party competition achieve as intervening variables between socioeconomic characteristics and expenditure decisions depends on the extent to which the policies involved are redistributive in nature, i.e., taking from the haves and giving to the have-nots.

> Given the advantages possessed by the haves, the organization, continuity, and visibility of alternatives provided through inter-party competition are important for the capacity of have-nots to attain policies in their own interests.[45]

Finally, none of the academic debate over economic vs. political factors notes a relationship that is sensed by political practitioners. Politics tend to focus on how the political decisions reached by key decision makers, especially legislators, can be influenced by the way in which those decision makers and their constituents making a living.[46]

Levels of Spending and Service Quality

It is generally thought that increases in expenditures for a given function are associated with increases in the quantity or quality of services offered in that function. The quality of public services may be reflected in such measures as the percentage of selective service registrants who pass mental examinations and the percentage of infants who survive their first year. Yet at least one prolific researcher contends that neither the quantity nor the quality of public service is related to government spending in any simple or direct fashion.[47] If this is true, expenditure increases may become very hard to justify.

> In contrast to the assumptions of several authors, it is evident that the levels of state and local government spending do not exert pervasive influence upon the nature of public services.[48]

Many factors other than spending affect the quality of services. These include the nature of agency leadership, the type of clientele being served, and the organizational structure of the agency itself. It does appear that states with high per capita income and those with large administrative corps relative to population are likely to be high producers of public services, and states with both fiscal and administrative decentralization are more inclined to have high-quality service. In general, the quality of services provided within a state appears to be primarily a function of its overall socioeconomic status.

The level of spending has one important characteristic that should not be ignored in trying to affect the quantity and quality of public services: It can be manipulated. Expenditures are subject to actions by government officials whereas other underlying factors, such as economic conditions or the type of clientele are not readily modified in the short run.[49]

Regionalism

There are distinct regional variations in the expenditures of American states, but they seem not to arise from any political characteristics or factors that are unique within those regions.[50] Although the findings are not statistically significant, researchers feel that when state officials make interstate comparisons in reaching their decisions, the comparisons tend to be heavily regional in nature.[51]

> The likelihood of a state adopting a new program is higher if other states have already adopted the idea. The likelihood becomes higher still if the innovation has been adopted by a state viewed by key decision makers as a point of legitimate comparison. Decision makers are likely to adopt new programs, therefore, when they become convinced that their state is relatively deprived, or that some need exists to which other states in their "league" have already responded.[52]

Summary on Expenditure Determinants

Research into comparative spending patterns among states has confirmed quantitatively some ideas and intuitive feelings that budget officials have long held based on experiences within their own jurisdictions. Relationships among various factors have been explored, but the most powerful of the relationships uncovered is better for predicting future state spending than for revealing the basic causes behind the spending levels that emerge. The relationships analyzed thus far can be very helpful in explaining what happens over time *within* a given state, but they are less help in explaining existing differences *between* states. Finally, the entire effort to establish determinants of state and state-local spending has been subjected to strong criticism on both substantive and methodological grounds.[53]

SUMMARY

State budgeting emerges as a noncomprehensive process that takes place in a highly charged political environment, is incremental and fragmented, and focuses more on policy agreement than on goal attainment. Despite efforts to simplify the required calculations and to determine factors that affect the levels of state spending, budgetary decisions remain extremely difficult to make, particularly when choosing between different programs that meet different needs and have different goals. The criteria used in making such allocations are, and ought to be, political.

In practical terms, state officials need consider not *all* alternatives, but rather those that are politically feasible. They must be ever sensitive to "what will go." Policies in a democracy are usually altered in small increments, thus making available a storehouse of relevant information based on prior experience with similar policies. Participants play generally definable roles and utilize limited perspectives rooted in their own particular interests on the assumption that the process as a whole provides opportunities for proponents of opposing views to present their case.

The following three facts need to be recognized:

A system for prioritymaking exists now and helps planners and budgeters to allocate billions of dollars annually. Second, prioritymaking is political. Third, there is no operational overall economic theory that provides the means for making decisions about priorities among major program areas at this time.[54]

But the mere fact that these truths represent realities about budgeting does not mean that they represent desirable practice or that the budgeting process operates as well as has been assumed. Certainly some aspects of budgeting have been underemphasized in the shortsighted stress on fiscal management and expenditure control.

NOTES

1. This section drawn heavily from S. Kenneth Howard, Analysis, rationality and administrative decision making, in *Toward a New Public Administration* (Scranton: Chandler, 1971), pp. 285-301.
2. Herbert A. Simon, *Administrative Behavior* (New York: Macmillan, 1957), p. 241.
3. In this discussion of intended rationality, we ask only that the actions an administrator takes seem likely to accomplish the goals he is pursuing. We are avoiding the issue of whether those goals are *worth* pursuing.
4. Interestingly, the narrower the range of interests the administrator needs to consider and the less complex his calculations need to be, the more helpful quantitative techniques may become. The differences among the alternatives from which he must select become less and less great with this narrowing, and noneconomic factors become more and more nearly equal, thus allowing

economic differences between alternatives to become dominant in indicating the "best" choice.

5. James R. Schlesinger, Uses and Abuses of Analysis. Memorandum prepared at the request of the Subcommittee on National Security and International Operations of the Committee on Government Operations, U.S. Senate, 90th Cong. 2d sess. (1968), p. 5.

6. It has been suggested that incremental changes or decisions assume fundamental decisions at various points. The type of evaluation of alternatives or scanning that the administrator needs to do may vary with the type of decision or exploration of the situation that he wants to make. There is the constant problem in this approach of separating the big potatoes from the small ones, but the idea is suggestive. See Amitai Etzioni, "Mixed-Scanning: A 'Third' Approach to Decision-Making," *Public Administration Review* 27(5) (Dec. 1967), pp. 385-392.

7. This point is well appreciated by some proponents of PPB. "In practice, comprehensiveness may be too costly in time, effort, uncertainty and confusion." Arthur Smithies, Conceptual framework for the program budget, in David Novick (ed.), *Program Budgeting: Program Analysis and the Federal Budget* (Cambridge: Harvard University Press, 1965), p. 45.

8. James W. Martin, training officer of the National Association of State Budget Officers, pointed this fact out in reviewing this manuscript.

9. The idea of simplifying the burden of calculations and much of the material presented here is drawn from Aaron Wildavsky, *The Politics of the Budgetary Process* (Boston: Little, Brown, 1964).

10. Ibid., p. 22.

11. Thomas J. Anton, Roles and symbols in the determination of state expenditures, *Midwest Journal of Political Science* 11(1) (Feb. 1967), pp. 30-31.

12. The notion of "contained specialization" has been developed by Ira Sharkansky, *The Politics of Taxing and Spending* (Indianapolis: Bobbs-Merrill, 1969), pp. 34, 38-49. He feels that this concept is less applicable to a state than the national government, particularly in the legislative branch, where professional expertise is less available in state legislatures.

13. The phrase "successive limited comparisons" is taken from Charles E. Lindblom, The science of "Muddling Through," *Public Administration Review* 19(2) (Spring 1959), p. 81.

14. Wildavsky, *The Politics of the Budgetary Process*, p. 125.

15. Efforts toward a similar A, B, and C budget system have been undertaken in Louisiana. See P.A.R. Legislative Bulletin 18(2) (May 22, 1970), pp. 3, 8.

16. Wildavsky, *The Politics of the Budgetary Process*, p. 62.

17. There are indications that earmarking's most sacred cow, highway trust funds, may be breaking down. See *State-Government News* 13(5) (May 1970), pp. 2-3.

18. Fragmentation is particularly scored on these grounds in D. J. Alesch, Improving Decisionmaking About Priorities in State Government (Santa Monica, Cal.: RAND, Paper No. 4187, delivered before the Joint National Association of State Budget Officers and Coundil of State Planning Agencies Institute on Urban Problems, September 4-6, 1969, Palo Alto, California).
19. Information in the following two paragraphs is taken from National Association of State Budget Officers, *Budgeting by the States* (Chicago: Council of State Governments, 1967), pp. 3-16.
20. This certainly has been true in Illinois and North Carolina. See Thomas Anton, *The Politics of State Expenditure in Illinois* (Urbana: University of Illinois Press, 1966), especially pp. 76-111.
North Carolina law provides:
If the Director (Governor) and the Commission (Advisory Budget Commission) shall agree in their recommendations for the budget for the next biennial period, he shall prepare their report in the form of a proposed budget, together with such comment and recommendations as they may deem proper to make. If the Director and Commission shall not agree in substantial particulars, the Director shall prepare the proposed budget based on his own conclusions and judgment and shall cause to be incorporated therein such statement of disagreement and the particulars thereof, as the Commission or any of its members shall deem proper to submit as representing their views. General Statutes of North Carolina, Chap. 143, Section 11.
Four of the six members of the commission were the chairmen of the key revenue and the appropriations committees in both chambers during the most recent legislative session. In this situation any dissent by the commission carries great weight and disagreements between the governor and the commission rarely become as public as the law would suggest.
21. I am indebted to James W. Martin for suggesting these ideas when reviewing the manuscript.
22. Anton, Roles and symbols, p. 31.
23. Mosher considers this one of the states' foremost "special" problems. See Frederick C. Mosher, Limitations and problems of PPBS in the states, *Public Administration Review* 29(2) (March-April 1969), p. 165.
24. Roy W. Bahl, Jr., and Robert J. Saunders, Determinants of changes in state and local government expenditures, *National Tax Journal* 18(1) (March 1965), pp. 50-57. Charles F. Cnudde and Donald J. McCrone, Party competition and welfare politics in the American states, *American Political Science Review* 63(3) (Sept. 1969), pp. 858-866. Richard E. Dawson and James A. Robinson, Interparty competition, economic variables, and welfare politics in the American states, *Journal of Politics* 25(2) (May 1963), pp. 265-289. Richard E. Dawson and James A. Robinson, The politics of welfare, in Herbert Jacob and Kenneth N. Vines (eds.), *Politics in the American States:*

A Comparative Analysis (Boston: Little, Brown, 1965), pp. 371-410. Thomas R. Dye, Inequality and civil-rights policy in the States, *Journal of Politics* 31(4) (Nov. 1969), pp. 1080-1097. Thomas R. Dye, Malapportionment and public policy in the States, *Journal of Politics* 27(3) (August 1965), pp. 586-601. Thomas R. Dye, Politics, economics and educational outcomes in the States, *Educational Administration* 3(1) (Winter 1967), pp. 28-48. Thomas R. Dye, *Politics, Economics, and the Public: Policy Outcomes in the American States* (Chicago: Rand McNally, 1966). Solomon Fabricant, *The Trend of Government Activity in the United States Since 1900* (New York: National Bureau of Economic Research, 1952). Glenn W. Fisher, Determinants of state and local government expenditures: A preliminary analysis, *National Tax Journal* 14(4) (Dec. 1961), pp. 349-355. Glen W. Fisher, Interstate variations in state and local government expenditures, *National Tax Journal* 17(1) (March 1964), pp. 57-73. Richard J. Hofferbert, The relation between public policy and some structural and environmental variables in the American states, *American Political Science Review* 60(1) (March 1966), pp. 73-82. Seymour Sacks and Robert Harris, The determinants of state and local government expenditures and intergovernmental flows of funds, *National Tax Journal* 17(1) (March 1964), pp. 75-85. Ira Sharkansky, Economic and political correlates of state government expenditures: General tendencies and deviant cases, *Midwest Journal of Political Science* 11(2) (May 1967), pp. 173-192. Ira Sharkansky, Government expenditures and public services in the American states, *American Political Science Review* 61(4) (Dec. 1967), pp. 1066-1077. Ira Sharkansky, Regional patterns in the expenditures of American states, *Western Political Quarterly* 20(4) (Dec. 1967), pp. 955-971. Ira Sharkansky, *The Politics of Taxing and Spending* (Indianapolis: Bobbs-Merrill, 1969). Ira Sharkansky and Richard I. Hofferbert, Dimensions of state politics, economics, and public policy, *American Political Science Review* 63(3) (Sept. 1969), 867-879. Richard Spangler, The effect of population growth upon state and local government expenditures, *National Tax Journal* 16(2) (June 1963), pp. 193-196.

25. Dye, Politics, economics and educational outcomes (see note 24).
26. Sharkansky, Economic and political correlates (see note 24).
27. Sharkansky, *The Politics of Taxing and Spending,* p. 113 (see note 24).
28. Ibid., p. 96.
29. Robert L. Harlow, Sharkansky on state expenditures: A comment, *National Tax Journal* 21(2) (June 1968), pp. 215-216.
30. These points are most incisively made by Philip L. Beardsley, The determinants of public policies in the American states: A critique of recent studies (Ph.D. diss., University of North Carolina at Chapel Hill, 1970), pp. 8-16.
31. Dye, *Politics, Economics and the Public,* p. 295 (see note 24).
32. Dye, Politics, economics and educational outcomes (see note 24).

33. Dye, Inequality (see note 24).
34. Sharkansky, Economic and Political Correlates (see note 24).
35. A point well made by Jack L. Walker, The diffusion of innovations among the American states, *American Political Science Review* 63(3) (Sept. 1969), p. 880.
36. This line of reasoning has been taken by Cnudde and McCrone, Party competition and welfare politics (see note 24). Sharkansky, *The Politics of Taxing and Spending* (see note 24). Herbert Jacob and Michael Lipsky, Outputs, structure, and power: An assessment of changes in the study of state and local politics, *Journal of Politics* 30(2) (May 1968), pp. 510-538.
37. Such a finding has been made at the local level. See James W. Clarke, Environment, process and policy: A reconsideration, *American Political Science Review* 63(4) (Dec. 1969), pp. 1172-1182.
38. Sharkansky, *The Politics of Taxing and Spending,* pp. 124-125 (see note 24).
39. Ibid., p. 121.
40. Sharkansky and Hofferbert, Dimensions of state politics (see note 24).
41. Ibid., pp. 867, 878.
42. Brian A. Fry and Richard F. Winters, The politics of redistribution, *American Political Science Review* 64(2) (June 1970), pp. 508-522.
43. Walker, The diffusion of innovations.
44. Ibid.
45. Cnudde and McCrone, Party competition and welfare politics, p. 865 (see note 24).
46. Another insight attributable to James W. Martin.
47. Ira Sharkansky makes this point in his work. See especially *The Politics of Taxing and Spending,* Chap. 6, and Government expenditures (see note 24).
48. Sharkansky, Government expenditures, p. 1074 (see note 24).
49. This point is well made in Sharkansky, *The Politics of Taxing and Spending,* p. 198 (see note 24).
50. Sharkansky, Regional patterns (see note 24).
51. This conclusion is suggested by both Sharkansky, ibid., and Walker, The diffusion of innovations.
52. Walker, The diffusion of innovations, p. 897.
53. The most thorough of these critiques is contained in Beardsley, The determinants of public policies.
54. Alesch, Improving decisionmaking, p. 1.

7
MOTIVATION THEORIES*

Roger N. Blakeney

Motivation is one of the most studied areas in relating the behavioral sciences to management. While motivation is a complex topic, it can generally be thought of as an internal pressure prompting us to act in certain ways that may serve to reduce the tension underlying this pressure. However, the internal state is influenced by the external environment, and modern organizations provide complex work environments. The historical background just developed will be used to organize the presentation of a limited number of motivational theories that have received a lot of attention in management theory and organizational behavior writings.

CLASSICAL THEORY

Implicitly underlying the classical management theories was the concept of the human being as a rational-economic creature. Many assumptions associated with

---

*From *Organization and Behavior, Including Ethical Considerations,* Grant Newton, ed. Copyright © 1978 by Harper & Row, Publishers, Inc. Reprinted by permission of the publisher. References have been renumbered.

this concept derive from the philosophy of hedonism—the seeking of pleasure and avoidance of pain. Therefore, human beings were seen as maximizing their own self-interest. Adam Smith's economic philosophy justified the pursuit of self-interest by describing the marketplace as a regulator (1). He felt that if individuals pursued their own self-interest in a free market relationship, the result would be the maximum overall social well-being for all. Adam Smith's philosophy was both economically descriptive and morally prescriptive, thus providing a basis for classical theories of management.

The general line of management thought toward employees that grows out of the classical concept of the rational-economic human being has been described as follows (2):

1. Humans are primarily motivated by economic incentives and will do that which gives them the greatest economic gain.

2. Since economic incentives are under the control of the organization, the employees are essentially passive agents to be manipulated, motivated, and controlled by the organization.

3. Human feelings are essentially irrational and must be prevented from interfering with the individual's rational calculation of self-interest.

4. Organizations can and must be designed in such a way as to neutralize and control human feelings and, therefore, the individual's unpredictable traits.

The major weakness of the classical theory was that it was too simple to account for the complexities of human motivation. Therefore, let us turn to a more complex theory that is associated with the beginnings of modern organizational behavior.

MASLOW'S HIERARCHY OF HUMAN NEEDS

Everyone has many goals and motives and no two persons' sets are exactly the same. Broadly speaking, however, the needs underlying motivation are similar for all members of the organization. Each person has basic needs that she or he seeks to satisfy. Since work is such a major and integral part of life in our society, members try to meet many of their needs in the work organization (3). The differences that develop in ways of meeting needs are a result of each member's past experiences.

Maslow arranged these basic needs in a hierarchy (with one lowest and five highest) as follows (4):

1. Need for physiological satisfaction—food, air, water, shelter, i.e., those things basic to life

2. Need for safety and security

3. Need for love and social fulfillment

4. Need for self-esteem and the esteem of others

5. Need for self-actualization (self-realization)—to develop one's abilities and capabilities to the fullest

In general, each lower need has to be met to a minimum degree before the next level of need begins to influence the individual. Thus, if an individual is constantly having to worry about lower level needs throughout childhood and into adulthood, his or her development is likely to be stopped at that level. If, however, as individuals mature they have the lower level needs met, they can progress to higher levels of need. If a lower level need is threatened, there is a strong tendency to revert to a primary concern for the lower level. However, if the individual has functioned at a higher level for an extended period of time, she or he may continue to attempt to meet that level of need at the expense of the lower level needs. For example, individuals may sacrifice their own life to save a loved one. They are functioning at the social-love level at the expense of their own survival. Or, their self-esteem may be tied to a cause in which they believe. If they give their life for that cause, they are functioning at a higher level at the expense of a lower level—survival.

Physiological Needs

The physiological needs are primary and, therefore, necessary for existence. When there is a threat to the meeting of the needs for air, water, food, body temperature control, excretion, rest and sleep, and so on, there is a very strong tendency for the human to attend to the meeting of these needs at the expense of all others. Therefore, an organization needs to provide adequate ventilation with cooling and heating, drinking fountains, lighting, rest rooms, and such other facilities as are necessary for the satisfaction of basic physiological needs.

Safety and Security Needs

When individuals have met their basic physiological needs to a minimum degree, safety and security needs become an important determinant of behavior. They are met by ensuring a continuation of the means for meeting the physiological needs for survival and by action to protect oneself. Society, through laws, is making increasing demands on organizations regarding physical health and safety. The problems of modern management also are focused on the psychological aspect of security. A balance is required within the work organization. If too much security is provided, individuals may become too dependent and lose initiative. However, if too little is present, then individuals are overly concerned with security and have little time or energy to be effective members of the organization.

Social Needs

In planning his incentive system, Frederick W. Taylor failed to take into account the complexities of human motivation. One of the key elements that he neglected was social needs. His attempts at improving efficiency often had the effect of isolating workers. When the workers had met their lower level needs, their social needs came to the fore. Thus, in the Hawthorne studies, Mayo found social needs to be an important determinant of worker behavior. Because social interaction was effectively blocked, the worker's social needs diverted energy from job performance. Once individuals have met physiological and security needs to a minimum degree, their social needs are very important. Failure to satisfy them, at least partially, within the work organization will probably result in ineffective performance, personal dissatisfaction, turnover, accidents, illness, and the like.

Esteem Needs

A firmly based self-esteem rests on real capacity and the esteem of others. When the social needs are met to the minimum degree, then a striving for such esteem by self and others begins to emerge. If these needs are met on the job, they can lead to the development of employees who are self-confident, capable, and adequate. If their satisfaction is blocked, employees are likely to become discouraged, hostile, and ineffective.

Self-Actualization Needs

As employees meet their esteem needs and begin to become self-confident and respected by others, a need for a sense of meaning and accomplishment begins to emerge. Argyris pointed out that when individuals reach this level of maturity, they strive for self-motivation and self-control (5). Individuals on this level seek to be mature and capable in their job performance. Management-imposed controls are likely to produce less mature and less effective behavior in job performance, which manifests itself in actions such as restricting output, goldbricking, cheating, and so on. In general, the result of such controls is a lowering of employees' expectations of themselves and the organization. Indeed, Argyris sees a conflict between the traditional organization based on classical theory and a healthy, mature personality.

SUMMARY OF MASLOW'S HIERARCHY OF HUMAN NEEDS

There are four major points about basic human needs in Maslow's theory:

1. Human needs are hierarchical in nature.
2. The lower needs have to be met before the higher level needs influence behavior.

3. If a lower level need is threatened, there is a tendency to revert to that level.

4. It is the unmet needs that "motivate" human behavior.

HUMAN RELATIONS THEORY

The beginning of the human relations movement is generally associated with Elton Mayo, (6) especially his work with the Hawthorne studies. These studies clearly challenged the adequacy of the assumptions of classical theory. Even though human relations theory historically came before Maslow's work, we covered the needs hierarchy first in order to use it in discussing human relations.

One of the reasons that scientific management achieved the results it did was because of the human conditions of the workers in the early 1900s. The workers were operating at the physiological and safety-security level of needs. Their way of meeting those needs was the money they earned on the job. Thus, much of their on-the-job behavior fit the rational-economic assumptions reasonably well. However, by the time of Mayo's work, much of the work force was successfully meeting a minimum level of those needs. As a result, the unmet social needs were beginning to much more strongly influence behavior on the job.

McGREGOR'S THEORY X AND THEORY Y

Immediately after World War II, Mayo concluded his contribution. Then Maslow presented his hierarchy of human needs. Thus, by the mid 1950s two approaches to management based on two different sets of assumptions had emerged. In an article, "The Human Side of Enterprise, (7) followed in 1960 by a book of the same name, (8) Douglas McGregor clearly presented the contrast. Theory X was the label he gave to the approach growing out of classical theory, theory Y the label he gave to the broad outlines of a theory of management based on the emerging behavioral knowledge. McGregor realized the need for much further behavioral research and for cultural change if theory Y were to be put into practice. He said:

> It is no more possible to create an organization today which will be a full, effective application of this theory than it was to build an atomic power plant in 1945. There are many formidable obstacles to overcome (8).

Assumptions of Human Nature and Motivation

The sets of assumptions of theory X and theory Y are listed in Figure 1. Under theory X, it is assumed that the personnel coming into the organization just

Theory X	Theory Y
Lazy	Want to do something
Prefer directions	Have initiative
Unambitious	Ambitious
Irresponsible	Responsible

Figure 1 Assumptions of theory X and theory Y.

naturally dislike work and will try to avoid it. They prefer to be directed in their work, wanting to be told the what, how, when, and where of their jobs. In addition, they are unambitious, irresponsible, and have no sense of self-direction. Associated with these assumptions is the concept of human beings as rational-economic creatures, on which the economic doctrine of Adam Smith was built. The basis is the philosophy of hedonism, which says that human beings seek pleasure and avoid pain. Work is seen as unpleasant, and the human works only for economic gain. The money earned is used to provide necessities and pleasure. However, a distinction is made between the mass of workers and the small group that manages the masses. The elite, of course, are not lazy or untrustworthy.

Theory Y assumes that the individuals entering an organization want to do things and are looking for meaningful work. For them, spending effort to work is as natural as spending effort for play. Thus, satisfying work will be voluntarily performed. They are seen as having initiative with the will and ability to exercise self-direction in the pursuit of achieving objectives to which they are committed. The individuals coming into the organization are therefore recognized as being ambitious and responsible.

Nature of Jobs

Logically enough, the acceptance of either theory X or theory Y by management will influence the way in which jobs are structured, as shown in Figure 2. The job design for theory X is clearly work-centered, as is the organizational structure within which the job is set. Direction and control of work flow is the primary concern, which leads to an overemphasis on unity of command, span of control, and so on. Authority and decision making reside at the top of the organizational structure.

Under theory Y's set of assumptions, job design and organizational structure consider people as well as work. The organizational structure is built to provide for two-way communication—both up and down—rather than only for the flow of orders from the top. Superiors and their subordinates are considered a functional group. With an approach that centers on employee commitment as the

Theory X	Theory Y
Simple	Complex
Unskilled or semiskilled	Requires skill
Dull	Interesting
Seldom requires initiative	Often requires initiative
Provides little:	Provides great deal of:
personal satisfaction	personal satisfaction
feeling of accomplishment	feeling of accomplishment

Figure 2 Job designs under theory X and theory Y.

basis for self-direction, the consent theory of authority, which contends that authority emanates from those led rather than from the delegation process in a hierarchical system, becomes very important.

Responsibilities of Management

If the people are different, and if the jobs are structured differently, then the responsibilities of management are different, as contrasted in Figure 3. Under theory X, the full responsibility for the organization and its output falls on management. In theory Y, management's attention focuses on getting people to work together to achieve the objectives of the organization. The workers participate in the decision-making process and share the responsibility for achieving organizational goals.

Resulting Behaviors

The behaviors facilitated by, and likely to develop under, the two approaches also differ. Thus, people working under the two different approaches are likely

Theory X	Theory Y
Close supervision	General supervision
Punish errors (coercion)	Reward
Place blame	Give recognition
Control	Encourage
Direct	Develop
Tell what and how to do	Set organizational objectives

Figure 3 Management responsibility under theory X and theory Y.

Example 1

The assumption that does not belong to theory Y is

a. the average human being prefers to be directed and wants security above all.

b. the expenditure of physical and mental effort in work is as natural as play or rest.

c. people will exercise self-direction and self-control in the service of objectives to which they are committed.

d. the average human being learns, under proper conditions, not only to accept but to seek responsibility.

---

to respond differently. Under theory X people are likely to be cautious and only follow the rules. As a result they appear to be unambitious and hiding behind the rules. Uncreative and passive behavior is adaptive in the theory X environment. In addition, close supervision and tight controls can lead to hostility that may be expressed as passivity. Since passive-aggressive behavior is an extremely effective counter to coercion and pressure, it is commonly found in theory X organizations.

The opposite is also true. People assumed to be as theory Y suggests, and treated accordingly, are likely to appear ambitious and creative. They learn to exercise judgment, assume responsibility, and be actively involved in cooperative efforts. Since there is intrinsic satisfaction in the work performed, the personnel develop self-direction and self-control. They are likely to take the initiative in getting a job done because of the recognition involved. In general, the individual is encouraged to become a participating member of a functional group.

A sample question on McGregor's theories is shown in Example 1. Response a, "The average human being prefers to be directed and wants security above all," is not in keeping with theory Y. It is more in keeping with classical theory, or theory X. Thus, a is the correct answer. Choices b, "The expenditure of physical and mental effort in work is as natural as play or rest," c, "People will exercise self-direction and self-control in the service of objectives to which they are committed," and d, "The average human being learns, under proper conditions, not only to accept but to seek responsibility" are all assumptions of theory Y.

HERZBERG'S TWO FACTOR (MOTIVATOR-HYGIENE) THEORY

While McGregor was formulating and writing *The Human Side of Enterprise,* Frederick Herzberg was engaged in behavioral research related to both Maslow's and Mayo's previous works. Maslow was dealing with motivation in general; Herzberg studied the motivation to work. In the work environment, he found that behavior was influenced by needs that appear similar to the ones described by Maslow. Maslow's concept of unmet needs being the ones that influence goal-directed behavior is reflected also in Herzberg's work.

Herzberg concluded that there were two major sets of factors in work motivation. One set of factors, associated with job dissatisfaction, he called *hygiene* (or *maintenance*) *factors* (9). The other set, associated with job satisfaction, he called *motivator factors*. He also referred to them as *dissatisfiers* and *satisfiers*. The dissatisfiers included such things as supervision, company policy and administration, working conditions, interpersonal relations, status, job security, and salary. The motivators included such items as achievement, recognition, the work itself, responsibility, advancement, and the possibility of growth. Generally, Herzberg's dissatisfiers correspond to Maslow's first three levels of need. The motivators roughly correspond with the esteem and self-actualization levels.

Herzberg does not see job dissatisfaction-satisfaction as a single continuum (10). Rather he describes two separate continua with one running from "very dissatisfied" to "not dissatisfied" and the other from "not satisfied" to "very satisfied." When the hygiene factors are present in very inadequate amounts, the workers are "very dissatisfied." As the presence of the hygiene factors improves, the workers become progressively less dissatisfied until they reach the point of being "not dissatisfied." A continued improvement in the hygiene factors will not produce satisfaction, which is dependent on the motivators. When the motivators are present in inadequate amounts, the workers are "not satisfied." And, as the presence of the motivators improves, the workers become more satisfied until they reach the point of being "very satisfied."

Basically, Herzberg says that the dissatisfiers must be present to the required degree for workers to provide "a fair-day's work for a fair-day's pay." If they are not, the workers will restrict effort below that level. He sees any increase in performance that results from improving the maintenance (hygiene) factors to be a restoration to that level. If the dissatisfiers are present to the required degree, the more the motivators are present the more the workers are willing to perform above the "fair-day's work for a fair-day's pay" level. Thus, the presence of motivators is the key to a desire for significantly improved performance (11).

Job Enrichment

As Herzberg began to translate his research findings into management prescriptions, he focused on job enrichment. He differentiated between job enrichment and job enlargement, which was one of McGregor's suggestions as a movement toward theory Y. Job enlargement involves horizontal job loading (an increase in job scope). Herzberg sees job rotation as a form of enlargement. Job enrichment involves vertical job loading (an increase in job depth). He sees the key to job enrichment as the incorporation of motivators into the job.

Example 2

As used by management theorists, the term *job enrichment* refers to:

a. increasing the workload.
b. horizontal changes in job content.
c. a greater degree of self-management.
d. an increase in pay rate for the job.
e. all of the above.

Experience and research have shown that job enrichment can increase the motivational potential of a job by increasing participation and self-management (12). However, job enrichment programs often fail because of a lack of costly and time-consuming changes in the behavioral system of the job. Alone, the technical changes that go with job enlargement are insufficient. The workers must also be prepared technically and psychologically to perform and gain satisfaction for the more demanding, enriched jobs. These changes usually involve changes in the psychological climate of the organization as well.

A sample question related to job enrichment is given in Example 2. The correct answer is c, "A greater degree of self-management." The removal of controls, increasing accountability, and the granting of additional authority all involve a greater degree of self-management. Choice a, "Increasing the workload" does not add any motivators to the job. Answer b, "Horizontal changes in job content" is simply an increase in scope, and thus is job enlargement, not job enrichment. Choice d, "An increase in pay rate for the job" only increases a hygiene factor. Though Herzberg says pay is the most important hygiene factor, it is not a motivator. Its increase, then, is not job enrichment.

SPECIFIC NEEDS APPROACH

Another approach to motivation that has been important in the organizational behavior area is based on the work of Henry A. Murray (13). Murray viewed human motivation as being made up of a number of specific needs. He developed the Thematic Apperception Test (TAT), a projective test, to measure them. The TAT involves a series of ambiguous pictures of people about which a person is asked to make up a story. The content of the story is used to measure the strength of the need. Three of Murray's needs have become important in studying individual behavior in the organization. They are the need for achievement, the need for affiliation, and the need for power (14).

The Need for Achievement

The need for achievement (*n*-Ach) is the most widely known and studied. David C. McClelland (15) has done a substantial amount of the work and has described individuals with a high *n*-Ach as thriving on immediate and concrete feedback to try to improve their performance and gain satisfaction for getting things done. They therefore choose situations with a moderate degree of risk.

The Need for Affiliation

The need for affiliation (*n*-Aff) is concerned with positive affective relationships —friendships. Most, if not all, of us feel the need to socialize with other people. When upset, threatened, or stressed in some other way, we have a tendency to seek the company of others in a similar condition. The individual with a high *n*-Aff feels and responds to these things even more. She or he feels a need to share personal beliefs with someone who agrees in order to confirm them.

The Need for Power

The need for power (*n*-Pow) is not related to economic growth as *n*-Ach is. Rather, *n*-Pow is related to style of leadership. Both the *n*-Aff and *n*-Pow are interpersonally oriented whereas *n*-Ach is oriented toward the situation. When a high *n*-Pow and a low *n*-Aff are combined in the same person, there is a tendency toward an authoritarian style of leadership. Individuals with a higher *n*-Pow spend more time planning and thinking about the obtaining of power and authority. They expend energy in winning arguments and persuading others. If they do not prevail, they feel uncomfortable and experience a loss of personal power.

Application

The above needs can be useful in relating individuals to jobs. For example, difficulties can be foreseen if individuals with high *n*-Aff are placed in jobs which are physically isolated from others. Likewise individuals with high *n*-Ach are likely to be frustrated in jobs that provide inadequate feedback or that do not allow them to control their own performance. Another example might be individuals with high *n*-Pow being unsatisfied in situations where they have little influence over others.

BASIC EXPECTANCY THEORY

Basic expectancy theory is the result of work by Victor Vroom (16). It is process theory dealing with choice behavior. It describes individuals as assessing

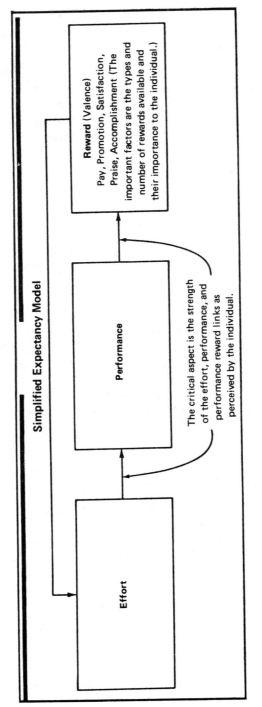

Figure 4 A simplified expectancy model.

various tactics (patterns of behavior) and then choosing the one that they feel will get them what they want from the work situation. The motivation to pursue the chosen pattern of behavior is called *force*. The force, or motivation, is a function of a set of variables, or elements. The basic variables in expectancy theory are outcomes, instrumentality, valences, expectancies, and choice (17).

Figure 4 is a simplified model that reflects that the effort workers put into performance (motivation) is contingent on (1) their *expectancy* that effort will lead to an *outcome* of performance, (2) their belief that performance will be *instrumental* in an outcome of their receiving rewards, (3) how much they value the reward (*valence*). The individual subjectively assesses the expectancies, valences, outcomes, and instrumentalities and then chooses (*choice*). Thus, individuals will be "motivated" only if certain conditions are met:

1. If they feel that increased effort will lead to increased performance

2. If they believe that the increased performance will lead to reward, and

3. If they value the reward

REFERENCES

1. Smith, Adam. *The Wealth of Nations*. New York, Modern Library, 1939.
2. Schein, Edgar H. *Organizational Psychology*. Englewood Cliffs, N.J., Prentice-Hall, 1965, pp. 48-49.
3. Neff, Walter S. *Work and Human Behavior*. New York, Atherton, 1968.
4. Maslow, Abraham H. *Motivation and Personality*. New York, Harper & Bros., 1954.
5. Argyris, Chris. The individual and organization: Some problems of mutual adjustment. *Administrative Science Quarterly*, June 1957, *2*, 1-24. Reprinted in *The Individual and the Organization*, Donald R. Domm, Roger N. Blakeney, Michael T. Matteson, and Robert Scofield (eds.). New York, Harper & Row, 1973, pp. 94-103.
6. Mayo, Elton. *The Human Problems of an Industrial Civilization*. Boston, Harvard University Press, 1933.
7. McGregor, Douglas. The human side of enterprise. *The Management Review*, November 1957, *46*, 22-28, 88-92.
8. McGregor, Douglas. *The Human Side of Enterprise*. New York, McGraw-Hill, 1960.
9. Herzberg, Frederick, Mausner, Bernard, and Schneidern, Barbara B. *Motivation to Work*. New York, John Wiley, 1959. Herzberg, Frederick. *Work and the Nature of Man*. Cleveland, Work, 1966.
10. Herzberg, Frederick. New approaches in management organization and job design—1. Reprinted in Domm, pp. 189-192.

11. Herzberg, Frederick. *Motivation Through Job Enrichment* (film). Silver Springs, Md., Bureau of National Affairs.
12. Chung, Kae H. *Motivational Theories and Practice.* Columbus, Ohio, Grid, 1977, pp. 202-203.
13. Murray, Henry A., et al. *Explorations in Personality.* New York, Oxford University Press, 1938.
14. Wainer, Herbert A., and Rubin, Irwin M. Motivation of research and development entrepreneurs: Determinants of company success. *Journal of Applied Psychology,* June 1969, *53.* Reprinted in Domm, pp. 177-181.
15. McClelland, David C. That urge to achieve. *Think Magazine,* Nov.-Dec. 1966, *32,* 18-32. Reprinted in Domm, pp. 172-176. McClelland, David C., Atkinson, J. W., Clark, R. A., and Lowell, E. L. *The Achievement Motive.* New York, Appleton-Century-Crofts, 1953.

8

AN EXPECTANCY THEORY APPROACH TO THE MOTIVATIONAL IMPACTS OF BUDGETS*

J. Ronen
J. L. Livingstone

In this chapter we discuss the implications of budgets for motivation and behavior in the context of expectancy theory as developed in the psychology of motivation. We argue that propositions from expectancy theory can be used to integrate and accommodate the fragmented research findings on budget and behavior in the accounting literature. We discuss how the expectancy model reconciles what might appear to be contradictory findings from prior studies.

THE FUNCTIONS OF BUDGETS

Budgets serve three decision-making functions: planning, control, and motivation. Budgets aid planning in that they incorporate forecasts which reflect the anticipated consequences of different combinations of plans (actions) made by management and the relevant uncontrollable events that may occur in the environment. Budgets also serve the planning function through being utilized as a tool for sensitivity analysis, which includes the examination of how slight changes in management plans affect the consequences (budgets). Many budgets could be thus

*Reprinted from *The Accounting Review,* vol. 50, no. 4 (October 1975), pp. 671-685.

generated as a result of alternative plans so that the most desirable plan could then be chosen.

The control function is typically a feedback process whereby information about past performance (both anticipated and actual) is provided to those who "control," to be utilized by them for making decisions. As a motivational tool, the budget conveys information to the subordinate about expectations of superiors regarding what constitutes successful task performance and the consequent reinforcement contingencies. These characterizations of the control and motivation processes probably apply whether the budget is imposed on subordinates, whether developed through the participation of the "controlled," or whether they result from a dynamic, interlevel bargaining process over goals and resource allocations (1).

The three functions of budgets are interdependent. The motivational effect must be explicitly considered in planning and control. Similarly, knowledge by subordinates of superiors' plans and control styles have motivational effects. Furthermore, the budgeting process is likely to cause subordinates to bargain for increases in the resources they command. This may result in dysfunctional budgetary slack (1,2).

THE DYSFUNCTIONAL ASPECTS OF BUDGETS

Budgetary slack is not the only potential dysfunctional aspect of budgets. The literature is filled with exhortations to consider the behavioral effects of standards and budgets on motivation and, consequently, on performance (3-6). These effects could be either dysfunctional or positive. Many articles deal specifically with the behavioral impacts of budgets on employees; some base their conclusions on generalizations from the psychological literature, and others show findings from empirical experiments (7-9). Mostly, these discussions were launched in terms of specific principles taken from various areas of psychology such as aspiration level, participation, and attitude change.

To gain better understanding and insight into how these behavioral effects are created, we propose the expectancy model as a unifying framework within which the effects could be analyzed. While the universal usage of budgets implies that their benefits are perceived to exceed the possible dysfunctional effects, the latter can be minimized if the budget's behavioral impacts are better understood.

By choosing the expectancy model (a description of the model appears below) as a framework, we do not wish to imply that it accurately described behavior even though some recent progress has been made.[1] Rather, we view it as a framework that facilitates the generation of hypotheses about the behavioral effects of budgets. The testing of these hypotheses would indicate whether subordinates' behavior is consistent with the model.

In the following section we describe the expectancy model. After that, we reinterpret the budget's behavioral implications discussed in the literature within the expectancy framework.

THE EXPECTANCY MODEL

The expectancy model is viewed as underlying the superior-subordinate budget relationship in two respects: (1) as the model according to which the subordinate's motivation to perform the task is influenced via the budget and (2) as the model which the superior regards as determining the subordinate's motivation (it is assumed that the superior can and may affect the subordinate's motivation via the budget in accordance with the expectancy model).[2]

The particular expectancy model version that we use in this chapter is the one advanced by House (10), which in turn is derived from the path-goal hypotheses advanced by Georgopoulos, Mahoney, and Jones (11) and from previous research supporting the class of expectancy models of motivation (12-19). The basic tenet of expectancy theory is that an individual chooses his behavior on the basis of (1) his expectations that the behavior will result in a specific outcome and (2) the sum of the valences, i.e., personal utilities or satisfaction that he derives from the outcome. A distinction is made (13) between valences that are intrinsic to behavior itself (such as feelings of competence) and those that are the extrinsic consequences of behavior (such as pay). Behavior that is intrinsically valent is also intrinsically motivational because the behavior leads directly to satisfaction, whereas extrinsic valences are contingent on external rewards.

House's formulation can be expressed as follows:

$$M = IV_b + P_1 \left(IV_a + \sum_{i=1}^{n} P_{2i} EV_i \right),$$
$$i = 1, 2, \ldots, n$$

where

$M =$ motivation to work
$IV_a =$ intrinsic valence associated with successful performance of the task
$IV_b =$ intrinsic valence associated with goal-directed behavior
$EV_i =$ extrinsic valences associated with the ith extrinsic reward contingent on work goal accomplishment
$P_1 =$ the expectancy that goal-directed behavior will accomplish the work goal (a given level of specified performance); the measure's range is $(-1, +1)$
$P_{2i} =$ the expectancy that work goal accomplishment will lead to the ith extrinsic reward; the measure's range is $(-1, +1)$

The individual estimates the expectancy P_1 of accomplishing a work goal given his behavior. For the estimate he considers factors such as (1) his ability to behave in an appropriate and effective manner and (2) the barriers and support for work goal accomplishment in the environment. Also, he estimates the expectancy P_2 that work goal accomplishment will result in attaining extrinsic rewards that have valences for him such as the recognition of his superiors of his goal accomplishment. He also places subjective values on the intrinsic valence associated with the behavior required to achieve the work goal IV_b, the intrinsic valence associated with the achievement of the work goal IV_a, and the extrinsic valences associated with the personal outcomes that accrue to him as a result of achieving the work goal EV_i.

The superior can affect the independent variables of this model:

1. He partially determines what extrinsic rewards (EV_i) follow work goal accomplishment, since he influences the extent to which work goal accomplishment will be recognized as a contribution and the nature of the reward (financial increases, promotion, assignment of more interesting tasks or personal goals, and development).

2. Through interaction, he can increase the subordinate's expectancy (P_2) that rewards ensue work goal accomplishment.

3. He can, through his own behavior, support the subordinate's effort and thus influence the expectancy (P_1) that the effort will result in work goal achievement.

4. He may influence the intrinsic valences associated with goal accomplishment (IVa) by determining factors such as the amount of influence the subordinate has in goal setting and the amount of control he is allowed in the task-directed effort. Presumably, the greater the subordinate's opportunity to influence the goal and exercise control, the more intrinsically valent is the work goal accomplishment.

5. The superior can increase the net intrinsic valences associated with goal-directed behavior (IV_b) by reducing frustrating barriers, by being supportive in times of stress, and by permitting involvement in a wide variety of tasks and being considerate of the subordinate's needs (10).

Three classes of situational variables that determine which particular superior behaviors are instrumental in increasing work motivation were hypothesized by House and Dessler (20):

1. *The needs of the subordinate:* The subordinate views the superior's behavior as legitimate only to the extent that he perceives it either as an immediate source of satisfaction or as instrumental to his future satisfaction. For example, subordinates with high needs for social approval find warm, interpersonal superior behavior immediately satisfying and therefore legitimate. On the other hand, subordinates with high need for achievement desire clarification of path-goal relationships and goal-oriented feedback from superiors. The perceived legitimacy

of the superior's behavior is thus partially determined by the subordinate's characteristics.

2. *Environmental demands:* When the task is routine and well defined, attempts by the superior to clarify path-goal relationships are redundant and are likely to be viewed as superfluous, externally imposed control, thus resulting in decreased satisfaction. Also, the more dissatisfying the task, the more the subordinate resents behavior by the superior directed at increasing productivity and enforcing compliance with organizational procedures.

3. *The task demands subordinates:* The superior's behavior is assumed to be motivational to the extent that it helps subordinates cope with environmental uncertainties, threat from others, or sources of frustration. Such behavior is predicted to increase the subordinate's satisfaction with the job content and to be motivational to the extent that it increases the subordinate's perceived expectancies that effort will lead to valued rewards.

THE RELATION BETWEEN THE EXPECTANCY MODEL AND THE ACCOUNTING BUDGETING PROCESS

Budgets have long been recognized as a managerial tool of communication between superiors and subordinates with respect to the parameters of the task. As a tool of communication, the budgets are perceived by subordinates as an aspect of their superior's attitudes toward them, the task and the work environment.

First, the budgets reflect management's expectations about what constitutes successful task performance; implicit in this is the promise of extrinsic rewards for the subordinates if the budget is accomplished. The imposition by management of a particular budget implies that its accomplishment will be recognized by management because it is in accordance with what management views as desirable goal attainment. To the extent that subordinates value the superior's recognition of their accomplishment, the budget communication constitutes a specification of the potential level of some of the extrinsic valences associated with work-goal accomplishment (EV_i). The budgeting process, when coupled with subordinate knowledge of the external reinforcement contingencies (i.e., the set of rewards contingent on effective performance), clarifies the set of external valences associated with work goal accomplishment or at least helps the subordinate to subjectively assess these valences.

Second, the perceived difficulty of the budget affects the expectancy of the subordinate that his effort would lead to budget achievement. Thus, the content of the budget also serves as an input for the subordinates to formulate their P_1 expectancies. Comparison of past levels of performance with past budgets generates a record of deviations which clearly influences P_1.

Third, the degree to which superiors were consistent or inconsistent in delivering the contingent rewards following budget accomplishment may induce the subordinates to revise their estimates of P_{2i}. Also, the degree to which superiors show recognition of past accomplishments will affect the subordinate's expectation of the level of future extrinsic valences (EV_i) associated with work goal accomplishment.

The budget may also fulfill the role of providing structure to an ambiguous task as well as coordinating activities, so that merely working toward accomplishment of the budget provides satisfaction. To the extent that the budget content facilitates the derivation of this satisfaction, the budget also affects the intrinsic valence associated with the goal-directed behavior (IV_b).

Thus the budgeting process can crucially affect the parameters of the expectancy model. Consequently, we can gain insights into the effect on motivation—the dependent variable in this model—by examining the effects of the budgets on the independent variables of the model, such as the subordinate's expectations, perceived valences, etc. Such an examination should increase the likelihood of identifying the psychological mechanisms underlying the effects of budgets on work motivation. Among the psychological states of subordinates that deserve exploration are the subordinate's intrinsic job satisfaction, his expectancies that effort leads to effective performance, and his expectancies that performance leads to reward.

In the next section, it is shown that reinterpretation of previous experimental and other empirical investigations regarding the effects of budget on behavior make it possible to integrate and reconcile the otherwise fragmented findings cited in the literature within the expectancy model framework.[3]

INTEGRATION OF PRIOR STUDIES WITHIN THE EXPECTANCY FRAMEWORK

It is useful to reconcile prior findings and assumptions regarding impacts of budgets by focusing on the underlying behavioral assumptions assumed (although not necessarily valid) by accountants in the budgetary process:

1. The budget should be set at a reasonably attainable level.

2. Managers should participate in the development of budgets for their own functions in the organization.

3. Managers should operate on the principle of management by exception.

4. Personnel should be charged or credited only for items within their control.

5. Dimensions of performance that cannot be conveniently measured in monetary terms are outside the budgetary domain.

The possible invalidity of these assumptions has been extensively discussed in the accounting literature. The generalizations offered can be summarized as follows.

Achievement of budgeted performance may not satisfy the needs of the subordinates, who thus need not be motivated by the budget. Also, the individual's goals and the organization's goals may not be identical. For an individual to internalize or accept the budget, he must believe that achieving it will satisfy his needs better than not achieving it. A goal that an individual has internalized is known as his aspiration level—the performance level that he undertakes to reach (see, e.g., Ref. 5). The probability that an individual will internalize the budget is influenced by his expectations of what he is able to achieve (21), his past experience of success in reaching budgeted goals, and the priority that he assigns to the need for a sense of personal achievement.

These assumptions are now closely examined in an attempt to show how the expectancy model can be used to integrate findings and assertions related to them within a cohesive framework.

The Assumption That Standards Should Be Reasonably Attainable

Summary of Existing Studies. The assumption implies that as long as the standards do not exceed what is reasonably attainable, the subordinate will internalize them. If too tight, presumably the subordinate will regard the budget as unrealistic and either cease to be motivated or be negatively motivated by it. Thus, while loose standards (as opposed to reasonably attainable standards) will lead to slackening of effort, tight standards could be perceived as unrealistic and therefore fail to motivate personnel, except perhaps in a negative direction (22). For example, Stedry (8) suggested that under certain conditions performance could be improved if management would impose unattainable standards on subordinates. Under laboratory conditions, he found that his measurements of the subjects' aspiration levels were influenced by the level at which the imposed standards were set. He also found that performance that was significantly different from the aspiration level led to an adjustment of the aspiration level in the direction of the performance level that was actually achieved. Thus, he suggested that standards be changed from period to period so that they are met some of the time and are slightly above the attainable level the rest of the time. Hofstede (23) also found that motivation is highest when standards are difficult to reach but are not regarded as impossible.

Other discussions and evidence in the literature support these findings. When an individual barely achieves the level of aspiration, he is said to have subjective feelings of success; subjective feelings of failure follow nonachievement of the level of aspiration (24). In particular, Child and Whiting (25) argue that (1) success generally raises the level of aspiration, failure lowers it; (2) the probability of rise in level of aspiration is positively correlated with the strength of success or failure; (3) changes in the level of aspiration partially depend on changes in the subject's confidence in his ability to attain goals; and (4) failure is more likely than success to lead to avoidance of setting a level of aspiration.

From their review of the literature, Becker and Green (5) conclude that "level of aspiration not only describes a goal for future attainment but also it partially insures that an individual will expend a more than minimal amount of energy, if necessary, to perform at or above the level." Indeed, although not in a business budgeting setting, Bayton (26) found that higher performance followed higher level of aspiration in testing the performance of 300 subjects on seven arithmetic problems. Also, Cherrington and Cherrington (7) experimentally found that when supervisors imposed either a minimum or a specific standard of performance, the subordinate's estimate of their performance (level of aspiration) was higher than when supervisors imposed either lenient minimum standards of performance or imposed none at all. They also found that the higher estimates of performance also were followed by higher actual performance. Cherrington and Cherrington's findings seem somewhat to contradict some of Stedry's (8) results. In Stedry's study, one group was first given the standard and then asked to indicate its own goal for performance in the subsequent period. The second group was asked to indicate its goals *before* it knew what the experimental manager's goals were. The group setting its personal goals first set higher goals and performed better than the group which was informed of management's goals first, although it must be noted that in Cherrington and Cherrington's study high estimates and performance were achieved when the group also formulated its estimates before knowledge of the supervisor's imposed minimums. Thus, in a sense, the situation is not unsimilar to Stedry's except that revision of the estimate after knowledge of the supervisor's higher standards proved to be beneficial.

Reconciliation with the Expectancy Model. In terms of the expectancy model, the conclusion that standards regarded as impossible are not motivational or negatively motivational can simply be explained by the fact that P_1, the expectancy that goal-directed behavior would lead to work goal accomplishment, was low or even negative and, to show this more clearly, Stedry's conclusions are examined in light of the expectancy model.

As indicated, Stedry found that his measurements of the subject's aspiration levels were influenced by the level at which the imposed standards were set. The results of the Cherringtons' study partially confirm Stedry's results in that the experimental group's estimate of their performance was highest under nonparticipation conditions, i.e., when high minimum standards were imposed. If the aspiration level is taken to reflect the level which the subordinate sets out to achieve, then it is understandable that (within limits) the higher the imposed standards by superiors, the higher would be the aspiration level. In comparison with other levels of attainment, P_{2i}, the expectancies that work goal accomplishment will lead to extrinsic valences would be higher the nearer the performance level is to the imposed standard. Thus, if the subordinate's task is viewed as a selection among different aspiration levels, it is only natural that he will choose the aspiration level that maximizes the dependent variable M in the model.

However, if the imposed standards are too high, the aspiration level will lag behind since, although P_{2i} will increase, P_1, the expectancy that goal-directed behavior will lead to work goal accomplishment, is likely to be negatively correlated with the perceived difficulty of attaining the standard.

The assessment of P_1 is also likely to be affected by feedback on past performance; P_1 will tend to be positively correlated with prior levels of performance and consequently the dependent variable and the aspiration level will tend to move in the same direction as performance. This "expectancy model" induced observation could explain Stedry's other finding that performance which differed significantly from the aspiration level led to the latter's adjustment in the direction of the performance level actually achieved.

It is particularly important and interesting to relate the level of aspiration conceptualization of the budgeting process with the expectancy approach. The expectancy model's dependent variable—motivation to exert effort in the task—is a direct function of the expected valences. The model's underlying assumption is that the higher the expectation of valences, the greater the effort the subordinate is likely to exert and, thus, the higher the performance level. In other words, the subordinate's effort exerted in task performance is assumed to change along a continuum as a function of the expectation of valences.

Level of aspiration, on the other hand, is operationally defined as "the goal one explicitly undertakes to reach," where "maximum effort will be exerted to just reach an aspiration goal" (5). According to this view, effort is seen not as a continuum but as changing discretely where the level of aspiration goal of performance is that for which a maximum—a specifically defined amount of effort—is spent in order to derive the subjuective feeling of success. If we attempt to interpret the meaning of the level of aspiration within the expectancy framework, it seems that it corresponds to the performance level consciously chosen by the subordinate (among alternative performance levels) so as to maximize the expectation of valences—the value of the expectancy equation. That is, the subordinate behaves as if he computes the expected values associated with different performance levels, which clearly depend on the model's parameters (P_1, P_2, IV_b, IV_a, and EV_i) and selects the one that maximizes M as the level of aspiration. The implications of this relationship between the level of aspiration and the expectancy model's dependent variable to the specification of desirable attributes of the budgetary process could be far reaching.

Participation

Summary of Existing Studies. Participation means that decisions affecting a manager's operations are, to some extent, jointly made by the manager and his superior. As such, it is more than mere consultation by which the superior informs himself of the manager's views but makes the decisions himself. The participation of subordinates in budgeting setting is usually regarded as effective in getting subordinates to internalize the standards embodied in the budgets and thus in achieving goal congruence (27).

The role of participation can perhaps be best understood in the context of group dynamics. Aspiration levels are said partially to depend on the levels of aspiration prevailing in the groups that the individual belongs to (28). The amount of influence that group members are said to have on the individual's aspiration level depends on the group's cohesiveness, i.e., the degree to which individual members value their group membership.

The value of group membership to an individual derives from the degree to which the individual believes that group membership will help him attain his own goals (29,30). Perceived value of membership seems to be correlated with the likelihood that different members in the group will have similar goals—thus the individual's likelihood of continued membership in the group. The relationship between the two appears to be reciprocal. Similarity of goals among the group's members will make membership in the group more attractive. On the other hand, if membership in the group is highly valued, the individual will tend to assimilate the group's goal to be able to maintain the valued membership. As a result of valuing his own membership and his desire to maintain it, the individual will tend to reject goals that he believes conflict with those prevailing in the group and accept those that appear to be consistent with the group's goals (29, 30).

Thus, participation does not seem to automatically produce congruence between the group's goal and that of the firm. Conditions may be such that a more authoritarian managerial style will be more effective in raising the aspiration levels of subordinates. Becker and Green (5) describe these conditions in greater specificity. Their position could be summarized as follows: If greater interaction of individuals leads to greater group cohesiveness, and if this cohesiveness plus some incentive to produce either at higher or lower levels are positively correlated, then participation can be an inducement for higher or lower levels of performance. Also, if participation at an upper level generates positive attitudes on the part of supervisors, then they will try to induce higher individual and group aspirations in the subgroup which will hopefully lead to higher rather than lower levels of performance.

There is also some evidence that participation improves morale. Coch and French (31) found a much lower turnover rate, fewer grievances about piece rates, and less aggression against the supervisor as individual participation in planning job changes increased. Vroom (32) argues that participation makes employees feel more a part of the activities and less dominated by a superior, more

independent, and thus improves their attitude toward the job. But while participation enhanced satisfaction, it did not necessarily increase productivity. Or at
least the results are ambiguous. Literature to date shows no direct correlation
between participation and improved productivity (e.g., 7,31,33).

Personality variables can also affect the relation between participation and
performance. For example, Vroom emphasizes the affective consequences of
the degree of consistency between a person's performance and his self-concept:
persons were found to perform better on tasks perceived to require highly valued
ability or intelligence which they believed themselves to possess (32).

Reconciliation with the Expectancy Model. It was indicated that participation
tends to increase performance if interaction of individuals leads to greater group
cohesiveness and if the group norms are such that they are conducive to higher
levels of production. These particular effects of participation can be accommo-
dated within the expectancy model. A group is cohesive when the individual
members value their acceptance within the group. Participation in the context
of a cohesive group would be a process of reaching consensus within the group
on the desirable standards of performance within the group. Once such a consensus has been reached as a result of the group's participation, it would be
viewed by the individual as reflecting the group's own norm. Striving to attain
that goal would therefore increase the individual's likelihood of maintaining his
acceptance in the group. In terms of the expectancy model, the existence of a
cohesive group of which the subordinate is a member enhances the extrinsic
valence associated with work goal accomplishment. With the attainment of the
goal, the individual achieves not only the extrinsic and intrinsic valences that
exist in the absence of a group context, but, in addition, he maintains his acceptance in a cohesive group which can be regarded as an extrinsic valence associated
with goal accomplishment.

In addition, participation may create intrinsic valences that are absent in nonparticipative environments. These intrinsic valences may be due to a tendency
for individuals to become "ego-involved" in decisions to which they have contributed, as would be the case in participative decision making. A similar process
is suggested by evidence that participation by a single person in decision making
with a superior affects the subsequent performance of that person (34).

Thus, only when groups are cohesive and their norms support the organization would participation be likely to increase motivation and hence the aspiration level and hence performance. When groups are not cohesive, no additional
valence is introduced and therefore motivation is not likely to be increased, although participation may increase group cohesiveness, as stated above. In fact,
participation in certain environments can lead to negative results as related, for
example, by Shillinglaw (35). The introduction of participative budgeting in a
large electrical equipment factory years ago was received coldly by most of the

first level supervisors. The reason offered was that foremen were reluctant to accept the risk of censure for failure to achieve targets that they had set themselves (9). In terms of this expectancy model, this phenomenon can be explained in terms of the effect of undesired participation on IV_b. Since participation under this environment induced anxiety and thus a decrement in the intrinsic valence associated with goal-directed behavior, motivation and performance were likely to decline.

Management by Exception

Summary of Existing Studies. The fact that accountants and managers emphasize deviations (we use this term instead of variances) in accounting reports implies that, by and large, attention is merited when significant deviations are observed and not when standards are met. Such a system, however, may be perceived as emphasizing failure with only exceptional success attracting management attention. The response to favorable deviations not requiring corrective actions often seems to be weaker than that to unfavorable deviations. As a result, subordinates may be led to view the system as punitive rather than as informative. This may lead to defensiveness, overcautious behavior, and other dysfunctional effects (36). This suggests that effort should be made to emphasize positive as well as negative aspects of performance to provide "positive reinforcement" (37).

Reconciliation with the Expectancy Model. In terms of the expectancy model, it is easy to predict the effect of these practices. Nonreinforcement or mere attainment of the budget will tend to decrease P_{2i}, the expectancy goal that accomplishment leads to extrinsic valences. The same effect would be produced by relative nonreinforcement of performance that is superior to the budget. On the other hand, punitive response to unfavorable deviations, while it may accomplish some results since subordinates have no alternatives, may also result in resistance, sabotage, and other kinds of conflict. Punishment is known to have generally negative effects (30). The Cherringtons' (7) finding that only appropriate reinforcement contingencies (i.e., when subordinates can control the performance on which rewards are contingent) were motivational can also be explained in terms of the effect on P_{2i}.

The Controllability Criterion

Summary of Existing Studies. Controllability refers to the ability of the subordinate to make decisions and execute them in his attempt to accomplish specified goals or a budget. A distinction must be made between *actual* control and *perceived* control. The motivational variable of interest is perceived control, which may differ from the actual degree of control that the subordinate can apply to a task. Personality as well as sociological factors can affect the degree of deviation between perceived control and actual control (38).

It is generally asserted that only controllable activities in the budget should constitute the basis for evaluation and reinforcement of the subordinate. For example, according to Vroom (34):

> The effectiveness of any system in which rewards and punishments are contingent on specified performance outcomes appears to be dependent on the degree of control which the individual has over these performance outcomes. The increment in performance to be expected from an increase in the extent to which the individual is rewarded for favorable results and/or punished for unfavorable results is directly related to the extent to which the individual can control the results of his performance.

Several sources can contribute to the lack of control over results which appears from existing evidence to reduce the effectiveness of organizationally administered reward-punishment contingencies. The first source is the existence of interpersonal and interdepartmental interdependencies within the formal organization. The jointness of the inputs in terms of subordinate's effort makes it extremely difficult to measure and assess a particular subordinate's contribution to the results. In such an interdependence setup, only the effort of a group as a whole can be adequately evaluated and each person has but partial control over the group's outcome.

The second source for lack of control is the operation of "chance" events that perturb the otherwise one-to-one relationship between the subordinate's efforts and his accomplishments. States of nature that are beyond his control affect the results of his effort. The existence of these "chance" events is partially a function of the nature of the task itself. Shooting at a fast-moving target, for example, is subject to far more external and uncontrollable events than performing a standard manufacturing operation.

The degree of skill of a subordinate to perform a job constitutes a third source of lack of control over results. While the degree of skill tends to be inversely related to the incidence of "chance" events, the two variables (skill and chance) are usefully viewed as distinct from each other (38). The degree to which "chance" factors affect performance depends on the skill of the performer as well as on the nature of the task. Thus, a very competent and skillful performer may still fail because the task is subject to many external perturbances, and at the same time an unskilled worker may fail to perform effectively even if his task is highly structured and subject to no external disturbances.

As indicated above, the perceived and not the actual degree of control is the variable of interest from the standpoint of predicting motivation and performance. And, as suggested, perceived control may differ from actual control, and the difference can depend on personality variables such as degree of achievement motivation, risk-taking behavior, as well as on cultural variables such as black vs. white, etc. (39-41).

Reconciliation with the Expectancy Model. Using the expectancy model, it can be explained why only activities in the budget that are perceived as controllable by the subordinate should constitute the basis for evaluation and reinforcement. Only activities that are perceived as controllable are likely to be associated with a relatively high P_1. In addition, performing tasks that are perceived as controllable could be associated with higher intrinsic valences (42).

Unfortunately, since it is difficult to discriminate finely between controllable and noncontrollable activities, dysfunctional decisions may result:

1.   Excluding from the evaluation basis activities that are partially controllable but classified as uncontrollable will direct the subordinate not to exert effort in those activities and eventually to jeopardize the accomplishment of the organization's goals. When basically controllable activities are excluded from the evaluation basis, the dependent variable M of the expectancy model operates on only some of the activities that are instrumental to the firm's overall goal attainment and it bypasses other beneficial activities.

2.   Including in the evaluation basis activities that are perceived by the subordinate as noncontrollable can result in lowering his expectancy that effort will lead to work accomplishment, i.e., P_1.

Also, the intrinsic valence associated with goal accomplishment may decrease if the task is perceived as partially beyond the subordinate's control. Under both cases, the subordinate's motivation to exert effort in his performance will tend to decrease.

The Exclusion of Criteria That Are Not Easily Measured in Monetary Terms

Summary of Existing Studies. Because of the difficulty of measuring nonmonetary dimensions of performance, the accounting structure usually restricts itself to reporting financial performance. As a result, managers may be motivated to emphasize the things that are measured to the neglect of those that are not. One suggested solution to this problem is the development of a composite measure of performance, with each dimension assigned a weight in proportion to top management's perceived priority. But this solution is deficient because the weighting schemes are implicit, difficult to translate into numerical form, and possibly nonstable over time. However, a useful step is said to be to identify the major dimensions of performance, whether measurable or not, so that they could be incorporated into the performance review process. The motivational problem involved is that the subordinates lack knowledge of the precise managerial reward structure and the weighting schemes implicit in the evaluation system.

Reconciliation with the Expectancy Model. The exclusion of nonmonetary criteria from the evaluation basis can be interpreted in terms of the expectancy model as motivating subordinates on the basis of only one dimension. In other words, the dependent variable M is characterized by only one dimension—the maximization of monetary profits. Since the work goal accomplishment that is expected to secure extrinsic rewards EV_i, is only defined by the criterion of maximizing monetary profits, the kinds of effort spent by the subordinate in the task will be only directed to that, and other objectives will be neglected.

Using the expectancy model, the subordinate can be motivated to spend effort to accomplish nonmonetary objectives if these are formally introduced into the control system by (1) making extrinsic rewards contingent on their accomplishment, (2) facilitating their accomplishment through task clarification, i.e., through increasing P_1, and (3) attempting to make the accomplishment of the nonmonetary criteria intrinsically valent to the subordinate.

As suggested by Vroom (34), one of the conditions needed to improve productivity by making effective performance on a task instrumental to the attainment of organizationally mediated rewards or the avoidance of punishments is that

> there is no conflict, either actual or perceived, between those behaviors necessary to attain a short term reward (for example, higher wages this week) and those required to avoid a longer term punishment (for example, a tightening of standards) (34).

However, merely introducing the nonmonetary criteria into the expectancy model through the explicit specification of effective performance via the budget does not in itself facilitate the attainment of goal congruence, unless the importance attached by top management to the attainment of various criteria is also made explicit to subordinates and internalized by them. If the weights to be attached to the criteria that are implicit in management's preference function are not made explicit to the subordinate, he may impose his own preference ordering on the criteria. That may not coincide with the management's preference ranking. In this case, goal congruence will not be attained in spite of the incorporation of the nonmonetary criteria into the model.

SUMMARY AND CONCLUSIONS

The literature on the effects of budgets on behavior is quite fragmentary and draws upon many diverse and partial areas of behavioral science. We have shown that this is the case for five general assumptions made in accounting with respect to budgets and behavior. These assumptions are

1. That standards should be reasonably attainable
2. That participation in the budgeting process leads to better performance

3. That management by exception is effective

4. That noncontrollable items should be excluded from budget reports, and

5. That budgetary accounting should be restricted to criteria measurable in monetary terms

We then introduced an expectancy model of task motivation within which, with some refinement, it was possible both to reconcile the fragmentary and contradictory past research findings and to explain the five assumptions in a consistent manner. To summarize, the following relations between the assumptions and variables in the expectancy model were discussed:

- Standards: P_1, P_2 (expectancies of performance and of reward)
- Participation: IV_a, IV_b, EV_i (intrinsic and extrinsic valences)
- Exception management: P_2
- Controllability: P_1, IV_a
- Monetary criteria: P_1, EV_i

We examined not only the budget's impact on behavior per se, but also the effects of the superiors' responses contingent on given levels of budget achievement on the part of the subordinate. Thus, the administration of extrinsic rewards contingent on successful budget achievement and the facilitation of intrinsic values are both related to the budgeting process and affect the subordinates' performance. As a result, the expectancy model could be also used as a framework for evaluating the effect of the accounting reports that compare actual performance with the budget on the subordinates' future performance.

Of course, there is a wealth of other relations which fall outside the immediate scope of this paper. The literature of expectancy theory is large, rich in empirical research, and fast growing. We recognize that the expectancy theory and its assumptions have come under criticism and that tests of the model's predictive ability have produced ambiguous results (see note 1). Nonetheless, recent progress in the testing and the operationalization of the model has apparently been made.[4]

Further research should be concerned with the derivation of testable hypotheses that apply the expectancy framework to the budgeting process as well as with further improving the predictive validity of the model through better operationalization of its variables. Also, the moderating effects of situational variables that are part of the working environment on the relation between budgets and motivation should be explored and tested. These situational aspects include variables such as the needs of subordinates, the environmental pressures and demands that subordinates must cope with to accomplish work goals and satisfy their needs, and the task demands of subordinates. Another particularly promising avenue for future research is the rigorous formulation of an expectancy model version which ties in with the SEU (Subjections Expected Utility) model, and with the level of aspiration theory.

Motivation, the dependent variable in the expectancy model, can be used as an indication of the probability that the task will be performed, given the ability of the subordinate. In other words, the probability that a task will be performed is a function of motivation and ability. To the superior it is important to assess this ability in order both to evaluate the merit of competing activities and to allocate effectively people to tasks. Hypotheses generated and tested within an expectancy framework should be helpful toward that end.

NOTES

1. Indeed, the model has been found wanting with respect to its description power (see, e.g., Ref. 43). But there is some recent evidence of progress (see note 4).
2. Clearly, motivation is only one variable that is likely to affect performance. Others are the subordinate's general ability as well as specific skills. To improve the subordinate's performance, the superior may choose to initiate training programs or take other actions to enhance the subordinate's skill, in addition to affecting his motivation.
3. Cherrington and Cherrington (7) tested experimentally the effect of various conditions of budget participation and reinforcement contingencies on performance and on psychological states of subordinates such as satisfaction with job and perceived superior consideration. However, they did not test an expectancy model per se but merely investigated the effects of their manipulated conditions in the context of reinforcement and operant conditioning theory.
4. Reviews of recent empirical studies in nonbudget contexts which were designed either to test directly the expectancy model or to provide an inferential basis for assessing the model's validity indicate some empirical support for the relationships stipulated by the expectancy theory (20,44-46). In fact, Kopelman (46) observed coefficients of correlation between the model's independent variables and performance indicators as high as .53. Furthermore, operational tools for measuring the model's parameters are available and are in the process of being continually improved and refined (47).

REFERENCES

1. Schiff, M., and Lewin, A. Y. The impact of people on budgets. *The Accounting Review, April 1970,* 259-268.

2. Williamson, O. E. *The Economics of Discretionary Behavior: Managerial Objectives in a Theory of the Firm.* Englewood Cliffs, N.J., Prentice-Hall, 1964, pp. 28-37.
3. Argyris, C. *The Impact of Budgets on People.* Controllership Foundation, 1952.
4. Benston, G. The role of the firm's accounting system for motivation. *The Accounting Review, April 1963,* 351-353.
5. Becker, S., and Green, D. Budgeting and employee behavior. *Journal of Business, October 1962,* 392-402.
6. Usry, M. Solving the problem of human relations in budgeting. *Budgeting Nov.-Dec. 1968,* 4-6.
7. Cherrington, D. J., and Cherrington, J. O. Appropriate reinforcement contingencies in the budgeting process. Presented at the Accounting Empirical Research Conference, University of Chicago, May 1973.
8. Stedry, A. *Budgetary Control and Cost Behavior.* Prentice-Hall, 1960.
9. Stedry, A., and Kay, E. The effects of goal difficulty on performance: A field experiment. *Behavioral Science,* 1966, *2,* 459-470.
10. House, R. J. A path-goal theory of leader effectiveness. *Administrative Science Quarterly,* Sept. 1971, *16*(3), 321-338.
11. Georgopoulos, B. S., Mahoney, G. M., and Jones, N. W. A path goal approach to productivity. *Journal of Applied Psychology,* 1957, *41,* 345-353.
12. Atkinson, J. W. Toward experimental analysis of human motivation in terms of motives, expectations and incentives. In J. W. Atkinson (ed.), *Motives in Fantasy, Action and Society.* New York, Van Nostrand, 1958.
13. Galbraith, J., and Cummings, L. L. An empirical investigation of the motivational determinants of past performance: Interactive effects between instrumentality, valence, motivation and ability. *Organizational Behavior and Human Performance, 1967,* 237-257.
14. Graen, G. Instrumental theory of work motivation: Some empirical results and suggested modifications. *Journal of Applied Psychology, 1969, 53,* 1-25.
15. Lawler, E. E. A correlation causal analysis of the relationship between expectancy attitudes and job performance. *Journal of Applied Psychology,* 1968, *52,* 462-468.
16. Lawler, E. E. *Pay and Organizational Effectiveness: A Psychological Perspective* (Wiley, 1971).
17. Lawler, E. E., and Suttle, J. K. Expectancy theory and job behavior. *Organizational Behavior and Human Performance,* 1973, *9,* 482-503.
18. Porter, L., and Lawler, E. E. *Managerial Attitudes and Performance.* Irwin-Dorsey, 1967.
19. Vroom, V. H. *Work and Motivation.* Wiley, 1964.
20. House, R. J., and Dessler, G. The path-goal theory of leadership: Some post

hoc and a priori tests. Paper presented at the Second Leadership Symposium: Contingency Approaches to Leadership; Southern Illinois University, Carbondale, April 1973.

21. Costello, T., and Zelking, S. *Psychology In Administration: A Research Orientation.* Englewood Cliffs, N.J., Prentice-Hall, 1963.

22. National Association of Accountants. *How Standard Costs Are Used Currently.* New York, 1948, pp. 8-9.

23. Hofstede, G. H. *The Game of Budget Control.* Assen, The Netherlands, Koninklijke Van Corcum and Comp. N. V., 1967, pp. 152-156.

24. Lewin, K., Dembo, T., Festinger, L., and Sears, P. Level of aspiration. In Vol. 1 of J. McV. Hunt (ed.). *Personality and Behavior Disorder.* Ronald Press, 1944, pp. 338-378.

25. Child, J. L., and Whiting, J. W. M. Determinants of level of aspiration: Evidence from everyday life. In H. Branch (ed.), *The Study of Personality.* New York, Wiley, 1954, pp. 145-158.

26. Bayton, J. A. Inter-relations between levels of aspiration, performance, and estimates of past performance. *Journal of Experimental Psychology,* 1943, *33,* 1-21.

27. Welsch, G. A. *Budgeting: Profit Planning and Control,* 3rd Ed. Englewood Cliffs, N.J., Prentice-Hall, 1971, pp. 17, 22-23.

28. Lewin, K. The psychology of a successful figure. In *Readings in Managerial Psychology,* H. S. Leavitt and L. R. Pondy (eds.). University of Chicago Press, 1964, pp. 25-31.

29. Caplan, E. Behavioral assumptions of management accounting. *The Accounting Review, July 1966,* 476-509.

30. Vroom, V. H. Some psychological aspects of organizational control. In Cooper, Leavitt & Shelly (eds.), *New Perspectives in Organizational Research.* Wiley, 1961.

31. Coch, L., and French, J. R. P. Overcoming resistance to change. *Human Relations,* 1948, *1,* 512-532.

32. Vroom, V. H. *Some Personality Determinants of the Effect of Participation.* Englewood Cliffs, N.J., Prentice-Hall, 1960.

33. French, J. R. P., Kay, E., and Meyer, H. H. *A Study of Threat and Participation in a Performance Appraisal Situation.* General Electric Co., 1962.

34. Vroom, V. H. Industrial social psychology. In *Handbook of Social Psychology.* Boston, Addison, Wesley, 1970.

35. Shillinglaw, G. *Cost Accounting, Analysis and Control,* 3rd Ed. Homewood, Ill., Irwin, 1972.

36. Sayles, L. R., and Chandler, M. K. *Managing Large Systems: Organizations for the Future.* New York, Harper & Row, 1971.

37. Birnberg, J. G., and Nath, R. Implications of behavioral science for managerial accounting. *The Accounting Review, July 1967,* 478

38. Feather, N. T. Valence of outcome and expectation of success in relation to task difficulty and perceived locus of control. *Journal of Personality and Social Psychology,* 1967, *7,* 372-386.
39. Lefcourt, H. M. Risk taking in Negro and white adults. *Journal of Personality and Social Psychology,* 1965, *2,* 765-770.
40. Rotter, J. B., Liverant, S., and Crowne, D. P. Growth and extinction of expectancies in chance controlled and skill tasks. *Journal of Psychology,* 1961, *52,* 151-177.
41. Sutcliffe, J. P. Random effects as a function of belief in control. *Australian Journal of Psychology,* 1956, *8,* 128-139.
42. Ronen, J. Involvement in tasks and choice behavior. *Organizational Behavior and Human Performance,* February 1974, *2,* 28-43.
43. Kerr, S., Klimoski, R. J., Tolliver, J., and Von Glinow, M. A. Human Information Processing and Problem Solving. Paper presented at the Workshop in Behavioral Accounting: Annual Meeting of the American Institute for Decision Sciences, Atlanta, Ga., Oct. 30, 1974.
44. Dessler, G. A Test of the Path-Goal Theory of Leadership, Doctoral Dissertation, Bernard M. Baruch College, City University of New York, 1973.
45. House, R. J., and Wahba, M. A. Expectancy Theory as a Predictor of Job Performance, Satisfaction and Motivation: An Integrative Model and a Review of the Literature. Paper presented at the American Psychological Association Meeting, Hawaii, August 1972; Working Paper 72-21, Faculty of Management Studies, University of Toronto, 1972.
46. Kopelman, R. Factors Complicating Expectancy Theory Prediction of Work Motivation and Job Performance. Paper presented at the meeting of the American Psychological Association, 1974.
47. House, R. J. Some Preliminary Findings Concerning a Test of the Path Goal Theory of Leadership. Unpublished manuscript, University of Toronto, April 1972. House, R. J. *Notes on Questionnaires Frequently Used by or Developed by R. J. House,* Faculty of Management Studies, University of Toronto, July 1972.

9

ORGANIZATIONAL MODELS OF SOCIAL PROGRAM IMPLEMENTATION*

Richard F. Elmore

I will develop four organizational models representing the major schools of
thought that can be brought to bear on the implementation problem. The *system
management model* captures the organizational assumptions of the mainstream, rationalist tradition of policy analysis. Its point of departure is the
assumption of value-maximizing behavior. The *bureaucratic process model* represents the sociological view of organizations, updated to include recent research by students of "street level bureaucracy" that bears directly on the analysis of social program implementation. Its point of departure is the assumption
that the essential feature of organizations is the interaction between routine and
discretion. The *organizational development model* represents a relatively recent
combination of sociological and psychological theory that focuses on the conflict between the needs of individuals and the demands of organizational life.
Finally, the *conflict and bargaining model* addresses the problem of how people
with divergent interests coalesce around a common task. It starts from the

*Reprinted from *Public Policy,* vol. 26, no. 2 (Spring 1978), pp. 185–228. Copyright ©
1978 John Wiley & Sons, Inc. Reprinted by permission of the publisher. References have
been renumbered.

assumption that conflict, arising out of the pursuit of relative advantage in a bargaining relationship, is the dominant feature of organizational life.

The most important aspect of these models, however, is not that they represent certain established traditions of academic inquiry. As we shall see, their major appeal is that each contains a common sense explanation for implementation failures. And each explanation emphasizes different features of the implementation process.

The format of the discussion will be the same for each model. I will first present a list of four propositions that capture the essential features of each model. The first proposition states the central principle of the model; the second states the model's view of the distribution of power in organizations; the third states the model's view of organizational decision making; and the fourth gives a thumbnail sketch of the implementation process from the perspective of the model. I will then discuss how these assumptions affect the analyst's perception of the implementation process. In Allison's words, I will develop "a dominant inference pattern" that serves to explain why certain features of the implementation process are more important than others and to predict the consequences of certain administrative actions for the success or failure of implementation efforts. Finally, I will draw some examples from the current case literature on social program implementation that demonstrate the strengths and weaknesses of each model.

Some readers will no doubt chafe at the idea that highly complex bodies of thought about organizations can be reduced to a few simple propositions. My defense is that this is an exercise in the *application* of theory, not an exercise in theory building. The premium is on capturing the insights that each model brings to the problem, not on making the theory more elegant or defensible. I have tried mightily to avoid creating straw men. Each model is offered as a legitimate analytic perspective.

MODEL I: IMPLEMENTATION AS SYSTEMS MANAGEMENT

Propositions

1. Organizations should operate as rational value maximizers. The essential attribute of rationality is goal-directed behavior; organizations are effective to the extent that they maximize performance on their central goals and objectives. Each task that an organization performs must contribute to at least one of a set of well-defined objectives that accurately reflect the organization's purpose.

2. Organizations should be structured on the principle of hierarchical control. Responsibility for policy making and overall system performance rests with top management, which in turn allocates specific tasks and performance objectives to subordinate units and monitors their performance.

3. For every task an organization performs there is some optimal allocation of responsibilities among subunits that maximizes the organization's overall performance on its objectives. Decision making in organizations consists of finding this optimum and maintaining it by continually adjusting the internal allocation of responsibilities to changes in the environment.

4. Implementation consists of defining a detailed set of objectives that accurately reflect the intent of a given policy, assigning responsibilities and standards of performance to subunits consistent with these objectives, monitoring system performance, and making internal adjustments that enhance the attainment of the organization's goals. The process is dynamic, not static; the environment continually imposes new demands that require internal adjustments. But implementation is always goal-directed and value maximizing.

A frequent explanation for failures of implementation is "bad management." We generally mean by this that policies are poorly defined, responsibilities are not clearly assigned, expected outcomes are not specified, and people are not held accountable for their performance. Good management, of course, is the opposite of all these things, and therein lies the crux of the systems management model. The model starts from the normative assumption that effective management proceeds from goal-directed, value-maximizing behavior. Organizations are thought of as problem-solving "systems"—functionally integrated collections of parts that are capable of concerted action around a common purpose.[1]

Integration presupposes the existence of a controlling and coordinating authority. In the systems management model, this authority is called the "management subsystem," "the source of binding pronouncements and the locus of the decisionmaking process."[2] It provides "a means of insuring role performance, replacing lost members, coordinating the several subsystems of the organization, responding to external changes and making decisions about how all these things should be accomplished."[3] Hierarchical control is the single most important element ensuring that organizations behave as systems.

The translation of policy into action consists of a deliberate, stepwise process in which goals are elaborated into specific tasks. Robert Anthony's discussion of planning and management control gives a succinct statement of the transition from policy to operations:

> Strategic planning is the process of deciding on objectives, on resources used to obtain these objectives, and on the policies that are to govern acquisition, use and disposition of these resources. . . . Management control is the process by which managers assure that resources are obtained and used effectively and efficiently in the accomplishment of the organization's objectives . . . [and] operational control is the process of assuring that specific tasks are carried out effectively and efficiently.[4]

These functions are distributed in descending order from the highest to lowest levels of the organization. Taken together, they describe a general set of decision rules for the optimal allocation of resources, tasks, and performance criteria among subunits of an organization.

For all its emphasis on hierarchical control, one would expect that the systems management model would make little or no allowance for the exercise of lower level discretion by subordinates carrying out policy directives. In fact, this is not quite the case. The problem of subordinate discretion figures prominently in the literature of systems management. Understandably, the issue arose in a very visible way during the initial attempts to apply systems analysis to national defense planning. Defense planners found almost immediately that the ability of the management subsystem to control the performance of subunits was limited by the enormous complexity of the total system. Hence, a great deal hinged on discovering the correct mix of hierarchical control and subordinate discretion. Hitch and McKean call this process *suboptimization,* which they define as an "attempt to find optimal (or near optimal) solutions, but to sub-problems rather than to a whole problem of the organization in whose welfare or utility we are interested."[5] In organizational terms, suboptimization consists of holding subunits responsible for a certain level of output but giving subunit managers the discretion to decide on the means of achieving that level. In business parlance, these subunits are called "profit centers," in the public sector they have been called "responsibility centers." Suboptimization provides a means of exercising hierarchical control by focusing on the output of subunits rather than on their technically complex internal operations.

In practice, suboptimization raises some very complex problems—selecting appropriate criteria of subunit performance, accounting for the unintended consequences, or spillovers, of one unit's performance on another's, and choosing the appropriate aggregation of functions for each subunit.[6] But the notion of suboptimization gives the systems management model a degree of flexibility that is not often appreciated by its critics. It is *not* necessary to assume that all organizational decisions are centralized in order to assume that organizations are functionally integrated.[7] If the outputs of delegated decisions are consistent with the overall goals of the organization, then there is room for a certain degree of latitude in the selection of means for achieving those outputs.

A great deal of behavior in organizations can be explained by examining devices of control and compliance. Some are easy to identify, some blend into the subtle social fabric of organizations. One common device is what Herbert Kaufman calls the "preformed decision." He argues that "organizations might disintegrate if each field officer made entirely independent decisions," so organizations develop ways of making decisions for their field officers "in advance of specific situations requiring choice":

[Events] and conditions in the field are anticipated as fully as possible, and courses of action [for each set of events and conditions] are described. The field officer then need determine only into what category a particular instance falls; once this determination is made, he then simply follows a series of steps applicable to that category. Within each category, therefore, the decisions are "preformed."[8]

Much of the work of high-level administrators in the implementation process consists of anticipating recurrent problems at lower levels of the system and attempting to program the behavior of subordinates to respond to these problems in standardized ways.

But not all devices of control are so obvious. In a casual aside, Robert Anthony remarks that "the system [of management controls] should be so constructed that actions that operating managers take in their perceived self-interest are also in the best interests of the whole organization."[9] An important ingredient of control, then, is to be found in the way people are socialized to organizations. Social psychologists Katz and Kahn observe that all organizations have "maintenance subsystems" for recruitment, indoctrination, socialization, reward, and sanction that "function to maintain the fabric of interdependent behavior necessary for task accomplishment."[10] These devices are the basis for "standardized patterns of behavior required of all persons playing a part in a given functional relationship, regardless of personal wishes or interpersonal obligations irrelevant to the functional relationship."[11] In plain English, this means that organizations often require people to put the requirements of their formal roles above their personal preferences. The effect is to enhance the predictability and control of subordinate behavior in much the same way as preformed decisions and suboptimization. The difference is that instead of shaping decisions, it is the decision *makers* who are shaped.

The major appeal of the systems management model is that it can be readily translated into a set of normative prescriptions that policy analysts can use to say how the implementation process ought to work. From the model's perspective, effective implementation requires four main ingredients: (1) clearly specified tasks and objectives that accurately reflect the intent of policy; (2) a management plan that allocates tasks and performance standards to subunits; (3) an objective means of measuring subunit performance; and (4) a system of management controls and social sanctions sufficient to hold subordinates accountable for their performance. Failures of implementation are, by definition, lapses of planning, specification, and control. The analysis of implementation consists of finding, or anticipating, these breakdowns and suggesting how they ought to be remedied.

Analysis is made a good deal easier in this model by virtue of the fact that organizations are assumed to operate as units; a single conception of policy governs all levels of an organization. Success or failure of the organization is judged by observing the discrepancy between the policy declaration and subordinate behavior. The analyst focuses on the "clarity, precision, comprehensiveness, and reasonableness of the preliminary policy," on "the technical capacity to implement," and on "the extent to which the actual outputs of the organization have changed in the expected direction after the introduction of the innovation."[12] But in order for this conception of analysis to make any sense in organizational terms, one must first assume that policy makers, administrators, and analysts have a common understanding of policy and have sufficient control of the implementation process to hold subordinates accountable to that understanding.

A great deal would seem to depend, then, on whether organizations can actually be structured on the assumptions of the systems management model. The empirical evidence is suggestive but hardly conclusive. Herbert Kaufman, who has made a career of studying administrative compliance and control, concludes his classic study of the U.S. Forest Service with the observation the "overall performance comes remarkably close to the goals set by the leadership."[13] This was accomplished using a set of management controls and social sanctions that closely approximate the systems management model. The net result is that "the Rangers want to do the very things that the Forest Service wants them to do, and are able to do them, because these are the decisions and actions that become second nature to them as a result of years of obedience."[14] Much the same conclusions is reported by Jeremiah O'Connell in his study of the implementation of a major reorganization of a large insurance company. He sets out to demonstrate the effectiveness of an implementation strategy based on "unilateral" action by top management and on "economic values."[15] The reorganization plan was a pristine example of suboptimization:

> Managers will have line responsibility for the accumulated results every week of a unit composed of seven to ten men. . . . Line responsibility makes each . . . manager accountable for determining the use of his personal time. His record will be the combined record of his agency unit. On this record his performance will be evaluated, he will be recognized, and he will be compensated.[16]

O'Connell argues that the plan had its intended effect of putting "the best resources possible in the most promising markets," hence presumably increasing company profits.[17]

The distinctive feature of both these cases is strong management control in the presence of wide geographic dispersion, which suggests that large organizations can approximate the ideal of value-maximizing units. But neither example comes from the literature on social program implementation, and in the existing literature there are no examples that come close to approximating the ideal. One explanation for this is that the literature records only failures. Another is that social programs are characterized by chronically bad management. If we could find successful examples of implementation, one could argue, they would manifest all the essential attributes of the systems management model. This is an empirical question that requires more evidence than we presently have.

But there are at least two other explanations for the lack of systems management examples in the implementation literature, and both point to weaknesses in the model. The first is that the model completely disregards a basic element common to all cases of social program implementation: federalism. Regardless of how well organized an agency might be, its ability to implement programs successfully depends, to some degree, on its ability to influence agencies at other levels of government. In both of the examples cited above, the implementing agent is a direct subordinate of management; he is selected, indoctrinated, rewarded, and penalized by the same people who articulate policy. Where more than one agency is involved in the implementation process, the lines of authority are much more blurred. It is not uncommon for implementors of social policy to be responsible to more than one political jurisdiction—to the federal government for a general declaration of policy and certain specific guidelines, and to a state or local unit for myriad administrative details. These jurisdictional boundaries are a permanent fixture of the American federal system; they exist not to enhance the efficiency of implementation but to protect the political prerogatives of state and local government. Insofar as it equates "success" of implementation with outcomes that are consistent across all levels of government, the systems management model is antifederalist. A good example of this antifederalist bias is Herbert Kaufman's study of management control in nine federal agencies. Six of the agencies in Kaufman's sample administered their own programs, three agencies administered programs through units of state and local government. Kaufman recognized the distinction, but chose to treat it as analytically unimportant:

> In the case of inter-governmental programs, we opted to treat the recipients of bureau-administered funds as though they were the subordinates of the administering agencies in order to sharpen the comparisons . . . between feedback practices in direct and intergovernmental administration, and we found this artificial convention useful even though it exaggerated some seeming shortcomings in some of the bureaus.[18]

Not surprisingly, Kaufman found that the two weakest agencies, in terms of his criteria of administrative feedback, were those that administered intergovernmental programs in areas where functions were understood to be primarily state and local—the Law Enforcement Assistance Administration and the U.S. Office of Education.[19] Far from an indictment of internal management in these agencies, his analysis turns out to be an unintentional affirmation of the strength of federalism in the face of administrative efficiency. The systems management model, then, fails to account for the weakness of management control across jurisdictional boundaries.

The second possible explanation for the lack of systems management examples in the literature on social program implementation is perhaps that the model is not intended to describe reality. Recall that all propositions on which the model is based are normative; they describe how organizations *ought* to function, not necessarily how they actually do. The distinction is not as disingenuous as it sounds. We frequently rely on normative models to help us evaluate performance, diagnose failure, and propose remedies, even though we understand perfectly well that they have very little descriptive validity. We do so because they provide useful ways of organizing and simplifying complex problems. In this sense, the test of a model is not whether it accurately represents reality, but whether it has some utility as a problem-solving device. The major utility of the systems management model is that it directs our attention toward the mechanisms that policy makers and high-level administrators have for structuring and controlling the behavior of subordinates.

It is dangerous, however, to focus on the normative utility of the model to the exclusion of its descriptive validity. To say that the model simplifies in useful ways is not the same thing as saying that the implementation process should be structured around the model. This is a mistake that policy analysts are particularly prone to make, and it involves a peculiar and obvious circularity. If the fit between model and reality is poor, the argument goes, then the model should be used to restructure reality. Only then, the analyst concludes triumphantly, can it be determined whether the model "works" or not. A special form of this argument claims that social programs fail because policies are poorly specified and management control is weak. To the extent that we remedy these problems we can predict a higher ratio of successes to failures. The problem with this argument is that the definition of success is internal to the model and it may or may not be shared by people who are actually part of the process. The systems management model will almost certainly "work" if everyone behaves according to its dictates. If we could make value maximizers of all organizations, then we could no doubt prove that all organizations are value maximizers. But the point is that participants in the implementation process don't necessarily share the norms of the model. And it is this fact that leads us to search for alternative models.

MODEL II: IMPLEMENTATION AS BUREAUCRATIC PROCESS

Propositions

1. The two central attributes of organizations are discretion and routine; all important behavior in organizations can be explained by the irreducible discretion

exercised by individual workers in their day-to-day decisions and the operating routines that they develop to maintain and enhance their position in the organization.

2. The dominance of discretion and routine means that power in organizations tends to be fragmented and dispersed among small units exercising relatively strong control over specific tasks within their sphere of authority. The amount of control that any one organizational unit can exert over another—laterally or hierarchically—is hedged by the fact that as organizations become increasingly complex, units become more highly specialized and exercise greater control over their internal operations.

3. Decision making consists of controlling discretion and changing routine. All proposals for change are judged by organizational units in terms of the degree to which they depart from established patterns; hence, organizational decisions tend to be incremental.

4. Implementation consists of identifying where discretion is concentrated and which of an organization's repertoire of routines need changing, devising alternative routines that represent the intent of policy, and inducing organizational units to replace old routines with new ones.

We reach instinctively for bureaucratic explanations of implementation failures. "There was a major change in policy," we say, "but the bureaucracy kept right on doing what it did before." Or alternatively, "When the bureaucracy got through with it, the policy didn't look anything like what we intended." Bureaucracy was not always a pejorative term; for Max Weber, it was a form of organization that substituted impersonal, efficient, and routinized authority for that based on personal privilege or divine inspiration. Lately, though, bureaucracy has become an all-purpose explanation for everything that is wrong with government. We use terms like "the bureaucracy problem"[20] and "the bureaucratic phenomenon"[21] to describe behavior of public officials that is "inefficient, unresponsive, unfair, ponderous, or confusing."[22]

When we look behind these characterizations, the problems of implementing policies in bureaucratic settings can be traced to two basic elements: discretion and routine. As bureaucracies become larger and more complex, they concentrate specialized tasks in subunits. With specialization comes an irreducible discretion in day-to-day decision making; the ability of any single authority to control all decisions becomes attenuated to the point where it ceases to be real in any practical sense. In the words of Graham Allison, factored problem solving begets fractionated power.[23] With the growth of discretion also comes the growth of routine. Individuals and subunits manage the space created by discretion so as to maintain and enhance their position in the organization. They create operating routines in part to simplify their work but also to demonstrate their specialized skill in controlling and managing their assigned tasks. Individuals and subunits resist attempts to alter their discretion or to change their operating routines—in other words, they resist hierarchical management—because these things are a concrete expression of their special competence, knowledge, and status in the organization. The central focus of the bureaucracy problem, according to J. Q. Wilson, is "getting the front-line worker—the teacher, nurse, diplomat, police officer, or welfare worker—to do the right thing."[24] The job of administration is, purely and simply, "controlling discretion."[25]

The standard techniques of hierarchical management—budget and planning cycles, clearance procedures, reporting requirements, and evaluation systems— are the means by which high-level administrators attempt to structure the behavior of subordinates. To the front-line worker, though, these techniques are often incidental to the "real" work of the organization. The front-line worker's major concern is learning to cope with the immediate pressures of the job, and this requires inventing and learning a relatively complex set of work routines that go with one's specialized responsibility. This split between high-level administrators and front-line workers accounts for the quizzical, sometimes sceptical, look one often gets from teachers, social workers, and other front-line workers when they're asked about the implementation of policy. "Policy?" they reply, "We're so busy getting the work done we haven't much time to think about policy."

The bureaucratic process model, then, traces the effect of lower level discretion and routinized behavior on the execution of policy. The central analytic problem is to discover where discretion resides and how existing routines can be shaped to the purposes of policy. The major difference between systems management and bureaucratic process models is that former assumes that the tools of management control can be used to program subordinate behavior, while the latter posits the existence of discretion and operating routines as means by which subordinates resist control. The systems management model assumes that the totality of an organization's resources can be directed at a single, coherent set of purposes—that organizations can be programmed to respond to changes in policy. The bureaucratic process model assumes that the dominant characteristic of organizations is resistance to change—not simply inertia (the tendency to move in one direction until deflected by some outside force), but, as Donald Schon observes, "dynamic conservatism" (the tendency to fight to remain the same).[26] In the systems management model one assumes that given the right set of management controls, subunits of an organization will do what they are told; in the bureaucratic process model, one assumes that they will continue to do what they have been doing until some way is found to make them do otherwise.

In the implementation of social programs, new policies must typically travel from one large public bureaucracy to another, and then through several successive layers of the implementing agency before they reach the point of impact on the client. Whether or not the policy has its intended effect on the client depends in large part on whether the force of existing routine at each level of the process operates with or against the policy.

It is frequently at the final stage of this process—the point of delivery from agency to client—that the forces of discretion and routine are most difficult to overcome. This problem is the central concern of students of "street-level bureaucracy." The growth of large public service agencies has created a distinguishable class of bureaucrat—one who shoulders virtually all responsibility for direct contact with clients, who exercises a relatively large degree of discretion over detailed decisions of client treatment, and who therefore has considerable potential impact on clients.[27] From the client's perspective, the street-level bureaucrat *is* the government. Clients seldom, if ever, interact with higher level administrators; in fact, most public service bureaucracies are deliberately designed to prevent this. Because of the frequency and immediacy of the contact between street-level bureaucrats and their clients, it is usually impossible for higher level administrators to monitor or control all aspects of their job performance. Consequently, a significant distance opens up between the street-level bureaucrat and his superiors. This distance breeds autonomy and discretion at lower levels of the organization. The distinctive quality of street-level bureaucracy is the "discretion increases as one moves down the hierarchy.[28]

But this concentration of discretion at lower levels has a paradoxical quality. For while street-level bureaucrats occupy the most critical position in the delivery process, their working conditions are seldom conducive to the adequate performance of their jobs. More often than not, they find themselves in situations where they lack the organizational and personal resources to perform their jobs adequately, where they are exposed regularly to physical or psychological threat, and where there are confilcting and ambiguous expectations about how they ought to perform their work.[29] Social service delivery jobs are among the most stressful in our society. Street-level bureaucrats are expected to treat clients as individuals, but the high demand for their services forces them to invent routines for mass processing. High-level administrators and policy makers are preoccupied with the way policy is expressed in legislation, regulations, and guidelines. But the major concern for the street-level implementor is how to control the stress and complexity of day-to-day work. Out of this concern grows a whole set of informal routines that students of street-level bureaucracy call "coping mechanisms."

Learning to cope with the stresses of service delivery means learning to rely on simple, standardized sources of information to clients—case histories, employment records, permanent school records, test scores, eligibility forms, and the like. It means developing a facility for classifying and labeling people simply and quickly—"an alcoholic parent," "a broken family," "a history of drug abuse," "violence-prone and resistant to authority," "can't hold a job," and so on. It means developing one's "faculties of suspicion" in order to spot people who pose a threat either to oneself or to the system one is administering. And it means using the formal procedures of the organization to strike an impersonal distance between oneself, as an individual, and the client.[30]   All these mechanisms have the effect of reducing and controlling the stress and uncertainty of daily work, and for this reason they figure prominently in the implementation of social policy. On the other hand, they are not typically included in the policy maker's or the high-level administrator's definition of "policy." More often than not, they're either ignored or regarded as external to the implementation process.

Concentrating on formal declarations of policy at the expense of informal coping routines means that "even the most imaginative manipulations of goals, structure, staff recruitment, training and supervision may . . . represent only superficial changes . . . rather than the fundamental reforms hoped for."[31] From the perspective of the bureaucratic process model, major shifts in policy have little or no effect until they reach the final transaction between service giver and client. The elaborate superstructure of regulations, guidelines, and management controls that accompany most social programs tend to have weak and unpredictable effects on the delivery of social services because street-level bureaucrats and their clients develop strong patterns of interaction that are relatively immune to change. Implementation failures, from this point of view, are the result of a failure on the part of policy makers to understand the actual conditions under which social services are delivered.

Empirical evidence demonstrating the effect of organizational routines on the implementation of social policy, while not extensive, is certainly compelling. Probably the first serious attempt to document the street-level effect of a major shift in policy was Miriam Johnson's study of how national manpower policy influenced the operation of local employment service offices in California.[32]

The major advantage of the bureaucratic process model is that it forces us to contend with the mundane patterns of bureaucratic life and to think about how new policies affect the daily routines of people who deliver social services. Policy makers, analysts, and administrators have a tendency to focus on variables that emphasize control and predictability, often overlooking the factors that undermine control and create anomalies in the implementation process. Bureaucratic routines operate against the grain of many policy changes because they are contrived as buffers against change and uncertainty; they continue to exist precisely because they have an immediate utility to the people who use them in reducing the stress and complexity of work. Failing to account for the force of routine in the implementation of policy leads to serious misperceptions.

Walter Williams argues that most implementation problems grow out of a division of labor between what he calls the "policy and operations spheres."[33] In the policy sphere, people tend to focus on global issues and general shifts in the distribution of power among governmental units. Consequently, when the responsibility for implementation shifts to the operations sphere there is little in the way of useful guidance for implementors. The limited case literature on the role of bureaucratic routines bears out this observation. The unresponsiveness of large public bureaucracies to new policy initiatives is more often than not attributable to a failure to connect the "big ideas" of policy makers with the mundane coping mechanisms of implementors.

Unlike the systems management model, the bureaucratic process model does not give any clear-cut prescriptions for improving the implementation process. About the only normative advice offered by students of street-level bureaucracy is the rather weak suggestion that "bureaucratic coping behaviors cannot be eliminated, but they can be monitored and directed" by rewarding "those that most closely conform to preferred public objectives [and] discouraging objectionable practices."[34] What this prescription overlooks is that coping routines derive their appeal and resilience from the fact that they are rooted in the immediate demands of work: they are, then, almost generically immune to hierarchical control. It's difficult, within the context of the bureaucratic process model, to think of ways to change street-level behavior in a predictable fashion. But, as we shall see in the following section, it's not at all difficult to solve this problem when we adopt the perspective of another model.

The utility of the bureaucratic process model shouldn't hang entirely on its limited normative power, although, since its major advantages are descriptive, it captures a very common pattern of implementation failure, in which hierarchical controls generated by top management to alter the behavior of subordinates, or by one government agency to structure the behavior of another, simply fail to affect the important street-level transactions that determine the success of a policy.

MODEL III: IMPLEMENTATION AS ORGANIZATIONAL DEVELOPMENT

Propositions

1. Organizations should function to satisfy the basic psychological and social needs of individuals—for autonomy and control over their own work, for participation in decisions affecting them, and for commitment to the purposes of the organization.

2. Organizations should be structured to maximize individual control, participation, and commitment at all levels. Hierarchically structured bureaucracies maximize these things for people in upper levels of the organization at the expense of those in lower levels. Hence, the best organizational structure is one that minimizes hierarchical control and distributes responsibility for decisions among all levels of the organization.

3. Effective decision making in organizations depends on the creation of effective work groups. The quality of interpersonal relations in organizations largely determines the quality of decisions. Effective work groups are characterized by mutual agreement on goals, open communication among individuals,

mutual trust and support among groups members, full utilization of members' skills, and effective management of conflict. Decision making consists primarily of building consensus and strong interpersonal relations among group members.

4. The implementation process is necessarily one of consensus building and accommodation between policy makers and implementors. The central problem of implementation is not whether implementors conform to prescribed policy but whether the implementation process results in consensus in goals, individual autonomy, and commitment to policy on the part of those who must carry it out.

Another frequent explanation of implementation failures is that those who implement programs are seldom included in decisions that determine the content of those programs. The closer one gets to the point of delivery in social programs, the more frequently one hears the complaint that policy makers and high-level administrators don't listen to service deliverers. What grates most on the sensibilities of teachers, social workers, employment counselors, and the like is the tacit assumption in most policy directives that they are incapable of making independent judgments and decisions—that their behavior must be programmed by someone else. It's difficult for persons who see themselves as competent, self-sufficient adults to be highly committed to policies that place them in the role of passive executors of someone else's will.

The prevailing theories of organizational behavior represented by the systems management and bureaucratic process models encourage and perpetuate this pathology. Hierarchy, specialization, routine, and control all reinforce the belief that those at the bottom of the organization are less competent decision makers than those at the top. High-level administrators can be trusted to exercise discretion while those at the bottom must be closely supervised and controlled. Policy is made at the top and implemented at the bottom; implementors must set aside their own views and submit to the superior authority and competence of policy makers and high-level administrators.

Not surprisingly, this view has become increasingly difficult to defend as the work force has become more professionalized and better educated. It's now relatively clear that there are basic conflicts between the individual's need for autonomy, participation, and commitment and the organization's requirement of structure, control, and subordination. Concern for this conflict has led some to posit a "democratic alternative" to established theories of organization.[35] The label we attach to this alternative is "organizational development." A number of schools of thought coexist within this tradition, but we will concentrate primarily on the work of Chris Argyris, who has spent an unusually large amount of effort specifying the assumptions on which his view is based.

Argyris begins with the observation that what we define as acceptable adult behavior outside organizations directly contradicts what's acceptable inside. On the outside, adults are defined as people who are self-motivating, responsible for their own actions, and honest about emotions and values. Inside organizations, adults are expected to exhibit dependency and passivity toward their superiors, they resort to indirection and avoid taking responsibility as individuals, and they are forced to submerge emotions and values.[36] Resolving this tension requires a fundamentally different kind of organization and a different theory of organizational behavior. Rational or bureaucratic theories of organization stress abstract, systemic properties—structure, technology, outputs—at the expense of the social and psychological needs of individuals.[37] The reasonable alternative is a theory that begins from the needs of individuals rather than the abstract properties of organizations. Such a theory leads "not only to a more humane and democratic system but to a more efficient one."[38]

The essential transactions of organizational life occur in face-to-face contacts among individuals engaged in a common task, i.e., in work groups. Organizational effectiveness and efficiency depend more than anything else on the quality of interpersonal relations in work groups. As stated earlier, effective work groups are characterized by agreement on goals, open communication, mutual trust and support, full utilization of member skills, and effective management of conflict.[39] The cultivation of these attributes requires a special kind of skill, which Argyris calls "interpersonal competence" to distinguish it from the purely technical competence that comes from the routine performance of a task. Individuals are interpersonally competent when they are able to give and receive feedback in a way that creates minimal defensiveness; to give honest expression to their own feelings, values, and attitudes; and to remain open to new ideas.[40] The trappings of bureaucracy and rational decision making—routines, management controls, objectified accountability—undermine interpersonal competence and group effectiveness, encouraging dependence and passivity while penalizing openness and risk taking. Hence, "the very values that are assumed to help make [an organization] effective may actually . . . decrease its effectiveness."[41]

Nowhere in the literature on organizational development is there a simple composite of the well-structured organization. It's fair to infer from the theory, though, that an effective organization would have at least the following features: most responsibility for decisions would devolve to lower levels of the organization; the focus of organizational activity would be the work group, formed of people engaged in a common task; and information—statements of purpose, evaluative judgments, and expressions of needed changes—would be readily exchanged without negative social consequences at all levels of the organization. All these features originate from the simple assumption that people are more likely to perform at their highest capacity when they are given maximum control over their own work, maximum participation in decisions affecting them, and hence maximum incentives for commitment to the goals of the group.

The organizational development model gives quite a different picture of the implementation process than either the systems management or bureaucratic process models. In the systems management model, implementation consists of the skillful use of management controls to hold subunits accountable for well-defined standards of performance. In the bureaucratic process model, implementation consists of changing the formal and informal work routines of an organization to conform with a declaration of intent. In both instances, *policy is made at the top and implemented at the bottom.* But in the organizational development model the distinction is much less clear. If major responsibility is actually devolved to work groups at lower levels of the organization, it makes very little sense to think of policy as flowing from top to bottom. More about this in a moment.

Implementation failures are not the result of poor management control or the persistence of bureaucratic routines, but arise out of a lack of consensus and commitment among implementors. The features of the implementation process that matter most are those that affect individual motivation and interpersonal cooperation, not those that enhance hierarchical control. Success of an implementation effort can be gauged by looking at the extent to which implementors are involved in the formulation of a program, the extent to which they are encouraged to exercise independent judgment in determining their own behavior, and the extent to which they are encouraged to establish strong work groups for mutual support and problem solving.

Empirical evidence on the underlying assumptions of the organizational development model is relatively scarce.

The real significance of the organizational development model is that it effectively turns the entire implementation process on its head. It reverses what we instinctively regard as the "normal" flow of policy, from top to bottom. The message of the model is, quite bluntly, that the capacity to implement originates at the bottom of organizations, not at the top. In each of the two previous models the central problem was how policy makers and high-level administrators could shape the behavior of implementors using the standard devices of hierarchical control. What the organizational development model suggests is that these devices explain almost none of the variation in implementation outcomes. The factors that do affect the behavior of implementors lie outside the domain of direct management control—individual motivation and commitment, and the interaction and mutual support of people in work groups. Hence, the closer one gets to the determinants of effective implementation, the further one gets from the factors that policy makers and administrators can manipulate. The result is that, in terms of the effective structure of organizations, *the process of initiating and implementing new policy actually begins at the bottom and ends at the top.* Unless organizations already have those properties that predispose them to change, they are not likely to respond to new policy. But if they have those properties, they are capable of initiating change themselves, without the control of policy makers and administrators. The role of those at the top of the system, then, is necessarily residual; they can provide resources that implementors need to do their work, but they cannot exert direct control over the factors that determine the success or failure of that work.

If one accepts this view, the important business of implementation consists not of developing progressively more sophisticated techniques for managing subordinates' behavior but of enhancing the self-starting capacity of the smallest unit. The organizational capacity to accept innovations necessarily precedes the innovations themselves, so one can't expect individuals to respond to new policies unless they are predisposed to do so. But once this predisposition exists, it is no longer practical to think of imposing changes from above. The only conception of implementation that makes sense under these conditions is one that emphasizes consensus building and accommodation between policy makers and implementors. Mutual adaptation exists not because it is a pleasing or democratic thing to do, but because it is the only way to ensure that implementors have a direct personal stake in the performance of their jobs. This is what the advocates of organizational development mean when they say that more democratic organizations are also the more efficient ones.

The organizational development model focuses on those aspects of an organization's internal structure that enhance or inhibit the commitment of implementors. The chief determinants of success are the sort of microvariables identified by the Rand analysts: material development by implementors, strong interpersonal and professional ties among implementors, nonmanipulative support by high-level administrators, and explicit reliance on incentives that elicit individual commitment from implementors rather than those designed to enforce external conformity. To the extent that the implementation process actually becomes these things, it is neither accurate nor useful to think in terms of a single declaration of policy that is translated into subordinate behavior. Policy does not exist in any concrete sense until implementors have shaped it and claimed it for their own; the result is a consensus reflecting the initial intent of policy makers and the independent judgment of implementors.

The organizational development model also forces us to recognize the narrow limits of one organization's capacity to change the behavior of another. When an agency at one level of government attempts to implement policy through an agency at another level, the implicit assumption is that the former controls factors that are important in determining the performance of the latter. The organizational development model suggests that those factors that have the greatest influence on the success or failure of implementation are precisely the ones over which external agencies have the least control. The maximum that one level of government can do to affect the implementation process is to provide general support that enhances the internal capacity of organizations at another level to respond to the necessity for change, independent of the requirements of specific policies. So to the extent that the implementation process actually took the shape of the model, the federal government, for example, would invest most of

its resources not in enforcing compliance with existing policies, but in assisting
state and local agencies to develop an independent capacity to elicit innovative
behavior from implementors.

The most powerful criticism of the organizational development model comes,
surprisingly, from its strongest supporters. The bias of the model toward consensus, cooperation, and strong interpersonal ties leads us to ignore or downplay
the role of conflict in organizations. The model, one of its advocates argues,
"seems most appropriate under conditions of trust, truth, love, and collaboration.
But what about conditions of war, conflict, dissent, and violence?" "The fundamental deficiency in models of change associated with organization development," he concludes, is that they "systematically avoid the problem of power,
or the *politics* of change"[42] The same criticism may be leveled, to one degree
or another, against each of the three models discussed thus far, because none
directly confronts the issue of what happens in organizations when control,
routine, and consensus fail. A wide range of implementation problems can be
understood only as problems of conflict and bargaining.

MODEL IV: IMPLEMENTATION AS CONFLICT AND BARGAINING

Propositions

1. Organizations are arenas of conflict in which individuals and subunits
with specific interests compete for relative advantage in the exercise of power
and the allocation of scarce resources.

2. The distribution of power in organizations is never stable. It depends
exclusively on the temporary ability of one individual or unit to mobilize sufficient resources to manipulate the behavior of others. Formal position in the
hierarchy of an organization is only one of a multitude of factors that determine
the distribution of power. Other factors include specialized knowledge, control
of material resources, and the ability to mobilize external political support.
Hence, the exercise of power in organizations is only weakly related to their formal structure.

3. Decision making in organizations consists of bargaining within and among
organizational units. Bargained decisions are the result of convergence among actors with different preferences and resources. Bargaining does not require that
parties agree on a common set of goals, nor does it even require that all parties
concur in the outcome of the bargaining process. It only requires that they agree
to adjust their behavior mutually in the interest of preserving the bargaining relationship as a means of allocating resources.

4. Implementation consists of a complex series of bargained decisions reflecting the preferences and resources of participants. Success or failure of implementation cannot be judged by comparing a result against a single declaration of
intent because no single set of purposes can provide an internally consistent state-

ment of the interests of all parties to the bargaining process. Success can only be defined relative to the goals of one party to the bargaining process or in terms of the preservation of the bargaining process itself.

Social programs fail, it is frequently argued, because no single unit of government is sufficiently powerful to force others to conform to a single conception of policy. With each agency pursuing its own interest, implementation does not progress from a single declaration of intent to a result, but is instead characterized by constant conflict over purposes and results and by the pursuit of relative advantage through the use of bargaining. This diversity of purpose leads some participants to characterize programs as "failures" and some to characterize them as "successes," based solely on their position in the bargaining process. Conflict and bargaining occur both within and among implementing agencies. Single organizations can be thought of as semipermanent bargaining coalitions, and the process of moving a declaration of policy across levels of government can be understood as bargaining among separate organizations.

Bargaining can be explicit or tacit. We tend to associate the notion of bargaining only with direct confrontations between well-defined adversaries—labor negotiations, arms limitation talks, and peace negotiations, for example. But many forms of bargaining, especially those in implementation, occur without direct communication and with an imperfect understanding by each party of the others' motives and resources.[43] Seen in this light, implementation becomes essentially a series of strategic moves by a number of individual units of government, each seeking to shape the behavior of others to its own ends.

The key to understanding bargaining behavior is recognizing that conflict implies dependency. Even the strongest adversaries must take account of their opponents' moves when they formulate a bargaining strategy. "The ability of one participant to gain his ends," Schelling observes, "is dependent to an important degree on the choices or decisions that the other participant will make." Furthermore, "there is a powerful common interest in reaching an outcome that is not enormously destructive of values to both sides."[44] In implementation, as in all important bargaining problems, parties with strongly divergent interests are locked together by the simple fact that they must preserve the bargaining arena in order to gain something of value. Failure to bargain means exclusion from the process by which resources are allocated. But the mutual advantage that accrues to participants in bargaining has little or nothing to do with their ability to agree explicitly on the goals they're pursuing or their means for pursuing them. Mutual advantage results only from the fact that by agreeing to bargain they have preserved their access to something of value to each of them.

Lindblom uses the general term "partisan mutual adjustment" to characterize the variety of ways in which individuals with divergent interests coordinate their actions. The common element in all forms of bargaining behavior, he argues, is that "people can coordinate with each other without someone's coordinating them, without a dominant purpose, and without rules that fully prescribe their

relations to each other."[45] This point is essential for understanding the usefulness of the conflict-and-bargaining model in the analysis of social program implementation. The model permits us to make conceptual sense of the implementation process without assuming the existence of hierarchical control, without
asserting that everyone's behavior is governed by a predictable set of bureaucratic routines, and without assuming that concerted action can proceed only
from consensus and commitment to a common set of purposes. In short, the
model provides a distinct alternative to the limiting assumptions of the previous
three. Implementation can, and indeed does, proceed in the absence of a mechanism of coordination external to the actors themselves, such as hierarchical control,
routine, or group consensus.

   Bargained decisions proceed by convergence, adjustment, and closure among
individuals pursuing essentially independent ends. Allison makes this point when
he says that "the decisions and actions of governments are . . . political resultants
. . . in the sense that what happens is not chosen as a solution to a problem but
rather results from compromise, conflict, and confusion of officials with diverse
interests and unequal influence."[46] The term *resultant,* appropriated from
physics, emphasizes the idea that decisions are the product of two or more con-
verging forces. The mechanism of convergence depends on what Schelling calls
"interdependence of expectations." Parties to the bargaining process must predi-
cate their actions not only on predictions of how others will respond but also on
the understanding that others are doing likewise. So bargaining depends as much
on shared expectations as it does on concrete actions.

> The outcome is determined by the expectations that each player forms
> of how the other will play, where each of them knows that their ex-
> pectations are substantially reciprocal. The players must jointly dis-
> cover and mutually acquiesce in an outcome or a mode of play that
> makes the outcome determinate. They must together find "rules of
> the game" or together suffer the consequences.[47]

   In concrete terms, this means that much of the behavior we observe in the
implementation process is designed to shape the expectations of other actors.
An agency might, for example, put a great deal of effort into developing an
elaborate collection of rules and regulations or an elegant system of management
controls, knowing full well that it doesn't have the resources to make them binding on other actors. But the *expectation* that the rules *might* be enforced is sufficient to influence the behavior of other actors. The important fact is not whether the rules are enforced or not, but the effect of their existence on the outcome
of the bargaining process.

   The outcomes of bargaining are seldom "optimal" in any objective sense.
More often than not, they are simply convenient temporary points of closure.

Asking "what it is that can bring . . . expectations into covergence and bring . . .
negotiations to a close," Schelling answers that "it is the intrinsic magnetism of
particular outcomes, especially those that enjoy prominence, uniqueness, simplicity, precedent, or some rationale that makes them qualitatively differen-
tiable" from other alternatives.[48] In other words, the result of bargaining is
often not the best nor even the second or third best alternative for any party;
all parties can, and frequently do, leave the bargaining process dissatisfied with
the result. As long as an opportunity to resume bargaining remains, there is seldom a single determinant result; all resolutions are temporary. So one should
not expect the mechanisms of bargaining to lead teleologically from a single
purpose to a result.

The real structure of organizations, then, is to be found in their bargaining
processes rather than in their formal hierarchy or operating routines. Notions of
top and bottom have very little meaning. Formal position is a source of power,
but only one of many, and it does not necessarily carry with it the ability to
manipulate the behavior of subordinates. Many other sources of power—mastery
of specialized knowledge, discretionary control over resources, a strong external
constituency, and so on—can be used to enhance the bargaining position of subordinates relative to superiors, and vice versa. No simple rules can be set forth
for determining the distribution of power in organizations. Stability, if it exists
at all, is the short-term product of bargaining on specific decisions.

This view leads to a conception of implementation considerably different
from any of the other models. One understands the process by focusing on conflict among actors, the resources they bring to the bargaining process, and the
mechanisms by which they adjust to each others' moves. Most important, the
distinguishing feature of the conflict-and-bargaining model is that *it doesn't rest
on any assumptions about commonality of purpose.* In each of the previous
models, it was possible to say that successful implementation was in some sense
dependent on a common conception of policy shared by all participants in the
process. In the systems management model, agreement was the product of management control; in the bureaucratic process model, it resulted from incorporation of a new policy into an organization's operating routines; and in the organizational development model, it resulted from consensus among policy makers
and implementors. But in the conflict-and-bargaining model, the outcomes of
implementation are temporary bargained solutions—resultants—that reflect no
overall agreement on purposes.

Success or failure of implementation is therefore largely a relative notion,
determined by one's position in the process. Actors who are capable of asserting
their purposes over others, however temporarily, will argue that the process is
"successful." Those with a disadvantage in the bargaining process will argue that
the process is "unsuccessful." It is entirely possible for the process to proceed
even when all actors regard it as unsuccessful because the costs of refusing to

bargain may exceed the costs of remaining in a disadvantageous bargaining relationship. Under these circumstances, the only objective measure of success or failure is the preservation of the bargaining process itself. So long as all parties agree to bargain and mutual benefit is to be gained from bargaining, preservation of the bargaining arena constitutes success. Regardless of the level of conflict in social programs, all actors have an interest in maintaining the programs as long as they deliver benefits that are not otherwise accessible.

The empirical evidence on conflict and bargaining in social program implementation is abundant. The implementation of federal educational programs provides some of the best examples because the process occurs in a system whereby power is radically dispersed across all levels of government.

The extremely diffuse and fluid nature of organizational relationships in the field of education has led Karl Weick to characterize educational organizations as "loosely coupled systems."[49] Although conflict and bargaining do not figure prominently in Weick's model, the characteristics of loosely coupled systems that he identified lead to the same conclusions as the conflict-and-bargaining model. The lack of structure and determinancy, the absence of teleologically linked events, the dispersion of resources and responsibilities, and the relative absence of binding regulation all add up to the kind of system in which concerned action is possible only through tacit or explicit bargaining among relatively independent actors.

NOTES

1. This account of the systems management model is drawn from the following sources: Daniel Katz and Robert Kahn, *The Social Psychology of Organizations* (New York: Wiley, 1966). William Baumol, *Economic Theories and Operations Analysis,* 3rd ed. (Englewood Cliffs, N.J.: Prentice-Hall, 1972). Robert Anthony, *Planning and Control Systems: A Framework of Analysis* (Boston: Harvard Graduate School of Business Administration, 1965). C. West Churchman, *The Systems Approach* (New York: Delta, 1968). Charles Hitch and Roland McKean, *The Economics of Defense in a Nuclear Age* (Cambridge, Mass.: Harvard University Press, 1963).
2. Katz and Kahn, *The Social Psychology of Organizations,* p. 79.
3. Ibid., p. 203. Cf. Churchman, *The Systems Approach,* p. 44.
4. Anthony, *Planning and Control Systems,* pp. 16-18.
5. Hitch and McKean, *The Economics of Defense in a Nuclear Age,* pp. 128-129, 396-402. Their choice of the term *suboptimization* is perhaps unfortunate because to most of us it communicates the meaning "less than optimal," which is quite opposite from the meaning they wish to convey. It is clear from their discussion that they intend the term to mean "optimizing at lower levels." Some writers, however, insist on using the term to mean

less than optimal. See, e.g., Anthony, *Planning and Control Systems,* p. 35. Two other sources in which the term is used consistently with the meaning of Hitch and McKean are, Baumol, *Economic Theories and Operations Analysis,* p. 395n, and Richard Zeckhauser and Elmer Schaefer, Public policy and normative economic theory, in Raymond Bauer and Kenneth Gergen (eds.), *The Study of Policy Formation* (New York: Free Press, 1968), pp. 73-76. A more recent treatment of suboptimization in policy analysis may be found in E. S. Quade, *Analysis for Public Decisions* (New York: Elsevier, 1975), pp. 95-98.

6. Hitch and McKean, *The Economics of Defense in a Nuclear Age,* p. 129.
7. Nor is it necessary to assume, as Graham Allison does, that a "rational" model of decision making is one that treats all decisions as if they were the product of a single decision maker (Allison, *Essence of Decision,* pp. 3, 28, 36). Most theories of rational choice encourage this view by using stock phrases like "the decision maker's problem," "the decision makers's preference," etc. In organizational terms, though, the important issue is not whether the peculiar fiction of the single, value-maximizing decision maker can be maintained, but whether it is possible to construct a set of organizational controls sufficient to integrate subunits of an organization into a functional whole. This is a point of difference between Allison's discussion and mine. In his rational actor model (*Essence of Decision,* pp. 10-38), he treats all decisions as the product of a single decision maker, and this makes it very easy to criticize the model. My intention is to demonstrate that a substantial body of theory treats organizations as rational, value-maximizing units but does not depend on the fiction of the single decision maker.
8. Herbert Kaufman, *The Forest Ranger: A Study of Administrative Behavior* (Baltimore: Johns Hopkins University Press, 1960), p. 91.
9. Anthony, *Planning and Control Systems,* p. 45.
10. Katz and Kahn, *The Social Psychology of Organizations,* P. 40.
11. Ibid., p. 40.
12. Walter Williams, Implementation analysis and assessment, in Williams and Elmore (eds.), *Social Program Implementation,* pp. 281-282.
13. Kaufman, *The Forest Ranger,* p. 203.
14. Ibid., p. 228.
15. Jeremiah O'Connell, *Managing Organizational Innovation* (Homewood, Ill.: Irwin, 1968), p. 10.
16. Ibid., pp. 72 and 74.
17. Ibid., p. 13.
18. Herbert Kaufman, *Administrative Feedback: Monitoring Subordinate's Behavior* (Washington, D.C.: The Brookings Institution, 1973), p. 17.
19. Ibid., p. 68.
20. James Q. Wilson, The bureaucracy problem, in *The Public Interest* 6 (Winter 1967), pp. 3-9.

21. Michel Crozier, *The Bureaucratic Phenomenon* (Chicago: University of Chicago Press, 1964).
22. James Q. Wilson, *Varieties of Police Behavior* (New York: Atheneum, 1973), p. 1.
23. Allison, *Essence of Decision*, p. 80.
24. Wilson, *Varieties of Police Behavior*, pp. 2-3.
25. Ibid., p. 9; see also pp. 64ff.
26. Donald Schon, *Beyond the Stable State* (New York: Random House, 1971), p. 32.
27. Michael Lipsky, Toward a theory of street-level bureaucracy, in Willis Hawley and Michael Lipsky (eds.), *Theoretical Perspectives on Urban Politics* (Englewood Cliffs, N.J.: Prentice-Hall, 1976), p. 197.
28. Wilson, *Varieties of Police Behavior*, p. 7.
29. Lipsky, Toward a theory of street-level bureaucracy, pp. 197-198.
30. Ibid., pp. 201ff.
31. Richard Weatherly, Toward a Theory of Client Control in Street-Level Bureaucracy. Unpublished paper, School of Social Work, University of Washington, 1976, p. 5.
32. Miriam Johnson, *Counter Point: The Changing Employment Service* (Salt Lake City, Utah: Olympus, 1973).
33. Walter Williams, Implementation problems in federally funded programs, in Williams and Elmore (eds.), *Social Program Implementation*, pp. 20-23.
34. Weatherly and Lipsky, Street-level bureaucrats and institutional innovations, p. 196.
35. See, e.g., Katz and Kahn, *The Social Psychology of Organizations*, pp. 211ff.
36. Chris Argyris, *Personality and Organization: The Conflict Between System and Individual* (New York: Harper, 1957), pp. 53ff.
37. Chris Argyris, *The Applicability of Organizational Sociology* (London: Cambridge University Press, 1972), passim.
38. Warren Bennis, *Organization Development: Its Nature, Origins, and Prospects* (Reading, Mass.: Addison-Wesley, 1969), p. 28.
39. Ibid., p. 2 (quoting Douglas McGregor, *The Professional Manager* (New York: McGraw-Hill, 1967)).
40. Chris Argyris, *Interpersonal Competence and Organizational Effectiveness* (Homewood, Ill.: Irwin, 1962), p. 42.
41. Chris Argyris, *Integrating the Individual and the Organization* (New York: Wiley, 1964), p. 138.
42. Bennis, *Organization Development*, p. 77; emphasis in original.
43. An elegant account of tacit bargaining and coordination is given in Thomas Schelling, *The Strategy of Conflict* (London and New York: Oxford University Press, 1963), pp. 53ff.
44. Ibid., pp. 5-6.

45. Charles Lindblom, *The Intelligence of Democracy: Decision Making Through Mutual Adjustment* (New York: Free Press, 1965), p. 3. In the interest of economy of expression, I have taken some liberties with Lindblom's terminology. Lindblom actually develops no fewer than 12 distinguishable types of partisan mutual adjustment, based on different assumptions about the ability of parties to determine the effect of their actions on others, the level of communication among parties, their ability to use conditional threats, and their ability to elicit behavior using unilateral action (pp. 33-84). I have equated bargaining with partisan mutual adjustment, where in Lindblom's scheme bargaining is one particular type of partisan mutual adjustment involving the use of conditional threats and promises (pp. 71ff).
46. Allison, *Essence of Decision,* p. 162.
47. Schelling, *The Strategy of Conflict,* pp. 106-107.
48. Ibid., p. 70; Lindblom, *The Intelligence of Democracy,* pp. 205-225.
49. Karl Weick, Educational organizations as loosely coupled systems, in *Administrative Science Quarterly* 21 (1976), pp. 1-18.

III

SOME TECHNICAL CONTEXTS: Toward More Effective Control via Analysis

This chapter focuses on tools of analysis, but we trust it does so with a moderate perspective. Basically, we join with James R. Schlesinger who—along with the McNamara "whiz kids"—introduced much sophisticated analysis to government. Despite his technical interests, he stated that "analysis is not a scientific procedure for reaching decisions which avoid intuitive elements, but rather a mechanism for sharpening the intuitions of the decisionmaker" (1).

The distinctions between analysis and intuition often have been pushed too far. Indeed, an analysis/intuition dichotomy has all but dominated the decision-making and budgeting arenas since the mid-1950s and continues to be potent. Here we seek to avoid resurrecting that dichotomy even as we focus on several of the powerful constraints that limit many of the analytic tools used today.

ANALYSIS vs. INTUITION

Many observers might take exception to Schlesinger's notion that analysis only helps "sharpen" intuition, so let us dwell on the theme of that duality for the moment. The literature of public administration is replete with instances when analysis failed. Often such failure is linked to deficiencies in the underlying model of analytic procedures: the rational-comprehensive (R-C) model of decision-making. Essentially, goes the argument, the R-C model does not take into consideration the unanticipated consequences that result when the model relates to human decision processes. The very comprehensiveness of the R-C model is often judged to be its fatal presumption, i.e., by assuming that a method or procedure (which rests on the R-C model) has encompassed all relevant variables, one has made a serious value judgment. Critics allege that the claim of comprehensiveness is unsupportable because analysis often neglects major human variables: logrolling, politics, error, misunderstanding, self-interest, and so on.

Is this criticism of analysis by public administrationists fair? Have we and Charles Lindblom (2) created straw men? Have the protagonists of analysis ignored human variables? As we shall see in the following two chapters on the technical contexts of budgeting and finance, the human factor has not been omitted. However, it will be up to the reader to determine whether the authors truly understand that their methods of analysis seriously may be limited. No doubt that judgment will vary from case to case.

Given what we have just considered, is public administration still saddled

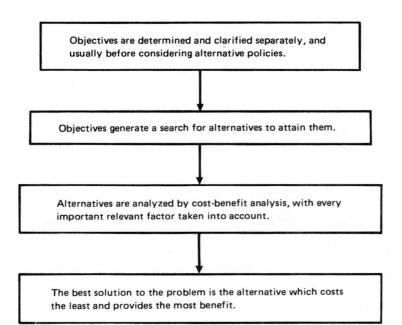

Figure 1 Rational-comprehensive model of decision making. (From J. Rabin, State and Local PPBS, in *Public Budgeting and Finance,* R. T. Golembiewski and J. Rabin, eds., 2nd ed. Itasca, Illinois: Peacock, 1975, p. 432. Modified from Ref. 2.)

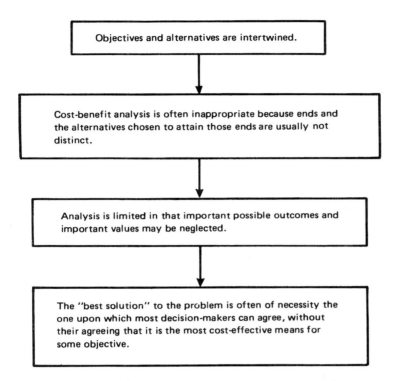

Figure 2   Incremental model of decision making.   (From J. Rabin, State and Local PPBS, in *Public Budgeting and Finance,* R. T. Golembiewski and J. Rabin, eds., 2nd ed.   Itasca, Illinois: Peacock, 1975, p. 434.   Modified from Ref. 2.)

with an analysis-intuition dichotomy?   Is there a way out?   Let us review graphically the R-C model; its antagonist, the incremental (successive limited approximations) model; and a variant which may be one way of merging the R-C approach with the incremental.   That variant intermingles analysis with intuition.

Figure 1 presents the familiar step-by-step approach to decision making and budgeting assumed by the R-C model.   The definition and clarification of objectives or goals is the first step in the process, which includes comparisons of appropriate alternatives and a choice between them on the basis of calculations of relative costs and benefits.   Some observers might wish to add a prior step: They argue that the "definition of the problem or situation" is a more appropriate first step, on which the development of objectives or goals can rest.

The incremental model of decision making, as pictured in Figure 2, sees objectives and the range of means to obtain them as intertwined.   The point is

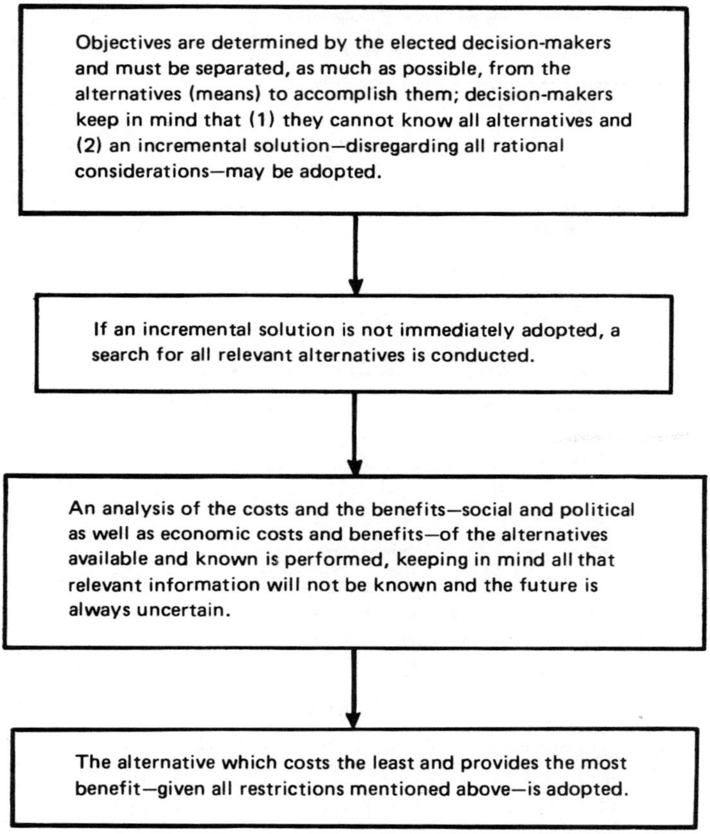

Objectives are determined by the elected decision-makers and must be separated, as much as possible, from the alternatives (means) to accomplish them; decision-makers keep in mind that (1) they cannot know all alternatives and (2) an incremental solution—disregarding all rational considerations—may be adopted.

If an incremental solution is not immediately adopted, a search for all relevant alternatives is conducted.

An analysis of the costs and the benefits—social and political as well as economic costs and benefits—of the alternatives available and known is performed, keeping in mind all that relevant information will not be known and the future is always uncertain.

The alternative which costs the least and provides the most benefit—given all restrictions mentioned above—is adopted.

Figure 3 Modified rational model of decision making. (From J. Rabin, State and Local PPBS, in *Public Budgeting and Finance,* R. T. Golembiewski and J. Rabin, eds., 2nd ed. Itasca, Illinois: Peacock, 1975, p. 435.

critical because it denies the practicality of the first step in the R-C model—determining and clarifying objectives in isolation from the ways and means of approaching those objectives.

A third model—a modified rational model—may help to resolve the conflict in approaches between the R-C and incremental models. The modified rational model (Figure 3) attempts to define objectives, but this attempt takes into account the needs-means problem and also incorporates an easy way of choosing an incremental solution to the problem of defining objectives. The simplifying assumptions should be relatively clear. For example, the search to be conducted in the modified rational model is for "relevant" alternatives; moreover, the model presumes that the costs and benefits of alternatives may be both unquantifiable or simply unknown.

MANAGERIAL CONTROL VIA ANALYSIS

Many of the analytic tools used by managers have at least two elements in common. They are based on the R-C model of decision making. Moreover, they seek to enhance control over the setting which confronts the manager. We consider each of the two common elements in turn.

R-C Model Foundation

Analytic procedures used by managers include tools to (1) identify responsibility and hold people accountable, as by accounting and auditing principles or practices, (2) effect common ways of producing the organization's products, as via standards, productivity measurement, or program evaluation, and (3) do organizational planning, as via program-evaluation-review-technique (PERT), the critical path method, or revenue and expenditure forecasting. All these tools rely in some way on the R-C model for their theoretical foundation, and the several chapters to come will provide substantial detail about them.

Effecting Control

Analytic tools may effect control in two basic ways. The direct purpose of any analytic tool is embodied in its objectives that seek to control explicit variables in the organization's environment. This central point gets multiple emphasis in a publication of the American Accounting Association reprinted as Chapter 10, "Concepts of Accounting Applicable to the Public Sector."

Analytic tools also can have indirect but still potent effects. Consider an objective which a manager cannot accomplish directly or overtly. For example, when faced with subordinates who are protected by civil service regulations, a manager in the public service can find that his power of command is negligible. One means for securing some compliance by subordinates is through the use of an analytic tool which, on its face, seems neutral. For instance, very few can argue with the goals of productivity measurement. Why not have a more productive organization? Tools exist which propose to measure productivity, and the use of productivity measures may help the manager circumvent that barrier between self and subordinates created by civil service regulations.

ANALYTIC TOOLS: FOR RESPONSIBILITY AND ACCOUNTABILITY

Many tools help effect responsibility and accountability in organizations. We shall concentrate on aspects of two such vehicles: accounting and auditing.

Accounting

The American Accounting Association (AAA) points out that the public sector's definition of "cost" is not the same as that of business. That point is clear in the next chapter, "Concepts of Accounting Applicable to the Public Sector." In fact, governmental costs and benefits often relate to the special nature of the public sector. For instance, as the authors of the AAA statement note in dealing with the subjects of accomplishment, benefits, and effectiveness:

> To justify its existence, every organization must accomplish something. It must have output in the form of tangible goods or intangible services. If the output is in the form of intangible services, as is true with most entities in the public sector, the output is often difficult, if not impossible, to identify.
>
> Even more difficult than the identification of output, however, is the search for answers to questions such as: Why does the organization do what it does? Are there alternative ways of accomplishing the same results? Were the activities performed effectively and efficiently?
>
> The problem of identifying and measuring accomplishment is compounded, however, when output is both intangible and not market oriented. Examples are public education and the protection of life and property. This situation exists with much of the output of the public sector.

At least, the AAA statement should encourage pause on the part of those who would take analytic tools directly from the private sector and apply them to the public sector. Are organizations in the two sectors similar enough that such techniques or tools can be installed adequately and used effectively? Too often, nothing of the sort is even attempted, so that "success" of a technique in the private sector is seen as a "guarantee" of similar, positive results in the public sector.

Auditing

Auditing also is a traditional way of obtaining control and accountability, i.e., by "requiring public officials to report the disposition and use of public resources." More specifically, auditing is

> an analytical *process* consisting of preparation, conduct (examination and evaluation), reporting (communication), and settlement. The basic elements of this process are: an independent, competent, and professional auditor who executes the process upon an auditee for an audit recipient. The *scope* or area of concern can involve matters of the following nature: financial (accounting error, fraud, financial controls,

fairness of financial statements, etc.), and/or compliance (faithful adherence to administrative and legal requirements, policies, regulations,
etc.), and/or performance (economy, efficiency, and/or effectiveness
of operational controls, management information systems, programs,
etc.). . . .

Kenneth S. Caldwell provides diverse evidence about the direct and indirect
impacts of auditing in the chapter, "Operational Auditing in State and Local
Government." For all its positive results, to suggest its direct limitations, auditing is primarily a post hoc process coming after decisions have been made and
money expended. Thus, auditing has real direct limits even for public organizations with yearly audits. But it can have profound indirect effects as it induces
self-fulfilling prophecies, because it encourages self-discipline at one time by
those concerned about what a later audit might show.

ANALYTIC TOOLS: THREE COMMON WAYS OF
FOCUSING ON THE ORGANIZATION'S PRODUCT

Looked at from another important perspective, analytic tools provide orientations for focusing on what organizations are constituted to do, i.e., to make a
product or deliver a service. Three chapters in this part illustrate how analytic
tools relate to an organization's complex production processes. In turn, attention will emphasize (1) a system for obtaining data and disseminating information, (2) standards of measurement, such as benefit-and-cost analysis, and (3)
analyses of output, such as productivity or effectiveness/efficiency measurement.

Information Systems

Assuming that "current information resources, if utilized properly, can greatly
enhance both program effectiveness and program management," Robert G.
Stanley describes the use of management information systems (MIS) in the U.S.
Department of Transportation. Of special import in Stanley's contribution—entitled "Data-Based Management: Initial Efforts to Develop DBM Capabilities in
a Federal Program"—is a description of how the "gee-whiz" syndrome was avoided in the implementation of the MIS. This problem exists when the hardware
and its potential applications overwhelm the people who will be using the system. Stanley and his group opted for a cautious approach, reflected on reporting
needs, and attempted to answer several questions concerning MIS:

1. Why an MIS? What objectives need to be served? What audiences need
   to be served?

2. What do we already do to meet those objectives? Serve those audiences?
   What are our current activities and information resources?

3. What existing systems are available to facilitate MIS development and operation? How can they be refined and upgraded to serve program management needs?

4. What should be the specific scope and scale of the system? What will be the contents in terms of inputs? What will be the products in terms of outputs?

5. What will be the key implementation and operational aspects of an MIS once basic design parameters are defined?

Keeping these key questions in mind helps avoid the gee-whiz and other traps, Stanley advises.

Benefits and Costs

One way of quantifying variables used in an MIS concentrates on benefits and costs. John Pennington and Heber Bouland's "Evaluating Benefits and Costs of Auto Safety Standards" describes the problems involved in placing dollar values on the benefits of an auto safety program, and then comparing benefits to costs. Such efforts provide useful perspective on a central question: Was it worthwhile?

The authors indicate the tradeoffs required to obtain benefit and cost data, as well as detail some of the exotica which the hunt for quantifiable data can entail. It is left to the reader to determine, in specific cases beyond the present scope,

- How often are problems affecting government susceptible to quantification?

- Can one "meaningfully quantify" benefit and cost information, or are we stretching the data to fit our wishes or requirements?

Output Analysis: Productivity Measurement

Brian L. Usilaner's "Productivity Measurement: A Management Tool" presents some important caveats with regard to output analysis and productivity. Unlike many output measures, "productivity examines trends and the reasons for changes in these trends. . . ." Thus, attention should be focused on the line manager, who must decide how to use productivity information.

Productivity measurement may help the manager sharpen operational goals, but many productivity objectives are not quantifiable. What then? Usilaner provides us with a useful way out:

> Since both in the short and long run the potential for improvements in productivity of an organization varies, both among units of the organization and from year to year, the actual percentage change in produc-

tivity of an organization should not be viewed as a direct indicator of the quality either of its management or of its labor force. Such an evaluation requires additional information and judgment regarding the difference between potential and actual change in productivity and an estimate of the contribution made to increase the potential.

This is refreshing. Analysis carries one a useful distance, Usilaner proposes. But one should not be "carried away" by too much of an otherwise good thing.

ANALYTIC TOOLS: FOR PROJECTING VARIABLES USED IN ORGANIZATIONAL PLANNING

There are very few variables about which we can be certain when we make decisions that require projecting plans and budgets into the future. By "certain" we imply a high probability that the circumstances will develop in the future as they are projected today. For instance, we try to project with some certainty what degree of military deterrence we will need 5 and 10 years from now. We hope that we will be close because the margin for error may be very small and the costs of miscalculation are measured in gruesome terms.

In a similar way, governments attempt to project what their future revenues and expenditures will be over a set period of time. In planning a project which contains numerous tasks, many of which can be performed concurrently, it would be useful to construct a "flow chart" of those tasks, their interrelationships, as well as the ponts where trouble may occur with special impact on the project.

Such pursuits are based on our attempt to obtain some degree of certainty, to determine the probability of events occurring within a vast area of uncertainty. We will concentrate on only two efforts for reducing the region of uncertainty: forecasting revenue and expenditure data; and constructing flow charts of complex events (critical paths).

Revenue and Expenditure Forecasting

The environment of uncertainty in which government exists makes some projection of revenues and expenses mandatory and problemmatic. Often, these forecasts are made in the executive branch and then become the subject of debate within the legislature. Often, even the best estimates will not be accepted and may become political issues resolved with variable regard to what knowledge exists about the relevant matter.

Nevertheless, an administrator can attempt to reduce uncertainty by resorting to very elementary forecasting techniques. For instance, one of the most common methods is extrapolation, i.e., continuing a curve on a chart from its last established points toward future states which, hopefully, the extrapolation

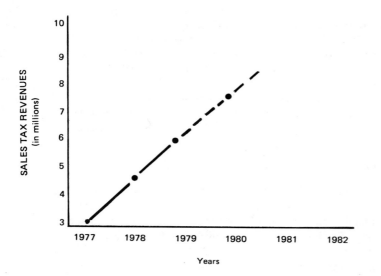

Figure 4 Extrapolation method in forecasting. A simplistic example in which sales tax revenues have been increasing by $1.5 million/year. Extrapolating from 1979, and given such a curve, we project that revenues will be $7.5 million in 1980.

will help anticipate. Figure 4 illustrates this method. Of course, the simplicity of the technique is also one of its major drawbacks.

Figure 4 presents an easy piece, as it were; and reality seldom can be described in linear terms with any great confidence. Perspective on this more complex and often wicked organizational reality gets provided by Albert C. Hyde and William L. Jarocki in "Revenue and Expenditure Forecasting: Some Comparative Trends." They discuss the importance of forecasting, sketch the forecasting environment, and also illustrate some of the technology, theory, and methods. They also emphasize the *limits* of forecasting, especially the politics of forecasting, in which "the perspectives of participants may often manipulate forecast results."

Critical Path Method

Critical path method (CPM) employs massive flow charts to network the relationships of important variables, with emphasis on the time required to complete tasks. Essentially, CPM calculates the "longest route through the . . . network in terms of calendar time" and the concurrent "minimum time for completing" all the tasks. These calculations help determine the "critical path" within the flow chart or network.

Rising above details for present purposes, the calculation of the critical path can be variously useful. According to John C. Karmendy and Thomas Monohan in "The Critical Path Method Applied to GAO Reviews," such calculations can help

1. Focus on time-critical tasks throughout the assignment

2. Identify tasks that can be performed concurrently

3. Quickly assess the impact of tasks added to the assignment, and

4. Establish more realistic incremental time goals and completion dates

Basically, CPM is another way to cope with uncertainty, not some be-all and end-all. Specifically, one must be sensitive as to whether meaningful probability statements can be made about the occurrence of events at specified times within the CPM network. The less certain the probability of the occurrence of events, the less useful the CPM scheme.

REFERENCES

1. Schlesinger, James R. Use and abuses of analysis. In Robert T. Golembiewski and Jack Rabin (eds.), *Public Budgeting and Finance,* Second Ed. Itasca, Ill., Peacock, 1975, p. 499.
2. Lindblom, Charles E. The science of muddling through. *Public Administration Review,* Spring 1959, *19,* 79-88.

10

CONCEPTS OF ACCOUNTING APPLICABLE TO THE PUBLIC SECTOR*

American Accounting Association Committee on Concepts of Accounting
Applicable to the Public Sector, 1970-71

Since the earliest formulation of accounting theory, an attempt has been made
to articulate the concepts of effort and accomplishment in order to provide the
proper matching or comparison of data for performance evaluation. In the commercial world, accountants have largely focused their attention on the matching
of revenues and expenses. In the public sector, however, the nature of operations
and the concepts of revenues and expenses are not relevant to this type of matching, except in those instances where public enterprises (such as municipal utility
companies) bill customers for their services and operate on a profit-seeking or
break-even basis. It is important, then, for this study to examine the relationship
of effort and accomplishment as measured in typical government programs.

   Effort, as used in this study, is defined as *the cost* of operations, and *accom-*

   *In Supplement to Volume XLVII of the *Accounting Review,* published by the American Accounting Association (1972), appears the report of the Association's Committee on
Concepts of Accounting Applicable to the Public Sector. Part III of the report discusses the
concepts of accounting for the cost and accomplishment of public programs and is thus of
special interest to GAO staff members.
   Reprinted from *GAO Review,* vol. 12 (Fall 1977), pp. 59-70. References have been
renumbered.

plishment is defined as *the resulting benefit* from operations. The term *operations* is used broadly here to refer to programs, activities, and all other actions undertaken by a governmental entity. In short, cost is what is given up; accomplishment is what results.

CONCEPTS OF COST

The starting point in distinguishing cost concepts related to the measurement of effort in government programs is to clearly distinguish the cost of acquiring an asset from the cost of using that asset in a program. The first concept is called *acquisition cost,* and it usually is composed of the purchase price of the good or service plus related expenses associated with the acquisition. The second concept is known as *applied cost;* it represents that portion of acquisition cost that is assigned to a particular program, project, or time period.

One of the most basic concepts of traditional accounting is that of asset acquisition cost. Under this concept, assets are recorded on the records at cost; and these amounts remain unchanged until they are written off to operations over appropriate periods of time.

Replacement cost is the amount that would now have to be sacrificed to acquire the equivalent asset; and in many decisions of choice, this concept is more relevant to managerial decisions than the recorded historical cost.

Another important distinction among cost concepts is that of *program cost* contrasted with *total cost to the government* and *social cost. Program costs* are the sum of the assigned historical costs that are applied during a particular period of operations. Thus, program costs include both direct and indirect costs associated with the particular program. *Total cost to the government* includes all program costs plus administrative overhead for general government. *Social cost* is the total sacrifice made by the public to support government programs.

Social cost may be measured as the *opportunity cost* to the public of paying taxes, using resources, and conducting the program in question. Included here, in addition to economic factors, are such items as pollution to the environment, increase in fear and apprehension, and loss of security and freedom. This concept of cost is highly relevant to planning government programs, and it therefore is equally important for control and performance evaluation. Yet, because of the difficulty of operationalizing the concept, we are seldom able to use it in accounting.

The second concept—*total government cost*—is again a relevant concept if we wish to know how much it costs the government in resources used to carry out a program. However, the problem is one of identifying meaningful concepts of cost association and allocation, so that the assignment of administrative costs becomes something more than an exercise in arbitrary calculations.

The most relevant of these concepts for responsibility center management is that of *program cost.* Here, direct costs associated with a program are calculated on the basis of resources used. Indirect but related costs can be assigned on the basis of positive correlation, as noted below. These costs are meaningful for management control and should be included in the design of the accounting system.

Where it is desirable to have interperiod comparisons of performance, as is usually the case in any organization, it is important to understand the concept of *positive correlation* as it relates to the matching of effort and accomplishment.[1] Very simply, this concept requires that costs, representing efforts, be recognized as expenses in the period when the resulting benefits, representing accomplishments, are realized. Where no cause-and-effect relationship can be established, there is no positive correlation. This concept is very important to accounting in both the public and private sector.

The assignment of cost of programs, organizations, or accounting periods always requires that some basis be established for computing the allocation and making the assignment. If the problem is merely one of assigning cost to periods of time, it is only necessary to determine which period benefited from the incurrence of the cost. If costs are to be distributed to programs, the question to be answered is: Which program benefited from each item of cost incurred?

Thus, the first step is to allocate the benefits to time periods, and this allocation requires an appropriate interpretation of the point in time when the benefit is realized. Efforts, in the form of costs, are then assigned to the periods in which the related benefits are recognized. A cause-and-effect relationship should be established as nearly as possible. Where no such relationship exists, costs should be charged off in the period in which they are incurred unless it can be clearly demonstrated that some decision or control purpose is served by assigning them or computing the allocation otherwise.

When assets are lost, destroyed, or discarded where no benefits result, the government has a *loss.* Such a loss must be distinguished conceptually from an expense, for by definition an *expense* is the use of or giving up of an asset to produce some benefit. To the extent that managers are responsible for the control of assets, losses are relevant for inclusion in management reports. They do not, however, become a part of the computation of effort when comparing effort and accomplishment.

Finally, while most assets are of a nature that requires that they be charged off to operations over their useful life, some are clearly not within this classification. One area along the center of debate on this point is the concept of depreciation. When long-lived assets are conceived to be of the same nature as unexpired costs, the difference being that of length of useful life span, the concept of depreciation can be satisfactorily resolved. For those governmental activities for which it is deemed advisable to evaluate on the principle of matching effort and accomplishment, the assignment of a portion of the cost of capital items to each period or program is justifiable and appropriate. Contrariwise, for those governmental services which are not to be measured and evaluated in terms of effort and accomplishments, depreciation accounting serves little useful purpose. It serves no useful purpose, for example, to depreciate a monument in a park. Unless the assets are related to operating entities and are used in doing the work of the entity, it is doubtful that their expiration has any significance to the measurement of effort and accomplishment in government.

Assets

The reconciling difference between accrued expenditures and accrued cost is the amount recorded as assets having some future service potential. Expenditures may be classified as either current operating expenses (applied cost) or capital asset acquisitions. Similarly, current operating expenses contain items of current expenditure as well as assets written off currently but acquired previously. The recording of assets defers the recognition of cost as an operating expense.

Normally, assets are defined as those resources or rights held by an entity which have future service potential or realizable (sales) value. In considering resources which are of concern to administrators of governmental units, three broad classes of assets may be distinguished:

1. Monetary or financial assets. These assets include cash, investments, and receivables—all being characterized by their liquidity and availability as sources of funds for future expenditures.

2. Assets acquired for resale. These assets consist of inventories which are held for direct and immediate resale or which are to be converted into other products and then marketed.

3. Consumable assets or unexpired costs. These assets include two major subclasses of assets: those expected to be used in the near future, such as supplies, etc., and those long-lived assets that will render useful service over several future periods of operations.

For most governmental units, the second category of assets (those held for resale) is not a very significant item. However, some governmental units do engage in manufacturing and retailing activities. In such cases, these assets need to be distinguished from those that are purchased and held for use or consumption within the governmental unit itself and which will ultimately become an important item of program cost. Similarly, many governmental units have few long-lived tangible assets; but where these are found, they need to be distinguished from the current operating items, such as supplies and prepaid expense.

It can be said that in a large measure administrative units operating in the public sector have been careful to exercise strict accountability for reporting on the acquisition and use of monetary assets in accordance with legal provisions governing the entities or funds. Much less attention has been given by most governments to current consumable assets and the utilization or expiration of such assets.

The prevailing practice in local governments has been to treat expenditures for supplies and services as expenses of the current fiscal period, with little effort being made to reflect residual amounts which will make some contribution to governmental activities in the following period. This practice has prevailed even though any reliable measure of operating efficiency must consider the effect of these assets. Moreover, the existence of a considerable investment in unexpired costs at the end of any fiscal period should be an important factor in decisions relating to budgets and appropriations.

Long-lived or fixed assets are a special category of consumable assets which have utility or value extending over a number of operating periods. For many governmental units, the investment in long-lived assets is substantial. It is imperative, therefore, in accordance with the overall objectives of accounting, that useful, reliable, and generally acceptable principles be adopted for planning, controlling, and reporting on the acquisition, use, and disposition of such resources. However, in a large number of situations, accounting practices and procedures relating to fixed assets are woefully inadequate. Too often, no records of the ownership, utilization, and ultimate disposition of fixed assets are kept beyond the information concerning the original acquisition transaction.

Expenses

In various sections of this chapter, distinctions have been made between expenditures and expenses. It has been noted that expenditures represent cash outlays or the creation of liabilities associated with the acquisition of goods and services. Expenses, on the other hand, have been defined as expired costs. Some of these costs expire simultaneously with the expenditures, and others expire gradually over more than one fiscal period.

One of the principal objectives of accounting is to assign expenses (applied costs) to the periods or programs which receive the resulting benefits. The use of accrual accounting, including the recognition of both deferred and accrued expenses, is necessary to achieve this objective. Such a system is an accrued cost system, however, as contrasted with the accrued expenditure system discussed in Part II. Accrued cost accounting is simply an extension of accrued expenditure accounting, and both types of information should be available from a full accrual accounting system.

ACCOMPLISHMENT, BENEFITS, AND EFFECTIVENESS

To justify its existence, every organization must accomplish something. It must have output in the form of tangible goods or intangible services. If the output is in the form of intangible services, as is true with most entities in the public sector, the output is often difficult, if not impossible, to identify.

Even more difficult than the identification of output, however, is the search for answers to questions such as: Why does the organization do what it does? Are there alternative ways of accomplishing the same results? Were the activities performed effectively and efficiently?

In the private sector, the amount of revenue a firm earns has traditionally been used as a measure of accomplishment. Even when the output of a business firm is in the form of service, a pricing schedule is used and quantities of service are determined that correspond to this schedule. Accomplishment is measured as the result of the quantity of services produced multiplied by the unit price, as determined by the pricing schedules. Likewise, in certain segments of the public sector, although the output is intangible, such as the generation and transmission of electrical energy, sales (quantity sold times price) may also be used as a measure of accomplishment.

The problem of identifying and measuring accomplishment is compounded, however, when output is both intangible and not market-oriented. Examples are public education and the protection of life and property. This situation exists with much of the output of the public sector.

Furthermore, effort (measured by accrued cost) and accomplishment (measured by accrued revenue) are used in the business world to derive a figure called "net income." This figure is important to a number of computations and calculations that are made in evaluating the performance of an enterprise operation. To the extent that government engages in enterprise operations, such a figure is also relevant to performance evaluation, although it is by no means the only relevant measure. In other operations, particularly where the organization or program is service oriented, it is both practically and conceptually impossible to derive a "net" figure in numerical terms. It is conceptually possible to speak of the net public gain or loss or the net public good, but it is conceptually impossible to measure the net difference unless both effort and accomplishment can be reduced to a common scale.

The Relationship of Accomplishment to Objectives

It is impossible to speak of accomplishment without some concept or notion of objectives, and it is therefore important here to look closely at the relationship of objectives to accomplishment.

Objectives in most organizations are hierarchical, and the accomplishment of one objective is often the means for achieving still higher objectives. Since the selection of measures of accomplishment depends on the objectives which are formulated, measures of accomplishment are also hierarchical in nature.

If our objective is to build highways, for example, one measure of accomplishment might be the number of miles of highway built during a period of time. If highways are thought of as being useful only because they serve a higher objective (such as transporting people and goods effectively, efficiently, and safely), a different measure or even multiple measures are suggested. Examples might be the reduction in travel time, the decrease in the accident rate, the increased number of vehicles moved, and the increased average speed of movement.

Not only does the statement of objectives influence the selection of measures of accomplishment, but the selection of measures of accomplishment may also influence the statement of objectives. Objectives often become meaningful only when alternative means of achieving them are considered and when a measure of accomplishment is established. For example, the analysis of alternatives A, B, and C may suggest alternative D, which in turn may be preferable to either A, B, or C. Moreover, the measures of accomplishment which are supplied to individuals may redirect their social and economic activities, actually changing their objectives. Therefore, the establishment of objectives and of criteria for the measurement of these objectives are actually interacting processes. Not only does the selection of the criteria for accomplishment, benefits, and effectiveness depend on the objectives which are formulated, but the process of selecting the criteria may also suggest the need for revision of the objectives.

Although analytically the determination of objectives and the measurement of accomplishment may be treated separately for purposes of discussion, operationally they are part of the same system of planning, programming, and budgeting. The recognition of this fact has culminated in recent years in the adoption by some governmental units of planning-programming-budgeting systems (PPBS). PPB is simply a systematic way of dealing with difficult problems of choice. It includes:

1. The consideration of alternative objectives and programs and the definition, with as much precision as possible, of programs, output, and resource requirements

2. The development of multiyear planning of desired objectives in relation to program costs

3. Careful consideration of the benefits and costs of existing programs

4. The comparison of alternative courses of action

The systematic analysis of alternatives and an enlarged planning horizon constitute the crux of a PPB system.

Criteria for Evaluation of Objectives

As long as the public sector was considered to be a necessary evil and government outputs were deemed to be of limited value, it may have made sense to emphasize control over inputs only. However, as the accomplishments of the public sector have more and more come to be regarded as public benefits, it has become necessary to shift the emphasis from the control of inputs to the effective allocation of resources for the attainment of objectives. The more sophisticated tools of program analysis, such as cost-benefit analysis, require quantified expressions of program objectives. Criteria for evaluation are needed in order to determine if the objectives have been accomplished and to bring to light problems that require managerial attention. Internally, criteria are needed by the lawmaking body, as the top policy-making group, as well as by the various levels of administration. Externally, criteria are needed by potential lenders, citizens, and other governmental units and organizations. Criteria for evaluation, therefore, must be designed with as much care as the program itself.

In a federated system of government, objectives are partially a function of the level of government. National prestige and national security, for example, while of interest to the states, are peripheral to state functions. However, within any level of government there are also different levels of objectives. Since there are different levels of objectives and, hence, different levels of indicators of accomplishment, one of the first problems is the identification of the different levels of criteria for the evaluation of objectives.

Indicators of accomplishment have been classified according to levels by one source as (1) operations indicators, (2) program impact indicators, and (3) social indicators.[2]

Operations Indicators. These measures are associated with outputs of activities. They are indicators in nonfinancial terms of what is produced for the money or effort expended. They are largely workload and performance statistics useful for activities below the program level. Examples are number of licenses issued, number of tests administered, etc. While often considered as outputs of departments, they are actually intermediate products of programs.

These measures may be classified as volume indicators, quality indicators, and comparative indicators. The activity "street lighting" can be used as an illustration of the three classes. "The number of street lights maintained" is a volume indicator. An "illumination index" (kilowatts) is an indicator of the quality of service. The aim is to specify quality in terms of characteristics—duration, content, intensity. While kilowatt hours of electricity per mile is an example of a comparative indicator, it can be thought of as variant of the other two classes.

Generally speaking, operations indicators provide very little aid in revealing how well the needs of the citizens are being met. These measures are often selected on the basis of simplicity of understanding and data availability rather than on the basis of relevance. They include the kind of data commonly used for the determination of unit costs by dividing the total cost of an activity for a period of time by the number of work units produced during the same period of time.

Program Impact Indicators. These indicators are related directly to a public need or policy. They are expressed in or implied by the program objectives. Outputs of programs should be described in terms that provide a basis for evaluating actual against planned accomplishment. Examples of this type of indicator are (1) vehicle accidents averted and (2) wages earned and welfare costs averted due to handicapped persons being made self-sufficient.

Some program impact indicators could possibly also be used as operations indicators at the departmental level; but they are usually too highly aggregated because a single organizational unit seldom has complete control of a program. To the extent that standards have been developed by specialists in the program areas, these standards may be used for program evaluation.

Social Indicators. These indicators reflect changes in social conditions resulting from a combination of programs but not solely attributable to any one of them. This type of indicator relates to the "quality of life." Examples are family living and home conditions, personal security, and community livability. To the extent that these indicators are available, they aid in answering such questions as: Are we getting healthier? To what extent is pollution increasing? Do children learn more now than they used to? Do people have more satisfying jobs?

Thus, the various performance indicators form a spectrum. At one end of the spectrum are indicators easily understood and applied (quantified) but giving little indication of accomplishment. As the spectrum is traversed, indicators of increasing relevance for program evaluation may be identified. However, they become increasingly more difficult to quantify. At the opposite end, indicators are more closely related to the social objectives of the program than at any point along the spectrum, but they are extremely difficult to identify and quantify.

Due to the adoption of performance budgeting by some units of government, accountants have in some instances already developed workload statistics (operations indicators). Conceptually, it should not be too difficult for accountants working with operating personnel to develop meaningful program impact indicators. However, there is a crucial link, sometimes termed a social production function, still to be forged between social indicators that are heavily laden with value systems and the measurement of program objectives and program accomplishment.[3]

Implications for Accounting

Since governmental programs are not normally undertaken to produce revenue, the accomplishment of any program must be measured in terms of the public good that results. And information disclosing the results of operations in terms of the public good must be collected and processed through the accounting system to the extent possible if effort and accomplishment are to be meaningfully related.

Ideally, one would like to know the ultimate social impact of certain program operations, but seldom can this impact be determined. How much does a particular program, for example, reduce the criminal tendencies in society? We need substantial research to see if it is even possible to come up with relevant answers; but even if we do, they are likely to be both controversial and indefinite.

In the absence of impact data, and even if we could get it, we must look to program achievement data as being the most relevant indicators of accomplishment for accounting. Some of this information may be collected and reported in the formal accounting process, but much of it must come from outside the formal system. To be included, this information must be quantifiable, verifiable, and objective. Otherwise, it will have to be derived by special analyses, studies, surveys, statistical methods, or other means. However, whether the accomplishment data are included in the formal accounting system or not, the concept relating effort and accomplishment is unchanged; and the accountant must understand this relationship in order to structure the "effort" information in such a way that it can be compared to "accomplishment" data, however the latter are derived.

Where it is impossible to relate cost data to achievement data, we are forced to fall back on operations indicators. However, operations indicators are something quite different conceptually from program achievement data. For example, the number of students taught is something quite different from the information needed to determine educational achievement in the public schools. Yet knowing the number of students taught is very useful for many decisions. It is simply one of several indicators necessary to reflect achievement in the overall program, and it must be recognized as such.

In cases of programs for which no really relevant output measures can be identified and quantified, nothing is to be gained by counting the uncountable. In these cases the best solution may be to use operations indicators (workload statistics). Although these relate to program inputs and shed little light on what is accomplished by the purchase and utilization of program resources, they do provide at least a measure of program magnitude. They should not, however, be substituted for program accomplishment data where such data are available.

These distinctions are important for another reason. If one operating statistic (such as number of students taught) is allowed to become the key statistic in a performance standard used to evaluate a program, it may lead to behavior patterns that are undesirable. One can maximize the number of students taught, for example, by lowering the demands made on students so that fewer students drop out of the system and more are able to enter it. Thus, decision makers need to be aware of these possibilities. The information and control system, including the selection of relevant indicators and standards, must promote the objectives that are sought. The selection of relevant indicators with which to measure and evaluate accomplishment is as important as anything done to compute the cost of effort related to that accomplishment.

Finally, we must not forget that the public sector is characterized by complicated systems in which institutional, economic, technical, and political factors interact with one another. Fragmented power is a characteristic of a democracy where government is a system of checks and balances and where decision making becomes a complex balancing of issues, pressures, facts, and politics. In a democracy, objectives are often expressions of conflicting value systems, and the "best solution" may be the achievement of consensus through adjustment of conflicting values rather than one which meets criteria of effectiveness and efficiency. Thus in measuring benefits of programs and combinations of programs, political consequences as well as social and economic benefits must be considered by many governmental decision makers.

Furthermore, in the allocation of resources by the legislative body, political tradeoffs must often be made between expenditures on one program and those of another. It is very difficult, if not impossible, to develop measures which permit direct quantitative comparisons of the benefits of expenditures for welfare programs, for example; and analysis will have to yield to the judgments of the decision maker in situations such as this one. The value judgments of many decision makers in the public sector must be based on the actual and projected outcome of issues which in a democracy are resolved in the political arena. However, analyses based on concepts of accomplishments, benefits, and effectiveness should make the political cost of ignoring these analyses higher for elected officials. Analysis plays a further role in translating general policy, which may have been derived by political processes, into specific objectives to which evaluation criteria can be applied.

In conclusion, it would appear that the greatest challenges for accountants in the public sector lie in finding ways to implement the concepts of effort and accomplishment so that meaningful relationships may be disclosed for managerial decision making as well as for public accountability on the part of all public officials. No area of concern offers accountants a greater challenge, but no other challenge offers greater promise of exciting rewards and meaningful public service.

NOTES

1. See Concepts and Standards Research Study Committee, The matching concept, *Accounting Review, April 1965,* pp. 368-372.
2. State-Local Finances Project, *Output Measures for a Multi-Year Program and Financial Plan—PPB Note 7,* Washington, D.C., George Washington University, 1967, p. 9ff.
3. For an example of two excellent studies that discuss these subjects in some depth, see: Charles L. Schultze, *The Politics and Economics of Public Spending,* Washington, D.C., The Brookings Institution, 1968; and U.S. Department of Health, Education and Welfare, *Toward a Social Report,* Washington, D.C., U.S. Government Printing Office, 1969.

11

OPERATIONAL AUDITING IN STATE AND LOCAL GOVERNMENT *

Kenneth S. Caldwell

I will explore in this chapter some of the basic concepts of accountability and the audit function and, in particular, the financial and compliance aspects of an operational audit—considerations which are not dealt with in the GAO standards or in the literature. I will also cover alternative approaches for organizing and conducting the operational audit and discuss some of the factors involved in developing and utilizing internal operational audit capabilities and in contracting for such services with outside organizations.

CONCEPTUAL FRAMEWORK FOR OPERATIONAL AUDITING

First, we should have some initial understanding of what we mean by the term *audit* or *auditing,* as the issue of accountability and how it can be properly discharged through the audit process in general—and operational auditing in particular—is a fundamental one.

The publication *Auditing Public Education* (1), prepared by the staff of the AIDE project in Alabama, sets forth a *conceptual framework* which identi-

---

*Reprinted from *Governmental Finance,* vol. 4 (November 1975), pp. 36-43.

fies the dual objectives of auditing: accountability and management control. It identified, from an examination of hundreds of differing audits and an examination of the literature, that for an activity to be classified as an audit, it must be (1):

1. An auditor, auditee, and audit recipient
2. An accountability relationship between the auditee (subordinate) and the audit recipient (higher authority)
3. Independence between the auditor and auditee
4. An examination and evaluation of certain of the auditee's accountabile activities by the auditor for the audit recipient

It further states that

these are essential elements or characteristics of an audit. There are also a number of other topics and concepts that relate to auditing, including: audit scope, audit networks, auditor competencies, auditor ethics and standards, behavioral relationships, and specific audit procedures and techniques. The authors found that all of these concepts could be logically organized for discussion and examination around the following conceptual framework.

   I. Objective (Why?)
      Accountability
      Management control

  II. Scope (What?)
      Financial
      Compliance
      Performance

 III. Parties (Who?)
      Auditor
         Independent
         Competent
         Professional
      Auditee
      Audit recipient

 IV. Process (How?)
      Preparation
      Conduct
      Reporting
      Settlement

This conceptual framework identifies four areas of reference (objective, scope, parties, process) that provide the answers to four frequently asked questions: Why, What, Who, and How? These are questions that every auditor, auditee, and audit recipient should know (or seek) the answers to. The framework may also be expressed in the form of a comprehensive definition of auditing

Auditing is an analytical *process* consisting of preparation, conduct (examination and evaluation), reporting (communication), and settlement. The basic *elements* of this process are: an independent, competent, and professional auditor who executes the process upon an auditee for an audit recipient. The *scope* or area of concern can involve matters of the following nature: financial (accounting error, fraud, financial controls, fairness of financial statements, etc.,), and/or compliance (faithful adherence to administrative and legal requirements, policies, regulations, etc.), and/or performance (economy, efficiency, and/or effectiveness of operational controls, management information systems, programs, etc.). The objective or purpose of auditing can be some combination of accountability and management control. . . .

This definition can be effectively used in defining what is really expected from the auditing function and in establishing basic "ground rules" for developing and/or expanding the audit function in a particular government.

A number of very practical issues relating to the traditional financial audit are raised and must be considered in structuring a meaningful operational auditing program.

These include:

To what extent, if any, can or should auditing concern nonfinancial, management activities? What authority do auditors have to make broad scope audits? Since most auditors have an accounting background, are they qualified to do more than a financial audit? How can a management audit be logically conducted in areas where no generally accepted standards exist, either for the management activity or the auditor himself? Is it possible for the auditor to be both (1) the critical representative of the audit user, and (2) a valued consultant to auditee management? Is it really possible for auditing to be a significant aid to management? (1)

There appear to be as many different opinions and interpretations regarding audit standards as there are public finance officers, governmental accountants and auditors, public accountants, management consultants, or specialized program evaluators, etc.

A brief explanation of what is meant by efficiency, economy, and effectiveness is in order so I'll start with performance evaluation.

Performance evaluation is the process of measuring and evaluating efficiency, economy, and effectiveness, using both quantitative and nonquantitative criteria. The term *efficiency*—which includes economy as well—describes how well a government utilizes its available resources or inputs in carrying out public service programs. Effectiveness, on the other hand, focuses on results—what a government actually accomplishes with the resources made available.

Efficiency and effectiveness measures are, in turn, used to evaluate governmental performance and to determine how well governmental managers discharge their financial, management, and program accountability responsibilities.

The word *accountability* is a key one, as the operational audit as promulgated by the GAO represents a direct means for discharging accountability and related performance evaluation responsibilities.

Mort Dittenhofer of the GAO, principal author of the GAO standards, has defined accountability as "the requirement placed on a public official to report the disposition of and use to which he has put the resources with which he has been entrusted."

He further identified three broad areas of accountability to which the GAO audit standards are intended to respond (2):

1. *Financial accountability:* This focuses on determining "whether financial operations are properly conducted, (b) whether the financial reports of an audited entity are presented fairly, and (c) whether the entity has complied with applicable laws and regulations."

2. *Management accountability:* This area involves the development and application of performance standards for use in determining "whether the entity is managing or utilizing its resources (personnel, property, space and so forth) in an economical and efficient manner and the causes of any inefficiencies or uneconomical practices including inadequacies in management information system, administrative procedures, or organizational structure."

3. *Program accountability:* This area of accountability focuses on program accomplishments to determine "whether the desired results or benefits are being achieved, whether the objectives established by the legislature or other authorizing body are being met and whether the agency has considered alternatives which might yield desired results at a lower cost."

There are, of course, other definitions of accountability. This definition, I believe, is a realistic one.

There are many different viewpoints regarding the operational audit and its use as a basic resource for better discharging accountability responsibilities. For example, in the February 1975 issue of *Public Management,* H. P. Hatry, Director, State and Local Government Research Program, The Urban Institute, differentiates between a performance [operational] audit and program evaluation (3). He states:

> The GAO report, however, provides no further guidance on the meaning of performance standards or how to develop and apply them. Some, in trying to interpret the intent, have suggested the development of performance standards for each local service. But, what aspects of service the standards should cover and how such standards should be derived thus far have been left to each state and local government's own imagination. Preliminary field work presumably will provide a start toward answering such questions, but attainment of meaningful standards appears to be a long way down the road.
>
> Performance auditing will be defined here as the assessment by an independent group of the performance of a governmental program or service to determine its success in efficiently achieving its explicit and implicit objectives. Its principal purposes are to identify whether public resources are being used effectively and efficiently in the program being audited and to identify whether or not changes are needed.
>
> What may distinguish performance auditing from program evaluation is the independence of the activity, and the attempt to verify the performance findings for external use. However, some will consider these as being identical. Wherever possible, performance audits also should identify desirable program improvements as well as assess performance.
>
> If a government has previously undertaken or has underway a systematic, documented evaluation of a program that is to be the subject of a performance audit, the audit can be primarily an audit of the evaluation. However, if an evaluation had not been undertaken, or if the program evaluation were inadequate, at least a partial evaluation for the purposes of auditing results may be necessary. . . .

This definition identifies the need for independence. However, the focus of the performance audit is primarily on effectiveness or program accountability. The operational audit is not put in a defined perspective with respect to the financial audit. Such an operational audit could be performed by an independent group within the government or under contract with any qualified outside organization.

This definition illustrates one well-defined need—the need for developing uniform terminology with respect to operational auditing so that, at least, we all can communicate when we discuss audits and the related issues of accountability and performance evaluation. Unfortunately, lack of well-defined and understood terminology is a problem which is not unique to this topic, but one which plagues the entire budgetary and financial planning and management process in government.

The GAO commented on terminology problems in an article published in the *Journal of Accountancy* as far back as 1971 (4). Things have not changed much since then:

> The terms, performance auditing or operational auditing, are usually used to establish a distinction between auditing of accounting and related records for the purpose of expressing professional opinions on financial statements and auditing which examines the operating, managerial or administrative performance of selected aspects of an activity or organization beyond that required for the audit of the accounts. The purpose of such expanded auditing is primarily to identify opportunities for greater efficiency and economy or for improving effectiveness in carrying out procedures or operations. The objective is improvement in relation to the goals of the organization.
>
> Unfortunately, such labels as performance auditing, operational auditing and financial auditing can cause confusion. The boundaries between them, even on a conceptual basis, are not sharp and clear. As good as our English language is, we have not been able to sharpen our terminology in many areas of accounting and auditing. Financial auditing requires the auditor to concern himself with aspects of management or administrative performance and control. He cannot confine his attention to accounting records. The auditor of financial statements, if he is doing the job properly, will find himself on much the same ground as the so-called operational auditor. . . .

In a sense, the same basic "communications gap" exists as was the case with respect to PPBS—another poorly defined concept. PPBS meant cost accounting to the accountant; information systems to the data processor; planning and management analysis to the budget analyst; and cost-benefit analysis to the management scientist. How the public administrator or legislator viewed it I'm not sure.

One of the real problems involved in attempting to define operational auditing is the use by the GAO of the term *audit* on a broad basis. The term *audit* connotes independence. Further, it implies a direct interdependence on or interrelation with the traditional financial auditing attest process. Further, the use of the term *audit* to encompass nonattest considerations poses practical problems for the independent CPAs, as it poses many unknowns and problems for which no answers are available at this time.

Significant problems also exist with respect to the term *compliance* as used in the standards. There were good reasons for the GAO to incorporate financial and compliance considerations in the first audit standard, and to consider evaluations of efficiency, economy and program results or effectiveness as logical extensions of the basic financial audit process.

Naturally, the independent accounting and auditing organizations, governmental and nongovernmental alike, tend to view operational auditing as a direct *extension and expansion of the financial auditing process.* This is the perspective within which the GAO standards were developed. However, internal management or program analysis and evaluation organizations in the executive branch of government, management consultants and organizations offering specialized resources management or program evaluations services, are *not* concerned with, and therefore do not necessarily view, the financial audit as the "foundation" for introducing or performing operational auditing.

Some recategorization and redefinition of the GAO standards is indicated if we are to avoid those problems which revolve around terminology and the tendency to use broad categorical definitions to cover functions which have more dissimilarities than similarities.

There are valid reasons to consider some recategorization of the GAO standards so as to overcome these problems, and to enable a government to develop an operational auditing program which can utilize all qualified resources without necessarily having to deal with operational auditing within the somewhat constrained perspective of the traditional financial audit. This is particularly important where a financial (opinion) audit is not required; or even where it is, yet where there is little likelihood that the financial audit can, in fact, be expanded to serve as the "foundation" for an ongoing operational auditing program.

I suggest that the GAO standards be redefined to include four, not three, elements as follows:

1. *Financial audit* in which the auditor performs the traditional attest function and expresses an opinion on the financial statements of the government or agency involved. Such an audit includes limited review of compliance, as well.

2. *Compliance audit or review* in which no formal opinion on the financial statements is required. Such an audit may have many of the characteristics of a traditional financial audit. But the scope and orientation of such an audit, as well as the specific auditing procedures to be followed, may differ substantially from opinion audits.

3. *Review of efficiency and economy* in which the focus is primarily on evaluating the use of resources.

4. *Evaluation of program results* (effectiveness) in which the primary focus is on evaluating program accomplishments or results.

The principal difference in this categorization is the establishment of the traditional financial (opinion) audit as a separate, defined category, and the corollary establishment of a new category of compliance audit or review.

This will enable the scope of an operational audit to be viewed from two separate perspectives: where a financial opinion audit is required, and where it is not. Where an opinion is required, it will be possible to precisely define financial audit objectives and scope and to better cope with those issues which concern the independent auditor, e.g., independence, format and content of auditor's opinion, questions of potential liability, etc., without clouding the issue with complexities relating to in-depth reviews of compliance or to matters of efficiency, economy, and effectiveness other than as customarily included in the traditional "management letter."

Audit scope and procedures covering additional work desired with respect to compliance and/or efficiency, or economy or program results, can be set forth in a supplement to the basic financial audit work plan or contract, or in a separate document.

Proper definition of operational audit objectives, scope, and procedures; format and content of the auditor's report; the need for expressing some form of an opinion regarding audit findings and recommendations; these are issues which are far easier to deal with in the operational audit context if they are kept outside the scope of the attest function. It will also be far easier, on this basis, to develop an operational audit program and procedures which will meet the specific audit objectives without introducing the other complexities inherent in the financial (opinion) audit.

As a matter of fact, the scope and procedures of the traditional financial audit in which the auditor is required to express an opinion on financial statements are adequately prescribed in the AICPA industry audit guide published last year, entitled *Audits of State and Local Governments* (5). While this guide sets forth some concepts and requirements which differ from those of *GAAFR* (6), the two books used together represent a well-defined body of knowledge which can be followed by governmental auditors and independent accountants alike in conducting financial audits on a consistent and comparable basis.

A significant problem exists, however, with respect to the integration by the GAO of the two subelements—financial and compliance—within a single audit element. Neither the AICPA audit guide nor the GAO standards, and/or subsequent explanatory and implementing memoranda, provide any clear-cut definitions with respect to what compliance really encompasses, even within the scope of the traditional financial audit. Nor do the GAO standards set forth any criteria or procedures for the auditor to follow in his examination to assure that when he expresses an opinion, he can comment fairly both on the adequacy of the financial statements and on whether the agency has complied with applicable constitutional charter, statutory and policy regulations, rules and requirements.

There is, however, a reasonable basis in fact and tradition for considering some aspects of compliance as an integral part of the financial audit. This appears to be largely based on the assumption that the auditor will be alert to and report on instances of noncompliance *to some extent* during the audit or secure some form of assurance from the client. Is this a practical assumption?

There are some areas where compliance aspects of a financial audit are well defined. These, however, are limited mostly to the rules and regulations prescribed for specific federal grant or assistance programs such as revenue sharing. The revenue-sharing audit guide issued by the Office of Revenue Sharing, for example, sets forth specific requirements which must be considered in performing the compliance aspects of an audit of federal revenue-sharing funds, as well as the format and content of the auditor's report thereon.

There are a host of federal laws, rules, and regulations governing both public and private corporations alike involving equal opportunity and discrimination, occupational health and safety, minimum wage levels, etc., as well as requirements imposed in connection with the specific federal grant or assistance programs which may be received and administered by the particular local government.

From the perspective of the independent auditor, what are the implications of failure to detect noncompliance? Specific penalties, including forfeiture and/ or repayment of the grant, fines for noncompliance, etc., exist and can be imposed for violations. To what extent does the independent auditor have an obligation to expand audit procedures to determine whether or not significant contingent liabilities may exist for noncompliance which may, in turn, be material in relation to the financial statements and the auditor's ability to express an opinion thereon?

This is another reason I suggest that the traditional financial (opinion) audit be established as a separate audit "element" within the broad framework of operational auditing, but with the requirement that adequate policies and guidelines be developed which set forth the extent of compliance-related reviews which should comprise an integral part of the financial (opinion) audit.

All in-depth reviews of compliance should be dealt with as a separate audit element or category with an accompanying defined audit scope and procedures. Significant problems exist in this area as well—problems which can be dealt with if the independent auditor properly defines compliance review objectives and scope. This is also an element of the operational audit which is of increasing interest to governing boards and which can be used as a direct means of better discharging legislative accountability responsibilities.

The GAO standards set forth only general guidelines and criteria, yet place specific responsibility on the auditor for

determining whether the organization, program function, or activity under audit has complied with the requirements placed upon it by pertinent laws and regulations. In reviewing compliance with pertinent laws and regulations, the auditor should consider not only statutes and implementing regulations but also the related legislative history, legal opinions, court cases, and regulatory requirements, including such documents as grant or loan agreements . . . .

Sources of appropriate information include:

1. Legal or legislative data, including:
   a. Basic legislation
   b. Reports of hearings
   c. Legislative committee reports
   d. Annotated references from reference services covering related court decisions and legal opinions
   e. Historical data relating to the movements to achieve the legislation
   f. State constitutions, statutes, resolutions, and legislative orders
   g. Local charters, ordinances, and resolutions

2. External administrative requirements, including:
   a. Memorandums from federal, state, or local administrative agencies
   b. Guidelines and other administrative regulations affecting program operations from federal, state, or local agencies

3. Grant arrangements, when grants are involved, including:
   a. Proposals from grantees
   b. Pertinent correspondence from grantors and grantees
   c. Memorandums of meetings held to discuss the grants
   d. The grant documents, including amendments
   e. Grant regulations
   f. Grant budgets and supporting schedules

The nature and purpose of the review of legal and administrative requirements will tend to vary with the element of auditing being performed .

The standards further state that "The auditor is to test the financial transactions and operations of the audited organization, program, function, or activity to determine whether that entity is in compliance with pertinent laws or regulations. The auditor also is to make a review to satisfy himself that the audited entity has not incurred significant unrecorded liabilities (contingent or actual) through failure to comply with, or through violation of pertinent laws and regulations. . . ."

These requirements sound simple. Yet without well-defined guidelines and criteria, they may be difficult to comply with. From the perspective of the independent auditor, the requirement that the auditor determine and express some form of opinion on compliance poses significant problems with respect to form and substance of the report, and the potential liability in connection with such a review or examination—an examination which may not involve rendering an opinion on the financial statements.

What potential liability is involved when an independent auditor performs a compliance audit or review and issues a report which contains an "opinion" that the agency is in compliance with the myriad of appropriate laws and regulations, yet future developments reveal noncompliance with a particular law or regulation which may involve a significant contingent, unrecorded liability?

Perhaps the issue of potential liability in connection with compliance falls in the same category as defalcations. Failure to detect defalcations is not necessarily a basis for taking punitive action against the auditor, provided the auditor has structured his audit program to comply with generally accepted auditing standards and criteria.

The same considerations may apply regarding compliance. If the auditor has properly identified applicable laws, regulations, etc.; categorized these in terms of their significant requirements or constraints; and structured his examination utilizing appropriate attribute sampling and other audit procedures, he will be able to demonstrate his competence through an orderly and well-planned approach. On this basis, it may be difficult for any third party to sustain an action against him in subsequently detected instances of noncompliance. In the absence of defined auditing standards and criteria governing compliance, the burden of proof would fall heavily on the third party plaintiff, not the auditor.

From work undertaken by our firm in this area, it appears that compliance can be subdivided into four broad categories, as follows:

- Compliance with identified agency fiscal, administrative, or management policies and procedures governing the receipt and expenditure of public funds

- Compliance with external fiscal, administrative, and reporting requirements covering the receipt and expenditure of federal and other external funds

- Compliance with applicable overall constitutional, charter, or statutory requirements

- Compliance with legislative intent or purpose underlying appropriations as set forth in the appropriations act or budget as adopted for the fiscal period concerned

Compliance with the first three categories (internal agency fiscal and other policies, rules, and regulations; external requirements; and constitutional, charter, and statutory requirements) appears to be the easiest to deal with in structuring an appropriate audit program. In most instances, a body of knowledge exists in written form. Implementing policies, rules, regulations and guidelines are usually available, although they may be subject to interpretation.

Written well-defined audit procedures are mandatory. However, compliance with legislative intent or purpose underlying appropriation and expenditure of public funds is a different and potentially far more difficult matter. Perhaps new audit procedures must be developed through which appropriations are categorized, and selected representative ones are examined on an attribute basis. The scope of such an examination must focus on the budget and on the entire budgetary and appropriation process, as the appropriation act, or the budget as adopted may not adequately set forth legislative purpose and intent.

The State of Illinois is one major jurisdiction that is developing initial standards and criteria for compliance audits based on the GAO standards (7). Illinois postaudit instructions state:

> One objective of all compliance audits is to test compliance with the statutes, laws, rules and regulations under which the agency being audited was created and is functioning. Each agency will usually be governed by statutes authorizing existence and operations, applicable appropriation acts, including supplemental appropriations and rules and regulations adopted to govern its own operations.

The instructions also identify the principal legislative and statutory provisions relating to compliance.

A number of the postaudits contracted for with independent accountants by the State of Illinois are being reoriented as compliance audits in which no opinion on financial statements is required. Significant problems are involved in structuring such compliance audits because, while the intent is clear, no defined policies and guidelines exist to guide the auditor. The scope and procedures of such a compliance audit may differ significantly from those of the traditional financial audit, which has as its primary objective determining whether the financial statements of the agency present its position fairly. This is an area of accountability in which no definitive or authoritative rules, policies, or guidelines have as yet been developed to guide the auditor.

The compliance audit will emerge, however, as an additional resource through which accountability can be better defined and determined, as well as a useful resource to the legislator and governmental manager alike in helping to discharge accountability responsibilities.

I now "shift gears" to explore a few of the considerations involved in developing and implementing an initial approach to operational auditing. My comments are applicable primarily to those governments which do not have independent financial (opinion) audits or where the scope of financial audits is extremely limited; where internal staff capabilities are limited or nonexistent; or where it may be necessary to develop internal resources and/or to rely heavily on the use of resources outside the government for operational audits.

Because of the limitations, I am purposefully bypassing the many basic issues involved in structuring a meaningful operational auditing program which considers the alternatives available through which a government may elect to discharge its financial, management, and program accountability responsibilities. I will also not attempt to generalize as to who has or should exercise accountability responsibilities. This would create more problems than it would solve. The differences between public jurisdictions as to constitutional or charter requirements, the "balance of power," e.g., the relative role and responsibilities of the executive vs. the legislative branches of government are so great as to almost defy placing them in any common perspective.

One basic assumption is that the legislative branch bears the ultimate responsibility for enacting legislation and introducing programs which are responsive to the needs of their constituency. Therefore, the legislative branch has a direct responsibility to determine that such programs are responsive to needs; are properly administered and managed; and that they actually accomplish their intended purposes. This we have already defined as the broad area of program accountability.

If so, what are the executive branch responsibilities for accountability? Can executive branch responsibilities be limited solely or primarily to management of the resources provided in the budget as enacted—the areas of financial and management accountability? Obviously not, as the executive branch must also concern itself with identifying public service needs in its planning efforts; in developing programs to meet these needs, and then in administering and managing these programs on an efficient and effective basis. This involves program accountability.

THE POSTAUDIT FUNCTION

I use the term *auditor* in the context of the GAO—that of an independent "audit" function performed by an elected auditor, a legislative postauditor, an independent public accountant, or similar organization. Such audit functions are characterized by a degree of independence (from the client agency or from the executive branch which is responsible for managing the government) which is not possessed by organizational units located in the executive branch who may perform internal audit, operational audit, or closely related management or program review, analysis, and evaluation functions.

The concept of an *independent* audit function to assure proper safeguarding and stewardship of public funds is one of long tradition, practice, and importance in government. However, it has only been in recent years that significant changes or improvements have come about in the organization, reporting relationships, duties, and responsibilities of the independent audit function in government or what is frequently referred to as the (legislative) postaudit function.

This is an important development, as well as one which may provide the vehicle for implementing a meaningful and responsive operational auditing program —at least from the legislative perspective. While this development has been limited primarily to state governments and larger local governments, the concept will undoubtedly be adapted by many medium sized and smaller local governments.

A long-term trend appears to exist to place the postaudit function within the legislative branch of state government and to develop a corollary capability for program performance review and evaluation.

Since 1950 the number of states with legislative postaudit involvement has grown from 8 to 36, while legislative performance auditing has been introduced in 12 states since 1960 (8).

Here, as with respect to the new audit standards, leadership has been provided by the GAO in stimulating and assisting state and local governments to improve their internal auditing practices through the development and issuance of audit legislation in its publication *Suggested State Auditing Acts and Constitutional Amendments* (9).

Now let's explore some of the alternative approaches to operational auditing available to a typical government.

There are many factors which affect how such a state/local government may elect to develop and implement an initial operational auditing program. Two basic organizational and policy issues are involved.

Should the agency develop an *internal* operational auditing capability or expand on existing audit function? If so, where should this function be organizationally located and to whom should it report—the executive branch, legislative branch, or both? Should it involve existing governmental financial audit functions, or should it be established as a separate function? This depends partly on the size of the agency; whether auditing functions presently exist and where they are organizationally located; their staff capabilities; the economics involved; and a myriad of other factors, including the key issue of independence.

To what extent can or should the agency rely on operational auditing services provided by *outside* organizations under contract? If so, should such functions complement, supplement, or supplant internal capabilities? Should they focus primarily on the financial audit, on matters of efficiency, economy, or effectiveness, or both? How should an agency go about contracting for such services and ensuring that such contracts attain their objectives?

These are not necessarily alternatives, as such. Such decisions really depend on a number of practical, political, and other considerations which include:

- Constitutional or charter requirements governing audits and the audit function
- The need, size, and complexity of the government
- "Balance of power," e.g., the comparative strength, role, and responsibilities of the executive vs. legislative branches
- Ability to secure and retain qualified staff
- Ability to contract for and availability of outside professional contract resources

- Extent of direct third party involvement, e.g., grand juries, special investigating boards or commissions, etc.

- Sensitivity of the issues which must be dealt with and/or degree of probable exposure of audit findings to the public and media

Remember, for purposes of initiating an operational auditing program, independence is a key factor. Further, it is important that all governments develop some degree of internal capability to either undertake operational audits or reviews, or to effectively plan and manage the use of outside resources.

This, in turn, requires that each government—excepting perhaps those whose size and budget are extremely small—develop a *planned approach* to better discharging its financial management and program accountability responsibilities. Initially, a legislative policy should be formulated which sets forth or clarifies requirements or policies governing (operational) auditing. Such a policy could be quite restrictive, or broadly based and include provision for

- *Financial (opinion) audits,* and how these can be properly and most effectively discharged—through use of governmental auditors, independent auditors, or a combination of both

- *Expanded scope audits* or reviews which focus on compliance and/or matters of efficiency, economy, and effectiveness

- *Organization and management of the independent operational audit function* within the government, and definition of the comparative role and responsibilities of the legislative and executive branches of government for evaluating financial, management, and program performance and accountability

- *Priority* establishment to help identify the departments, agencies, functions, or activities on which the program should initially focus, and the primary focus of such audits, e.g., compliance, efficiency, and economy, or program results

- *Procedures for qualifying and contracting* with outside independent audit organizations for financial (opinion) and expanded scope audits or reviews

- *Adequate financing* for initiating the operational auditing program

- *Incorporating legislation*

Such policies could also include a requirement for including in key legislation a requirement for operational audits or other means for determining accountability.

This issue was partially addressed in Ohio in the June 1972 report of the Ohio Citizens Committee on the State Legislature, created by the General Assembly in 1970, which recommended that (10):

General Assembly bills contain requirements for program where appropriate, and provision for financing such program review and analysis;
The General Assembly establish a bi-partisan joint standing Program
Review and Evaluation Committee to develop standards and criteria
for program measurement, and to conduct performance audits of selected state program; and The Program Review and Evaluation Committee
develop guidelines for program evaluation of all legislation proposed by
the executive branch, including the biennial budget. . . .

A soundly conceived legislative *mandate* can provide the direction, motivation, and resources necessary to establish and sustain such a program and on a
basis which will provide results.

Here, cooperation and assistance will be required from both executive and
legislative branches in planning such an approach so that it will meet legislative
needs, as well as serve as a framework within which the executive branch can
better discharge its responsibilities in the areas of financial and management accountability.

Following the adoption of some legislative framework and policies regarding
operational auditing, the agency faces the practical problem of "getting something going." The important consideration here is to identify those specific problems or issues which the legislative branch views as having the highest priority, and
to determine initially whether these can be best explored from the perspective of
the independent financial (opinion) audit (where such an audit exists) or whether
it is more practical to explore such problems or issues apart from the financial
audit.

This determination largely depends on the scope of the existing financial
audit function and/or the availability of required personnel resources. Do audit
personnel possess the skills and experience required to cope with the specific
problems or issues involved? If accomplishments of a specific program are the
basic issue, then appropriate program skills are mandatory. If an evaluation must
be made regarding agency-wide computer hardware and software, centralization
vs. decentralization, relative merits and costs of competing manufacturers, etc.—
then appropriate data-processing and system skills are required.

On a practical basis, perhaps the greatest short-range benefits from any initial
operational auditing program can be realized where (1) a significant return can be
anticipated for the investment required and (2) no significant staff is required to
administer the program. Typical areas which may offer potentials for improving
governmental performance include:

- Mechanizing, streamlining, and improving highly intensive labor, clerical, and
  other operations
- Improving the systems used for managing resources, e.g., purchasing, inventory management, personnel administration, maintenance, etc.

- Cost vs. benefit studies of alternative ways of providing public services which lend themselves to measurement and evaluation on a quantitative basis
- Introduction of high-speed data-processing equipment for high-volume operations
- Improving facilities layout and utilization
- Independent studies and evaluations of identified problems within specific agencies or departments

Labor productivity measurement and improvement programs may also offer significant potentials. However, implementation of such programs requires a substantial continuing commitment of staff resources, even where the initial system may be designed by an organization outside government.

The foregoing areas primarily involve the improvement of financial and management performance in the use of resources appropriated, not on program results. In my opinion, it is unrealistic and impractical for a government to structure an initial operational auditing program which focuses, or attempts to focus, on evaluating program accomplishments. Not only is the "body of knowledge" required to make such evaluations nonexistent with respect to the many important and controversial programs with which legislators must cope; such evaluations require a commitment of resources that only the larger governments appear able or willing to meet.

This is difficult for many legislators to appreciate. Many of the more controversial socially oriented programs involve large expenditures. Understandably, legislators want to get answers to their questions. Unfortunately, however, the state of the art is such that most operational auditing programs, particularly in the initial stages, must concentrate on the more mundane resource management issues of highway, road, street building or vehicle maintenance, solid waste collection and disposal; and those other programs and activities which can be fairly readily quantified.

The legislative branch should be encouraged to initiate a legislative policy which imposes a direct responsibility on the executive branch for developing appropriate evaluation guidelines, criteria, and procedures and incorporate these requirements in legislation when enacted. This will impose a significant burden on the executive branch, particularly the departments and agencies involved.

However, the focus of the operational audit could then be directed to determining whether a department or agency had complied with defined legislative requirements and developed evaluation procedures; whether these procedures are being followed; and what corrective or other actions are being taken by management regarding problems and deficiencies. This is a different approach than where attempts are made to conduct independent evaluations of program results.

Initially, it is reasonable to assume that many agencies will contract for operational audits with other governmental audit agencies and/or independent public accounting or management consulting firms who possess the necessary skills and experience. Certain other possibilities should also be explored. In addition to the services provided by a wide range of public accounting and other professional firms, the utilization of the services of individuals and organizations independent of the government who have a high degree of capability and knowledge in specialized program areas should be explored.

It is possible, for example, to create advisory groups of professionals to assist in designing evaluation procedures and in making evaluations. Independent "peer review," such as employed to review utilization in health care facilities, could be an important element of an operational auditing program, as one means of focusing on program results.

However, even such an approach requires some commitment of staff as well as financial resources. Otherwise it will be difficult to implement the recommendations of outside auditors, consultants, and others.

The services of at least one staff individual are required to provide necessary internal direction and coordination among outside consultants or auditors, executive branch departments and agencies, and the legislative branch. It may be possible to supplement such efforts by temporarily drawing on the personnel resources and skills within particular departments, agencies, and program areas. Departmental involvement is important. It is comparatively easy to take people who are knowledgeable in a program or activity area and to train them in specific analysis techniques. Again, ongoing internal direction and guidance is mandatory from both a legislative and executive perspective.

The organizational location of this function is not critical. Initial support and direction can be provided from within the executive branch.

The government should avoid complete reliance on independent third parties, e.g., elected state auditors, legislative postauditors, independent accountants, etc., as the operating management of the particular department or agency will be at a real disadvantage when it comes to implementing recommendations for change or improvement.

Obviously, these are short-term considerations. Any long-term program directed to improving governmental performance must involve the development not only of a meaningful program and of the staff resources required, but modernization and improvement of an agency's basic budgeting and financial management systems and procedures, including introduction of program accounting and responsibility accounting. Otherwise the government will continue to encounter serious problems because of inherent deficiencies in its attempts to make more than immediate, or short-term, improvements. This means strengthening the executive branch's capabilities to develop and implement appropriate continuing programs for improving performance.

Long-term improvement in assessing and discharging accountability responsibilities must be shared by both the legislative and executive branches. This is a responsibility in which much of the initiative must then come from the executive branch. On a comparable basis, the legislative branch also takes direct action to improve governmental performance using the operational audit as a key resource.

Development or expansion of an internal operational auditing capability may be difficult to achieve in the short run, even where some audit capabilities exist. Many existing internal governmental audit agencies have a significant backlog of traditional audits; problems securing legislative authorization for new positions; and extreme difficulty in attracting and retaining qualified personnel. Under these circumstances, the independent auditor can play a vital and constructive role. He can help to identify long-term financial management needs and help the agency to develop and implement basic financial and related management systems, procedures, and controls.

He can make an immediate contribution to improving governmental performance and accountability through the operational audit. Effective use of outside audit resources, on the other hand, depends largely on the government's ability to

- Properly identify the problems
- Develop a set of specifications which clearly define desired objectives, the scope of the project, and the basic skills required
- Secure a contractor who possesses the proper combination of functional and technical skills and who can make these skills available when needed
- Execute an appropriate contractual agreement which clearly defines project objectives, scope, procedures, and costs from the perspective of both the agency and the contractors
- Secure the cooperation of the key personnel in the executive branch whose activities may be involved and establish appropriate liaison with the legislative branch where legislative issues are involved
- Provide the internal continuity and support necessary to successfully "sell" recommendations to key agency heads and the legislature, and then implement them

These considerations apply, regardless of whether a project is undertaken as a part of an operational audit as defined by the GAO or as a special audit or review independent of the financial audit involved.

There are many good reasons why the audit should serve as the basic vehicle for independent evaluations of performance and determinations of accountability, and why the auditor is exceptionally well qualified, by virtue of his knowledge and experience, to undertake an expanded role—provided he can provide the staff resources needed and properly discharge his responsibilities.

There are also occasions when it will be in the best interest of the government to contract separately for (1) the financial (opinion) audit and (2) any supplemental audits or reviews focusing on compliance or on efficiency, economy, and effectiveness. The important issue is that operational "audits" be undertaken on a planned and coordinated basis within whatever organizational context is most appropriate, and that basic policies and procedures governing such audits be clearly defined.

Referring back to the GAO standards, the Comptroller General of the United States, in explaining the intent underlying the GAO standards, has made it clear that he does not expect that the typical state and local government will, by some magic process, expand its auditing activities to encompass all the accountability objectives underlying the standards. He suggests that each government structure its approach to implementing operational auditing on a basis which recognizes the practical limitations involved.

A key issue is how you define the role of the independent auditor and where this function is organizationally located in the government. Even where heavy reliance is placed on the use of outside independent audit resources, continuity in planning and managing these audits is required within the government.

If the role of the auditor is to be expanded beyond the attest function statements and related systems of internal control, then the scope and procedures of the (typical) audit must be significantly expanded.

The vehicle may already partially exist. The scope of the management letter can be expanded so as to give increased emphasis to identifying problems and developing constructive recommendations for change or improvement. This, in turn, will call for development of the audit staff capabilities necessary to adequately and professionally discharge these added responsibilities. In the final analysis, the responsibility for developing a successful program for measuring performance and better assessing accountability is a shared one—shared by the legislative branch, the client agency, and the independent audit organization alike. This is the basis on which development of a successful long-term operational auditing program depends.

REFERENCES

1. McMickle and Elrod, *Auditing Public Education.* AIDE Project, Alabama, 1974.
2. Office of the Comptroller General of the United States, *Standards for Audit of Governmental Organizations: Programs, Activities and Functions.* Washington, D. C., 1972.
3. Hatry, H. P. *Public Management, February 1975.*
4. Morse, Ellsworth H. Performance and operational auditing. *Journal of Accountancy, June 1971.*

5. Committee on Governmental Accounting and Auditing, *Audits of State and Local Governmental Units.* New York, American Institute of Certified Public Accountants, 1974.
6. Municipal Finance Officers Association, *Governmental Accounting, Auditing, and Financial Reporting.* Chicago, 1968.
7. *Illinois Post-Audit Guide.* Springfield.
8. *Book of the States,* Brookville, Maryland, American History Research Associates, 1972.
9. General Accounting Office, *Suggested State Auditing Acts and Constitutional Amendments.* GAO Model Post-Audit Legislation, Washington, D. C.
10. Report of the Ohio Citizens Committee on the Ohio State Legislature, Columbus, June 1972.

12

DATA-BASED MANAGEMENT: Initial Efforts to Develop DBM Capabilities in a Federal Program[*]

Robert G. Stanley

Program management typically requires both a sound understanding and effective orchestration of relationships among a great number of actors. At a minimum, these include program recipients, regional offices, headquarters program
managers, agency executive staffs, congressional committees, and outside interest
groups. Each of these actors maintains direct and indirect relationships with one
or more of the others. A major characteristic of these relationships is the flow of
increasing amounts of information and data.

Unfortunately, more often than not, the typical pattern of information management involves nothing more than routine accumulation and storage, intermittent perfunctory analysis, and crisis-oriented year-end summarization. In other
words, the vast quantities of information produced during the normal administration of many federal programs is generally not *used* in any effective way for regular, day-to-day program management.

Based on the underlying assumption that our current information resources,
if utilized properly, can greatly enhance both program effectiveness and program
management, this chapter briefly describes ongoing efforts to develop a data-

---

*Reprinted from *The Bureaucrat,* vol. 9, no. 1 (Spring 1980), pp. 3-10.

based management information system for the $55 million technical studies program administered by the U.S. Department of Transportation's Urban Mass Transportation Administration (UMTA).

BASIC CHARACTERISTICS OF THE PROGRAM

Although the specific actors may be different, the basic process of delivering the UMTA technical studies program (provided for in the Surface Transportation Assistance Act of 1978) is typical of many federal programs. The fundamental components include:

- $55 million in grants, distributed annually to . . .
- 279 urbanized areas (UZAs) and 50 states, by . . .
- 10 regional offices, in accordance with . . .
- regulations and guidelines describing both the activities to be carried out and the process to be followed, all overseen by . . .
- headquarters program staff and agency executive staff, and . . .
- regularly reported to Congress through the oversight, budget, and appropriations processes

Figure 1 graphically illustrates the basic program structure and scope. Each of the linkages represents either actual or potential flows of discrete and distinct bits of information, only some of which is routinely collected, stored, analyzed, or reported during the program cycle.

Although this structure is hardly unique within the federal system, I think it is safe to assume that there are few, if any, instances in which the collection and analysis of information goes beyond basic project file record keeping and traditional expense accounting.

CHANGING PROGRAM MANAGEMENT
AND INFORMATION NEEDS

The initial impetus for improving the flow and use of program information and data stems from decentralization of the national program to 10 regional offices. Prior to this decentralization, all critical program information was housed in headquarters. Within typical limits, data could be assembled by hand, aggregated, and analyzed with relative ease. However, only very rarely was available information used for program management purposes aside from annual congressional legislative and budget review sessions.

Within the last year (1979), however, decentralization of the program has provided both the opportunity and the need to reassess the nature of overall program

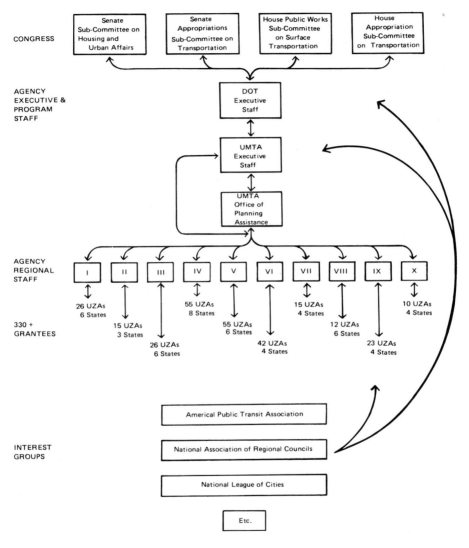

Figure 1 Program structure and actors.

management roles and responsibilities, including the need for upgraded program
reporting. Three hundred grantees no longer interact directly with a central program office. Instead, each is establishing a more personalized relationship with
its various regional offices. The record of these relationships is now widely dispersed among project and grant files in each of the regions.

At the same time that decentralization has created more sensitivity to local
and regional circumstances—the reason for the decentralization—the requirements,
guidelines, and policies for conducting local transportation and transit planning
have grown more complex and demanding through the heightened concern over
air quality, energy, and elderly and handicapped accessibility. National policy in
these areas and the local implementation of those policies demands careful coordination and much closer monitoring than was previously the case.

Finally, the windfall profits tax notwithstanding, the program budget has
not been growing in proportion to either the complexity or the number of issues
to be addressed.

In summary, within UMTA there is the desire and the organizational structure for greater sensitivity to local and regional concerns, the somewhat contradictory need to reinforce national consistency in key emphasis areas, all within
a strained budget subject to increasing scrutiny. The challenge implied here is
how to upgrade program management to meet these circumstances. One important opportunity is through a well-reasoned approach to data-based management.

DEVELOPMENT OF A MANAGEMENT INFORMATION SYSTEM
TO AID IN PROGRAM MANAGEMENT

In consideration of circumstances outlined above, managers of the UMTA technical studies programs have placed renewed emphasis on program monitoring in
a way which could encourage more effective delivery of program resources and,
at the same time, provide a mechanism for more fully monitoring the total scope
of regular program activities as they are routinely carried out in 10 regional offices.
One of the first steps in this process was to explore development of a very basic
data-based program management information system (MIS) in hopes of providing
a variety of new and essential insights on the growing number of critical program
activities. In the absence of centralized program administration, this approach required starting from scratch in conceptualizing, designing, and implementing an
effective MIS.

The responsibility for defining the concept and nature of an MIS is being
shouldered by the headquarters staff in close consultation with the regional staffs.
At the outset, there was no clear picture of what a useful MIS might look like or
how it would operate, although there was a typical initial fascination with the
potential for high-technology, "gee-whiz" hardware applications. Despite these
initial flights of fancy, we have successfully resisted the preoccupation with overly

detailed and exotic ADP approaches. It may be interesting to note that no one involved in this effort to date carries professional systems design or programming credentials per se.

In lieu of a premature commitment to heavily automated system concepts, a more cautious approach has been taken. A significant amount of time was devoted early on to a broad and reflective examination of program reporting and related management responsibilities, generally between headquarters and the regions. As a result, a number of critical questions arose which have provided a sound, working definition of the problems at hand, and at the same time helped to structure much of the MIS development work.

1. Why an MIS? What objectives need to be served? What audiences need to be served?

2. What do we already do to meet those objectives? Serve those audiences? What are our current activities and information resources?

3. What existing systems are available to facilitate MIS development and operation? How can they be refined or upgraded to serve program management needs?

4. What should be the specific scope and scale of the system? What will be the contents in terms of inputs? What will be the products in terms of outputs?

5. What will be the key implementation and operational aspects of an MIS once basic design parameters are defined?

The major phases of MIS development that have been carried out to date in response to these questions are briefly described below, along with some key observations and insights that have come to light in the process.

OUTLINING THE OBJECTIVES AND ASSUMPTIONS

Objectives

The initial issue which led to the exploration of MIS concepts, as expressed by executive management, was the need to monitor more closely grant expenditures in several of the growing list of critical national emphasis areas. Achieving regular, consistent reporting on these areas would have the added benefit of facilitating the summary of selected expenditure information for use in responding to various congressional inquiries and requests.

In reviewing the intended audience for this information (Congress and agency executive staff), it became apparent that this very narrow problem definition involved only a very limited and specialized stream of information flowing from the regions to headquarters. While this initial need was certainly legitimate, it rather conspicuously overlooked the equally legitimate need for monitoring other specific actions in a half dozen areas besides grant flow, findings from which should logically be of great significance and use to other audiences, including the regional program staffs.

Consequently, it was decided that a more useful and meaningful approach required a restatement of the initial grant flow problem in broader terms to reflect the more basic need to improve overall information flow and program reporting generally. This is particularly important because the regions have just recently undertaken complete program authority, and processes, workload, roles, and responsibilities for administering the program are still evolving.

This reassessment of a rather narrowly conceived problem or objective has had major implications and has created a much better context for investigation of MIS applications.

Three major objectives have emerged which provide a logical focus for an appropriately conceived MIS. These objectives include:

1. Provide regular monitoring of financial grant activity in specific areas of study (i.e., national emphasis areas)

2. Provide a means by which to develop timely responses to congressional and related inquiries on financial as well as other program activities, and

3. Improve overall program management in the areas of
   a. Meeting national program objectives
   b. Improving the delivery of federal resources
   c. Identifying problems and/or successes in areas of (a) and (b), and
   d. Highlighting actions that could be used in remedying those problems or shortcomings

Assumptions

Along with the development of a workable set of objectives came the recognition of several key assumptions that require verification and continuing attention in each step of MIS development.

1. Although the concern for improved management and related reporting within the technical studies program should be closely integrated with programs and responsibilities in other UMTA offices (e.g., capital assistance program, operating assistance program, demonstration programs, policy development and analysis, etc.), it was decided that the initial effort in program reporting should focus directly on the flow and use of information within the technical studies program only. Biting off too big a piece at the outset was likely to be counterproductive and lead to unnecessary floundering in the typical quagmire of multiprogram and multioffice "cooperation and coordination."

2. It was questionable whether any of the existing information systems available within the agency would prove useful in meeting the newly emerging program management and MIS needs. It was equally doubtful that these existing systems could be easily expanded or augmented to meet these needs.

3. If the system were properly conceived, the nature of the basic information needed for input and output was thought to be simple enough to allow very effective automation at any time, but not at the outset (see assumption 2, above).

4. Because regional program activities are conducted on the basis of individual grants and actions for each urbanized area, input for any MIS must logically draw from individual project files. The regional offices would have to provide much of the basic MIS inputs directly from their daily activity. Severe workload problems and understaffing in the regional offices clearly suggest that the quality, consistency, and timeliness of inputs would be unacceptable if the input process became an independent time-consuming administrative burden above and beyond normal daily program activities. Consequently, it is assumed that major support and assistance from headquarters would be needed in the provision of MIS inputs for some time into the future.

5. It is also assumed that regular MIS input and report would not be made self-sustaining in a meaningful way unless there were some direct applicability and benefit to the regions in system operations. The system has to provide a direct resource and service to the regions as the inputters if it is to be successful.

6. The administrative pitfalls of implementing any type of new reporting or data-based management system present potentially major problems, including (1) the need to arrive at a consensus on the need, value, use, and proposed mechanics of a reporting system among all levels of program staff, (2) the obvious but only partially recognized fact that a substantial commitment in dollars and time would be needed to design an MIS and manage its operation, (3) the likelihood that a new, independent fully automated system was not going to be developed in the immediate future because of cost implications and administrative difficulties.

ASSESSING THE PROGRAM ACTIVITIES
IN TERMS OF INFORMATION NEEDS

The next step has been to analyze the various actions and activities within the program as a means of establishing the scope and scale of the reporting system.

Delivery of the technical studies program entails four primary activities, each of which requires a specific formal review and approval action in the regions.

1. Annual review and "certification" of the urbanized area planning process and its conformity to basic regulatory and administrative requirements

2. Annual review and approval of a program of proposed technical studies agreed on by all participating local units of government for the upcoming year (a *U*nified *P*lanning *W*ork *P*rogram—UPWP)

3. Annual review and approval of a technical studies grant application to fund the year's work program

4. Annual review and approval of a capital improvement program for transportation projects, the justification for each of which is expected to be based on the findings of past technical study efforts (*T*ransportation *I*mprovement *P*rogram/*A*nnual *E*lement—TIP/AE)

These actions typically are taken based on findings coming out of considerable negotiations with various grantees. Information and data from each of these separate actions is routinely accumulated within the regional project files. (Effective records management is therefore a critical factor affecting MIS operations but will not be discussed in this chapter.) However, no mechanism exists to allow either useful analysis or aggregation of information for any of the objectives outlined above, short of exhaustive special efforts to dig back into the files well after the fact.

Each of these four transactions is carried out for each of the 279 urbanized areas in the country. (Two of these actions, UPWP review and approval and grant approval, are also required for each of the 50 states.) The principal issues of concern to program managers at both the regional and national levels, and therefore within the MIS, include:

1. The duration and type of "deficiencies" found within the local planning processes with respect to current regulations and guidelines, in various regions, and for cities of various sizes, etc.

2. The distribution of funds among various categories of technical activity, in various regions and for cities of various sizes, etc. (Technical activity categories include planning program support and administration, long-range transportation planning, five categories of short-range, project-specific planning, etc.)

3. The link between technical study activities and the actual capital projects that are requested, funded, and implemented

4. The identification of particularly noteworthy local programs, policies, plans, or projects, that may have application or relevance in other areas, and

5. The timeliness of responses and grant delivery to local and regional client agencies and grantees

After a relatively straightforward review of the basic program activities, the general scope and scale of the MIS became apparent and generally agreed on among executive staff, headquarters program staff, and regional program staff. To reach this point has taken approximately 8 months. In the process it has become apparent that the system must include the ability to manipulate four or five discrete sets of information (files) based on key program actions for each of approximately 330 areas or grantees. It also must be capable of providing periodic status reports based on inputs received continuously throughout the fiscal year.

ASSESSING EXISTING INFORMATION SYSTEMS AND PROBLEMS

Another of the initial steps in the development of an effective data-based MIS was a preliminary assessment of current data and information systems in use within the agency. The purpose was to discover whether or not they offered the potential to meet the new reporting and program management objectives being formulated.

An initial assessment of the current flow (or lack) of program information and of the supporting data systems indicated clearly that the information and data necessary to address the issues outlined above by and large lies buried, on paper, within the individual area grant files housed in each region. With the exception of the basic financial data necessary for centralized requisitioning and disbursements, very little of the available information is being aggregated, distilled, and/or analyzed in a systematic way, either within the regions or at the national level.

This observation is not an indictment of the existing systems per se, but rather a reflection of the fact that traditional accounting systems have not yet caught up with decentralization of program authority to the regions.

A very basic records system is being maintained which serves no useful purpose for regular program management and oversight. Financial information which is routinely transmitted via remote terminals from the regions is processed and stored in an archaic system of computer accounts. This system appears to provide very little flexibility or interactive capability to meet the newly articulated needs for regular program reporting and analysis.

In many instances simple operational problems and shortcomings within these systems and the associated hardware have reduced the reliability of the current system to the point where backup paper records are still essential to guarantee accurate and up to the minute information.

In addition to the general systemic problems mentioned above, there are operational and definitional problems as well with the financial information that is currently being submitted. First, the summary of proposed grant budget expenditures which are broken down among various categories of technical activities has frequently been provided by the regional staff rather than the grantees themselves. This reflects the sensitivity of the regional staff to foisting added informational and/or reporting responsibilities on their clients. However, because the summarization of grantee costs is a time-consuming and relatively low-priority task for the regions, even the current technical activity expenditure data, the quantitative heart of the MIS, is uneven and untimely in its current form.

Second, the 10 or so categories of activities being used to summarize the costs of work programs (which each individually may contain as many as 100 discrete technical studies) do not provide logical, clear, or consistent distinctions between categories, nor do they provide an accurate expression of many of the factors of concern to program managers.

DETAILED MIS DESIGN ACTIVITIES

In recognition of the objectives, assumptions, and problems outlined above, a preliminary MIS design effort has been undertaken in-house to define the specific components of the system. As implied earlier, the overall objective has been and continues to be to improve program management, with data-based management applications viewed as a major vehicle toward this end.

Within the technical studies program, six specific types of information have been identified that are felt to be of critical importance in the MIS effort. Each of these is briefly described below to give some idea of the nature of the MIS development process and the proposed content of the system.

Grant Flow

One of the key steps in the initial design of the MIS has been to redefine the categories used as the basis for reporting grant budget breakdowns. This is currently being done in two major steps.

First, significant changes are being made in the administrative program guidance to grantees to facilitate the necessary reporting. Grantees themselves, during the normal course of the grant application process, will be required to provide the necessary budget breakdowns. This should relieve the regional staff of the need to do additional, time-consuming financial analysis on each work program. At the same time little or no additional burden should be imposed on grantees because they already typically provide aggregated budget summaries in the process of preparing their work programs.

Second, the technical activities reporting categories are being redrafted in close consultation with the regional staffs to arrive at a clear and complete framework for aggregating and analyzing grant expenditures in a way that reflects the structure of typical work program elements and the breakdowns considered necessary from a program management standpoint.

Certification

The certification process can be monitored through a relatively simple report of individual certification actions at the time they are carried out. Although a few regions currently provide such summaries, the formats are inconsistent and no regular way to tabulate and analyze the results exists.

Work Program

Work program reviews and approvals can be handled through the use of four or five pieces of key information.

TIPs

Because the transportation improvement programs contain projects for which capital funding requests will be made, they represent the link between project planning and implementation. There are some conceptual difficulties, however, in how this linkage should be described within an MIS. First, the dollar value of specific projects is not always an accurate indicator of the effectiveness of the project or of its impact. Frequently, less capital-intensive projects have more significant impacts which would be severely underrepresented if absolute cost were the only measure monitored.

Second, many projects have streams of costs and benefits that are both difficult to measure and which vary widely over time. Determining when and what cost should be reported for projects within a given year or quarter is a difficult question.

Finally, the fact that projects are "programmed" guarantees neither their timely implementation nor their ultimate success, which is the ultimate test of the planning process. At this point in the preliminary design of the MIS, there is no clear answer on how TIP programming and the critical linkages between planning, project implementation, and success can be monitored. However, it is possible to both record the timing aspects of TIP review and approval and note specific deficiencies or problems encountered in the process.

Success Stories

An alternative to the dilemma raised above is to actively seek narrative descriptions of significant planning and project successes.

One option being explored at this time is requesting a simple periodic report from each region noting only the location (city) and the type of project or planning that is being suggested as an exemplary effort. These notations would be filed in headquarters and specific descriptive information would be sought from the regions and grantees by headquarters staff, as needed.

System Capabilities

The intention of instituting an MIS is to go beyond mere record keeping in the accumulation and use of information flowing out of the program. In general terms, this implies that whatever "system" evolves must provide certain specific capabilities to be useful.

1. The system must be fully interactive, i.e., it should be capable of addressing a wide range of program-oriented questions on command.
2. System access and interactive capabilities should be provided to the regional office to facilitate system inputs and to encourage regular MIS use at the regional level.
3. The system should be designed to provide specific status reports on various program activities on a regular basis (e.g., quarterly) as well as on request.
4. The system should incorporate adequate logic and error checks to ensure maximum reliability and dependability.

These concepts, and particularly the way in which they are described, imply an automated system. However, with some imagination and desk work, these capabilities can be translated into functions that can be carried out even if inputs and information flow occur on paper. This flexibility is critical since for several reasons initial operation of the MIS is likely to be based on paper flow and hand calculations for at least a full program cycle and perhaps longer.

NEXT STEPS

At this point we have only identified and described the basic MIS concept for the first time. Preliminary proposals on MIS content are circulating for hard review and discussion.

A work program has been developed identifying the steps and responsibilities necessary in proceeding beyond these preliminary steps into final MIS development, implementation, and operation. Though it may be premature, the prospects are mildly exciting and offer potentially great improvements in a number of areas of program management. Interest in the MIS effort is growing steadily, both in headquarters and in the field, as the concept and value of the data-based management approach crystalizes.

USEFUL CONCEPTS

It seems helpful to mention some useful concepts that have been gleaned from
the literature that is developing on information resource management or that
have surfaced in the process of actually trying to outline an effective MIS.

System Perspective

Before effective steps can be taken in managing and using our vast information
resources, the entire system from which these resources are generated and within
which they may find use must be carefully reviewed and fully understood. Unless
a broad perspective is adopted at the outset in terms of problem definition and
objective setting, we run the risk of focusing prematurely on narrow subsets of
our information management problem and settling for a "quick fix" in terms of
the disjointed use of hardware, equipment, or unnecessary additional administrative procedures.

The problems identified above in terms of the inability of existing ADP systems to accommodate our emerging data-based management needs stem in part
from this problem; our current ADP systems have tended to grow piecemeal
through the periodic addition of new, small components without proper recognition that program management roles and responsibilities have changed or are
changing, and along with them our basic data and information needs.

Relationship to Decision Making

To become an effective and self-sustaining function, information resources management and mechanisms must be responsive and accessible to, and of direct
benefit to, decision makers. The information management function must go beyond simple records maintenance to provide regular analysis, insights, and recommendations on the ongoing, operational aspects of the program, whether the
decision maker is a regional office director, headquarters program manager, agency
executive, or congressional committee member.

Feedback and Follow-Through

Closely related to the concept of information systems as an aid to the decision
maker is the corresponding need to incorporate feedback to the various system
contributors explicitly as well as to promote consistent follow-through on issues
and problems raised in the analysis phases on MIS operation. Each contributor
or user of the system must be able to realize some benefit from its operation.
Intermittent one-way streams of information must be appropriately converted
to regular two-way information flows to knit program elements and actors together in serving overall program management objectives.

Audiences

The fact that many different participants with different needs and interests are likely to be part of a stream of program information and data requires that careful attention be paid to these audiences and to what specific types of information are needed to meet their needs. Care in identifying the audiences to be served and their respective needs can go a long way in establishing the basic scope and scale of systematic information management activities.

Transactional Activities

The basic use of an MIS for program management involves monitoring a series of continuing transactions. The implication is that system inputs will be continuous and that system outputs will be required at both regular intervals and intermittently throughout the program cycle. Attention to this dynamic character is also fundamental in determining the scope, scale, and complexity of the system.

Output vs. Outcome

At the root of all public expenditure analysis lies the problem of selecting measures of effectiveness by which to assess program performance. The same problem lies beneath the concept of data-based management, i.e., what are we measuring and what is its significance? While many programs have a large "output," i.e., dollars for particular types of goods and services, these large outputs may have significantly smaller impact of "outcome" than programs whose outputs are much smaller. Care must be taken in MIS development that these factors are not confused.

13

EVALUATING BENEFITS AND COSTS OF AUTO SAFETY STANDARDS*

John Pennington
Heber Bouland

In August 1974, the Chairman, Senate Commerce Committee, asked GAO to analyze the benefits and costs of motor vehicle safety standards. In essence, we were to place a dollar value on the benefits of the automobile safety program, i.e., fatalities and injuries prevented, and to compare this with its costs—to give the ultimate or bottom line in program results auditing. The chairman emphasized his request by pointing out that the Legislative Reorganization Act of 1970 specified that we conduct studies of the costs and benefits of federal programs at the request of a congressional committee.

　　We were concerned about this request because our previous work had identified many obstacles which could thwart such an undertaking.[1]

- No nationally representative accident-cause data were available. Such data are necessary to "quantify" program benefits.

- Separating the benefits of improved automobiles from the benefits of improved highways and driver-oriented safety programs was a problem.

- Manufacturers usually did not reveal the costs of safety features.

---

*Reprinted from *GAO Review,* vol. 11 (Fall 1976), pp. 36–42.

- There were no universally acceptable dollar values for lives saved and injuries and accidents avoided. Such values are necessary to "price" program benefits.

DEVELOPING AN APPROACH

Although we recognized all these problems, we also recognized the Congress's pressing need for facts to evaluate this multimillion dollar program. Consequently, we decided to seek the best accident data available and analyze and evaluate it to the best of our ability.

We also knew we would have to make certain assumptions and indicate them in our evaluations. We assumed that each model year of a car would reflect changes in safety because succeeding models incorporated previous safety features. The relationship between model year and some of the major standards is shown in Table 1.

Features such as better brakes and windshield wipers and improved highways are designed to prevent accidents; seat belts, padded dashes, etc., are designed to save occupant lives and reduce injuries once an accident has occurred. Since we would be dealing with data from accidents, we were limited to an evaluation of the occupant protection standards.

We also had to limit our analyses to drivers because the number of uninjured occupants involved in accidents often is not reported. Thus, our basic premise was that occupant protection safety could be evaluated by how often drivers involved in accidents were killed or injured in different model year cars.

Table 1   Relationship Between Model Year and Major Standards, 1966-1974

Model year introduced	Major safety features
1966	Manufacturers installed most items required by GSA standards—seat belts, safety glass, impact-absorbing steering column, safety door latches, recessed dash instruments, padded dash and sun visors, etc.
1969	Head restraints
1970	Strengthened windshield mounting
1972	Seat belt warning/light buzzer
1973	Side door beams
1974	Crush-resistant roof, ignition interlock

Table 2 North Carolina Study Data

	North Carolina	North Carolina	New York
Calendar years in which accidents occurred	1966-72	1973-74	1971-73
Number of accident-involved cars	1,020,000	424,000	861,000

ANALYSIS OF DATA

We decided to analyze North Carolina's accident data because it is relatively accurate, complete, and consistently gathered. We also wanted statistics from a more urbanized state, so we selected New York, whose accident data we considered reasonably good.

We contracted with the Highway Safety Research Center of the University of North Carolina to analyze the North Carolina data; our staff analyzed New York's data.

The North Carolina data base was divided into two independent groups because of changes in the accident-reporting system in 1973. The data groups we used are shown in Table 2.

Two types of analysis were performed on the data. The first involved raw or unadjusted statistics. Raw data are simple and uncomplicated to use, and results are obtained each year. A second, more complicated series of analyses was performed to adjust for factors—such as speed, weight of vehicles—which might unduly influence the model year safety results.

Raw Data

Figure 1 is a graph of the unadjusted statistics from the three data groups. In both states the safety of cars showed a continuing improvement in successive model years until the 1969 or 1970 model.

Because there were different definitions of "serious injury" and because New York has a different environment and different types of accidents, the three files show different percentages of drivers killed or seriously injured.

Adjusted Data

We adjusted the raw data to compensate for factors which might possibly distort the model year results. For example, the severity of an accident depends on many factors, such as speed, weight of the vehicles, and point of impact. Other less apparent factors are a single vehicle crash contrasted to two or more vehicles colliding; inebriated drivers or sober drivers in accidents; day or night accidents;

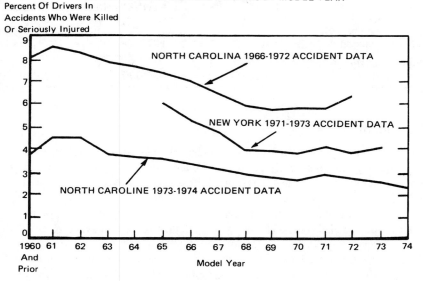

Figure 1 Fatalities and serious injuries by model year.

accidents on high-speed rural highways compared with those in the dense traffic of cities; women drivers vs. male drivers.

To equalize the factors, we used regression analysis—a statistical technique for measuring the relationship among variables.[2] Some of the more important variables used in the regression analyses were:

- Driver injury level
- Calendar years
- Weather conditions
- Locality
- Type of accident (single or multiple vehicle)
- Speed
- Driver's age
- Driver's sex
- Sobriety
- Model year

Table 3 Survivability Auto Safety Standards

Major standards	Model years	Improvement in safety compared to 1965 and prior models (%)
Seat belts, door locks, padded dash, energy-absorbing steering column	1966-68	15.3
Head restraint, strengthen wind-shield mounting	1969-70	26.9
Side door beams, crush-resistant roof, seat belt warning devices	1971-73	27.5

- Seat belt usage
- Vehicle damage index (TAD)

To thoroughly investigate the relationship between model years and crash survivability, 11 different analyses were performed using different data, files, variables, etc. For example, several analyses used only physical factors that *logically* affect accident severity—factors such as speed, weight of the vehicles, and point of impact. Another group of analyses used only factors that satistically affect accident severity (based on a modified chi-square technique). These factors included the driver's sex, weather, and time of day.

Table 3 shows the results of 1 of the 11 analyses. In general, most of the analyses showed the same pattern of improvement, i.e., improvements in the early and intermediate model year cars, then a leveling off of improvements in later model cars.

COST OF SAFETY STANDARDS

Federally mandated safety features have been incorporated in about 86 million passenger cars sold in the United States—from the 1966 models through the 1974 models—at a total estimated cost of $14.6 billion. This amount is based on the three major American automobile manufacturers' estimated average cost per car of complying with each federal standard (including changes) for each model year. The unit cost of all standards grew from about $40 on the 1966 model to about $368 on the 1974 model. Of these amounts, the estimate for crash survivability standards alone—those which we were evaluating—grew from about $22 to about $177. We computed the amortized cost of these standards at over $3 billion, as shown in Table 4.

Table 4   Costs of Crash Survivability Standards, 1966–1974

Model year introduced	Unit costs of standards	Amortized 1966–1974* (millions)
1966	$ 22	$ 928.2
1967	21	709.3
1968	36	941.3
1969	18	380.3
1970	2	28.8
	99	2,987.9
1971	2	19.1
1972	15	95.2
1973	14	46.7
	31	161.0
1974	$177	$3,193.4

*Based on an estimated 10-year car life.

BENEFITS OF SAFETY STANDARDS

To estimate the benefits of crash survivability safety features, reductions in fatalities and injuries have to be measured. We took a twofold approach to this because we believed that the probable reduction in fatalities was the only effect that could be reasonably measured nationwide for comparison with costs. We compared the benefits of safety features and the cost of both fatalities and injuries in North Carolina and then compared the benefits and costs of only fatalities nationwide.

Before we could do either, we had to select a cost to society of a fatality and an injury—not an easy thing to do. The Safety Administration, a special ad hoc committee of the executive branch, and the National Safety Council have made such estimates. They vary widely, depending on assumptions and exclusions of such factors as lost wages, days of hospitalization, value of pain and suffering, and other factors. The three estimates were:

	Dollars per death	Dollars per injury
National Safety Council	52,000	3,100
Ad hoc committee	140,000	2,750
Safety Administration	200,700	7,300

Table 5 Comparison of Benefits and Costs (Estimated)

Model year	Benefits of fatalities and injuries prevented			Unit cost of standards	Benefit-cost ratio
	Fatalities	Injuries	Total		
1966	$ 70	$38	$108	$ 22	4.9/1
1969	126	98	224	97	2.3/1
1972	154	95	249	116	2.2/1

The value of human life or injury is obviously a very subjective matter. We did not judge which one of the estimates was "best." We leave it to the reader to make the final judgment or to select his own set of values.

A North Carolina Automobile

Our first approach was to estimate the benefits and costs that occur over the useful life of different model year cars in North Carolina. The benefits of fatalities and injuries prevented are the product of (1) the number of fatalities and injuries prevented per accident, (2) the number of accidents a car is expected to be involved in over its life, and (3) the cost to society of a fatality or injury.

Table 5 compares the benefits and costs for selected model years using the ad hoc committee's estimate of benefits. (Using similar computations for the Safety Administration's values almost doubles the benefit-cost ratios, whereas using the National Safety Council's values decreases them by about one-third.)

Injuries are important in the benefit-cost ratios. Reductions in injuries account for about 36 percent of the benefits when the ad hoc committee's values are used, by 52 percent when the Safety Administration's values are used, and by 64 percent when the National Safety Council's values are used.

Nationwide Estimate

Since North Carolina's accident picture was not too atypical of the nation's, we applied North Carolina's rates of improvement to nationwide statistics on automobile fatalities, as follows:

1. The relative chance of being killed in different model year cars was estimated using 1 of the 11 analyses.
2. The percentage of total cars registered by model year was determined.
3. The chance of being killed for the various model years was multiplied by the percentage of cars registered for any year. This provided annual safety indices for each year.

Table 6 Nationwide Statistics

Value of each	Total (millions)
$ 52,000	$1,468.0
140,000	3,952.2
200,700	5,665.8

The estimated amortized costs of the 1966-1970 standard
in all 1966 and later models over the same period are about
$2,988 million. Estimated lives saved = 28,230.

4. Actual national fatality figures were divided by the annual safety indices
   to compute the estimated fatalities that would have occurred if there had
   been no safety features.

5. The difference between actual fatalities and the estimated fatalities that
   might have occurred without standard safety features is an estimate of the
   lives saved each year.

6. Lives saved each year are totaled, valued at three different societal cost
   estimates, and divided by the amortized costs to provide a benefit-cost
   ratio.

The results of this approach are shown in Table 6.

The following are the estimated benefit-cost ratios:

- At $ 52,000 $\dfrac{\$1,468.0}{\$2,987.9} = 0.5/1$

- At $140,000 $\dfrac{\$3,952.2}{\$2,987.9} = 1.3/1$

- At $200,700 $\dfrac{\$5,665.8}{\$2,987.9} = 1.9/1$

We did not attribute any benefits to 1971-1973 safety standards because our
study showed little, if any, improvement from these model cars. The total estimated costs of these requirements are nearly $850 million for model years 1971-
1973.

We also did not attempt to estimate benefits for the 1974 occupant safety
requirements because there were not enough accidents to analyze.

The data in this article are based on the Comptroller General's report to the
Senate Commerce Committee entitled "Effectiveness, Benefits, and Costs of
Federal Safety Standards For Protection of Passenger Car Occupants" (CED-76-
121) dated July 7, 1976.

CONCLUSIONS

Although there are limitations to our study, we believe the results have power-ful policy implications for both the Congress and the Safety Administration. For example, although this program does not have to be justified on the basis of cost, there still remains the question of whether additional occupant protection standards should be required, since added costs in recent model years have pro-duced little, if any, additional benefits.

So far as we know, this is the first time GAO has conducted its own benefit-cost analysis. Because benefit-cost analysis is a useful tool for providing the Congress with needed program information, we believe GAO will be called on more and more to perform these evaluations in the future. Such undertakings are risky. The auditor must be willing to defend his work and accept the criticism which is inevitable when one is pushing the state of the art.

NOTES

1. Report to the Senate Committee on Commerce on Need to Improve Benefit-Cost Analyses in Setting Motor Vehicle Safety Standards, B-164497 (3), July 24, 1974.
2. William P. Johnston, Jr. and Allan Rogers, Regression analysis: Does it have practical use? *GAO Review,* Summer 1975.

14

PRODUCTIVITY MEASUREMENT: A Management Tool*

Brian L. Usilaner

Despite significant progress in recent years, productivity improvement in the federal government has had a relatively low level of impact. It has been affected by inflated rhetoric and shifting emphases from one fashionable managerial technique to another.

In federal experience, productivity improvement has been weak in motivation, purpose, and achievement primarily because it has been accorded very low status by political and career executives. The reason for this is simple—there are few, if any, incentives for these executives to focus their concerns and resources on efforts to improve productivity of programs they administer. Not only do managers lack incentives, but they are likely to encounter built-in penalties if they attempt to bring about improvements.

Operating officials regard arbitrary productivity cuts, taking away all savings achieved and across-the-board reductions, as disincentives to using productivity data. Undoubtedly some cases of apparently arbitrary actions result from lack of meaningful productivity data or failure to present available data effectively. In other cases there may have been inappropriate action in applying general pro-

---

*Reprinted from *GAO Review,* vol. 11 (Fall 1976), pp. 54-59.

ductivity goals to specific situations where they do not fit or in mandating unrealistic productivity goals. Budget and program officials at all levels need to
work together to find ways to deal with the problems of incentives and make
productivity an institutionalized management tool.

Experience has shown that there is no great mystery about the "how" of
achieving significant and measurable productivity improvements. Most, if not all,
of the management techniques involved are old, familiar tools of financial management, industrial engineering, and behavioral science. But it should be noted
that productivity is an after-the-fact evaluation tool. Unlike many work measurement systems that are used as daily measurement tools, productivity examines
trends and the reasons for changes in these trends. However, few agencies have
active productivity improvement programs, and the concept of productivity as
a pervasive consideration in the management process remains comparatively rare.

The following is a summary of some of the major areas in which productivity
measures can be useful in the management process.

SETTING GOALS

Most agencies, either through established management-by-objectives programs or
other means, are accustomed to establishing goals for their current and future
operations. Too often, however, these goals are general in nature and difficult to
assess in terms of accomplishment. A productivity measurement system can be a
means of making the goals more specific and meaningful by showing direction toward attaining the goals, recognizing, of course, that not all goals are quantifiable.

Productivity goals, in order to be meaningful, have to be specific to the organization. The productivity goals established in any given period for individual
agencies should be based on the specific potential for productivity improvement
in each agency. There is no logical basis for identical percentage targets that
would apply uniformly to each agency and program. Experience shows that productivity changes have occurred at very different rates in different agencies and
at different times for a variety of reasons.

Therefore, since both in the short and long run the potential for improvements
in productivity of an organization varies, both among units of the organization and
from year to year, the actual percentage change in productivity of an organization
should not be viewed as a direct indicator of the quality either of its management
or of its labor force. Such an evaluation requires additional information and judgment regarding the difference between potential and actual change in productivity
and an estimate of the contribution made to increase the potential.

With the development of a productivity measurement system and productivity goals, the next step is to integrate the measures and goals into the budget
process.

BUDGET JUSTIFICATION

For many years there has been a requirement that agencies submit productivity improvement data in support of the annual budget estimates (OMB Circular No. A-11, sec. 24). Implementation of productivity measurement techniques produces the technology necessary to satisfy this requirement. However, past measures of productivity data by budget reviewers have discouraged program managers from providing productivity data in the budget review process. Such actions as arbitrary productivity reductions, lack of rewards for self-imposed productivity improvement, and across-the-board cuts have all added toward inhibiting the full integration of productivity measurement into the budget process. Significantly increased use of productivity data is unlikely to occur unless changes in budget policies are made which will encourage the use of such data and counteract the negative factors.

The use of productivity data and specific goals can contribute to better projections of resource needs and the review by others of those needs. In particular, with the help of productivity data, it may be possible to analyze budget estimates in terms of volume of output projected, productivity rates anticipated, and prices of resources. Separate analyses can be made of the major components of output and input. Such analyses can be carried out at different levels of detail, which may be appropriate at the different stages of the review.

COST REDUCTION AND ORGANIZATIONAL IMPROVEMENT

The greatest immediate value of productivity measurement is its potential to contribute to improvements in productivity and hence savings of manpower and money. Productivity data may be helpful in at least two eays. First, they provide a history of what actually happened to productivity under a variety of conditions. This information may be drawn on in formulating plans for increasing efficiency in the future. Second, measures of productivity may be used as a follow-up device to determine how well the goals for productivity improvements are actually being achieved.

Analysis of productivity data can make possible more informed judgments about the effects on productivity of various actions or events, such as introduction of a new type of equipment, centralization of operations, changes in legislation, or changes in systems and procedures. Such analysis may be used both as a part of the postaudit and in formulating plans for organizational improvements.

Management analysis studies usually project improved operating situations resulting in reduced resource requirements in terms of reduced dollar costs, reduced material consumption, and reduced staffing requirements. Productivity measures can be used in preimplementation and postimplementation audits or analyses. The first assures the accuracy of the assumptions and calculations, while the second evaluates the actual savings realized.

Reduced resource requirements should result in achievement of the previous level of output with fewer resources or increased output with the same resources. This improvement should be reflected in a productivity index. The productivity index thus offers another means of validating management improvement studies. Requests for capital investments to replace existing facilities or equipment or to improve a physical process are stated in terms of reduced operating costs and productivity improvement. Managers should be held accountable for the forecasted productivity gains. Productivity measurement would serve as an aid in determination of whether forecast operating conditions are being achieved. It will also serve to highlight lagging areas in need of review.

ONGOING CONTROL OF OPERATIONS

A functioning system containing one or several measures of productivity will provide a periodic report on the efficiency of the organization and will bring to the attention of management departures from the past trends, from the planned goal, or from the pattern of change in comparable organizations.

Productivity measures may be used as a unifying framework for bringing together the various fragmented management components such as budget, personnel, internal audit, and management analysis. Each component can contribute to management improvement through the use of productivity data. However, coordination of efforts is essential if any significant impact on performance improvement is to be made.

Productivity measures may also be used to bring together the different types of management information, particularly for data generated through budgeting, cost accounting, work measurements, or personnel management evaluations. Sometimes, the diverse information already on hand is not fully used because of the lack of common focus and comparability of form.

The financial data, when related to the measures of output, can indicate the actual cost of the output produced and its changes on the per unit basis in the course of time. Also, the total unit costs may be broken down by types of cost. Changes in the total may be analyzed in terms of components. Further, as a byproduct of productivity measurement, trends in prices paid by the organization for its inputs can be established, and the separate effects on unit cost of change in the quantity of resource inputs and of changes in prices paid can be ascertained.

Where a detailed work measurement system exists, it may be possible to analyze the end-product outputs in terms of their component work process or units. Similarly, on the input side (with the help of accounting data) the detailed use of the individual resources, such as various labor skills or types of machinery, may be analyzed in terms of their effect on productivity, possibly in some degree of organizational detail. An integrated arrangement of management information, including both organizational productivity measurement and detailed cost accounting and work measurement, can be used both in detailed analysis of past changes in productivity and in developing plans for future productivity improvement.

IMPROVEMENT MOTIVATION

To improve productivity, individuals with government agencies must take strong action. They must commit themselves to specific productivity goals, specify performance criteria, and make decisions in an open and participative manner. People will persist in behavior which is aimed toward increased productivity when the activity is individually satisfying and rewarding. For this behavior to persist, it has to be consistently rewarded. The consistency and effectiveness of reward is a function of reinforcement. Positive reinforcement means that rewards are used to encourage people to perform in a desired manner. There are three necessary conditions for successfully motivating people:

1. Desired level of performance should be known and clearly stated.

2. People should be rewarded for specific increases in level of performance.

3. Rewards should follow desired performance as closely as possible.

Therefore, the objective of positive reinforcement must be considered in developing a productivity program. The measures will help to gage performance. For people to be encouraged and motivated, they must know where they stand. Productivity measures provide an objective means for rewarding performance. The most obvious incentive is money, where higher pay or salary is to be a reward for higher productivity. This can be in the form of either individual or group incentives.

There are, however, several constraints to implementation of monetary incentives. The first, and most obvious, is scarce funds. The second is the automatic longevity pay increase structure. The third is restraints imposed by job classification systems.

There have been several attempts to overcome these obstacles. One approach has been a concept called "productivity bargaining." This is a joint method of negotiating pay increases for employees based on increases in productivity. Productivity bargaining means that employees share directly in the savings realized through joint labor-management productivity efforts. Several local governments are trying this approach. In addition, the Bureau of Engraving and Printing is exploring a "Scanlon Plan" approach whereby federal employees would share in productivity savings. The key to any of these approaches is that a suitable productivity measurement system must first be developed.

The setting of productivity goals within the framework of a management-by-objectives system will help motivate managers to take an interest in productivity. Once goals are established there is accountability, commitment, and involvement on the part of managers. However, the system must be used by top management in reviewing organizational performance if managers are to be motivated to reach their productivity goals.

ACCOUNTABILITY

A sound productivity measurement system fosters accountability on the part of managers. Productivity measures the rate of change in efficiency. It measures the change in the relationship of products or services produced to resources used. It gives visibility in terms of specific numbers as to the change in efficiency of a program's operations. By giving visibility in terms of rates of performance, productivity measurement makes managers accountable for performance. It forces managers to explain poor performance and provides a vehicle for documenting good performance.

A good system also prevents sweeping statements about inefficiencies in government by providing factual data on efficiency to the Congress and the public.

CONCLUSIONS

The real payoff in the use of productivity measurement will come from the analyses by individual agency managers of their areas of responsibility. Effective use of productivity measurement will result in a determination of

- The trend of productivity over time
- Obstacles to productivity improvement
- Actions responsible for improvement
- Identification of future improvements
- Budget application of productivity data
- Validity of other performance measurement systems, such as work measurement
- Impact of changes in the relationship of overhead to direct production workers
- Impact of changes in the relationship of labor costs to staff years

Some of the potential uses of productivity measurement have been examined in this chapter. These surely are not all of the uses that may be made, and some of the uses are no more than concepts of utility at the present time. Productivity measurement, like other management data, must be kept in its proper perspective in the overall management information scheme. It should be used with care and caution, not to the abandonment of existing management information, but as an overall integrating factor.

Various approaches to developing the proper methodology of productivity measurement should be thoroughly explored to find the most reasonable approach for each organization to obtain an acceptable relationship of resources and outputs. These approaches should provide the foundation for an overall productivity improvement program.

15

REVENUE AND EXPENDITURE FORECASTING: Some Comparative Trends *

Albert C. Hyde
William L. Jarocki

In recent years, both public administrators and legislators have shown increasing interest in the external environment of the budgetary process. Whereas budgetary systems may adapt and evolve, providing one type of process change,[1] the external effects on the budget provide a different set of parameters for the budget process. Perhaps the most influential effect is the limitation imposed by the level of finite resources available to accomplish expenditure programs. Thus, the forecasting of available resources or revenues is viewed as an integral and essential element in the budgetary process. Conversely, predictions of specific levels of "necessary" expenditure can be equally significant.

The importance of aggregate revenue and expenditure estimation is perhaps most apparent at the state and local government levels, where by law budgets are required to balance. Over the past decade, state and local government jurisdictions have experienced significant increases in the demand for public goods and services. Since the late 1960s, this demand has outstripped the ability of state

*Reprinted by permission from Albert C. Hyde (ed.), *Government Budgeting: Theory, Process, Politics,* pp. 532-548. Copyright © 1978 Moore Publishing Company, Inc., Oak Park, Illinois.

governments to simply adjust appropriate tax policies to provide the necessary
revenues for increased spending policies. The growth rates of state and local
public expenditures have increased dramatically from 97.2 billion in 1969 to
185.0 billion in 1976 (estimated).[2] Concurrently, New York City and a host of
other state and local governments have faced grave budgetary/fiscal crises. This
resulting environment has focused new attention on budgeting and fiscal planning
to lessen the element of surprise and the inevitable shock of adjustment.

PLANNING TECHNIQUES

Revenue Forecasting

Two techniques have constituted governmental units' attempts to provide for
this element of planning for the budgetary process. The first, revenue forecasting,
is a well-established tool of budgeting involving the making of specific predictions
—tax by tax, of the *probable* next year's receipt of revenues. Methods range from
the extremely complex, making use of extensive computer and socioeconomic
dynamic models to the equally simplistic, using some form of statistical routine.
The crux of revenue forecasting is, of course, the degree of accuracy of the prediction. To some extent, all revenue-forecasting techniques except one are subject to error. Jesse Burkheadt describes, in *Government Budgeting,* the use by
the French of "the rule of the penultimate," whereby the fiscal cycle for revenues
is one year ahead of the budgeting cycle for expenditures.[3] Literally, the sum of
revenues collected the previous year becomes the budgeting ceiling for the current
year. Obviously, such an approach is highly accurate. It is also of questionable
utility because governments are not restricted solely to tax revenue sources; they
can borrow, advance, or postpone payments, sell services and public goods, etc.
Such options mean that more flexibility is *possible* in balancing budgets, provided sufficient lead time is available to make adequate arrangements. The purpose of revenue forecasting is primarily to provide guidance for such adjustments.
   Revenue forecasting, then, attempts to analyze the variables which can be
linked to the generation of revenues and provide accurate parameters for budgetary decisions. The ability of forecasting models to correctly pinpoint the behavior
of those variables is directly related to the forecasting methodology employed. Although long-range revenue estimating has been addressed previously,[4] little has
been done to examine revenue-forecasting methodologies in a comparative context. This chapter will attempt to provide a comparative frame of reference for
an analysis of some of the methodologies employed in revenue forecasting.

Expenditure Forecasting

Even less work has been accomplished with the second technique, expenditure
forecasting, which attempts to determine future levels of expenditures for pro-

grams and departments given a stated set or a variety of conditions. To some extent, the planning-programming-budgeting systems incorporated an element of expenditure forecasting with their 5-year forecasts of projected program budget costs. But it seems fair to note that for the most part such projections were straight-line extrapolations from current expenditure levels plus some factor for inflation. This hardly qualifies as real forecasting. Claudia DeVita Scott's major study of a pioneering expenditure-forecasting effort in the City of New Haven, Connecticut summarizes the current state of the art aptly:

> During the many years that city budget officers and planners have been making expenditure projections, their techniques, except for those few in the forefront, have remained virtually unchanged. Some simply make best guesses about the future level of expenditures. More common is the tendency to allow the previous pattern of expenditures to greatly influence projections. Next year's expenditures are determined by applying the observed percentage change in expenditures between this year and last year to this year's expenditures. Alternatively, a trend line is fitted to a series of historical data and then extrapolated to obtain the projections.[5]

The New Haven project resulted in a "real forecasting" prototype for expenditure forecasting. A computer model was constructed that considered population, salary, and service variables for nine major categories of public expenditures. The New Haven model was extremely flexible in that it could produce 5-year forecasts for aggregate departmental programs or examine various subdivisions and major activities of different programs. The expenditure model was also incorporated into a revenue-forecasting model and produced a truly prophetic conclusion: The city's expenditures were increasing more than the rate of revenues. This became a strong argument for employing the model, despite its cost and some problems with variable accuracy, because it could "foresee financial difficulties while there is still enough time to devise and execute actions to remedy, if not remove, the problem."[6]

Expenditure forecasting has been further experimented with, but the fiscal crisis of the mid-1970s has focused the bulk of the attention on the revenue side of the budgeting equation. Although Scott's analysis seems clearly appropriate, the political implications of social equity and decreasing service levels, mounting union pressures, and escalating inflation have strongly mitigated against effective expenditure remedies.[7] The promise of expenditure forecasting remains largely unrealized.

THE FORECASTING ENVIRONMENT:
TIME AND POLITICAL PERSUASION

Before any specific forecasting methodologies can be examined, the principle variables of the forecasting environment should be determined. Two are especially significant—time and participants and politics. The major limiting factor for forecasting invariably involves participants. In state governments, the revenue forecast is usually generated by the division of the budget, an administrative unit within the state executive branch. Once a specific forecasting methodology is determined, actual revenue estimates are developed. As the estimation process is an administrative function, the final responsibility lies with the governor, who reviews the revenue estimates and makes recommendations for the adjustments of the forecasts, if necessary. The governor, then, will deliver the revenue forecasts to the legislative branch as part of his or her budget.

The legislature may accept or challenge the administration's forecasts. In challenging the estimates, the legislature may opt to generate its own revenue forecasts or demand adjustments to the current estimates. Because elements of disagreement are prevalent in this process, the political implications influence both the adjustment of revenue estimates and expenditure plans. Inherent in this discussion of participants is the fact that the perspectives of participants may often manipulate forecast results.

It is important to note the impact of revenue forecasting on tax policy and expenditure planning. As expenditure plans are prepared, the legislative body must determine whether proposed expenditure programs can be financed with the existing revenue structure and whether revenue policy changes are needed to provide for any higher levels of spending required to meet growing demands for public goods and services. For state governments, the ceiling on expenditures is directly linked to the ceiling on revenues, and the ability of most states to incur debt is limited by existing statutes that require balanced budgets. Tax policy changes usually provide for revenue structures that will coincide with increasing expenditure plans. However, modification of tax policy becomes politically volatile, and the lag period between proposed and enacted policy changes affect the enactment of short-term expenditure programs.

Because changing state tax policy is a highly volatile political issue, the relationship between the administrative and legislative branches becomes a factor in the budget negotiation process. In states where one party dominates, agreement with regard to the changing of tax policy is more likely and the rearrangement of existing revenue structures will reflect partisan attitudes. In states where opposing parties control the legislative and administrative bodies, the political implications of adjusting tax policies tend to be more pronounced.

Although the adjustment of tax policies to reflect long-range expenditure programs is a political process, the technical evaluation of the impact of selected policies is a difficult and time-consuming process. The intricacies of dependent economic variables must be evaluated in order to study the impact of policies on the revenue process. These studies contribute to the lag period, mentioned earlier, which cause short-term expenditure programs to be affected. A lag period dramatically demonstrates the time variable, especially if a fiscal dimension is involved. The prediction is worth little if the action for it is significantly delayed. In fact, as has been demonstrated with national fiscal policy, current responses to economic forecasts at one time period can, if delayed, result in aggravation rather than remediation.[8] It is the embodiment of the old Will Rodgers saying: "Just because you're on the right track, doesn't mean that you won't get run over if you just sit there."

FORECASTING TECHNOLOGY: AN INTRODUCTION

State governments have attempted to divorce political considerations from the actual methodologies employed in developing revenue forecasts. The demand for accuracy in the forecasts has resulted from the realization of the role of estimation in the budgetary process. Robert S. Herman, in describing the development of revenue estimation for the State of New York, presents an excellent summary of the general evolution of revenue forecasting in state governments.[9]

Serious considerations of estimates began in the 1920s, although initial estimation procedures did little to provide any systematic methodology for deriving revenue forecasts.[10] Revenue estimation played a secondary role to crude expenditure estimation, and estimates were presented in broad, generalized terms. As revenue yields decreased during the Depression years, revenue estimation was of prime importance and new measures were conceived. As these new measures were employed, a general distrust of administrative estimates prompted legislatures to require more detailed information about the forecasts.[11] The first attempts to determine the relationships between policy and revenue estimates were made during these years.

The requirements of detailed information systems to be associated with estimation procedures and the legislative interest in relating tax policy decisions to revenue and expenditure estimates enabled legislatures to play an important role in dictating systematic methodologies and procedures for revenue estimation.[12] In many cases this has led to the legislative designation of forecasting responsibilities within budget agencies.

An example of legislative involvement in selecting methodologies is the State of Indiana. Through the budget agency, two committees are formed to deliver estimates. A five-member, revenue-forecasting, technical committee translates the economic estimates of an independent Indiana economic forum committee into state revenue estimates through a specified forecast methodology. This technical committee is composed of representatives of two members of the state assembly, two state senators, and an appointee of the budget agency administrator. The composition of this committee implies that estimates will be jointly accepted within the legislature and by the administrative bodies.

In theory, this arrangement seems to eliminate the possibilities for disagreement concerning the generated estimates. In reality, the ability of the revenue forecast technical committee to compromise on a specific methodology has proven to be difficult. The balance of administrative to legislative participants implies the relatively lower level of administrative influence on choices of methodology. Therefore, adjustment of estimates by the administration is limited. In view of this situation, the administration may have less control over the legislative expenditure process.

Current developments in the revenue estimation process include the increasing use of modeling theory in forecasting revenues. In these models, the specific economic environment of the state is simulated and estimates are directly related to the simulation. This type of estimation methodology suggests the trend of increased technological application, especially computerized variations, in forecasting revenues and expenditures.

In studying this evolution, the important point to be made is that the increased need for improving forecasting techniques was and is related to the growing complexity of tax structures and revenue-expenditure relationships. Generally, then, the process by which revenue estimates are generated by administrative agencies and received by legislatures in the budgetary process has been determined. In this analysis, the major participants have also been identified; in general, the budget agency retains the primary responsibility for generating revenue estimates on a tax-by-tax basis. A closer look at the forecasting techniques normally used is now in order.

THE THEORETICAL FRAMEWORK OF FORECASTING

The past decade has witnessed a number of developments in the area of forecasting methods as applied to governmental revenue and expenditure estimating. In general, governmental application of forecasting methodologies has lagged in respect to business sector applications. Although the reasons for this delay can be addressed, it is more useful to describe the basis of forecasting, the applicable methods, the choice of methodologies, all in a comparable framework.

As a key element of the decision-making process, especially in the case of budgeting, forecasting allows for the prediction of circumstances that surround decisions. In the budgetary context, forecasting and planning are to be considered as separate functions. Forecasting determines the parameters from which planning decisions can be made. In the opposite context, decision makers can determine how their decisions will affect outcome forecasts. Thus, the importance of the forecast is determined by its accuracy and applicability to situations and choices.

In a broad sense, forecasting methodologies can be separated into two distinct groupings—qualitative methods and quantitative methods. Qualitative methods rely on managerial judgment where data are usually not readily available or applicable to the forecasting situation. Quantitative techniques generally require historical data, through which patterns are identified to predict future values. These categories are not all-inclusive, however, and in some cases techniques are combined. For the purpose of this discussion, only quantitative and qualitative techniques will be analyzed with the emphasis on quantitative techniques.

Chambers, Mullick, and Smith have identified three questions in determining the choice of forecasting methods.[13] First, "What is the purpose of the forecast —how is it to be used?" This question determines, from the specific application, the accuracy required of the forecast. In budgetary considerations where accuracy is crucial and of primary importance, the predictive quality of the technique selected should provide a high degree of accuracy.

Second, "What are the dynamics and components of the system for which the forecast will be made?" This question addresses the need to identify the interacting variables and components of the forecasted environment. Once interacting variables can be identified, a model of causal relationships can be designed to form the basis of the forecasting situation.

The third question, "How important is the past in estimating the future?" must be answered in ascertaining the necessity of historical data requirements. As explained earlier, quantitative forecasting techniques require historical data points in extrapolating future values. However, if the past will probably not relate to any future values, a qualitative technique would most likely be selected. Alternatively, present or recent policy changes may require a significant qualitative input to augment the quantitative technique. A recent change in tax policy, for example, may not be apparent in the historical data. Therefore, adjustments in the historical data may be needed before the data base can be manipulated and then extrapolated. These three questions provide the manager and the forecaster with appropriate information about the specific forecasting situation.

In addition, the basic characteristics of each forecasting technique should be considered before selecting an effective forecasting methodology. Wheelwright and Makridakis present six major characteristics of forecasting methods: (1) time horizon, (2) pattern of data, (3) type of model, (4) cost, (5) accuracy, and (6) ease of application.[14]

The time horizon refers to the period being forecasted. Different forecasting methodologies are applicable to certain forecasting horizons. The data pattern, specifically historical data, should be a key consideration in technique selection. Methodologies that are applied to erratic data patterns should be able to predict the turning points in those data patterns. A turning point refers to the reversal of trend line direction. The "type-of-model" characteristic has been addressed

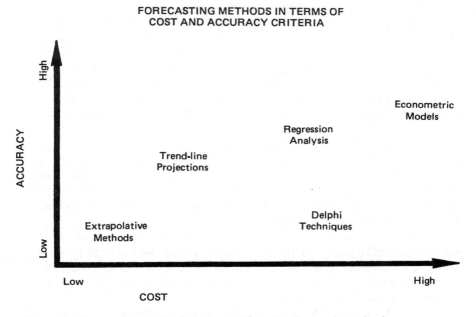

Figure 1   Forecasting methods in terms of cost and accuracy criteria.

earlier. Wheelwright and Makridakis confirm the importance of determining the model and its underlying assumptions.[15]   The capabilities of forecasting methodologies depend on the matching of the method to the model situation.

The cost and accuracy characteristics can be considered together. The component costs in any forecasting method are development, storage, and operation. Accuracy can be viewed as a dependent variable to cost and vice versa. The reliability of the forecast and its cost to produce have an impact on methodology selection. Figure 1 illustrates some of these methodologies in terms of accuracy and cost.[16]

Generally both cost and accuracy are maximized as causal forecasting methodologies are employed. Accuracy and cost of forecasting are minimized, however, when simple, statistical models, such as time-trend extrapolation, are used.

Ease of application is a characteristic that demands that decision makers be able to understand the forecasts before they can have confidence in their ability to apply the forecasts to a particular situation. This is an important consideration in determining revenue forecasts, because decision makers are generally one step away from the forecasting machinery. As increasingly scientific and more complex methodologies are employed in determining revenue estimates, the ability of governmental decision makers to understand the derivation of those estimates decreases; therefore confidence in those estimates may diminish even though accuracy increases.

The selection of forecasting methodologies is most appropriate when "purpose-of-the-forecast" criteria are matched properly with the characteristics of the individual forecasting techniques. The reader should be aware, however, that the characteristics of forecasting techniques discussed above are intertwined and these dependencies should be considered.

Revenue forecasting has primarily employed quantitative forecasting methodologies. Although qualitative methods have been used in the past,[17] the demand for accuracy has led to the increased use of quantitative models. Within quantitative methods, two broad categories can be identified—trend extrapolative models and causal models. These categories will now be examined in detail and some consideration of how state governments have made use of these techniques in generating revenue estimates will be added.

SPECIFIC METHODOLOGIES

In state governments today, specific methodologies being employed in making revenue estimates generally fall into two distinct categories. The first includes the extrapolative methods (also known as trend projections).[18] The second, causal methods, as used in revenue estimating, consists of regression analysis and econometric simulation models. These classical types have been adjusted to specific state environments, thus evidencing a qualitative mixing or hybridizing of models.

Thus three distinct methodologies can be distinguished within the two broad categories—trend-time projection, regression, and econometric. A study of these three provides a clear understanding of how state governments apply the classical techniques in forecasting revenues. It is interesting to note that these techniques follow the direction of Herman's evolutionary analysis of revenue forecasting in state government.[19] The increase in sophistication as these methods are studied seems to correlate with the need for greater accuracy in developing estimates. It is fitting, therefore, that an examination of these forecasting methodologies begins with the less scientific, extrapolative methods.

Extrapolation methods have been labeled as trend projection, time-series, and smoothing models.[20] By any name, however, the process by which the forecast is made remains the same. Simply stated, extrapolative methods rely on the extension or extrapolation of the existing time trend. This method considers the outputs or past observations of a specific system, the budget environment, and projects into the forecast horizon what the continuation of the trend will bring.

Wheelwright and Makridakis portray this process in Figure 2.[21] Inputs enter the system and exit as outputs. The system is considered as a "black box," and

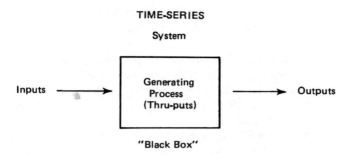

Figure 2 Time series.

no attempt is made to examine or discover its underlying behavior. In terms of forecasting state government revenues, this explanation holds true. The complexity of the state's economic environment actually helps to prevent the analysis of the black box. In reality, state governments are more concerned with how much revenue is going to be available, not how the revenue is derived.

Extrapolative methods take no account of factors other than time. The system, or generating process, is assumed to be constant. If not constant, adjustments can be made with a minimum of effort. For example, GNP (gross national product) may be a major factor in the system, and since past systems are assumed as being constant, GNP information should be available.

Extrapolative methods require only that the indices used to predict future revenues be available for certain historical periods. A typical functional equation using gross national product would be set up as follows:

$$GNP_{1978} = f(GNP_{1977}, GNP_{1976}, GNP_{1975}, \ldots)$$

CAUSAL METHODS

While extrapolative methods rely on the extension of trend-time relationships, causal methods assume a cause-and-effect relationship between the inputs of the system and the output generated. In state revenue forecasting, the successful application of any causal method must be related to the assumed relationships between the input factors. Such functional relationships are assumed in revenue forecasting between a specific tax and the various economic factors which can possibly be matched to it. Thus a set of independent variables are related to a dependent variable, and changes from year to year in the independent variables should accurately determine the change in the dependent variable. Causal methods also differ from extrapolative methods in that the generating system is analyzed and assumed relationships are determined (see Figure 3).

CAUSAL METHODS

Systems

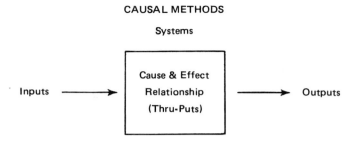

Figure 3 Causal methods.

The dominant causal methods used in state governments are regression analysis and econometric modeling. While the former has proven most popular, recent increases in the use of econometric models have resulted from decreased costs in the technology required to operate such models, which have made the latter increasingly attractive. Regression and econometric methods have many similarities in that functional relationships between economic variables and specific taxes are determined.

In general, three major elements compose the list of independent variables used to produce tax revenue estimates—GNP, United States personal income, and state personal income. With regression analysis, state percent of GNP is difficult to determine because of inadequate data, hence the use of state personal income. These three indices, in various combinations, are used to produce tax estimates. In Indiana, as well as other states using regression-type causal models,[22] other adjustments must be made to the input side of the model. These adjustments are reflective of economic elasticities related to the yearly changes in the major indices.[23] Other indices are derived from the list of appropriate economic indicators, such as corporate income and population measures.

Econometric methods are distinct from regression methods in that the relationships between economic factors and specific taxes are determined through statistical techniques. The statistical technique most commonly used, however, is regression analysis. Econometric models make use of a system of linear equations in which a variety of independent variables can be analyzed simultaneously. Referring to Figure 1, econometric models, although the costliest to perform, have the greatest accuracy associated with them.

In Table 1 these methodologies are compared according to the six criteria identified before—accuracy, identification of turning points, data patterns, cost-and-time horizon, and ease of application in developing and making a forecast.[24] Against these basic criteria, currently applied methodologies can be compared to determine relative weaknesses and strengths.

Table 1 Comparison of Forecasting Methodologies

	Qualitative and time series analysis and projection			Causal methods	
	Delphi method	Extrapolative	Trend-line analysis	Regression analysis	Econometric models
Description	A panel of experts make independent judgments on a common question. Independence in the decision process eliminates group influence. As expert opinions are evaluated, forecasts are generated.	This method relies on historical performance of the forecast indicators. The historical values are evaluated and the forecast is determined by extending the historical trend into the forecast period.	This technique fits a trend line to a mathematical equation and then projects it into the future by means of this equation.	The most popular of the causal methods, appropriate variable indices are combined into functional equations as historical data is evaluated. The functional relationships then are projected to produce the forecast values.	A system of interdependent regression equations which describe some part of the economy. The parameters of the regression equations are simultaneously estimated. Econometric models express causalities more accurately than ordinary regression equations.
Accuracy (medium-term forecast horizon 3 months–2 years)	Fair to very good. Note: This range of accuracy should be considered as a negative aspect.	Good	Good	Good to very good	Very good to excellent
Identification of trend turning points	Fair to good	Poor to fair	Poor	Very good	Excellent
Computer cost of forecasting	$2,000 +	Varies with application	Varies with application	$100. Note: Regression analysis can be performed without a computer.	$5,000 +
Time required to generate forecast	8 weeks +	1 day +	1 day +	Depends on time required to identify the functional relationships.	8 weeks +

One other aspect of the forecasting methodology should be explained. Although the various techniques employ aggregate data for initial calculations, the forecast results are generally cast in separate tax-by-tax, revenue-source-by-revenue-source displays. The budget will present a specific estimate for each tax source. It is unclear whether this results in more accurate total forecasts, and it is beyond the scope of this effort to ascertain whether 20 small guesses are better than one large guess excepting for psychological benefits. So that the essence of this tax-by-tax concept can be clarified, Appendixes A and B are added for further examination.

A more significant reason for tax-by-tax analysis is the prevalence of earmarked taxes and funds in so many states. For example, states must make separate forecasts of gasoline taxes because many earmark the tax revenues (on a benefits-received concept) to provide solely for highway maintenance. In some states, the use of earmarked taxes severely hamstrings the executive budget, literally controlling as much as 60 to 80 percent of total expenditures. This has been decreed by strong budgeting advocates as a major reason for increasing "uncontrollable budgets." Whatever the outcome of this longstanding debate on budget control between general and special revenues, the practice of tax-by-tax revenue estimates is firmly entrenched.

Ironically, one of the bastions of earmarked tax sources is now in perilous straits. If Indiana's experience is at all typical, states that have earmarked gas tax revenues for highway maintenance are finding their forecasts increasingly deficient. As the auto industry strives for better gas mileage through smaller, more efficient cars, states find tax revenues falling behind increasing use rates and inflated maintenance costs for highways. Adjustments through a tax increase to an already very high cost of gasoline (although not comparatively with other countries) are highly vulnerable politically. This illustrates the flexibility problem of earmarked taxes without even considering the converse case made for some time about highways and public mass transit.

THE CASE FOR THE BEST FORECASTING METHOD—A CLEAR DECISION?

As has been discussed thus far, trend projections, regression analysis, and econometric modeling are all being used in state governments today. From previous discussion it is also apparent that these methods can be ranked somehow. Why, then, do states continue to employ very different methodologies? One explanation lies in the way each method satisfies the various evaluative criteria found in Table 1. The combination of those elements and their applicability to the forecasting situation presents a key to explaining the "why" of method selection in state government forecasting efforts.

Early use of extrapolative methods has been documented in Missouri,[25] Connecticut,[26] and Maryland,[27] to name a few, with some measure of success.

The extrapolative techniques were applied on a fund-by-fund, tax-by-tax basis, allowing for replacement, when needed, with more reliable techniques. By using a fund-by-fund application, extrapolative techniques could easily be adjusted to adapt to historical data.

In terms of accuracy, the most applicable time frame—3 months to 2 years—receives only a "good" rating because accuracy usually decreases as the forecast horizon is increased, and forecasting accuracy is essential. Thus, in a fund-by-fund analysis, methodology replacement is understandable. Under the "identification-of-turning-points" criterion, extrapolative methods are, at best, only poor. Trend projection methods are accurate only as the identifiable direction of the trend is continued. The change in direction can be attributed to changes in the interacting factors of the forecasting environment. A change in policy, for example, will place considerable influence in trend-line direction, as input variables are affected. The limiting assumption of projection methods such as extrapolation is that the interacting factors are constant, whereas in reality they are not. Consequently, policy decisions cannot be analyzed in terms of their future impact in the budgetary process.

Certainly, the merits of extrapolative methods must be linked to the decisions to use such methods. The data required to generate the forecasts are easily obtained as long as the historical information exists. Because the generating system is not usually analyzed, the time requirement for developing the application and making the forecast is reduced in comparison with other methodologies. Generally, extrapolative methods are inexpensive to apply; calculations are possible without the use of a computer. On the other hand, it might be said that the quality of the forecasts reflects the resources committed to it.

The keyword in this choice of methodology is simplicity. As a simple system based on the laws of incrementalism, trend projection methodologies are easily understood by administrators and the general public. Still, in practice, this methodology has proven somewhat inadequate because of the variable relationships involved, leading to the use of causal methods for forecasting revenues.

REGRESSION ANALYSIS

Regression analysis has become the most popular method of forecasting state government revenues, and the wide application of regression methodologies is testimony to its effectiveness. Regression analysis attempts to forecast based on the identification of the functional relationships between variables. Thus, the characteristics of causal methodologies are inherent in regression. Basically, equations are developed for each tax based on those socioeconomic variables thought to be associated with each tax. Once these functional equations are developed, regression analysis projects the functional relationship. Although this method is attractive to administrators for a number of reasons, its application can be problemmatic.

As opposed to trend projection, which is dependent on the variable of time, regression is not necessarily time-dependent, producing medium-term forecast horizons of up to 2 years that are fairly reliable (Table 1). Additionally, because this technique is not time-dependent, adjustments in the revenue forecasts can be implemented. This becomes important as policy decisions are required to coincide with changes in the economic outlook. An example of this was Indiana's revenue forecast revision due to the projected negative impact on the state economy by the coal miners' strike of 1978. Regression, then, becomes more flexible as both a policy tool and a planning tool.

In terms of data requirements, the data base depends on the type of information needed. Each tax forecasted in regression has certain information, which may be available on a daily, monthly, or quarterly basis, associated with it. In order to provide adequate forecasts, several years of data should form the data base. Associated with this data requirement is the use of computer technology. The statistical and mathematical characteristics of causal forecasting methods are enhanced through the use of high-speed electronic data-processing equipment (EDP). The costs of using regression analysis techniques will be relative to the amount of computer time needed to generate the forecasts.

It appears that causal methods such as regression analysis have certain advantages in that they can better identify turning points in the data, are statistically based, and are generally accurate in forecasting revenues. However, the application of regression depends on the development of functional relationships in setting up regression equations for each tax. In Indiana, three major economic indices are used to make up the functional equations—gross national product, U.S. personal income, and Indiana personal income. Two problems arise in balancing these indices. First, it is difficult to set the balance between these information sources; second, these indices may not always be applicable, timely, or accurate. In other words, the accuracy of the forecasts will reflect the accuracy of the economic index outputs. In the political arena of revenue forecasting, the identification of relationships between variables may result in compromising the weights of the input variables. This, then, becomes the other negative aspect of this technique, namely, the time required to develop an application and make a forecast depends on the ability to identify the proper relationships.

In summary, regression analysis has advanced the quality of revenue forecasts, although certain application problems exist. The advantages of improved accuracy in the forecasts probably outweigh the disadvantages and certainly supersede the use of trend projection methodologies. However, recent developments in yet another causal method may then outweigh both of these methodologies: econometric modeling.

ECONOMETRIC MODELING

The era of computerization has permitted the development of comprehensive models for entire economies. Such models are called "econometric models" because of the statistical techniques which are used in their construction.[28] The recent applications of econometric modeling in state governments have come about through the use of more complicated models at the national level. Econometric methods go one step further than regression analysis. They determine the weights of the independent variables so that estimation is not needed. This aspect is perhaps the fundamental difficulty in regression.

The uses of econometric models are twofold. Although they can be used for forecasting purposes, they are primarily used to *understand* the local economy. Makridakis and Wheelwright cite this example:

> If a government . . . would like to know the results of a 10% tax reduction aimed at stimulating a recessionary economy, it has few alternatives other than econometric models. A tax cut will have direct and immediate effects on increasing personal disposable income and probably decreasing government revenues . . . through a series of chain reactions, the 10% decrease will affect almost all economic factors. These interdependencies must be considered if the effect of the tax cut is to be accurately predicted.[29]

As a policy tool, then, econometric modeling can advise in determining impact of policy decisions. The use of such a model for forecasting purposes is a side benefit. In Wisconsin and Washington, the primary purpose of developing an econometric model was to simulate the states' economic system. These two states developed their models with a private econometric consulting firm and adjusted and developed proven applications of the model as they used them. In Illinois, the comptroller's office (although not given statutory responsibility for developing forecasts) has also used the same econometric package in developing a revenue forecast "module" as a subset of a larger econometric model.

Econometric revenue-forecasting models are generally simpler than the entire econometric model and use fewer regression-type (causal) equations. In general, econometric models can determine "internal" independent variables. External variables, such as GNP, and U.S. personal income, still need to be supplied from outside the system. Because state forecasting systems rely on external data to make forecasts, disparities and inaccuracies in the forecasts will exist. Michael J. Bakalis demonstrates the effects of this on the Illinois forecasting effort:

> In 1975 United States real personal income declined (–1.8%). In the following year, Illinois' real personal income expanded more rapidly than national real personal income by a margin of 6.4% to 4.8%.[30]

Econometric tax revenue modules can help to eliminate the fluctuations and uncertainties of revenue estimates. Through this improvement in long-range revenue-forecasting accuracy, improvements in long-range expenditure decisions seem clearly feasible.

According to the criteria outlined in Table 1, econometric forecasting models demonstrate the highest accuracy whether the forecast horizon is short term or long term. As in regression, econometric models are not time-dependent, allowing for those same advantages mentioned in the regression discussion. Because econometric models are systems of interdependent regression equations, the characteristics of econometric systems are similar to regression methodologies. However, econometric methods identify turning points in the data better than the other two methodologies.

Although accuracy is rated highly, the aspect of cost must be addressed. First, the general costs associated with regression in terms of data collection are present in econometric forecasting techniques. Costs linked to performing the actual analysis are minimized through the use of EDP systems, and EDP costs are expected to decrease as computer technologies increase. Development opportunity costs are significant, however, and although basic state econometric models may be similar, the fine tuning needed may require several years to complete. These requirements result from the duplication of the state economy into a model simulation. Developmental costs are clearly related to the setup of the system and are not continuously fixed to the operation of the model. One should bear in mind that revenue-forecasting modules are usually a component of the larger econometric model and development costs are usually attributed to the larger models.

The advantages of increased accuracy should justify the costs of developing an overall econometric model, where these costs can be absorbed by large organizations that use policy analysis extensively. Most state governments would satisfy these requirements, and useful econometric models would not be restricted to the budget agency because the resulting economic information can be important to other state government divisions. Consequently, it seems that state governments can best justify the costs of econometric forecasting systems. Further, these costs could be absorbed by the increased accuracy of revenue forecasts and their relationship to the expenditure policies of the budgetary process.

Still, in answering the initial question, "Is there a clear decision as to which methodology is the best?" a clear decision cannot be made. Each methodology has advantages and disadvantages that must be considered against the degree of appropriateness to individual forecasting situations. In addition, individual forecasting situations will have certain limitations associated with them which can result in further mixing of the forecasting methodology choice.

The trend in applying forecasting methodologies is easier to identify. As the demand for increased accuracy in revenue forecasts becomes stronger, state government administrators will be encouraged to apply more sophisticated, statistical forecasting techniques. As recent years have evinced, the cost of EDP systems should decrease through the advancement of EDP hardware technology. In addition, the need to keep the forecasting process free of politics should contribute to the use of econometric forecasting modules. Whether this last variable becomes a contribution or constraint remains to be seen. The political obstacles still remain. To paraphrase Allen Schick's words about budgeting and evaluation, "the hardest part is not doing it, but using it."

APPENDIX A

In revenue-forecasting methodologies, a tax-by-tax forecast is usually performed. With econometric models, the formulation of equations used to determine the liability base of a specific tax is a complicated process. A closer look at the Illinois econometric-forecasting module, proposed by the state comptroller, displays the equations which constitute the corporate income tax liability base.

Annual Equations

- Corporate tax declarations + offsets (one year ago) = F (Illinois total tax liability).
- Illinois corporate profits tax liability base = F [U.S. Corporate before tax profits × (Illinois nonfarm employment ÷ U.S. nonfarm employment)].
- Corporate tax refunds = F [(1 ÷ (percent change in Illinois corporate tax liability)^2] × [Illinois corporate tax liability – corporate declarations – corporate offsets (one year ago)].
- Corporate tax offsets = F (corporate tax refunds).
- Corporate tax final payments = corporate tax liability + refunds + offsets – offsets (one year ago) – corporate tax declarations.

Quarterly Equations

- Corporate declarations = F (Seasonal dummies)
- Corporate final payments = F (Seasonal dummies)
- Corporate tax refunds = F (Seasonal dummies)

These equations operate in conjunction with 34 other equations making up other tax liability bases in the performance of the Illinois tax revenue module.

APPENDIX B

Each tax has had its impact on the state budget process and the proposed legislation necessary in spanning the revenue-expenditure gap. These excerpts from the Governor's annual budget message (1975-1976) for the state of New York explain how the state sales tax is analyzed.

Sales and Use Tax

New York imposes a state sales and use tax at the rate of four percent. In 1965, New York had become the 39th state to impose a general state sales and use tax (45 states now impose general sales taxes). The initial rate has been raised twice; from two percent to three percent on April 1, 1969, and to the current rate on June 1, 1971. With one exception, the maximum combined state and local rate in any community in New York is seven percent. As a result of 1974 legislation enabling New York City to temporarily raise its rate, the combined rate in the City is eight percent, effective from July 1, 1974 to June 30, 1975.

Base of Tax. This broad-based tax applies to receipts from sales and use within the state of most tangible personal property and from restaurant meals charges, admissions charges, hotel and motel occupancy charges, utility service billings, and charges for specified services.

To soften the impact of the tax on low-income families, a broad exemption is provided for rent, most food for home consumption, drugs (including non-prescription drugs formerly subject to local sales taxes in the state), medical services, and public transportation services.

The Outlook. State sales and use tax revenues during the first 9 months of the current fiscal year totaled $1,493 million. This represents an average growth of about 7½ percent over the comparable period in the prior year—or substantially less than the rate of price inflation. The growth rate appeared to peak at over 9 percent for the second fiscal quarter (July-September collections), partly reflecting price rises, new car sales this past summer, and increased fuel purchases.

In light of the widespread weakness pervading the economy at the turn of the year, state sales and use tax receipts are expected to total $1,990 million for 1974-1975. This estimate assumes continuation of the decline in real economic activity for the balance of the fiscal year and reflects the initial effects of the expanded exemptions granted in 1974.

The outlook for the economy in 1975 is uncertain. The pace of inflation has moderated in recent months, but underemployment has continued to rise. This budget assumes that employment and production will begin to rise after midyear, with the exact timing dependent on the direction and thrust of federal fiscal and monetary actions and the pace of improvement in consumer confidence. It is expected that the recession will have more adverse effects on employment and personal income in New York than in the nation as a whole.

Under these conditions, and taking into account the full-year impact of the new exemptions adopted in 1974, state receipts from the sales and use tax under present law would be estimated at $2,125 million in 1975-1976, reflecting

Table 2 State Sales and Use Tax Revenue
(thousands of dollars)

	Actual
Actual	
1966–67	$ 604,327
1967–68	630,912
1968–69	698,759
1969–70	1,012,036
1970–71	1,175,898
1971–72	1,532,795
1972–73	1,734,093
1973–74	1,863,241
Estimated	
1974–75	1,990,000
1975–76 (under present law)	2,125,000
1975–76 (under proposed legislation)	2,165,000

growth of more than 7 percent and adjustment for the impact of the broadened exemptions.

Proposed Legislation. Legislation submitted to implement this budget, however, will expand the base of state and local sales and use taxes to include selected business and personal services, admissions, and related charges not now taxes. A portion of the gain from this extension will be offset by revenues foregone under other provisions to exempt from taxation certain medical equipment, supplies, and prostheses required by sick and disabled persons.

Under this legislation, state revenues from the sales and use tax are expected to increase by an additional $40 million during the coming fiscal year, bringing total state receipts from this source to $2,165 million in state fiscal year 1975–1976 (Table 2).

NOTES

1. Allen Schick, The road from ZBB, *Public Administration Review* (March-April 1978).
2. Advisory Commission on Intergovernmental Relations, *Significant Features of Fiscal Federalism 1976* (Washington, D.C.: ACIR, 1976), p. 7.
3. Jesse Burkhead, *Government Budgeting* (New York: Wiley, 1956).

4. McLoone, Lupo, Mushkin, *Long-Range Revenue Estimation* (Washington, D.C.: George Washington University, 1967).

5. Claudia DeVita Scott, *Forecasting Local Government Spending* (Washington, D.C.: Urban Institute, 1972), p. 3.

6. Scott, op. cit., p. 100.

7. The article by Roy Bahl in this same section continues further on this theme.

8. A. C. Hyde, Fiscal policy, federal budgeting, and the chief executive. State University of New York, at Albany, unpublished manuscript, 1974, p. 23.

9. Robert S. Herman, Revenue Estimating in New York State Government (Albany, New York, 1960), discussion paper, pp. 1-11.

10. Ibid. p. 2.

11. Ibid. pp. 2-3.

12. Ibid. p. 4.

13. John C. Chambers, Satinder K. Mullick, and Donald D. Smith, How to choose the right forecasting technique, *Harvard Business Review: On Management* (New York: Harper and Row, 1975), pp. 502-506.

14. Steven C. Wheelwright and Spyros Makridakis, *Forecasting Methods for Management,* 2nd Ed. (New York: Wiley, 1977), pp. 8-9.

15. Ibid.

16. The concept of this figure was adapted from Chambers, Mullick, and Smith, How to choose the right forecasting technique, p. 503.

17. Herman, op. cit.

18. McLoone, Lupo, Mushkin, op cit.

19. Herman, op. cit.

20. Donald L. Harnett, *Introduction to Statistical Methods,* 2nd Ed. (Reading, Mass: Addison-Wesley, 1975).

21. Wheelwright and Makridakis, op. cit.

22. Those other states include Kansas, Minnesota, Illinois, and formerly Wisconsin and Washington.

23. McLoone, Lupo, Mushkin, op. cit.

24. The concept of this figure was adapted from Chambers, Mullick, and Smith, op. cit.

25. Paul E. Junk, *A Fiscal Profile of Missouri* (Columbia, Mo: School of Business and Public Administration, University of Missouri, 1964).

26. John E. Maher and Robert E. Hunter, *Selected Revenues of Connecticut to 1975* (Middletown, Conn: College of Quantitative Studies, Wesleyan University, 1961).

27. Maryland Legislative Council Committee on Taxation and Fiscal Matters, *A Long-Range Projection of General Fund Revenues and Appropriations* (Annapolis, Md: December 1959).

28. Michael J. Bakalis, *Issues in Public Finance—Illinois Economic Model,* Phase 1: Vol. No. 5 (Office of the Comptroller—State of Illinois).

29. Wheelwright and Makridakis, op. cit.
30. Michael J. Bakalis, *Issues in Public Finance—the Illinois Tax Revenue Module,* Vol. 6 (Office of the Comptroller—State of Illinois).

16

THE CRITICAL PATH METHOD APPLIED TO GAO REVIEWS*

John C. Karmendy
Thomas Monohan

INTRODUCTION

GAO can use the critical path method (CPM), a project management technique long employed in the construction, aerospace, and weapons development industries, to reduce the cost of our reviews and shorten review time. Such savings can be achieved because CPM enables us to (1) focus on time-critical tasks throughout the assignment, (2) identify tasks that can be performed concurrently, (3) quickly assess the impact of tasks added to the assignment, and (4) establish more realistic incremental time goals and completion dates. CPM has already proven itself in the San Francisco region and we think that such success can be repeated throughout GAO.

WHAT IS CPM?

CPM is a technique for project planning, analysis, coordination, and control. Simply stated, CPM is a flow chart showing an entire project in terms of a network of "events" connected by "activities."

*Reprinted from *GAO Review,* vol. 13 (Spring 1978), pp. 66-72.

A CPM NETWORK

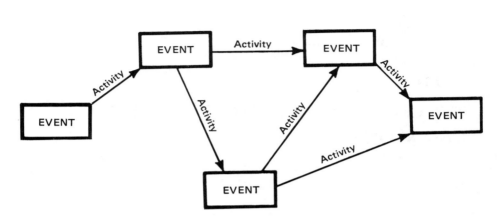

Figure 1   Model CPM.

An event represents an instant of time and is usually described as the start or completion of an activity, such as the start of field work, the completion of a product outline, or the completion of an audit. (On a CPM diagram, events appear as geometric shapes or nodes.) An activity is the amount of work in calendar days occurring between two events. (On a CPM diagram, activities are arrows or lines.) Figure 1 is a model CPM diagram.

Constructing a CPM diagram, usually an audit team effort in San Francisco, centers around the events and activities of the planned review. The first step is to determine the events and activities required to meet assignment objectives and estimate the time needed to complete each activity. Then the team decides on a sequence, i.e., on which activities must be completed before others can begin. Activities that can be performed concurrently are also identified at this time. Figure 2 and Table 1 illustrate a CPM diagram for a hypothetical GAO review.

HOW CPM DIFFERS

Although similar to GAO's traditional management of assignments, CPM emphasizes the relationships between activities and how these relationships affect the completion of the audit. GAO assignment supervisors not using CPM are *aware* of these relationships, but supervisors using CPM *manage* by them, thereby seeing better how the commitment of valuable resources to one activity affects other

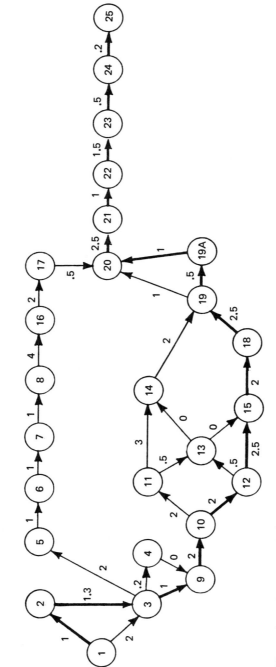

Figure 2 A hypothetical, final CPM review.

Table 1   Final CPM

	Event	Activity	Duration in weeks
1.	Assignment started, leader assigned		
2.	Staff assigned	1-2	1
3.	Research, initial contacts completed	1-3	2
		2-3	1.3
4.	Job conferences planned	3-4	0.2
5.	Questionnaires designed	3-5	2
6.	Questionnaires tested	5-6	1
7.	Questionnaires printed	6-7	1
8.	Questionnaires distributed	7-8	1
9.	Audit visits scheduled	3-9	1
		4-9	0
10.	Site A completed	9-10	2
11.	Site B completed	10-11	2
12.	Site C completed	10-12	2
13.	Initial outline prepared	11-13	0.5
		12-13	0.5
14.	Site D completed	11-14	3
		13-14	0
15.	Site E completed	12-15	2.5
		13-15	0
16.	Questionnaires returned	8-16	4
17.	Questionnaires coded, analyzed	16-17	2
18.	Site F completed	16-18	2
19.	Site summaries completed	14-19	2
		18-19	2.5
19a.	Training for two team members	19-19a	0.5
20.	Product outline prepared	19-20	1
		19a-20	1
		17-20	0.5
21.	Product drafted	20-21	2.5
22.	Product reviewed	21-22	1
23.	Product referenced	22-23	1.5
24.	Product final typed	23-24	0.5
25.	Product forwarded, completed	24-25	0.2

activities. This increased visibility gives the supervisor greater control over the assignment.

Focusing on the Critical Path

CPM diagrams quickly focus management attention on the critical path. The critical path is the longest route through the CPM network in terms of calendar time and is the minimum time for completing the assignment. All other activities are concurrent to critical path activities and take less time to complete. (The critical path is shown as the dark line in Figure 2.)

Focusing on the critical path is an important advantage of CPM because it gives information needed for good assignment management. The supervisor knows he must closely watch progress on the critical path because each day's delay there causes a corresponding delay in overall assignment completion. This knowledge enables the supervisor to identify possible slippage early and correct problems before they get out of hand, either by requesting additional staff or by dropping lower priority activities. With traditional management, slippage may not be recognized until the 80 or 90 percent completion mark, when the supervisor can do little but accept a delay in assignment completion.

But what if the assignment deadline is earlier than the completion date determined by CPM? Assuming the team has identified all possible opportunities for concurrent performance of activities, either the completion date must be pushed back or some critical path activities must be dropped or modified. The advantage of using CPM here is that the supervisor *knows* where he stands and can make an informed decision as to what must give.

Concurrent Performance of Activities

The time-saving potential of performing activities concurrently must not be overlooked. A team can save time by identifying and taking advantage of concurrent performance opportunities. For example, during a recent San Francisco regional office review, the team needed to visit 25 sites in 9 geographic clusters throughout the western states. If done sequentially, site work would have consumed 17 weeks—well beyond the assignment's deadline. Therefore, the team visited three site clusters concurrently, reducing site work time to 6 calendar weeks. Because of learning curve and coordination limitations, three concurrent visits was the team's practical upper limit in this case. Obviously, realistic upper limits for concurrent performance will vary, depending on the assignment and the staff available.

In contrast to critical path activities, concurrent activities *can* be delayed without delaying final product completion, as long as they are not delayed beyond the critical path activities with which they are concurrent. Otherwise, they become the critical path and dictate the assignment completion date.

For example, Figure 2 shows that the time required to reach event 20, "product outline prepared," via the questionnaire route (events 3-5-6-7-8-16-17-20) is only 11.5 weeks, compared with the critical path route (events 3-9-10-12-15-18-19-19a-20) of 13.5 weeks. The questionnaire portion of the review can be delayed, therefore, up to 2 weeks without delaying overall assignment completion. However, questionnaire delays beyond 2 weeks will push back the completion date by the amount of delay in excess of the 2-week "slack."

The bottom line is this: A team can use CPM to save by (1) identifying all possibilities of concurrent performance, (2) "staffing up" to take advantage of such opportunities, and (3) spotlighting delays either along the critical path or in concurrent activities that would lengthen the critical path.

But what if adequate staff are not available to take full advantage of concurrent performance? CPM has advantages here, too, as the diagram is an easily understood document useful for staffing purposes as well as for tactical assignment planning and control. The supervisor can use the diagram to vividly demonstrate the impact on the completion date if more personnel are not committed.

Assessing the Impact of New Tasks

Few GAO audits ever go exactly as originally planned. Analysis and information needs not foreseen at the start of the assignment often become apparent. With CPM the supervisor can determine if the new activities can be done concurrently, thus minimizing the need for additional time. However, even if concurrent processing is not possible, CPM allows the supervisor to determine when the new activities should be done so as to minimize the delay.

Setting Realistic Time Goals and Completion Dates

Setting realistic time goals for completing a job is difficult. However, when CPM is used, time frames become more clearly defined because they are related to specific activities. This in turn forces the supervisor and the team to plan better. Also, CPM breaks assignment time into visible, manageable segments, allowing a team to concentrate on meeting successive, incremental target dates, as opposed to one final, make-it-or-break-it completion date.

As the assignment progresses, the supervisor will be able to compare the team's original estimate with the actual time it takes to perform each activity. This evaluation allows the team to continuously update and redefine its goals so they remain realistic. It will also help team members estimate time more accurately for future assignments.

CONCLUSIONS

Completing assignments faster, a major GAO goal, requires effective and continuous assignment planning and control at the audit team level. CPM gives a team an edge in planning, coordinating, and controlling an assignment in an uncertain and complex environment.

CPM supplies a much needed methodology to reduce the time it takes to complete an assignment. CPM enables a team to focus on critical activities, take advantage of concurrent performance opportunities within staffing limitations, assess quickly the impact of new tasks, and set more realistic incremental time goals and completion dates. Consequently, we think CPM can be a valuable management technique for GAO assignment supervisors and audit teams.

IV

SOME TECHNICAL CONTEXTS: Toward More Effective Control via Systems

WHOSE PERSPECTIVE? WHOSE REALITY?

The preceding chapter may in effect neglect the forest by focusing on the trees, but that possible outcome must be averted. When confronted with the myriad tools and techniques involved in public budgeting, we need always to ask two versions of the same question. Which system or broad perspective is the proponent representing? Or, alternatively, whose idea of "reality" is at the base of what is being presented?

As Einstein's notion of relativity is crucial for physics, so is this chapter's emphasis on systems or broad perspectives central in public budgeting. If we presume that government can be run like a business, for example, then it is logical to use and apply in government techniques developed in the private sector. For instance, private sector organizations may be centralized and tightly bounded, with someone having great authority at the top of the hierarchy. Many budgetary and finance techniques, such as zero-base budgeting, management-by-objectives, and so on, can be presumed to fit this centralized and hierarchical entity.

Can the techniques found so helpful in the private sector organization be transferable to the public arena? *Only* if the same systemic view or perspective applies in both sectors, *only* if the ideas of reality are similar. "Only" is a major limit because public agencies often are loosely bounded.

So what of such systems or broad perspectives, such ideas of reality? They commonly differ for different observers, a crucial point that can be illustrated no better than by a brief review of the "line-item budget." This type of budget involves listing all items for purchase by government during the next budget year. The list is created by the executive for approval by the legislature. The line-item budget is a "shopping list," detailing what government plans to buy. It contains little information about the purposes which the line items will accomplish, however.

The line-item budget may be said to be a control budget, then, one that controls details but not substance or purpose. And therein lies its differential attraction to different actors in the public sector. To help make this elemental but significant point, consider the fundamental pattern of control in American government that is sketched in Figure 1. Legislatures approve budgets which are implemented by executives; although both formal and informal arrangements may exist that lessen the probability, legislatures often lose much control over how the budget will be administered. How can the legislature seek a greater measure of accountability by the executive, short of beginning impeachment or cutting off money the next year? The basic approach has been through the line-item budget for the legislature, but much less so for the executive branch.

What accounts for this difference in attraction? The key to the answer inheres in the structure of the executive branch. The executive branch in American government is composed of at least two parts: the elected executive and its appointed political officials; and employees in the civil service, or merit system. The elected executive—presidents, governors, mayors—and their appointees stay in government for fixed periods of time. On the other hand, members of the

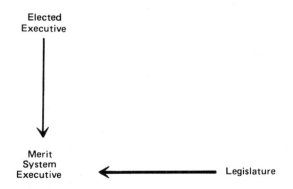

Figure 1   Basic control relations in American government.

merit system often remain in government for long periods of time and, most important, are protected against "political" interference by complex civil service rules. In addition, the day-to-day implementation of budgets is left to the merit system executives.

The legislature and the elected executive tend to respond to this major opportunity for discretion by the permanent bureaucracy in different ways. The elected executive often tries to control the merit system's implementation of the budget through the use of private sector budget techniques. In this way, the elected executive seeks to maximize its influence in order to assure accountability *within* the executive branch. Thus, nearly all "reforms" in budgeting—PPBS, MBO, ZBB, performance budgeting, charts of accounts, fund accounting—have issued from the office of the elected executive, i.e., from the office at the "top" of the elected executive pyramid.

Legislatures, on the other hand, emphasize accountability *between* branches of government. Hence they favor control mechanisms over implementation in which many of the day-to-day decisions are usually left to permanent administrators, but in a way that leaves much room for legislative influence. In summary, budget techniques such as PPBS or ZBB will be more attractive to the elected executive in government—given the substantial fit of such techniques within centralized, hierarchical organizations. Legislators tend to opt for more fragmented patterns, for "multiple access." Hence, they tend to favor line-item budgets to increase their control over the elected executive, the cost being that legislatures may contribute to a loss of control over the broader and comprehensive purposes of government.

SYSTEMS TO EFFECT CONTROL

Given this substantial but not complete tension between basic perspectives about budgeting and finance, we focus here only on several systemic approaches designed to increase executive control, whose early development typically was in the private sector. We will consider several of the most prominent of these systemic approaches—darlings of the elected executive but often objects of legislative suspicion.

Planning-Programming-Budgeting System (PPBS)

Harry S. Havens provides an "apology" for PPBS in his "Looking Back at PPBS," which is reprinted below. Havens points out that PPBS today should be used to make budgeting more "rational," to transcend the particularism of the line-item approach by focusing on major purposes. In doing so, PPBS focuses on such questions as:

- What happened in the past in pursuit of major purposes?
- Why did it happen?
- What are the options concerning major purposes for the future?
- What are the implications of each of those options?

The significance of these questions can be granted, but that does not settle matters. Consider a key question. Can PPBS exist with the two following major constraints which exist in American government?

1. Base. American budgets tend to be "historical" in that an agency's funding for one year determines fairly well what it will receive for the upcoming budget year. Last year's amount is known as the "base" and, while deviations up or down from that base can occur, budget review tends to focus on the incremental deviation rather than the far larger base. This reliance on the base in American budgeting often discourages any systemic analysis to determine how "effectively" funds were spent, whether the programs funded really were needed, and so on.

2. How controllable are expenditures? Budget line items may be divided into two categories: controllable and uncontrallable. Controllable expenditures involve monies which could be expended or not at someone's discretion. Interest paid on the national debt is basically uncontrollable in this sense because the best that can be done is to work in the long run to reduce the level of indebtedness. Uncontrollable expenditures are those which are dependent on previous and basically irrevocable decisions. As Murray L. Weidenbaum (1) explains:

> [I] n practice, the President and the Congress do not face each year's budget preparation and review cycle with a clean slate; they must take account of large accumulations of legal restraints within which they must operate.
>
> From the viewpoint of appropriations review, there are thus numerous exogenous forces and factors which they must take account of and cannot effectively control: the number of eligible veterans who apply for pensions or compensation, the amount of public assistance payments made by the states and for which they must be partially reimbursed according to prescribed matching formulas, and so forth. The relatively controllable portion of the budget, from this viewpoint, consists of those government spending programs where the determining factors are endogenous to the appropriations process, which may modify them, at least to a considerable extent.

A considerable amount of a budget may be uncontrollable. In that case, no amount of analysis will help unless the legislative body is ready to undertake a comprehensive review of previous decisions and is thus willing to place all budgets in jeopardy. This helps explain the lack of legislative enthusiasm for PPBS.

Management-by-Objectives

Harry Levinson provides an important caveat about the use of management-by-objectives (MBO), a useful approach under many circumstances. Basically, the technique involves goal setting—the development of work objectives and a commitment to achieve them. In this elemental sense, all effective management has MBO qualities.

But the technique does not dispose of all questions, not by a long shot. For example, the technique is dependent on *whose objectives* are considered. Are the objectives those of the legislature or the executive? That poses a critical issue of power. Or let us pose another key question. Are the objectives those of the organization or the individual? If an employee is viewed as having needs and goals, then "management by objectives should begin with *his* objectives. What does he want to do with his life? Where does he want to go? What will make him feel good about himself? What does he want to be able to look back on when he has expanded his unrecoverable years?" Levinson's ideas, at the least, should give MBO implementors some pause.

Zero-Base Budgeting

In regard to zero-base budgeting, we present both a positive and negative view. The positive viewpoint, found in Singleton's "Zero-Base Budgeting in Wilmington, Delaware," paints the successful implementation of ZBB in a city government. The negative point of view is presented by Robert N. Anthony, who proposes that "Zero-Base Budgeting Is a Fraud." The title leaves little doubt as to his basic argument. But also note Anthony's interest in finding ways of rescuing ZBB so that it does not have to be rejected *in toto*.

Whatever one's conclusion about efficacy, ZBB's intent seems direct. To David W. Singleton and colleagues, zero-base budgeting is an attempt to change the traditional, line-item budget operation

> through a process which divides all proposed activities (and expenditures) into cohesive units of manageable size, subjects them to detailed scrutiny, and ultimately establishes a rank-order of those units which, given unlimited resources, would be funded. A selected level of expenditure is then matched against the final rank ordering, and if funds are not sufficient to cover the entire listing, lowest priority items are left unfunded until the cumulative total of the funded priority list exactly matches the level of funding that is available. The final priority list, balanced with available funds, then becomes the budget.

Legislators might have a different systemic view or perspective, of course.

Contrasts to Singleton's optimism are not hard to find. Robert N. Anthony presents strong arguments that zero-base budgeting does not own up to three major defects in design and implementation, for example. These defects are reviewed here only briefly.

　　1.　Definition of "zero-base" in implementation. Not enough time exists to have all agencies justify all budget items each year, he argues, so that the real base hardly ever can be zero. Rather, a base is usually presumed. In the State of Georgia experience, the zero benchmark was equated with 80 percent of current spending limits.

　　2.　Size limitations of the budget. The immense nature of a budget makes individual program elements impossible to consider most of the time. Therefore padding is likely, perhaps even encouraged.

　　3.　Ranking process in ZBB. Whatever the base, and given that budgets will never cover all that might be done, ZBB clearly requires a ranking of projects. And this ranking process of budget purposes or projects is, in reality, a "political process." Discussions of ZBB can neglect two vital points—that no technique can make such decisions, and that data and figures often play secondary roles in such complicated bargaining processes. Legislators seldom will miss such points for very long, and hence their enthusiasm for ZBB may be quite limited.

Control Via Use of Human Resources

Control often is attempted through the use of machine-centered techniques, as PPBS and ZBB sometimes are. Machine-centered approaches utilize computers and other hardware, and often conceive of individuals as "cogs" in the organizational machine.

　　Michael O. Alexander's "Investments in People" proposes that this unfortunate simplification often occurs, at great cost. He asserts that current accounting and information systems ignore the human resource dimension in organizations. Alexander stresses the need for considering human variables though "human resource accounting." In this view, human resources in the organization would be viewed as assets, or investments, of the organization.

　　Jim Bohnsack's "EDP: An Organizational Question" concurs by stressing that before an information system can be installed in an organization, different views and approaches within the organization should be considered. All information systems—and perhaps especially those relying substantially on computers—will be no better than the assumptions and values on which they are built, either consciously or unwittingly. These various preferences and assumptions require direct attention in initial decision making rather than "down the track," when their impact would be negligible.

Control via Accounting Data

With the growth of government and nonprofit organizations, more attention is being paid to nonbusiness methods of accounting. Robert N. Anthony in "Making Sense of Nonbusiness Accounting" stresses the need for those who deal with governments to learn "a new accounting language," so that financial statements of nonbusiness organizations can be constructed according to useful principles. He stresses the importance of three general characteristics of nonbusiness accounting:

1. In nonbusiness financial statements, there is no "bottom line" that shows the overall result of operations.

2. Reports of operations are fragmented by the division into funds. Amounts for several funds must be combined to arrive at total spending for operating programs. Reports of operating performance are not separated from reports of capital transactions.

3. Some accounting numbers do not report the economic realities of the transactions. In addition to revenue and expenditure items that one would expect to find in a report of operations, there are items labeled "transfers," which are neither revenues nor expenditures, some having economic significance and some representing merely movements from one artificial pot to another with no effect on the entity as a whole.

One of the most common ways for organizations to keep track of funds is through the use of "fund accounting." Regina E. Herzlinger and H. David Sherman present arguments in favor of fund accounting in nonbusiness organizations in their "Advantages of Fund Accounting in 'Nonprofits.'" These authors see some critical differences between profit and nonprofit organizations. For example, a deficit "may mean that [the nonprofit] has invested in activities benefiting future generations. The deficit is not necessarily a signal of failure or a cause for concern, as it is in a business."

REFERENCE

1. Murray L. Weidenbaum, "Budget 'Uncontrollability' as an Obstacle to Improving the Allocation of Government Resources," in Robert T. Golembiewski and Jack Rabin (eds.), *Public Budgeting and Finance,* Second Edition (Itasca, Illinois: F. E. Peacock Publishers, Inc., 1975), pp. 97-98.

17

LOOKING BACK AT PPBS:
Image vs. Substance*

Harry S. Havens

Americans have a fondness for technological solutions to problems. It is an attachment which is easy to understand because over the years technology has served us well.

Sometimes, however, we find ourselves looking for technical fixes for problems which are not really amenable to technical solutions. Problems of social policy often fall into this category. We look for people to invent ways of providing clear, simple, and certain answers to questions for which such answers do not exist.

Budgeting, or the process of deciding how to allocate resources in the public sector, is a perfect example. It is hard to conceive of a more complex set of questions than those related to public sector resource allocations. But with our confidence in technology, we keep looking for solutions which are (or look like) technical fixes.

---

*Reprinted from *GAO Review,* vol. 12 (Winter 1977), pp. 10-14.

THE BLACK BOX SYNDROME

There is a predictable life cycle in these things, and it goes something like this: Someone comes up with an interesting and useful idea on improving the resource allocation process. He convinces others of its utility. In an effort to gain acceptance, however, the idea must be oversold. The rhetoric takes on an evangelical flavor. "If you accept this idea, and live by its rules, it will solve all your problems." The idea gains official acceptance and implementation is pushed. Suddenly some of the official sponsors begin to discover that the new technique doesn't quite live up to the promises. Somehow the answers are still a little fuzzy and uncertain. Disillusionment sets in and we criticize the new technique for not doing things which intelligent people should never have expected. We forget the things which the new technique really did accomplish.

Our experience with the planning-programming-budgeting system (PPBS) is a classic example of this pattern, which I call (with no particular originality) the "black box syndrome."

POPULAR HISTORY AND REALITY

The usual summary of PPBS's history at the federal level in the United States is that it started in the Department of Defense in the early 1960s, was adopted by the Budget Bureau in the mid-1960s, enjoyed a brief period of acclaim, and then was discarded. The "death" of PPBS is attributed by some to the ineptitude of those who promoted it. Others suggest that it was too sophisticated for use in the real world, that it was too much of a paperwork exercise, or that it was too divorced from the political realities of government decision making.

There is some merit in each of these explanations, but it really wasn't—and isn't—as simple as this.

The roots of PPBS go back well beyond Robert MacNamara, Secretary of Defense (1961-1968), and, to paraphrase Mark Twain, reports of its death are highly exaggerated. This difference in view is not just an idiosyncrasy on my part. Rather, it represents a differing idea of what PPBS is all about—what it represents and what is important about it.

This difference can be understood and reconciled if one conceives of PPBS as having two separate components. There is an analytic concept and there is an administrative process. The two parts were (and are) important to different people for different reasons.

THE PPBS ADMINISTRATIVE PROCESS

The administrative process is what most people are thinking about when they speak of PPBS. It encompasses procedures and requirements set forth in a series of Budget Bureau instructions to federal agencies.

Those instructions mandated such things as 5-year plans (updated annually), issue papers analyzing major policy alternatives, and crosswalks between the program structure in the 5-year plan and the account structure in the budget. Real decisions were supposed to be made in the 5-year planning context (with issue papers as the decision document). The first year slice of the 5-year plan would than be translated into the account structure of the budget and forwarded to the Congress as the President's budget for the ensuing fiscal year.

PROBLEMS AND LESSONS LEARNED

Most of the criticisms of PPBS have been directed at this administrative process—and most of them are valid. The process was initiated without adequate planning. Insufficient consideration was given to the nature and requirements of the existing budget process. The two processes were never really linked up. Those managing the existing process felt threatened by the new one. They were often excluded from participation with a not-too-subtle hint that budgeteers really aren't competent to do policy analysis and should stick to counting beans.

Unfortunately, when the budgeteers were excluded, they took with them a vital source of knowledge and understanding of the real world of resource allocation. It was partly because of this sharp distinction between PPBS and the existing budget process that PPBS sometimes was surrounded by an aura of unreality.

Incidentally, there was more wrong with this distinction than a tactical mistake. It reflected a serious misjudgment of both what was required to implement PPBS and what budgeteers were capable of doing. The sort of elitism and parochial outlook which underlay that misjudgment is all too common in other areas. It is one of the most serious impediments we face to the broad-scope, interdisciplinary analysis which may well be the only way we can ever find solutions to the complexities of present day problems.

DEATH AND REVIVAL OF THE PROCESS

Faced with these sorts of difficulties, it would have been surprising indeed if the administrative process of PPBS survived—and it didn't. The instructions were canceled and, superficially at least, the process stopped.

But that really isn't the end of the story. It would probably be more accurate to describe ensuing events as a metamorphosis of PPBS rather than its death. Rhetoric and labels changed, but much of the content remained. Budgeteers in the Office of Management and Budget (OMB) and the agencies had learned that it could really be useful to require explicit analysis of costs, benefits, and trade-offs and of outyear implications. They began doing it routinely. More important, they began doing it as part of the regular budget process rather than as a separate, disconnected process. PPBS became an effective part of decision making just when (and partly because) people stopped talking and thinking about it as something special and different.

The story goes even farther than this, however. Lo and behold, elements of the process have started reappearing in all sorts of unlikely places. In the Congressional Budget Act of 1974, for example, there is a requirement to project the results of action 5 years ahead. This is not a 5-year plan, but it has some of the necessary ingredients. If one looks closely at the Congressional Budget Act, one finds a great deal that looks suspiciously like **PPBS**.

The phoenix-like character of the **PPBS** administrative process is even more evident if one takes account of what management-by-objectives looked like and what would be necessary to implement the current proposals for periodic zero-based review of federal programs. The resemblances are great enough to be more than coincidental. They are all variations of the same central theme.

THE PPBS ANALYTIC CONCEPT

That theme—the analytic concept—is important enough that we keep looking for a perfect way of implementing it. Given the nature of our society and political system, we will never find that perfect way; but given the nature of our society, and particularly our fondness for technical solutions, we will keep looking.

The analytic concept underlying **PPBS** is nothing more than a fully rational way of deciding how much of the taxpayers' money should be spent on what.

This is certainly not a new concept. It is quite explicit in the utilitarianism of John Stuart Mill (the greatest good for the greatest number) and with a little effort the idea could undoubtedly be traced back further than that.

THE MYTH OF THE ULTIMATE BLACK BOX

The administrative process of **PPBS** was a means of getting some of the information necessary to implement that concept. It involved an effort to determine systematically the effectiveness of programs across the board. This information was to be used as a major element in the decision-making process of deciding on funding levels. Some people expected this ultimately to evolve into a system in which all the costs and benefits of all programs would be fully quantified.

In this ideal world, the computer would automatically spit out the distribution of funds among programs which would produce the greatest good for the greatest number, equitable distribution of income, maximum economic growth, minimum inflation, and all those other good things we expect from our government. The computer would replace all human judgment and constitute the ultimate black box.

Let me hasten to add that the number of people who really expected this ultimate evolution was quite small. The responsible people may have been a little naive in their thinking about **PPBS**, but they weren't that naive! Most of the people involved in the **PPBS** effort understood full well that there are very few programs in which either the costs or the benefits can be computed with precision. They understood that in many cases there isn't even consensus on which elements are costs and which are benefits.

Even more important, the central actors in the drama were acutely conscious of the fundamentally political nature of the resource allocation process. The thought of Lyndon B. Johnson espousing a system in which his freedom of action in the political arena would be constrained by technicians and computers is mind boggling, to say the least. Unfortunately, however, some earlier advocates of **PPBS** left the impression that they really did expect political choice to give way to technocratic decision making and we are still burdened with that image.

INFORMATION vs. DECISIONS

But if this image is wrong, what was the right image—what was **PPBS** really all about? Here it is important to make another conceptual distinction, this time between making a decision on the one hand and providing the information necessary for decisions on the other.

Nobody was going to take away Lyndon Johnson's prerogative to make decisions, but he knew full well that his base of information for making those decisions was not adequate. Johnson's thirst for information was reputedly almost unquenchable. His ideal was a situation in which he had access to all the information which was relevant to a subject (and he would define the limits of relevance) before he made a decision. In the end, however, the decisions were political. Information, while vital, was an adjunct to the exercise of political judgment.

Seen in this light, one can think of the central objective of **PPBS** as having been to take another step in the direction of giving decision makers the information they need in a form that is usable and at the time it is needed.

PPBS was one of many such steps taken over the years. The most obvious starting point was the creation of a single, more or less integrated budget in 1921. Until quite recently, most of the initiatives toward improving the information base for decisions came from the executive branch (**PPBS**, for example). Historically, those initiatives have been heavily oriented toward strengthening the President's ability to understand and direct the activities of the executive branch and to convince the Congress that his proposals should be enacted.

INFORMATION FOR CONGRESSIONAL DECISION MAKING

Within the past few years, however, it has become quite clear that the need for better information on which to base decisions is not unique to the President and the executive branch. As the Congress has sought a more active role in making policy—especially with respect to the allocation of resources—it has turned to some of the same tools used by the executive branch. Many of these tools, and the thinking behind them, look a lot like PPBS because the analytic concept is the same—the search for a rational way to allocate public resources.

The similarities are quite evident if one reviews the Congressional Budget Act of 1974. First, the Congress has established a single, integrated structure in which it will make aggregate resource allocation decisions in a coordinated fashion. Second, the Congress has recognized the need for a systematic flow of relevant information to support its decision-making process. Third, the Congress has recognized the need for special analytic studies structured around the specific decisions facing it. Fourth, the Congress has recognized the need to consider the implications of decisions in a time frame well beyond the traditional 1-year budgeting horizon. Finally, the Congress is recognizing the need to depart from the incremental approach to budgeting and to examine methodically the need to continue existing programs.

WHAT DO DECISION MAKERS NEED?

The similarities are not accidental between what the Congress is trying to do now and what the executive branch was trying to do with PPBS. But neither is the Congress slavishly copying the executive branch.

Both efforts are prompted by the fairly simple truth that society, and government's role in it, is just too complex today for fundamental policy choices to be made in a hit-or-miss fashion. And the choices are too interrelated to be made in isolation of each other.

We elect our political leaders to make decisions on our behalf. We expect—at least, we hope—that they will make those decisions wisely. To make an informed decision, any decision maker needs answers to the following general questions:

- What happened in the past?
- Why did it happen?
- What are the options for the future?
- What are the implications of each of those options?

PPBS represented a systematic effort to supply answers to those questions. The formal administrative process of PPBS was flawed in many respects, but the need to answer those questions remains. We will continue to look for better ways to supply the answers. With a little luck, and learning as we go along, each effort will be better than the one which preceded it.

We learned many things from the experience of PPBS, but two lessons stand out in my mind. First, I think we learned that these analytic processes work better if the participants bring a wide range of skills. No single academic discipline is uniquely qualified to do this work. Second, it is a lot easier to talk about doing good analysis than it is to do the work. Producing reliable, relevant, timely analysis involves a lot of hard work and we still have a lot to learn about doing it. The PPBS experience taught us that it is not as simple as the more naive supporters may have thought. But the experience also taught us that it is possible to do good analysis and important to try.

18

MANAGEMENT BY WHOSE OBJECTIVES? *

Harry Levinson

Despite the fact that the concept of management-by-objectives (MBO) has by
this time become an integral part of the managerial process, the typical MBO
effort perpetuates and intensifies hostility, resentment, and distrust between a
manager and subordinates. As currently practiced, it is really just industrial engineering with a new name, applied to higher managerial levels, and with the
same resistances.

Obviously, somewhere between the concept of MBO and its implementation,
something has gone seriously wrong. Coupled with performance appraisal, the
intent is to follow the Frederick Taylor tradition of a more rational management
process, i.e., which people are to do what, who is to have effective control over
it, and how compensation is to be related directly to individual achievement. The
MBO process, in its essence, is an effort to be fair and reasonable, to predict performance and judge it more carefully, and presumably to provide individuals with
an opportunity to be self-motivating by setting their own objectives.

*Reprinted by permission of the Harvard Business Review. "Management by Whose
Objectives?" by Harry Levinson, vol. 48 (July-August 1970), pp. 125-134. Copyright ©
1970 by the President and Fellows of Harvard College; all rights reserved.

The intent of clarifying job obligations and measuring performance against a person's own goals seems reasonable enough. The concern for having both superior and subordinate consider the same matters in reviewing the performance of the latter is eminently sensible. The effort to come to common agreement on what constitutes the subordinate's job is highly desirable.

Yet, like most rationalizations in the Taylor tradition, MBO as a process is one of the greatest of managerial illusions because it fails to take adequately into account the deeper emotional components of motivation.

In this chapter, I shall indicate how I think management-by-objectives, as currently practiced in most organizations, is self-defeating, and serves simply to increase pressure on the individual. By doing so, I do not reject either MBO or performance appraisal out of hand.

Rather, by raising the basic question, "Whose objectives?" I propose to suggest how they might be made more constructive devices for effective management. The issues I shall raise have largely to do with psychological considerations, and particularly with the assumptions about motivation which underlie these techniques.

THE "IDEAL" PROCESS*

Since management-by-objectives is closely related to performance appraisal and review, I shall consider these together as one practice which is intended

- To measure and judge performance
- To relate individual performance to organizational goals
- To clarify both the job to be done and the expectations of accomplishment
- To foster the increasing competence and growth of the subordinate
- To enhance communications between superior and subordinate
- To serve as a basis for judgments about salary and promotion
- To stimulate the subordinate's motivation
- To serve as a device for organizational control and integration

Major Problems

According to contemporary thinking, the "ideal" process should proceed in five steps: (1) individual discussion with his superior of the subordinate's description of his own job, (2) establishment of short-term performance targets, (3) meeting with the superior to discuss progress toward targets, (4) establishment of check-

---

*A bibliography for this section appears at the end of the chapter.

points to measure progress, and (5) discussion between superior and subordinate at the end of a defined period to assess the results of the subordinate's efforts. In *ideal* practice, this process occurs against a background of more frequent, even day-to-day, contacts and is separate from salary review. But in *actual* practice, there are many problems. Consider:

No matter how detailed the job description, it is essentially, i.e., a series of statements. However, the more complex the task and the more flexible a man must be in it, the less any fixed statement of job elements will fit what he does. Thus the higher a man rises in an organization and the more varied and subtle his work, the more difficult it is to pin down objectives that represent more than a fraction of his effort.

With preestablished goals and descriptions, little weight can be given to the areas of discretion open to the individual but not incorporated into his job description or objectives. I am referring here to those spontaneously creative activities an innovative executive might choose to do, or those tasks a responsible executive sees which need to be done. As we move more toward a service society, in which tasks are less well defined but spontaneity of service and self-assumed responsibility are crucial, this becomes pressing.

Most job descriptions are limited to what a man himself does in his work. They do not adequately take into account the increasing interdependence of managerial work in organizations. This limitation becomes more important as the impact of social and organizational factors on individual performance becomes better understood. The more a man's effectiveness depends on what other people do, the less he can be held responsible for the outcome of his efforts.

If a primary concern in performance review is counseling the subordinate, appraisal should consider and take into account the total situation in which the superior and subordinate are operating. In addition, this should take into account the relationship of the subordinate's job to other jobs, rather than to his alone. In counseling, much of the focus is in helping the subordinate learn to negotiate the system. There is no provision in most reviews and no place on appraisal forms with which I am familiar to report and record such discussion.

The setting and evolution of objectives is done over too brief a period of time to provide for adequate interaction among different levels of an organization. This militates against opportunity for peers, both in the same work unit and in complementary units, to develop objectives together for maximum integration. Thus both the setting of objectives and the appraisal of performance make little contribution toward the development of team work and more effective organizational self-control.

Coupled with these problems is the difficulty superiors experience when they undertake appraisals. Douglas McGregor complained that the major reason appraisal failed was that superiors disliked playing God by making judgments about another man's worth.[1] He likened the superior's experience to inspection of assembly line products and contended that his revulsion was against being inhuman. To cope with this problem, McGregor recommended that an individual should set his own goals, checking them out with his superior, and should use the appraisal session as a counseling device. Thus the superior would become one who helped the subordinate achieve his own goals instead of a dehumanized inspector of products.

Parenthetically, I doubt very much that the failure of appraisal stems from playing God or feeling inhuman. My own observation leads me to believe that managers experience their appraisal of others as a hostile, aggressive act that unconsciously is felt to be hurting or destroying the other person. The appraisal situation, therefore, gives rise to powerful, paralyzing feelings of guilt that make it extremely difficult for most executives to be constructively critical of subordinates.

Objectivity Plea

Be that as it may, the more complex and difficult the appraisal process and the setting and evaluation of objectives, the more pressing the cry for objectivity. This is a vain plea. Every organization is a social system, a network of interpersonal relationships. A man may do an excellent job by objective standards of measurement, but may fail miserably as a partner, subordinate, superior, or colleague. It is a commonplace that more people fail to be promoted for personal reasons than for technical inadequacy.

Furthermore, since every subordinate is a component of his superior's efforts to achieve his own goals, he will inevitably be appraised on how well he works with his superior and helps the latter meet his needs. A heavy subjective element necessarily enters into every appraisal and goal-setting experience.

The plea for objectivity is vain for another reason. The greater the emphasis on measurement and quantification, the more likely the subtle, nonmeasurable elements of the task will be sacrificed. Quality of performance frequently, therefore, loses out to quantification.

A case example. A manufacturing plant which produces high-quality, high-prestige products, backed by a reputation for customer consideration and service, has instituted an MBO program. It is well worked out and has done much to clarify both individual goals and organizational performance. It is an important component of the professional management style of that company, which has resulted in commendable growth.

But an interesting, and ultimately destructive, process has been set in motion. The managers are beginning to worry because when they now ask why something has not been done, they hear from each other, "That isn't in my goals." They complain that customer service is deteriorating. The vague goal, "improve customer service," is almost impossible to measure. There is therefore heavy concentration on those subgoals which can be measured. Thus time per customer, number of customer calls, and similar measures are used as guides in judging performance. The *less* time per customer and the *fewer* the calls, the better the customer service manager meets his objectives. He is cutting costs, increasing profit—and killing the business. Worse still, he hates himself.

Most of the managers in that organization joined it because of its reputation for high quality and good service. They want to make good products and earn the continued admiration of their customers as well as the envy of their industry. When they are not operating at that high level, they feel guilty. They become angry with themselves and the company. They feel that they might just as well be working for someone else who admittedly does a sloppy job of quality control and could hardly care less about service.

The same problem exists with respect to the development of personnel, which is another vague goal that is hard to measure in comparison with subgoals that are measurable. If asked, each manager can name a younger man as his potential successor, particularly if his promotion depends on doing so; but no one has the time, or indeed feels that he is being paid, to thoroughly train the younger man. Nor can one have the time or be paid, for there is no way in that organization to measure how well a manager does in developing another.

THE MISSED POINT

All of the problems with objectives and appraisals outlined in the example discussed in the foregoing section indicate that MBO is not working well despite what some companies think about their programs. The underlying reason it is not working well is that it misses the whole human point.

To see how the point is being missed, let us follow the typical MBO process. Characteristically, top management sets its corporate goal for the coming year. This may be in terms of return on investment, sales, production, growth, or other measurable factors.

Within this frame of reference, reporting managers may then be asked how much their units intend to contribute toward meeting that goal, or they may be asked to set their own goals relatively independent of the corporate goal. If they are left free to set their own goals, these in any case are expected to be higher than those they had the previous year. Usually, each reporting manager's range of choices is limited to his option for a piece of the organizational action, or improvement of specific statistics. In some cases, it may also include obtaining specific training or skills.

Once a reporting manager decides on his unit's goals and has them approved by his superior, those become the manager's goals. Presumably, he has committed himself to what he wants to do. He has said it and he is responsible for it. He is thereafter subject to being hoisted on his own petard.

Now, let us reexamine this process closely: the whole method is based on a short-term, egocentrically oriented perspective and an underlying reward-punishment psychology. The typical MBO process puts the reporting manager in much the same position as a rat in a maze, who has choices between only two alternatives. The experimenter who puts the rat in the maze assumes that the rat wants the food reward; if he cannot presume that, he starves the rat to make sure he wants the food.

Management-by-objectives differs only in that it permits the man himself to determine his own bait from a limited range of choices. Having done so, the MBO process assumes that he will (1) work hard to get it, (2) be pushed internally by reason of his commitment, and (3) make himself responsible to his organization for doing so.

In fairness to most managers, they certainly try, but not without increasing resentment and complaint for feeling like rats in a maze, guilt for not paying attention to those parts of the job not in their objectives, and passive resistance to the mounting pressure for ever higher goals.

Personal Goals

The MBO process leaves out the answers to such questions as: What are the manager's personal objectives? What does he need and want out of his work? How do his needs and wants change from year to year? What relevance do organizational objectives and his part in them have to such needs and wants?

Obviously, no objectives will have significant incentive power if they are forced choices unrelated to a man's underlying dreams, wishes, and personal aspirations. For example:

If a salesman relishes the pleasure of his relationships with his hard-earned but low-volume customers, this is a powerful need for him. Suppose his boss, who is concerned about increasing the volume of sales, urges him to concentrate on the larger quantity customers rather than the smaller ones, which will provide the necessary increase in volume, and then asks him how much of an increase he can achieve.

To work with the larger quantity customers means that he will be less likely to sell to the individuals with whom he has well-established relationships and be more likely to deal with purchasing agents, technical people, and staff specialists who will demand of him knowledge and information he may not have in sophisticated detail. Moreover, as a single salesman, his organization may fail to support him with technical help to meet these demands.

When this happens, not only may he lose his favorite way of operating, which has well served his own needs, but he may have demands put on him which cause him to feel inadequate. If he is being compelled to make a choice about the percent of sales volume increase he expects to attain, he may well do that, but now under great psychological pressure. No one has recognized the psychological realities he faces, let alone helped him to work with them. It is simply assumed that since his sales goal is a rational one, he will see its rationality and pursue it.

The problem may be further compounded if, as is not unusual, formal changes are made in the organizational structure. If sales territories are shifted, if modes of compensation are changed, if problems of delivery occur, or whatever, all of these are factors beyond the salesman's control. Nevertheless, even with certain allowances, he is still held responsible for meeting his sales goal.

Psychological Needs

Lest the reader think the example we have just seen is overdrawn or irrelevant, I know of a young sales manager who is about to resign his job, despite his success in it, because he chooses not to be expendable in an organization which he feels regards him only as an instrument for reaching a goal. Many young men are refusing to enter large organizations for just this reason.

Some may argue that my criticism is unfair, that many organizations start their planning and setting of objectives from below. Therefore, the company cannot be accused of putting the man in a maze. But it does so. In almost all cases, the only legitimate objectives to be set are those having to do with measurable increases in performance. This highlights, again, the question, "Whose objectives?" This question becomes more pressing in those circumstances where lower level people set their objectives, only to be questioned by higher level managers and told their targets are not high enough.

Here you may well ask, "What's the matter with that? Aren't we in business, and isn't the purpose of the man's work to serve the requirements of the business?" The answer to both questions is, "Obviously." But that is only part of the story.

If a man's most powerful driving force is composed of his needs, wishes, and personal aspirations, combined with the compelling wish to look good in his own eyes for meeting those deeply held personal goals, then management-by-objectives should begin with *his* objectives. What does he want to do with his life? Where does he want to go? What will make him feel good about himself? What does he want to be able to look back on when he has expended his unrecoverable years?

At this point, some may say that those are his business. The company has other business, and it must assume that the man is interested in working in the company's business rather than his own. That kind of differentiation is impossible. Everyone is always working toward meeting his psychological needs. Anyone who thinks otherwise, and who believes such powerful internal forces can be successfully disregarded or bought off for long, is deluding himself.

THE MUTUAL TASK

The organizational task becomes one of first understanding the man's needs, and then, with him, assessing how well they can be met in the organization, doing what the organization needs to have done. Thus the highest point of self-motivation arises when there is a complementary conjunction of the man's needs and the organization's requirements. The requirements of both mesh, interrelate, and become synergistic. The energies of man and organization are pooled for mutual advantage.

If the two sets of needs do not mesh, then a man has to fight himself and his organization, in addition to the work which must be done and the targets which have been defined. In such a case, this requires of him and his boss that they evaluate together where he wants to go, where the organization is going, and how significant the discrepancy is. The man might well be better off somewhere else, and the organization would do better to have someone else in his place whose needs mesh better with organization requirements.

Long-Run Costs

The issue of meshed interests is particularly relevant for middle-aged, senior level managers.[2] As men come into middle age, their values often begin to change, and they feel anew the pressure to accomplish many long-deferred dreams. When such wishes begin to stir, they begin to experience severe conflict.

Up to this point, they have committed themselves to the organization and have done sufficiently well in it to attain high rank. Usually, they are slated for even higher levels of responsibility. The organization has been good to them, and their superiors are depending on them to provide its leadership. They have been models for the younger men, whom they have urged to aspire to organizational heights. To think of leaving is to desert both their superiors and their subordinates.

Since there are few avenues within the organization in which to talk about such conflict, they try to suppress their wishes. The internal pressure continues to mount until they finally make an impulsive break, surprising and dismaying both themselves and their colleagues. I can think of three vice presidents who have done just that.

The issue is not so much that they decide to leave, but the cost of the way they depart. Early discussion with superiors of their personal goals would have enabled both to examine possible relocation alternatives within the organization. If there were none, then both the managers and their superiors might have come to an earlier, more comfortable decision about separation. The organization would have had more time to make satisfactory alternative plans, as well as to have taken steps to compensate for the manager's lagging enthusiasm. Lower level managers would then have seen the company as humane in its enlightened self-interest and would not have had to create fearful fantasies about what the top management conflicts were that had caused a good man to leave.

To place consideration of the managers' personal objectives first does not minimize the importance of the organization's goals. It does not mean there is anything wrong with the organization's need to increase its return on investment, its size, its productivity, or its other goals. However, I contend that it is ridiculous to make assumptions about the motivations of individuals, and then to set up means of increasing the pressures on people based on these often questionable assumptions. While there may be certain demonstrable short-run statistical gains, what are the long-run costs?

One cost is that people may leave; another, that they may fall back from competitive positions to plateaus. Why should an individual be expendable for someone else and sacrifice himself for something that is not part of his own cherished dreams? Still another cost may be the loss of the essence of the business, as happened in the case example we saw earlier of the manufacturing plant which had the problem of deteriorating customer service.

In that example, initially there was no dialogue. Nobody heard what the managers said, what they wanted, where they wanted to go, where they wanted the organization to go, and how they felt about the supposedly rational procedures that had been initiated. The underlying psychological assumption which management unconsciously made was that the managers *had to be made* more efficient; ergo, management-by-objectives.

Top management typically assumes that it alone has the prerogative to (1) set the objectives, (2) provide the rewards and targets, and (3) drive anyone who works for the organization. As long as this reward-punishment psychology exists in any organization, the MBO appraisal process is certain to fail.

Many organizations are making this issue worse by promising young people they will have challenges, since they assume these people will be challenged by management's objectives. Managements are having difficulty, even when they have high turnover rates, hearing these youngsters say they could hardly care less for management's unilaterally determined objectives. Managements then become angry, complain that the young people do not want to work, or that they want to become presidents overnight.

What the young people are asking is: What about me and my needs? Who will listen? How much will management help me meet my own requirements while also meeting its objectives?

The power of this force is reflected in the finding that the more the subordinate participates in the appraisal interview by presenting his own ideas and beliefs, the more likely he is to feel that (a) the superior is helpful and constructive, (b) some current job problems are being cleared up, and (c) reasonable future goals are being set.[3]

THE SUGGESTED STEPS

Given the validity of all the MBO problems I have been discussing to this point, there are a number of possibilities for coping with them. Here, I suggest three beginning steps to consider.

1. Motivational Assessment

Every management-by-objectives program and its accompanying performance appraisal system should be examined as to the extent to which it (1) expressed the
conviction that people are patsies to be driven, urged, and manipulated, and (2)
fosters a genuine partnership between men and organization, in which each has
some influence over the other, as contrasted with a rat-in-maze relationship.

It is not easy for the nonpsychologist to answer such questions for himself,
but there are clues to the answers. One clue is how decisions about compensation, particularly bonuses, are made. For example:

• A sales manager asked my judgment about an incentive plan for highly motivated salesmen who were in a seller's market. I asked why he needed one, and
he responded, "To give them an incentive." When I pointed out that they were
already highly motivated and apparently needed no incentive, he changed his
rationale and said that the company wanted to share its success to keep the men
identified with it and to express its recognition of their contribution.

I asked, "Why not let them establish the reward related to performance?"
The question startled him; obviously, if they were going to decide, who needed
him? A fundamental aspect of his role, as he saw it, was to drive them ever on-
ward, whether they needed it or not.

• A middle-management bonus plan tied to performance proved to be highly
unsatisfactory in a plastics-fabricating company. Frustrated that its well-inten-
tioned efforts were not working and determined to follow precepts of participative management, ranking executives involved many people in formulating a new
one: personnel, control, marketing executives, and others—in fact, everyone but
the managers who were to receive the bonuses. Top management is now dismayed that the new plan is as unsatisfactory as the old and is bitter that participation failed to work.

Another clue is the focus of company meetings. Some are devoted to inten-
sifying the competition between units. Others lean heavily to exhortation and
inspiration. Contrast these orientations with meetings in which people are ap-
prised of problems and plan to cope with them.

2. Group Action

Every objectives-and-appraisal program should include group goal setting, group
definition of both individual and group tasks, group appraisal of its accomplishments, group appraisal of each individual member's contribution to the group
effort (without basing compensation on that appraisal), and shared compensation based on the relative success with which group goals are achieved. Objectives should include long-term as well as short-term goals.

The rationale is simple. Every managerial job is an interdependent task.
Managers have responsibilities to each other as well as to their superiors. The

reason for having an organization is to achieve more together than each could alone. Why, then, emphasize and reward individual performance alone, based on static job descriptions? That can only orient people to both incorrect and self-centered goals.

Therefore, where people are in complementary relationships, whether they report to the same superior or not, both horizontal and vertical goal formulation should be formalized, with regular, frequent opportunity for review of problems and progress. They should help each other define and describe their respective jobs, enhancing control and integration at the point of action.

In my judgment, for example, a group of managers (sales, promotion, advertising) reporting to a vice president of marketing should formulate their collective goals, and define ways both of helping each other and of assessing each others' effectiveness in the common task. The group assessment of each manager's work should be a means of providing each with constructive feedback, not for determining pay. However, in addition to his salary, each should receive, as part of whatever additional compensation is offered, a return based on the group effort.

The group's discussion among itself and with its superior should include examination of organizational and environmental obstacles to goal achievement, and particularly of what organizational and leadership supports are required to attain objectives. One important reason for this is that often people think there are barriers where none would exist if they initiated action. ("You mean the president really wants us to get together and solve this problem?")

Another reason is that frequently when higher management sets goals, it is unaware of significant barriers to achievement, leaving managers cynical. For example, if there is no comprehensive orientation and support program to help new employees adapt, then pressure on lower level managers to employ disadvantaged minority group members and to reduce their turnover can only be experienced by those managers as hollow mockery.

3. Appraisal of Appraisers

Every management-by-objectives-and-appraisal program should include regular appraisals of the manager by his subordinates, and the appraisals should be reviewed by the manager's superior. Every manager should be specifically compensated for how well he develops people, based on such appraisals. The very phrase "reporting to" reflects the fact that although a manager has a responsibility, his superior also has a responsibility for what he does and how he does it.

In fact, both common sense and research indicate that the single most significant influence outside himself on how a manager does his job is his superior. If that is the case, then the key environmental factor in task accomplishment and managerial growth is the relationship between the manager and his superior.

Therefore, objectives should include not only the individual manager's personal and occupational goals, but also the corporate goals he and his superior share. They should together appraise their relationship vis-à-vis both the manager's individual goals and their joint objectives, review what they have done together, and discuss its implication for their next joint steps.

A manager rarely is in a position to judge his superior's overall performance, but he can appraise him on the basis of how well the superior has helped him to do his job, how well he is helping him to increase his proficiency and visibility, what problems the superior poses for him, and what kinds of support he himself can use. Such feedback serves several purposes.

Most important, it offers the superior some guidance on his own managerial performance. In addition, and particularly when the manager is protected by higher level review of his appraisal, it provides the supervisor with direct feedback on his own behavior. This is much more constructive than behind-his-back complaint and vituperative terminal interviews, in which case he has no opportunity either to defend himself or correct his behavior. Every professional counselor has had recently fired executive clients who did not know why they had been discharged for being poor superiors when, according to their information, their subordinates thought so much of them. In his own self-interest, every manager should want appraisal by his subordinates.

THE BASIC CONSIDERATION

When the three organizational conditions we have just seen do in fact exist, then it is appropriate to think of starting management-by-objectives with a consideration of each man's personal objectives; if the underlying attitude in the organization toward him is that he is but an object, there is certainly no point in starting with the man. Nor is there any point in trying to establish his confidence in his superiors when he is not protected from their rivalry with him, or when they are playing him off against his peers. Anyone who expressed his fears and innermost wishes under these circumstances would be a fool.

For reasons I have already indicated, it should be entirely legitimate in every business for these concerns to be the basis for individual objectives setting. This is because the fundamental managerial consideration necessarily must be focused on the question: "How do we meet both individual and organizational purposes?" If a major intention of management-by-objectives is to enlist the self-motivated commitment of the individual, then that commitment must derive from the individual's powerful wishes to support the organization's goals; otherwise the commitment will be merely incidental to his personal wishes.

Having said that, the real difficulty begins. How can any superior know what a subordinate's personal goals and wishes are if the subordinate himself—like most of us—is not clear about them? How ethical is it for a superior to pry into man's personal life? How can he keep himself from forming a negative judgment about a man who he knows is losing interest in his work, or is not altogether identified with the company? How can he keep that knowledge from interfering with judgments he might otherwise make and opportunities he might otherwise offer? How often are the personal goals, particularly in middle age, temporary fantasies that are better not discussed? Can a superior who is untrained in psychology handle such information constructively? Will he perhaps do more harm than good?

These are critically important questions. They deserve careful thought. My answers should be taken as no more than beginning steps.

Ego Concepts

Living is a process of constant adaptation. A man's personal goals, wishes, and aspirations are continuously evolving and being continuously modified by his experiences. That is one reason why it is so difficult for an individual to specify concrete personal objectives.

Nevertheless, each of us has a built-in road map, a picture of himself as his future best. Psychologists speak of this as an *ego ideal,* which comprises a man's values, the expectations parents and others have held out for him, his competences and skills, and his favorite ways of behaving. A person's ego ideal is essentially the way he thinks he ought to be. Much of a person's ego ideal is unconscious, which is another reason why it is not clear to him.

Subordinate's Self-Examination. Although a man cannot usually spell out his ego ideal, he can talk about those experiences that have been highly gratifying, even exhilarating, to him. He can specify those rare peak experiences that made him feel very good about himself. When he has an opportunity to talk about what he has found especially gratifying and also what he thinks would be gratifying to him, he is touching on central elements of his ego ideal.

Given the opportunity to talk about such experiences and wishes on successive occasions, he can begin to spell out for himself the central thrust of his life. Reviewing all of the occupational choices he has made and the reasons for making them, he can begin to see the common threads in those choices and therefore the momentum of his personality. As these become clearer to him, he is in a better position to weigh alternatives against the mainstream of his personality.

For example, a man who has successively chosen occupational alternatives in which he was individually competitive, and whose most exhilarating experiences have come from defeating an opponent or single-handedly vanquishing a problem, would be unlikely to find a staff position exhibarating, no matter what it paid or what it was called. His ideal for himself is that of a vanquishing, competitive man.

The important concept here is that it is not necessary that a person spell out concrete goals at any one point; rather, it is helpful to him and his organization if he is able to examine and review aloud on a continuing basis his thoughts and feelings about himself in relation to his work. Such a process makes it legitimate for him to bring his own feelings to consciousness and talk about them in the business context as the basis for his relationship to the organization.

By listening, and helping him to spell out how and what he feels, the superior does not do anything to the man, and therefore by that self-appraisal process cannot hurt him. The information serves both the man and his superior as a criterion for examining the relationship of the man's feelings and his, however dimly perceived, personal goals or organizational goals. Even if some of his wishes and aspirations are mere fantasy and impossible to gratify, if it is legitimate to talk about them without being laughed at, he can compare them with the realities of his life and make more reasonable choices.

Even in the safest organizational atmosphere, for reasons already mentioned, it will not be easy for managers to talk about their goals. The best-intentioned supervisor is likely to be something less than a highly skilled interviewer. These two facts suggest that any effort to ascertain a subordinate's personal goals is futile; but I think not.

The important point is not the specificity of the statement that any person can make, but the nature of a superior-subordinate relationship that makes it safe to explore such feelings and gives first consideration to the person. In such a context, both subordinate and superior may come closer to evolving a person-organization fit than they might otherwise.

Superior's Introspection. A person-organization relationship requires the superior to do some introspection, too. Suppose he has prided himself on bringing along a bright young man who, he now learns, is thinking of moving into a different field. How can he keep from being angry and disappointed? How can he cope with the conflict he now has when it is time to make recommendations for advancement or a raise?

The superior cannot keep from being angry and disappointed. Such feelings are natural in that circumstance. He can express his feelings of disappointment to his protégé without being critical of the latter. But if he continues to feel angry, then he needs to ask himself why another man's assertion of independence irritates him so. The issues of advancement and raises should continue to be based on the same realistic premises as they would have been before.

Of course, it now becomes appropriate to consider with the man whether—in view of his feelings—he wants to take on the burden of added responsibility and can reasonably discharge it. If he thinks he does, and can, he is likely to pursue the new responsibility with added determination. With his occupational choice conflict no longer hidden, and with fewer feelings of guilt about it, his commitment to his chosen alternative is likely to be more intense.

And if he has earned a raise, he should get it. To withhold it is to punish him, which puts the relationship back on a reward-punishment basis.

The question of how ethical it is to conduct such discussions as part of a business situation hinges on both the climate of the organization and on the sense of personal responsibility of each executive. Where the organization ethos is one of building trust and keeping confidences, there is no reason why executives cannot be as ethical as lawyers or physicians.

If the individual executive cannot be trusted in his relationships with his subordinates, then he cannot have their respect or confidence in any case, and the ordinary MBO appraisal process simply serves as a management pressure device. If the organization ethos is one of rapacious internal competition, backbiting, and distrust, there is little point in talking about self-motivation, human needs, or commitment.

CONCLUSION

Management-by-objectives and performance appraisal processes, as typically practiced, are inherently self-defeating over the long run because they are based on a reward-punishment psychology that serves to intensify the pressure on the individual while really giving him a very limited choice of objectives. Such processes can be improved by examining the psychological assumptions underlying them, by extending them to include group appraisal and appraisal of superiors by subordinates, and by considering the personal goals of the individual first. These practices require a high level of ethical standards and personal responsibility in the organization.

Such appraisal processes would diminish the feeling on the part of the superior that appraisal is a hostile, destructive act. While he and his subordinates would still have to judge the latter's individual performance, this judgment would occur in a context of continuing consideration for personal needs and reappraisal of organizational and environmental realities.

Not having to be continuously on the defensive and aware of the organization's genuine interest in having him meet his personal goals as well as the organization's goals, a manager would be freer to evaluate himself against what has to be done. Since he would have many additional frames of reference in both horizontal and vertical goal setting, he would need no longer to see himself under appraisal (attack, judgment) as an isolated individual against the system. Furthermore, he would have multiple modes for contributing his own ideas and a varied method for exerting influence upward and horizontally.

In these contexts, too, he could raise questions and concerns about qualitative aspects of performance. Then he, his colleagues, and his superiors could act together to cope with such issues without the barrier of having to consider only statistics. Thus a continuing process of interchange would counteract the problem of the static job description and provide multiple avenues for feedback on performance and joint action.

In such an organizational climate, work relationships would then become dynamic networks for both personal and organizational achievements. No incidental gain from such arrangements is that problems would more likely be solved spontaneously at the lowest possible levels and free superiors simultaneously from the burden of the passed buck and the onus of being the purveyors of hostility.

NOTES

1. An uneasy look at performance appraisal, *Harvard Business Review,* May-June 1957, p. 89.
2. See my article, On being a middle-aged manager, *Harvard Business Review,* July-August 1969, p. 51.
3. Ronald J. Burke and Douglas S. Wilcox, Characteristics of effective employee performance reviews and developmental interviews, *Personal Psychology,* 22 (3), 1969, p. 291.

BIBLIOGRAPHY FOR SECTION ON "THE IDEAL PROCESS"

In this part of the chapter, which defines the ideal process and the major problems inherent in it, I draw heavily on the work of these authors, in sequence:

Alva F. Kindall and James Gatza, Positive program for performance appraisal," *Harvard Business Review,* Nov.-Dec. 1963, p. 153.

Herbert H. Meyer, Emanuel Kay, and John R. P. French, Jr., Split roles in performance appraisal, *Harvard Business Review,* Jan.-Feb. 1965, p. 123.

Ishwar Dayal, Role analysis techniques in job description, *California Management Review,* Vol. XI, No. 4, 1969, p. 47.

Stanley Sloan and Alton C. Johnson, Performance appraisal . . . Where are we headed? *Personnel Administrator,* Vol. 14, No. 5, 1969, p. 12.

Philip R. Kelly, Reappraisal of appraisals, *Harvard Business Review,* May-June 1958, p. 59.

Robert A. Howell, A fresh look at management by objectives, *Business Horizons,* Vol. 10, No. 3, 1967, p. 51.

Albert W. Schrader, Let's abolish the annual performance review, *Management of Personnel Quarterly,* Fall 1969, p. 20.

George H. Labovitz, In defense of subjective executive appraisal, *Academy of Management Journal,* Vol. 12, No. 3, 1969, p. 293.

Larry E. Greiner, D. Paul Leitch, and Louis B. Barnes, Putting judgment back into decisions, *Harvard Business Review,* March-April 1970, p. 59.

George Strauss and Leonard R. Sayles, *Personnel: The Human Problems of Management* (Englewood Cliffs, N.J., Prentice-Hall, 1967), p. 564.

19

ZERO-BASE BUDGETING IN WILMINGTON, DELAWARE *

David W. Singleton
Bruce A. Smith
James R. Cleaveland

One of the major drawbacks in most budgeting systems is their primary focus on the increases from year to year in various accounting categories, with little systematic regard for programmatic priorities and results. A relatively new approach to planning and budgeting—zero-base budgeting—aims to overcome this drawback by subjecting all proposed activities and expenditures to the type of intensive scrutiny normally reserved for proposed new programs. Zero-base budgeting, or ZBB, originated in the private sector and has been little used in the public sector. This chapter presents a case history of its implementation in the municipal government of Wilmington, Delaware.

With a resident population of 80,000 and a daily commuter influx from the suburbs of another 60,000, Wilmington is by far Delaware's largest city, and its commercial hub. The city also houses half of the state's welfare recipients, a quarter of the senior citizens, a quarter of the persons with incomes below the poverty line, and nearly a third of the crime—although it represents only 15 percent of the state's population. Since 1960, the city's resident population has declined 17 percent.

*Reprinted from *Governmental Finance,* vol. 5, no. 3 (August 1976), pp. 20-29.

Wilmington's governmental structure, under home rule charter, is characterized as "strong mayor-council" form. The present mayor, Thomas C. Maloney,
has held office since 1973. During that time, Maloney has established a national
reputation for fiscal restraint, limiting the growth in the city's operating budget
to only 18.9 percent for all four of his budgets combined—compared with 16
percent annually under his predecessor. A mainstay of Maloney's approach has
been improved management of resources and dramatic productivity improvements in a variety of city services.

In their continuing review of the planning-budgeting-accountability process
in Wilmington, Mayor Maloney and his staff had identified a variety of disadvantages with the existing process—a fairly typical, although heavily detailed, line-
item approach. Among the more significant difficulties were:

- *Insufficient information:* The existing budget process provided little useful
  information about the nature and level of services provided, the reason for
  providing the service, the beneficiaries of the service, or the resources needed
  to provide a specific level of service.

- *Existing level assumed:* In general, the budgeting process took as given the
  level of funding from the current year, and focused almost entirely on the
  increase sought for the coming year. Expenditures included in previous
  budgets usually required no significant justification.

- *No tradeoffs:* Although the city did not have sufficient resources to fund
  all services at the requested—or even current—level, there was no meaningful
  process available to make choices and tradeoffs among the city's different
  services on anything even approaching a cost-benefit basis.

- *Impact of change unclear:* There was no mechanism to predict the impact of
  significant changes in the funding of particular services and no systematic
  way to identify the absolute minimum level of service (if any) which the
  city must provide. Similarly, there was no way to project the likely benefits
  of significant funding increases in a particular service.

Although these problems are relatively common to all levels of government,
they were exacerbated in Wilmington's case by the severe and continuing fiscal
problems which beset Wilmington and so many of America's older cities:

- Little or no growth in existing revenue sources, coupled with a high level of
  inflation and excessive unemployment

- Locked-in union wage settlements in the 5 to 7.5 percent range

- Relatively "fixed" expenses, such as pensions, debt service, insurance, and
  the public school subsidy, consuming roughly half the available revenues

- Continuing demands for new programs (or continuation of programs formerly federally funded), particularly social services

- Strong aversion to any tax increases, which tend to accelerate the erosion of the city's tax base

As a result of these concerns, members of Mayor Maloney's staff were attracted by the concept when they learned of the successful use of ZBB in the private sector.[1] After further research, discussions with a consulting firm having considerable ZBB experience and consultation with city officials in Garland, Texas, one of the few public jurisdictions which had utilized ZBB, a decision was made in the late autumn of 1975 to promptly implement ZBB in Wilmington.

In most organizations, the one type of budget request certain to receive intensive screening and analysis is the one that proposes to establish a new service. It is likely to be reviewed as to desirability and need for the service, beneficiaries of the service, reasonableness of proposed costs, potential future implications, and availability of funds—often in terms of relative priority of all proposed new services. Zero-base budgeting aims to apply this same type of process, in a more sophisticated manner, to all proposed expenditures.

Essentially, ZBB seeks to accomplish this through a process which divides all proposed activities (and expenditures) into cohesive units of manageable size, subjects them to detailed scrutiny, and ultimately establishes a rank order of those units which, given unlimited resources, would be funded. A selected level of expenditure is then matched against the final rank ordering, and if funds are not sufficient to cover the entire listing, lowest priority items are left unfunded until the cumulative total of the funded priority list exactly matches the level of funding that is available. The final priority list, balanced with available funds, then becomes the budget.

ZBB is a sophisticated management tool which provides a systematic method of reviewing and evaluating all operations of the organization, current or proposed; allows for budget reductions and expansions in a planned, rational manner; and encourages the reallocation of resources from low- to high-priority programs. Because of the nature of the process involved, ZBB also tends to have some important fringe benefits, such as involving more managers in the budgeting process, providing more information and options to decision makers, and establishing systematic basis for management by objectives and priorities.

The foundation of ZBB is a four-step analytic process. Conceptually, the steps are:

1. *Establish budget units:* A budget unit is a grouping of existing or proposed activities which might be identified as a "program." It may consist of only one distinct activity, as in the case of trash collection in Wilmington's budget, or it may consist of a group of closely related activities, as in the case of Wilmington's recreation program. In nearly every case in Wilmington, the budget units were smaller than a department, consisting of the previously established divisions within most departments. As a result, the budget units did not create a new and unfamiliar organizational structure, and each budget unit had a readily identifiable manager.

2. *Divide budget units into service levels:* Since the variety, quantity, and
quality of service to be provided is usually a more realistic question than whether
or not a given budget unit will be funded at all, each budget unit is divided into
several alternative levels of service. In most cases in Wilmington, this began with
a level at about half of current, and advanced in steps through a slightly reduced
level, the current level, and a possible expanded level. Each level represents a
forecast of the cost and service consequences of operating at that level. In Wilmington's budget, the 61 budget units were eventually divided into a total of 194
service levels, with from 1 to 7 levels per budget unit.

3. *Analyze service levels:* Given the relatively small size and programmatic
cohesiveness of the budget units and the service levels, it is then possible to analyze each segment of the proposed budget in considerable detail. The need to
provide a given level of a particular service may be explored. Potential alternative
approaches to meet a particular need may be identified. The manpower and other
costs proposed to provide a given level of service may be examined for reasonableness. A given level of marginal cost may be compared to a given marginal increase
in the quality or quantity of service.

4. *Priority ranking of all service levels:* Following the analytic process, all
of the potentially desirable service levels from all of the budget units, as revised
and finalized, are rank-ordered into a single list. The basic concept is that a given
service level is ranked higher than all of the service levels that would be foregone,
if necessary, to make available the funds for that given service level. Meanwhile,
a level of expenditure (typically the projection of revenue from existing sources)
is selected. Since generally revenues are not sufficient to cover the entire list, the
priority rankings determine which service levels will be funded and which will not.

In practice, the ZBB process is considerably more complex than this conceptual framework. Wilmington's experience with ZBB, in chronological order, is
presented in the following sections.

Following Mayor Maloney's decision in the late autumn of 1975 to implement ZBB in Wilmington, a variety of planning and decision making became necessary. In recognition of the priority ascribed to the project by the mayor, two
members of the mayor's staff were from the outset given essentially full-time
responsibility for ZBB. Also a consulting firm was retained to assist.

The first step was the development of a detailed time table, from the starting
point in mid-November 1975 to the charter-mandated City Council submission
date, April 1, 1976. From the outset, it was recognized that the schedule was
tight, with little allowance for slippage.

The major milestones of the schedule is shown at top of next page.

A fundamental decision was the comprehensiveness of the ZBB process. The
possibility of including only some departments or only certain expenditures
(such as personnel costs) was discussed. However, the ranking process which
culminates ZBB was judged to be far more meaningful if all requests competing
for the general fund were ranked competitively.

Task	Completion
Determination of agencies to be included	December 5
Review and approval of budget manual	December 12
Training program	December 19
Preliminary departmental ZBB submissions	January 16
Final departmental ZBB submissions	January 30
Departmental hearings	February 27
Preliminary ranking and revenue estimate	March 5
Mayor's approval of final ranking	March 19
Presentation of budget to council	April 1
Approval of budget by council	June 1

While Wilmington's water, sewer, and marine terminal funds are maintained independently of the general fund, it was decided to include all of these funds in the ZBB process—although they would be ranked separately. This was done to strengthen the overall resource allocation process, and because any year-end surpluses in these funds are transferred to the general fund, thus giving expenditures of these funds a direct impact on the general fund.

Likewise, federal and state grant funds, which had never previously been included in the budgeting process (except for federal revenue sharing), were to be included. In each case, federal and state grant funds were to be identified as such, but shown as part of the relevant budget unit and service level. The inclusion of grant funds would provide significant additional information not previously available to decision makers in a systematic manner. In many cases, these data would show major activities which had been little known to decision makers because they used no city funds. In some cases, the data identify critical areas with heavy dependence on grant funds, which might have to be assumed by city funds upon expiration of the grants.

The major exclusion from ZBB was to be the operating subsidy to the local school district. In view of the limited time available, the relative autonomy of the Board of Education, and the fact that the bulk of the schools' funding comes directly from state appropriations, it was considered unfeasible to include the schools in the first implementation of ZBB.

The other significant exclusion from ZBB was to be so-called fixed expenses. Due to the lack of short-term control and discretion over these expenditures, items such as pensions, debt service, and insurance were omitted from the process.

Once the extent of inclusion in ZBB had been determined, it was necessary to identify budget units. In the great majority of cases, budget units were selected to correspond with the established divisions within city departments. Thus, for example, Wilmington's Public Works Department was divided into 11 budget units,

corresponding to its 11 divisions, Planning and Development was assigned four
budget units matching its established divisional structure, and the Auditing and
Treasurer's Departments were each assigned one budget unit, since there were no
established divisions within those departments. In a few cases of very large divisions with highly varied functions, budget units were established to subdivide the
established divisions. Thus, in the Department of Public Safety, the police and
fire divisions were subdivided into, respectively, six and three budget units.

A critical step in the planning process was the development of forms. The
unique needs of every jurisdiction make it improbable that any set of standardized forms can be used for ZBB. In Wilmington's case, consideration was given
to such local factors as past budget practice, accounting system needs, availability
of data, and other factors in developing ZBB forms. Where possible, the forms
were designed to resemble the previously used budget forms. A total of seven
forms were designed and utilized, although later experience suggests that the process can and should be somewhat simplified, with the number of forms reduced.

The final planning step was the preparation of a budget manual, containing
ZBB instructions as well as traditional data, such as salary scales, hospitalization
insurance premiums, and submission deadlines. Although it was recognized that
the manual would have to be supplemented with training and technical assistance
support, the manual did serve a useful purpose as the only written compendium
of ZBB forms and instructions.

Recognizing the need for technical assistance, a team of nine budget analysts
was assembled from the Mayor's Office, the Finance Department, the Department of Planning and Development, and City Council staff. All had past experience in fiscal analysis. After a period of intensive training, one of the budget
analysts was to be assigned to each city department, to assist them in responding
to the demands of ZBB. With these steps completed, ZBB was ready for presentation to the city's departments for implementation.

The impending implementation of ZBB was formally announced to Wilmington's department heads by the mayor in late November 1975. Although as with
any radical departure from the past practice, there was some criticism and resistance, cooperation and support from the departments generally proved to be excellent.

Actually, the first involvement by most departments had been in early November, when the city's consultants met with department heads to gather their im-
pressions of the former budget process, suggestions to improve the process, and
sufficient information regarding departmental operations to identify budget units.
This information was all used in developing Wilmington's ZBB format.

Following the formal announcement, department heads and budget unit
managers (usually division managers) were split into two workshops of about 25
participants each for training. Each group received two half-day training sessions,
at which budget manuals and forms were also distributed. The first session was

an orientation to ZBB concepts and general procedures, while the second session was used to review specific instructions in the manual and to discuss samples of completed forms.

The first major process for departments—the preliminary analysis—focused largely on the definition of service levels. As the most radical and fundamental concept of ZBB, it is essential that service levels be soundly developed. Departments were given some guidance in defining service levels but functioned largely on their own. For each service level of each budget unit, departments were asked to submit basic information as shown on the sample form B-2 (Figure 1).

Some departments felt that a reduced service level might be misconstrued as a recommendation to operate at that level, and resisted proposing reduced levels. As a result, all budget unit managers were instructed that service levels represented options, not recommendations, and the first level must not exceed 40 to 60 percent of the current expenditure level. Generally, a second level below current service was to be proposed, then the current level, and finally an improved level of service (when desirable), yielding a recommended minimum of four service levels. In fact, budget units ultimately submitted averaged three service levels each.

The structuring of service levels is cumulative. If a given service level is funded for a department, those that precede it will also be funded—although those that follow will not necessarily be funded. This assumption means that the costs for each level are costs to be added to prior levels in a department in order to produce the higher level of service.

Service levels vary either the quantity or the quality of a department's operations, or both. For example, in firefighting, the first service level might reduce by 50 percent the number of fire companies but maintain manning on each company as at present (quantity variation); maintain the same number of fire companies as at present but reduce by 50 percent the manning of each (quality variation); or reduce both the number of companies and the manning on each by 25 percent (both).

Service levels were devised in all of these manners in Wilmington. Sanitation, in Public Works, varied primarily the frequency, and thus the quality, of service:

- Level 1: Once weekly pick-up at curb
- Level 2: Twice weekly pick-up at curb
- Level 3: Pick-up from rear or side yeard, plus special services and school pick-ups (current level)

The department apparently did not see sufficient marginal improvement to show possible service expansion to a fourth level (which could have been three times a week pick-up).

Other departments defined service levels largely in terms of the quantity of

PRELIMINARY
SERVICE LEVEL DESCRIPTION

Department Planning & Develop.	Division Development	Budget Unit Development
Rank 3	**Service Level Title** Extensive Planning & Development Activities	

Describe Services Provided and Activities Performed in this Service Level

Update Urban Renewal plans and the comprehensive plan for areas of the city, and prepare zoning ordinance amendments. Prepare plans for the expenditure of Community Development funds and coordinate the execution of those plans. Prepare designs for simple capital improvement projects. Develop housing programs and initiate downtown business improvement projects.

Briefly Describe Resources to be Used in this Service Level

1 Senior Planner
1 Community Development Coordinator
1 Renewal Technician
1 Draftsperson
Total Personal Services $57,797
"CURRENT LEVEL"

	Est. Fiscal 1977	
	City	Non-City
No. Pos.	2	2
Cost	$29	$29

Rank	**Service Level Title**

Describe Services Provided and Activities Performed in this Service Area

Briefly Describe Resources to be Used in this Service Level

	Est. Fiscal 1977	
	City	Non-City
No. Pos.		
Cost		

Figure 1 Preliminary service level description.

services provided on a prioritized basis, holding quality relatively constant. For example, the police patrol division budget unit in Public Safety divided current and proposed services into six levels:

- Level 1: Basic patrol and preliminary investigation of major crimes
- Level 2: Preliminary investigation of all criminal complaints; response to priority noncriminal calls
- Level 3: Follow-up on all criminal and noncriminal calls; operation of jail and selective parking enforcement
- Level 4: Increased parking enforcement; full-service response to noncriminal calls
- Level 5: Additional patrols, school crossing guards (current level)
- Level 6: Expansion of patrol, parking enforcement, and school crossing functions

Here, the department saw sufficient marginal improvement to show expansion to a sixth service level.

Whatever the approach, the objective was to show the department's assessment of what services should be provided if only a certain level of funding was available. Once levels were defined, an estimated cost for each level was calculated. This did not prove to be difficult because the bulk of the costs were personnel and fringe benefits, which could be readily correlated with the manner in which personnel were divided among the levels. The service levels and costs, along with certain additional data and a preliminary ranking by the department head, were submitted by the departments in mid-January 1976. This provided the mayor's staff with an estimate of the total budget and an opportunity to discuss possible revisions in the service level structure and priority rankings with the departments. As a result of this process, several significant revisions were made.

In the latter part of January, departments completed the detailed final service level descriptions, as shown on the sample form B-3 (Figure 2). In addition to the information reported in the preliminary phase, more precise data and certain supplemental information were required for the final submission.

A unique feature of ZBB is the "program measures" reported for each service level. Up to seven measures could be selected for each budget unit, which would be repeated for each service level and reflect the increasing quality or quantity of services provided at each higher service level. Unfortunately, many departments had not accumulated such data and were therefore unable to provide the desirable level of documentation of program measures. However, this process has established a foundation for future years and has led to efforts by several departments and the mayor's staff to begin the accumulation of more useful data.

SERVICE LEVEL ANALYSIS

RANK: 5

Department	2 of 15
Division	1 of 4
Budget Unit	1 of 4

Department: Planning	Division: Prog. Anal. Admin.	Budget Unit: Program Analysis	Service Level Title: Administrative, Budgeting, Plan & Grant Preparation	Bud Acct # 01-17-00

Describe Services Provided and Activities Performed in this Service Level

- general administration of the Dept. of Plan. & Devel.
- preparation of the Criminal Justice Plan
- preparation of the Capital Budget
- preparation of federal & state grant applications
- collection of data & other pertinent information necessary to complete the above mentioned tasks
- Fiscal management of Department Federal Grants
- Collection & dissemination of facts about the City for above functions
- Secretarial support for above functions

SUMMARY BUDGET DATA ($ 000's)

	This Serv. Level		Cumulative*	
	City	Non-City	Total	% FY76
No. Bud. Pos.	4	2	4	80
Pers. Serv.	86	38	86	96
M.S.E.	47	39	56	110
Total	142	77	142	101

PROGRAM MEASURES

	This Serv. L	Cumulative Total	% FY76
1. Federal Grants prepared	7	7	100
2. Value, Federal Grants	3,900	3,900	74
3. Special studies	1	1	NA
4. Capital Budget prep.	1	1	100
5. Criminal Justice Plan	1	1	100
6. Program Budgets Prep.	0	0	0
7. Programs Evaluated	0	0	0

Justification of Need for this Services Level

Preparation of the Criminal Justice Comprehensive Plan Description is required by contract #10-07-000-01-76 with DARC.

Preparation of the Capital Budget and program is an essential activity of city government. Section 5-700(e) of the City Charter states that the Department of Planning will prepare and submit the capital budget and program to the Planning Commission.

The city benefits substantially from the use of federal and state funds obtained by grant applications.

Fiscal & operational management of federal grants is necessary for effective and efficient utilization of funds. In order for the above mentioned functions to be completed effectively, data collection and analysis must be carried out. Overall department administration of the varied activities is necessary for effective management and control.

Describe and Justify Resources Required in this Service Level

1 Planning Director - needed for overall administrative control and expertise for all divisions and special projects.

1 Grants & Contracts Manager - needed for fiscal management of federal grants, other financial matters in department, and maintenance of census data and other Management Information Systems.

1 Criminal Justice Coordinator - prepares criminal justice plans and serves as expert on crime trends in Wilm.

1 Program Analyst

1 Director of Program Analysis - It is necessary to have these two people to prepare capital budget & assist in data collection for other above-mentioned professionals.

1 Clerk Stenographer III - Secretarial functions for above-mentioned professionals.

Contractual/other services: $87,645

Materials/supplies: $5,950   Equipment: $1,000

*Cumulative for City funds only.

Figure 2 Service level analysis.

The final service level description was accompanied by a detailed line-item listing of all costs associated with that service level, including personnel, fringe benefits, materials, supplies, and equipment. These forms resulted in a considerable bulk of paperwork and a significant workload to the departments, although the work was more time consuming than onerous.

In addition to the service level and line-item listings, each department also submitted a departmental priority ranking of all budget units and all service levels within the department. A running cumulative total was included to show the amount required to fund the department to a particular priority level. Also, departments were asked to include a memorandum indicating the rationale for the order of prioritization selected.

The focus then shifted to the mayor's staff for the preparation of the city's consolidated budget.

The Mayor's Office review of departmental budget submissions began with a preliminary assessment of the city's financial position. Departmental general fund requests,[2] including requests for new or expanded services, amounted to $19.9 million, an increase of 15.6 percent over the existing budget. With a 1 to 2 percent revenue growth likely, requests would exceed revenues by roughly $2.6 million.

Wilmington's ZBB process presented a number of alternatives, which could be used singly or in combination to deal with the $2.6 million gap: (1) raise taxes to increase revenues; (2) reduce the cost of providing a specified level of service; or (3) not fund lowest priority service levels.

The first alternative is generally least desirable. For policy reasons, it was ruled out in Wilmington at this time.

The second alternative is generally most desirable in that it tends to represent an increase in efficiency or productivity. In practice, this approach is most similar to traditional budgeting, with the prime emphasis on large or unusual expenditures, and expenditures showing significant increases from the current budget. Ultimately, Wilmington was successful in reducing the departmental budget requests by approximately $900,000 or 4.5 percent, through these line-item cuts.

Once revenues are established and the cost of each service level has been reduced as much as possible, the third alternative—prioritizing—comes into play. This alternative represents the unique characteristic of ZBB. For Wilmington, this provided the mechanism for identifying $1.2 million in departmental requests that were of lowest priority and would not be funded.

A major portion of the administration review process was consumed by departmental budget hearings. Each department was afforded a session of 3 to 6 hours duration, attended by both members of the mayor's staff and representatives of the City Council Finance Committee. At the hearings discussions focused on opportunities to reduce the cost of providing a specified level of service, as well as on the rationale for the structuring of the service levels and the prioritization of the department's service levels. Numerous minor changes in the costs of service levels were made at the hearings, generally with the consent of the department head. Changes in prioritization were not made at the hearings, although areas of disagreement with a department head's rankings were identified. Budget hearing discussions also covered program measures, beneficiaries of the service, involvement of grant funds, and marginal cost of increasing service levels.

The consensus of both departmental officials and members of the mayor's staff was that with the introduction of ZBB, the hearings provided a more comprehensive and penetrating view of a department's activities than hearings in previous years. Specifically, the basis for proposed expenditures was usually related much more directly and rationally to services provided than in the past. Also, more discussion of the value of specific services, and the need for specific services, was possible.

Separately from the hearings, members of the mayor's staff also reviewed the departmental submissions for completeness, clarity, arithmetic accuracy, and other largely technical considerations. This process, along with the hearings, resulted in minor adjustments to the total cost for most of the service levels.

Formal ranking of priorities is the crucial and distinctive step in ZBB. A variety of criteria may be used, both formally and informally. Some criteria are relatively general, probably applicable to any jurisdiction, while some are more related to local goals and objectives. Key criteria considered in Wilmington include:

- Importance of the service level in terms of the perceived health, welfare, safety, and satisfaction of city residents
- Statuatory, charter, and contractual commitments met by the service level
- Potential consequences of not providing the service level
- Federal and state funds received dependent on a particular expenditure of city funds
- Informal assessment of the quality of the service provided
- Cost effectiveness of the service level
- Preference, where feasible, to direct services to the public over administrative costs

The final analysis and ranking process began with the decision to lump together a group of services identified as essential, without further prioritization. Little benefit was seen in discussing whether the most fundamental service levels of police, fire, or sanitation service is more important. Clearly, all of these services will be provided, at least, at the first level of service. Thus, 34 of the 196 service levels were lumped together as a "basic" group and ranked above all other services. Since most budget units had developed a first service level of 40 to 60 percent of the existing funding level, the total cost of the "basic" group amounted to $10.0 million.

After isolating the "basic" group, $9.0 million in requested service levels remained, as against only $7.8 million in forecasted revenue. Efforts focused on analysis and ranking of the 162 service levels remaining.

Numerical ranking of 162 separate items is quite difficult—particularly when the 162 items are as varied as the service levels in Wilmington's budget. Consequently, the process began by dividing the remaining service levels into four groups: high-priority, medium-priority, low-priority, and service levels not to be funded for policy reasons.[3]

The initial ranking of the remaining service levels showed that revenues were sufficient to cover the entire high- and medium-priority groups and part of the low-priority group. Service levels undesirable for policy reasons were ranked below the low-priority group but were effectively eliminated from further consideration.

With the number of service levels to be ranked now reduced to groups of manageable size, all of the service levels in each group were then numerically prioritized. For the high and medium groups this was somewhat academic, since revenues were sufficient to fund all of the service levels in the group. However, it was judged important to establish these rankings as the first organized, comprehensive statement of the city's priorities.

For the low-priority group the specific numerical ranking was of critical importance. Of the 56 service levels within the group, funds were sufficient for only about half. After rankings were assigned, a cumulative funding total was calculated to determine the point at which revenues were exhausted. An analysis of the rankings showed that many of the service levels below the cutoff point were new or expanded levels of service, although 21 levels of service currently being provided also fell below the cutoff. Two levels of new or expanded service ended up above the cutoff.

The complete rankings as proposed by the mayor's staff were then presented to the mayor for his consideration. The mayor directed a number of minor changes, but generally expressed satisfaction with the priority order. However, the mayor was concerned that a number of existing service levels involving incumbent employees fell below the cutoff, necessitating immediate layoffs and service cutbacks.

As an alternative, the mayor's staff developed a factor known as "special attrition." A factor had already been allowed for normal attrition, representing funds that would not be spent for salaries and fringe benefits during the period positions remain vacant between incumbents. Now, in order to avoid layoffs and abrupt service cutbacks, an additional factor was calculated representing

anticipated savings from positions which would be left unfilled for the balance
of the fiscal year when they become vacant. Although this may still entail modest
service cutbacks, unless compensating productivity increases are achieved, they
would occur on a scattered basis throughout the year. While the exact positions
to be left vacant could not be identified, past turnover experience indicated that
the savings budgeted for "special attrition" were reasonable and attainable.

Following the addition of "special attrition" and minor priority adjustments,
the ranking was finalized. No layoffs would be required, although some existing
services without incumbent personnel still fell below the cutoff. All told, the
"basic" group and ranks 1-110 were shown as funded; ranks 111-162 were
shown as not funded.

With the completion of prioritization, the budget was then ready for final
housekeeping details, printing, and submission to City Council.

In a radical departure from most jurisdictions which have implemented ZBB,
Mayor Maloney decided that the council should receive the actual ZBB documentation. Other jurisdictions using ZBB have recast their budget in traditional format for legislative consideration and public distribution. Although this decision
was sure to significantly increase the complexity of City Council's work, Mayor
Maloney regarded the council's involvement in the actual ZBB process as critical.

City Council's exposure to ZBB had actually begun at the very start of the
city's involvement. The councilmen were thoroughly briefed before the decision
was made to adopt the process and had registered their support by adoption of a
resolution. In addition, Council's Finance Committee Chairman and a staff member had attended all of the departmental hearings.

Council's consideration of the completed ZBB budget began with an orientation session devoted to both the process and the output of ZBB. The ZBB budget represented such a total departure from past budgeting practice—in process
as well as appearance—that a thorough orientation was essential.

As in past years, City Council then proceeded to hold public budget hearings
for each department. The hearings, which lasted from 1 to 3 hours each, repeated some of the discussion from the administration's budget hearings, but
primarily served as a forum for the discussion of concerns of particular relevance
to the councilmen. Several departments used the hearing to appeal either a ranking or a line-item cut made earlier by the administration. In a number of cases,
members of the public or city employees raised questions about specific items
in the budget. Members of the mayor's staff attended all of the hearings and
were often asked to explain the rationale behind the prioritization of a particular service level.

Prior to the hearings, the council agreed that no actual changes in the rankings would be discussed until all of the hearings were complete and all comments
were heard. This avoided moving service levels up and down the ranking until
all the hearings were completed and the council could put all the levels in perspective.

Initially, many of the councilmen approached the budget much as they had approached past budgets. Most of the discussion concerned the incremental changes to line items. However, as the hearings proceeded, greater and greater attention focused on ZBB considerations. The rationale for a particular ranking, for example, was discussed more and more frequently. Much interest centered on the federal and state grant funds—information which the council had never before had available in a systematic manner. There was also steadily increasing discussion of program measures and the marginal costs associated with a higher level of service.

One problem was the greatly expanded amount of paperwork. As part-time city officials, many of the councilmen had difficulty finding the time to digest the large volume of information on a department prior to the hearing. The line-item budget detail, a 1,000-page document, was simply too heavy and bulky to be readily taken home for review.

At the conclusion of the hearings, council's staff checked with all of the councilmen to determine what changes in the administration's budget should be considered. After all had been polled, only five changes were proposed. Three proposed changes concerned service levels, with a total cost of $15,000, which had been ranked below the cutoff point but which council wished to see funded. One change was a line-item cut of $6,000 within a funded service level, which the department head had argued for convincingly. The final proposed change of $8,000 was a service previously provided which the department involved had not included in their budget submission.

The latter proposal was most easily resolved by the administration's commitment to continue the service with personnel under a federally funded Summer Youth Program, thus not requiring any additional city funds.

Council met at some length to consider possible rerankings to accommodate the other desired additions to the budget. The process proved difficult. Every service level suggested for deletion as a tradeoff had its own supporters among the councilmen. Most of the service levels just above the cutoff point included incumbent personnel, whom the councilmen were not anxious to see laid off. A tax increase was seen as unpalatable.

Ultimately, the small amount involved in the desired changes proved decisive. Council recommended to the mayor that the four service levels in question be reranked to include them in the budget and that all service levels then be reduced by 0.1 percent to provide the needed funds. Since extensive line-item cutting had already been undertaken, the mayor accepted the recommendation only with the understanding that the 0.1 percent savings would be achieved through attrition, by slightly increasing the time a position remained vacant between incumbents. Council agreed, and the appropriate rerankings were made. With these changes, the council soon thereafter gave its approval to the entire budget.

Generally, City Council appears to have found ZBB preferable to the city's former process. A major reason appears to be that council now gets more information, and more useful information, than they have ever had before. The ranked service level format, although not legally binding on the mayor, provides the council with a strong moral commitment as to what services will be provided —whereas the old process had provided only a commitment as to what the line-item expenditures would be. Many councilmen have expressed a desire to continue the ZBB process in future years and possibly expand it to other areas such as the operating subsidy to the school district and the city's capital budget.

It is important to establish the context in which zero-base budgeting was adopted in Wilmington. Essentially, it represented a logical step forward, in a well-established process of fiscal restraint and improved management of resources. It followed earlier experimentation with other budgeting innovations, particularly program budgeting. It drew heavily on analytic and management staff resources which had been developed over an extended period. And it relied on the cooperation and support of the mayor, City Council, and city department heads. The process and the results could differ significantly in a different context.

Insufficient time has passed to assess fully ZBB's impact on Wilmington. However, a number of conclusions may be drawn as to the benefits already derived, and the disadvantages.

On the positive side a key accomplishment has been the detailed identification of all the services provided by the city—regardless of funding source. Such information was never previously available in systematic form. Once identified, all programs and expenditures were reviewed to a level of detail usually reserved for proposed new programs.

Also beneficial is the establishment of a systematic prioritization of the city's services. This establishes a firm foundation for future years, when the city's financial situation may require extremely difficult decisions, and helps assure that those decisions will be based on a well-developed set of priorities.

The ZBB process itself was beneficial in that it involved nearly all management personnel in the budgeting process, considerably more than in the past. Also, as a planning and budgeting process, ZBB involved these personnel in a far more comprehensive resource allocation process.

The ranking of federal and state grant funds establishes a mechanism for identifying the importance of these funds to the city and anticipating the future demands to replace these funds with city funds when they expire. In effect, Wilmington had adopted a comprehensive planning and budgeting process for all its resources.

The statement of priorities and program measures by department heads serves as an excellent basis for a management-by-objectives program. In the past, the city's approach to management by objectives had been more general, making performance assessment more difficult. With the level of specific detail provided by ZBB, performance against objectives can be measured much more quantitatively.

ZBB has also involved City Council more meaningfully in the budget process. Specifically, it has given them a better picture of the issues involved and a direct involvement in the tradeoff process inherent to budgeting. Potentially ZBB could serve to very significantly increase the role of the legislative branch of government by providing more effective control of the planning and resource allocation process.

ZBB also has significant disadvantages. Foremost is the large increase in the time, effort, and paperwork required. Increased time devoted to the budget by city personnel, the need for consultants in the initial implementation, and increased printing costs probably resulted in a net increase of 100 percent in the cost of preparing the budget. The increased effort, and the high level of detail required, caused numerous complaints, especially from department heads. Particularly in the cases where a service is already rather well known to the city administration and City Council, such complaints are understandable.

The large size of the first service level in most budget units—40 to 60 percent of current spending—may also have provided an opportunity to effectively shelter costs which might, if listed as separate service levels, be more seriously questioned. In a number of departments it appeared that overhead-type costs were unduly heavy in the initial service level, although if more time had been available this could have been addressed by revisions in the proposed service levels.

Another limitation is the underlying assumption that the specified level of funding must be provided in order to obtain the specified level of service. Past experience suggests that improvements in efficiency and productivity may enable a specified level of service to be provided even with reduced funding levels. While the knowledge that reducing the cost of each proposed service level enables more service levels to be funded tends to encourage economy and stimulate productivity improvement, the stimulus may not be sufficiently strong to produce the desired results. Thus, it is desirable to undertake separate measures to promote efficiency and productivity in combination with the implementation of ZBB.

Wilmington's experience with ZBB has generally been quite positive and seems likely to lead to further use of ZBB in Wilmington. Combined with a variety of measures geared to improved organization effectiveness and economy, ZBB appears to be making a significant contribution. While ZBB would not necessarily prove beneficial in every jurisdiction, its implementation is certainly worthy of consideration.

NOTES

1. Peter A. Pyhrr, Zero base budgeting, *Harvard Business Review,* Nov.-Dec. 1970, pp. 111-121. *Zero Base Budgeting: A Practical Management Tool for Evaluating Expenses* (New York: Wiley, 1973).

2. Excluding fixed costs and the operating subsidy to the schools, which were not included in ZBB. These items were budgeted at $17.1 million.
3. For example, a proposed change in water-billing procedure that would initially result in serious cash flow problems.

20
ZERO-BASE BUDGETING IS A FRAUD*

Robert N. Anthony

Zero-base budgeting is supposed to be a new way of preparing annual budgets, which contrasts with the current way, which is called incremental budgeting. Incremental budgeting, it is correctly said, takes a certain level of expenses as a starting point and focuses on the proposed increment above that level.

By contrast, if the word *zero* means anything, it signifies that the budgeting process starts at zero and that the agency preparing the budget request must justify every dollar that it requests.

There is only one recorded attempt to take such an approach to budgeting in a government organization of any size. In 1971, the governor of Georgia hired a consultant to install such a system. He did so because of an article the consultant had written for *Harvard Business Review*.

A casual reader of that article could easily get the impression that the author had successfully installed a zero-base budgeting system in a large industrial company. A more careful reader would learn that the author had installed a system in certain staff and research units of that company, constituting an unspecified

*Reprinted by permission of the *Wall Street Journal* (April 27, 1977), © Dow Jones & Company, Inc. 1977. All rights reserved.

fraction, but less than 25 percent of the company's annual expenditures, and that the judgment that the system was a great success was entirely the author's and based on a single year's experience.

Anyway, the consultant started to work for the State of Georgia. He was well intentioned and probably sincere in his belief that it is possible to prepare and analyze a budget from scratch. This belief did not last long. Well before the end of the first budget cycle, it was agreed that expenditures equal to approximately 80 percent of the current level of spending would be given only a cursory examination and that attention would be focused on the increment.

Thus, even before one go-around of the new system, the "zero" bench mark was replaced by 80 percent. Moreover, amounts above this floor were in fact "increments" despite the claim that the process is the opposite of incremental budgeting. Eighty percent is a long way from zero and increments above 80 percent are just as much increments as increments above some other base. To put it bluntly, the name zero-base budgeting is a fraud.

FACTS DON'T SUPPORT

The facts don't even support the glowing reports about what happened with respect to the amounts above the 80 percent. In 1974, 13 heads of Georgia departments were interviewed, and only 2 went so far as to say that zero-base budgeting "may" have led to a reallocation of resources. (The whole idea of budgeting is to allocate resources.) None of 32 budget analysts reported that the system involved a "large" shifting of financial resources, and only 7 said it caused "some" shifting; 21 said there was no apparent shifting, and 4 were uncertain.

People experienced in budgeting know that zero-base budgeting won't work. Basically, the idea is that the entire annual budget request is to be broken down in "decision packages." These packages are to be ranked in order of priority, and budget decisions are made for each package according to the justification contained therein and its relative priority ranking. There are several things wrong with this approach.

Most important is that large numbers of decision packages are unmanageable. In Georgia, there were 11,000 of them. If the governor set aside 4 hours every day for 2 months he could spend about a minute on each decision package, not enough time to read it let alone analyze the merits. If he delegated the job to others, the whole idea of comparing priorities is compromised.

In the Defense Department, whose budget is 30 times as large as Georgia's, top management makes budget judgments on a few hundred items, certainly not as many as a thousand.

Even if the numbers of decision packages were reduced to a manageable size, it is not possible to make a thorough analysis during the time available in the annual budget process. In a good control system, basic decisions are made during the programming process, which precedes the budget process. And the annual budget process is essentially one of fine-tuning the financial plan required to implement these decisions during the budget year; there is not time to do anything else.

In zero-base budgeting, there is no mention of a programming process. The assumption evidently is that program decisions are made concurrently with budget decisions. This simply can't be done in an organization of any size; there isn't time.

Experience also shows that the idea of ranking decision packages according to priority doesn't work. Such rankings have been attempted from time to time in government agencies, as far back as 1960. They have been abandoned. Honest agency heads will admit that program priority is influenced by the amount of funds likely to be available rather than the other way around. If they are less than honest, they will deliberately structure priorities so that essential or politically popular decision packages are given low priority, knowing they will probably be approved and that their approval will automatically constitute approval of packages listed as having a higher priority. Only quite naive people would not expect this to happen.

The budget process is not primarily a ranking process. It is primarily the fine tuning of an approved program. The worth of programs can't be determined by reading words on a two-page form. Judgments about new programs are based on discussions with people involved, in which words on paper play some but not a dominant part. The budget analyst has a whole set of techniques for squeezing water out of budget requests for continuing programs; reading "decision packages" is not one of them.

Compared with the antiquated budget process which Georgia had at the time, zero-base budgeting was probably an improvement—almost any change would have been. Compared with the procedures that already are used in the federal government, it has nothing of substance to offer. The new parts are not good, and the good parts are not new.

Nevertheless, zero-base budgeting is rapidly becoming a highly prestigious term. I think there is a way of capitalizing on this prestige so as to give impetus to improvements in the budget process that really need to be made.

First, by a slight change in wording, the push behind the phrase might be transferred to a process called "zero-base review." This is an extremely valuable part of the control process. It is used by some agencies, but it is not widely used in a systematic way. It should be made systematic and extended throughout the government.

TIME CONSUMING AND TRAUMATIC

In a zero-base review, outside experts go into an agency, or some part of it, and carefully examine its reason for being, its methods of operation, and its costs.

It is a time-consuming and traumatic process, so it cannot conceivably be conducted annually. Instead, each agency should be examined about once every 5 years. It is by far the best way of controlling ongoing programs, just as benefit-cost analysis is the best way of making decisions on proposed new programs.

Next, the decision packages discussed so glibly could be used to give renewed emphasis to program budgeting in contrast to the old-fashioned line-item budgeting that persists in some agencies. Decision packages actually are what are called program elements in a program budget system. Budgeting by programs was a central part of what was called the PPB system, installed by Robert S. McNamara and Charles Hitch in the Defense Department in the early 1960s.

In 1965, an effort was made to extend this system to the entire government, but the extension was made without adequate preparation. Partly for this reason, and partly because it was developed in a Democratic administration, PPB was officially killed by the Republicans in 1969.

The basic idea of program budgeting remains sound, however. Indeed, in many agencies the basic idea continues to be used under other labels. The zero-base budgeting rhetoric could well be used to push for the complete installation of program budgeting throughout the government.

Third, the emphasis on stating measurable results in the budget proposal, which is implied in the form used to describe the decision packages, is a good one even though there is nothing new about it except the label. Under the term *management-by-objectives,* this idea has been common in industry and in certain parts of the government for years. Zero-base budgeting could be used to strengthen it, particularly to focus more serious attention on the development of better output measures.

So, even though zero-base budgeting is a fraud, and even though the good parts of it are not new, experienced budget people should not let the phrase make them nauseous. They should disregard the rhetoric and latch onto the term as a way of accomplishing what really needs to be accomplished anyway.

21

INVESTMENTS IN PEOPLE*

Michael O. Alexander

The resources of an enterprise are generally looked upon as its human, financial, and physical assets. Each is a vital part of the management process that can seldom be viewed alone. It is important, therefore, that accounting for human resources be conceived not as a separate process, but as a dimension of the management information system that can greatly assist the process of managing "total resources."

The human resources of an organization include the employees—the internal human resources who must make optimal decisions on the capital investment of the shareholders. The employees of the business interface with their suppliers and customers in performing their jobs. But all of these groups are surrounded by a larger, more loosely defined society of human resources—the public, which can include governments, other private institutions, the financial community, or various groups in society directly or indirectly affected by the actions of the business. In sum, they constitute the human resource dimension of an enterprise.

*Reprinted with permission from *Canadian Chartered Accountant* (now *CA Magazine*), vol. 99, no. 1 (July 1971), pp. 38-45. Published by the Canadian Institute of Chartered Accountants, Toronto.

Management is fully aware of the importance of its people to the growth and well-being of their organization. The majority of corporations make some reference to their employees in their annual reports—usually as important assets of the company. It is difficult, therefore, to understand why today's accounting and information systems still substantially ignore the human resource dimension. Capital expenditure budgets, inventory control systems, cash flow analysis, and profit contribution statements are examples of the type of information which is designed to assist in management of physical and financial resources. Present accounting concepts often do not reflect improvements or deterioration in the human resource capabilities until long after the event. It is difficult to find good information about investments in hiring, training, manpower development, and the related return on these investments during the period. Decisions on the people costs of employee layoffs, location or relocation of plants, development projects such as computer installations, and major investments in mergers or acquisitions are often made with a severe lack of appropriate information.

The influence of the information process on the effectiveness of an organization's structure and the behavior of its people toward their responsibilities is more fully recognized today than ever before. The success of an organization, its management structure, and human capabilities can be substantially enhanced by the existence of an appropriate information system. When organizational change takes place independently of or without regard for an appropriate information structure, the company may soon find that many of its managers will ignore their new responsibilities, and before long they will return to their old ways.

This chapter will outline some of the concepts of human resources accounting and describe some of its features that have received application in practice. The first application discussed will be an information system for human resource management in a service industry. In this case—a public accounting firm. Following this, the chapter will describe the various techniques which have been applied in manufacturing and commercial firms and government organizations. On a macro scale some proposals will be made for how human resource accounting concepts might be developed in various sectors of society at large.

THE TOTAL CONCEPT

What is human resource accounting? In simple accounting terms, the concepts of human resource accounting are merely an extension of the accounting principles of matching costs and revenues, and of organizing data so as to communicate it as relevant information in financial terms. The fundamental difference, of course, lies in the fact that human resources are viewed as assets or investments of the organization. The methods of measuring costs are similar to those used for other assets. However, the concepts of accounting for the condition of human capabilities and value introduce the measurement tools of the behavioral sciences. Such social measurements represent, if you will, the other side of the ledger from the cost-based system, and can provide important information on the condition and performance of the human organization by measuring the improvement or deterioration of these assets through time.

The importance of combining the concepts of social measurement with cost-based accounting for human resources is perhaps best illustrated by recognizing what can happen when managers are rewarded for high short-term cash flows and earnings. While cost reduction programs and increased pressure on people may produce favorable results in the short-term, such policies may contribute to a liquidation of the company's human resources with a much greater long-term cost. Unfortunately, these hidden costs do not become evident until several years later, and because the so-called successful men who benefit from these incentives generally get the reputation of being effective managers, they are moved by the company every 2 or 3 years from one job to another.

When people are recognized as assets of the business, at least for management-reporting purposes, investment expenditures in human resources are written off in the period to which they relate and net contribution reports can reflect a fairer picture of the performance during the period. Under present accounting practices these investments are considered as expenditures of the current year and, as a result, any curtailment of human resource acquisition or organizational development expenditures will cause a more favorable earnings picture. But even when human resource investments are amortized over their useful life, the resulting reports do not always tell the whole story; they do not necessarily reflect the degree of improvement or deterioration in the condition of the human assets during the period.

An effective modification of the performance-reporting system can be made by linking net contribution reports for the period to a report on the condition—improvement or deterioration—of the human assets. These measurements in social, organizational and behavioral terms cannot only provide a better measure of performance, but will also supply valuable information that can aid managers in their efforts to improve the motivation, perceptions, communications, and attitudes that their people require to achieve their objectives.[1]

While human resource accounting is conceived here as an integral part of the total accounting and information system, it has in its initial phases of application been viewed as a concept directed at improving the management of people. Some of the efforts that have been made in developing and applying this concept in practice have been directed toward assisting in specific people decisions. These applications are perhaps best described by way of example.

SERVICE INDUSTRY APPLICATIONS:
A PUBLIC ACCOUNTING FIRM

A public accounting firm is by its very nature human resource intensive and represents an ideal proving ground for the application of human resource accounting concepts. The primary assets of such a firm are its clients and the human capabilities of its people. The financial or physical assets represent a relatively minor part of the firm's total value and consist largely of cash, receivables, financial capital, and office equipment. As a result, conventional accounting systems which deal with these elements alone are of limited use for managing the all-important human resource.

The long-term survival of a public accounting firm is substantially enhanced by its efforts to develop its human resources; to do this requires adequate management information: the cost of employee turnover, the effectiveness of hiring and training policies, the adequacy of mix of professional skills, and the means for measuring human resource performances—information on these issues can be provided by a good human resource accounting system.

The high turnover rates usually experienced by a public accounting firm result from a variety of factors, including the perceived lack of opportunity, job satisfaction, and remuneration, etc. But the costs associated with this turnover are often elusive, and their elements cannot be readily determined from conventional accounting data. Accounting firms accept the fact that they have some responsibility to train professionals; nevertheless, it has become increasingly important for them to know how much and what kind of training should be provided—where it should be directed and what proportion of professional staff should be trained within the firm or hired fully trained at the senior level from outside.

The traditional yardstick of performance in a public accounting firm has normally been chargeable hours—the time an employee devotes to client service. Unfortunately, however, the use of this fact as a single measurement may discourage investment in human resources, since the latter is often seen as a feat which is only accomplished at the expense of chargeable hours.

The example that follows will hopefully illustrate how human resource accounting was designed to focus on some of these problems. The first step was to calculate the investment in each employee, in terms of both outlay (out-of-pocket expense) and opportunity (billings foregone) costs. These were used as a basis for calculating such things as employee contributions to profit and the costs of replacement turnover. The investments in employees could then be related to resulting benefits. For example, an assessment of organizational effectiveness could be related to the cost of developing that effectiveness—including the costs of familiarization, training, group relationship programs, etc. All of these include both dollar outlays and the cost of time spent by the employees involved.

Table 1 Cost of Time Analysis Report for the Year Ending Dec. 31, 1970

	Total office ($)			
	Plan	Man. var.	Hour var.	Actual
Chargeable	738,952	(7,230)	(24,724)	706,998
Investment				
Recruiting	11,500	622	868	12,990
Orientation	11,000	69	1,931	13,000
Counselling and dev.	10,000	579	1,421	12,000
Formal training courses	35,000	100	7,000	42,100
Research	15,500	42	(284)	15,258
Total	83,000	1,412	10,936	95,348
Maintenance				
Practice develop.	8,694	(124)	(5,850)	2,720
Prof. affairs and PR	3,064	19	6,825)	9,908
Administration	36,864	237	(310)	36,791
Holidays and vac.	102,000	(742)	(25,892)	75,366
Sickness and per.	28,932	(68)	8,877	37,741
Total	179,554	(678)	(16,350)	162,526
Total	1,001,508	(6,496)	(30,138)	964,872

The firm was already generating information that could be used as inputs to a human resource accounting system. The cost of time or opportunity costs were developed from time records regularly filled out by each employee. These records show how each hour of the day was spent, and whether or not it was chargeable to a client. The out-of-pocket, or outlay, costs were easily obtained with only minor reclassification of the existing cost accounts. This time and cost data, together with the planned amounts, were then incorporated into a series of human resource accounting reports showing planned and actual investments in employees. With these reports managers are better able to measure periodic changes in human resource investment and are encouraged to maintain or upgrade these investments.

Some of the human resource reports that are generated as part of the firm's internal management reporting system are illustrated below and include "The Cost of Time Analysis Report," "Summary of Human Resource Investments," "Statement of Human Resource Flows," and "Contribution Reports."

The Cost of Time Analysis Report illustrated in Table 1 is prepared from the employee time cards and indicates the value of actual and planned hours as well

Table 2 Human Resource Investments for the Year Ending Dec. 31, 1970

	Plan ($)			Actual ($)		
	Outlay	Opport	Total	Outlay	Opport	Total
Recruiting	500	11,500	12,000	1,420	12,990	14,410
Orientation	2,500	11,000	13,500	2,200	13,000	15,200
Counselling and development	1,600	10,000	11,600	400	12,000	12,400
Formal training courses	5,000	35,000	40,000	3,500	42,100	45,600
Research	1,400	15,500	16,900	1,200	15,258	16,458
Total	11,000	83,000	94,000	8,720	95,348	104,068

as resulting variances. Variances from plan recognize two basic causes. The main variance reflects a greater or lesser number of people on staff than plan, while the hour variance indicates the differences between actual and planned hours spent. The report distinguishes between the time spent on client work, recruiting and acquisition, courses and seminars, staff counseling, etc., and focuses on the need for good planning by managers for the development of the firm's total professional capability. Performance against the plan developed is continually assessed; each member of the professional staff receives his own monthly and year-to-date report showing his planned and actual hours. Reports are also prepared for different staff and service groups.

Table 2 illustrates in summary form the human resource investment made during a particular period, in terms of both opportunity and outlay costs on a plan and actual basis. The reports of this type are useful for determining the magnitude of investments made in various groups of professional staff during the period. The outlay costs are accumulated from the firm's accounting system, while the opportunity costs are provided by the Cost of Time Analysis Report.

The Statement of Human Resource Flows is shown in Table 3. This report shows in dollars and in people the human resource investment at the beginning of the period, and indicates how this investment was augmented or depleted throughout the year. The additions or reductions in investments during the year, resulting from expenditures on human resources, transfers in, transfers out, departures, and amortization, are considered in arriving at the closing balance of human resource investment at the end of the period. The purpose of this report is to emphasize the importance of human resource development, and it allows managers to assess their performance in this context. The amount shown as amortization reflects that part of human resource investment which expired during the period.

Table 3 Statement of Human Resource Flows for the Year Ending Dec. 31, 1970

	Manpower		Investments ($)	
	Plan	Actual	Plan	Actual
Opening balance	29	29	112,532	112,532
Add:				
Transfers in (other offices)	4	3	13,000	10,321
Investments:				
Recruiting	10	10	12,000	14,410
Investments in existing				
personnel during period	—	—	82,000	89,658
Total	14	13	107,000	114,389
Less:				
Transfers out (other offices)	6	5	30,000	26,449
Departures	9	8	34,000	33,498
Amortization	—	—	32,000	36,381
Total	15	13	96,000	96,328
Closing balance	28	29	123,532	130,594

Amortization for any investment category is based on the lesser of the individual's expected life with the firm or the useful life of the investment. For example, when an individual has a 4-year expected life—that is determined on the basis of employee turnover experience—an investment in a training course which only stands to benefit this individual for 2 years will be amortized over the 2-year period instead of the individual's expected life of 4 years.

Human resource amortization is based on the same principles as those used to systematically record the expiration or depreciation of a firm's other assets. Amortization, however, is not crucial information for the management decision-making process that human resource accounting is designed to facilitate. A more important question is the cost of turnover replacement.

The Contribution Report, which is illustrated in Table 4, provides a measure of profitability in terms of financial profits before overheads. The profit contributions of various service centers of the firm are measured and compared to plan.

The foregoing reports are directed at the normal operations of human resource management. Other reports and analyses are prepared as required to assist managers in planning and assessing manpower needs, directing training efforts, and allocating staff. These reports, together, are designed to provide information that will improve a manager's ability to make decisions in such areas as employee turnover, optimum staff mix, and hiring policies.

Table 4 Contribution Report for the Year Ending Dec. 31, 1970

	Total office ($)			
	Plan	Man. var.	Hr. var.	Actual
Chargeable hours X standard billing rates	738,743	(6,537)	(25,220)	706,986
Less:				
Salaries and fringe benefits	240,000	(13,107)		253,107
Amortization of human resource investment	32,000	(4,381)		36,381
Departures	34,000	502		33,498
Standard operating contribution before overhead	432,743	(23,523)	(25,220)	384,000

Human resource accounting information has provided the firm with a number of facts which have led to some reassessment of its traditional approach to staff mix and resource allocation. First, the new information indicated that the profit contributions per man for various levels of experience were somewhat different from what the firm had implicitly assumed. Second, the knowledge of employee replacement costs and measures of economic value are influencing the decisions that the firm must make in directing its training and development programs and determining the required investment in this effort. The firm is now in a better position to determine the optimal staff mix for various service areas and levels of staff experience.

APPLICATIONS IN INDUSTRY AND GOVERNMENT

While there are some natural differences between the people processes of a public accounting firm and those of a manufacturing firm, there are striking similarities between the former and the professional firms of law, consulting, and engineering, to name a few. Other service firms, such as advertising, insurance, banking and investment firms, or various government departments, may also find that human resource accounting techniques can be effectively applied in their management process. People are their most important profit-producing resource, and the performance or end-results of these organizations are highly sensitive to costs of staff turnover, investments in training and development, conditions of attitudes and motivational skills, and the ongoing value of the customer resource. The firm's monetary profit is, for the most part, an expression of its return on investment in human resources.

These kinds of issues can be just as important to industrial firms—manufac-

turing, commercial or government—where the cost of hiring, turnover, replacement cost, training, investments in customer resources, and the return on each of
these can be vital elements about which management must be informed. Accounting for human resources in industry and government is best discussed by illus-
trating some of the techniques which can be or are being applied in practice.

EMPLOYEE LAYOFF DECISIONS

A well-known approach to cost reduction is to lay off personnel not required in
the shorter term. Such layoffs can result in significant immediate benefits through
savings of payroll costs, overhead, and possibly reduction in inventories that may
be difficult to sell in a temporarily depressed market. But these decisions beg the
obvious question: What is the longer term cost to the company in terms of the
additional investment required to rehire, familiarize, or train such personnel in
the future? Because these costs are often substantial, some knowledge of them
is useful in making layoff decisions. Assume that the salary and payroll savings
related to shutting down an office and plant are estimated as follows for different
layoff periods:

Layoff period (weeks)	Related salary and payroll savings ($)
2	20,000
4	37,000
6	55,000
8	75,000
10	95,000

The human resource costs related to the shut-down would normally be the
startup costs for those employees who return to work and would include the
value of lost time in the startup process. For employees who do not return to
work, the costs of replacement would include the costs of hiring, familiarizing,
training new employees, and other associated opportunity costs of lost time in
the startup process.

Assume that if all employees return at the end of the shut-down period, the
estimated startup costs are $20,000. If, however, none of the employees return,
estimated startup costs, because of the need to hire from outside, are $150,000.

Because it may be necessary to consider layoff periods of varying lengths,
the human resource costs associated with each layoff period must be determined
along with the percentage of employees who can be expected to return to work
after each of these different layoff periods.

For example, the following schedule indicates that at the end of a 2-week

Table 5   Expected Human Resource Costs Related to Alternative Layoff Periods

Layoff period	Expected % of employees who will return	Startup costs ($)	Expected % of employees to be hired	Estimated startup and replacement cost ($)	Total expected costs
2 weeks	95	19,000	5	7,500	26,500
4 weeks	85	17,000	15	22,500	39,500
6 weeks	70	14,000	30	45,000	59,000
8 weeks	50	10,000	50	75,000	85,000
10 weeks	30	6,000	70	105,000	111,000

layoff period 95 percent of the employees would return, whereas after 10 weeks only 30 percent would return and 70 percent would have to be hired from outside. The expected percentage of personnel who would find employment elsewhere during the layoff period could be estimated on the basis of past experience, degree of skills, situation in the employment market, and the proximity of other opportunities for similar jobs.

The expected human resource costs related to alternative layoff periods are shown in Table 5. A comparison of the total expected costs with the savings in salaries and payroll related to the layoff shows that for each period these costs will exceed the savings and that the estimated minimum net cost of $2,500 will be incurred in a 4-week layoff period. Human resource costs and payroll savings might be considered for other alternatives, e.g., the layoff of a third or a half of the work force.

Availability of human resource cost information will help management to assess its courses of action and consider the costs and benefits of such issues as cutbacks in inventory production, service activities, or other ongoing programs.

MANPOWER PLANNING FOR AUTOMATION PROJECTS

In any business venture, the process of allocating resources must first recognize the importance of determining the needs and the availability of the resource, the investment required, and the potential return from alternative methods of allocating the resources. Examples of projects which require substantial allocation of human resources in addition to other resources are numerous; they include plant construction, branch office expansion, research and development projects, automation programs or computer installations. "Go-ahead" decisions for these projects cannot be made without a serious look at manpower needs, particularly with respect to the number of people and the types of skills required.

To illustrate how human resource accounting techniques can be applied in manpower planning and development, assume that an organization decides to make additional investment in its existing branch facilities by installing a companywide automation program, such as the installation of on-line computer systems and terminals that will be operated by branch personnel. Before the new automated system can become an effective operation, extensive hiring, training, and familiarizing of staff are required. These human resource costs are often ignored in the analysis of such ventures, or at very least the necessary information if not readily available. Indeed, ignoring the magnitude of these costs has quite possibly been the primary reason for major overruns in the initial cost estimates for this type of development project.

> The R. G. Barry Corp.
> "COLUMBUS, OHIO. In conventional terms, R. G. Barry Corp. had a fine year in 1970, when earnings rose 55%.
> From another view, however, the company concludes it paid a 'human' price for some of that gain."

This is how the *Wall Street Journal* of April 1, 1971 reported the results of the "leisure footwear maker" for the past year. It was not intended for "April Fools." During the past 4 years, this company has been developing a human resource accounting system that provides its management with better information on the total resources employed in the business and aids them in making decisions on the quality of profit performance, the human capabilities required to achieve objectives, and the degree to which people are being developed, maintained, and properly utilized by the organization.[2]

Although its accounting for human resources is primarily intended for its management process, Barry has also disclosed its investment in human resources in a separate balance sheet and income statement included in both its 1969 and 1970 annual reports.

In 1969, its "total concept" statement of income indicated that some $174,000 of human resource expenses incurred during that year were applicable to future periods. In 1970, it shows a net decrease in human resource investment of some $44,000, resulting mainly from losses due to turnover. The accompanying chart (Figure 1) indicates the amounts incurred for both new and expired investments during the 1970 year.

The R. G. Barry Corporation continues to develop its system of human resource accounting; its basic purpose of developing an operational information system to measure changes occurring in the human resources of the business that conventional accounting does not consider still continues—as does its objective to improve the effectiveness of management decision making and the profitability of the corporation over time.[3] In this connection, Barry's financial results seem

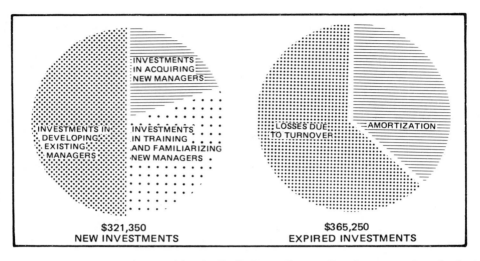

INVESTMENTS
IN ACQUIRING
NEW MANAGERS

INVESTMENTS IN
DEVELOPING
EXISTING
MANAGERS

INVESTMENTS
IN TRAINING
AND FAMILIARIZING
NEW MANAGERS

LOSSES DUE
TO TURNOVER

AMORTIZATION

$321,350
NEW INVESTMENTS

$365,250
EXPIRED INVESTMENTS

Figure 1 Amounts incurred by the R. G. Barry Corporation for new and expired investments in 1970.

to bear out the efforts that they have made—indeed, Barry's managers point out that their corporation's profitability has in no small way resulted from their efforts to develop the human resource as an integral part of this management process.

ACCOUNTING FOR HUMAN RESOURCES IN SOCIETY

Human capabilities have long been recognized as an important, if not the most important, resource of a nation. Paul Samuelson states, "Education is one of society's most profitable investments. Human capital yields a return as great or greater than capital in the form of tools and buildings."[4]

Education is now the largest category of total government spending in Canada; it exceeds $6 billion. As in the case of health care, a growing proportion of our education expenditures have been shifting from the private sector to the government sector of the economy. Expenditures on formal education and vocational training account for about 8 percent of our gross national product. Nearly one-third of Canada's population is involved in full-time education, and the proportion greatly exceeds this when we include those involved in part-time education.[5]

Our society has for a long time recognized the importance of education as an investment in the potential productivity of our nation's human resources. But because of the postwar growth in education expenditures, it has become increasingly important that the amounts we invest in these fields be subject to some form of accountability. Complex questions continue to surround the manner in which we should allocate our resources, assess performance of the investments made, and measure the elements involved in the selection of various alternatives.

In the United States, colleges are established at the rate of 20 or more per year. If this trend were to continue, by 1980 they would be founded at the rate of 1 per week. In 1967, the school age population in the United States was 70 million; in the year 2000 this may increase to 125 million. We must clearly be in a position to assess our methods of education and to have available to us the appropriate techniques for assessing alternatives that we confront in the allocation of our resources.

In a recent book, the Right Honourable Lester B. Pearson discusses the importance of human resources to the developing nations and points out that in some countries irrelevant education can breed discontent and frustration at all income levels.[6] The objective of education policy must be to make education an active and integral part of the effort to achieve development. Because the absolute numbers of educated people are growing in the developing nations, their presence immeasurably influences the organization of their societies and contributes to the growing awareness of the promise of development.

To the author's knowledge there has been little application of human resource accounting concepts to the question of education policy and human resource development on the macro scale. The point is that our investment in human capital has grown to a size and importance such that we can no longer afford to ignore the need for developing objective and suitable methods of accounting on this scale.

The answers to questions of manpower deployment in times of unemployment or full employment are important to our economic welfare; by developing more appropriate accounting techniques, a more effective allocation of our manpower resources of all ages and skills might be achieved. Questions of continuing education, programs to avoid obsolescence, and policies for immigration are further examples or reasons why we should seriously consider the role of accounting in national manpower planning and development programs.

The recent move by the President of the United States, in proposing four new departments for the executive branch of the government, is particularly interesting. The existing Departments of Agriculture, Labor, Commerce, Housing and Urban Development, Transportation, Interior, Health, Education and Welfare, would be eliminated and replaced by four new departments—Economic Affairs, Community Development, Natural Resources, and Human Resources. The Department of Human Resources would include the functions of health services, income maintenance and security, education, manpower, and social and rehabilitation services. This restructuring is of interest because of its recognition of human resources as a dimension of utmost importance to the nation. The question of human resource management on a national scale and the appropriate concepts and techniques of accounting for these resources is one to which all of us—and certainly accountants—can profitably address ourselves.

CONCLUSION

In a general sense the real value of an asset—if such a value exists—might be viewed as the present discounted value of the future income that the asset will yield. People, however, are vastly different from other types of assets, and their value cannot be viewed with the same concepts. Except, perhaps, for professional athletes, human resources are not legal property of their organization and cannot be sold. The principles of market or net realizable value, therefore, are only of limited interest. A further difference is that unlike physical assets, such as buildings or machinery, which normally depreciate in value with use, the value of human resources can substantially appreciate with experience.

Any quantification of the value of people to an organization should more properly be related to the reasons for knowing that value and the decision to be made. For example, what is the relative importance of one type of skill to others in the organization? If the job is to be left vacant, or if the person is irreplaceable, his value is more appropriately related to the resulting economic loss. Such values are often difficult to determine unless revenues or income can be directly associated with the activities of the employee, as in the case of salesmen, maintenance personnel, or those providing professional services for a fee.

As with other types of assets, concepts of human resource values are important questions to which answers can be found. But a good knowledge of the cost elements associated with investments in people can substantially improve management decisions involving the human resource. When human resource accounting employs measurements of the monetary investments in individual employees and organizational groupings, these measurements are generally familiar to accountants. Cost-based accounting and social measurement techniques, when applied to specific human resource problems such as those described in this chapter, can greatly aid the assessment of the condition of human resources, their utilization, and the return on this investment.

When human resource accounting is included as a dimension of the information system, managers will be better motivated toward improving the performance of people in their organization.

NOTES

1. For further reference on social measurements in human resource accounting see Rensis Likert, *The Human Organization: Its Management and Value* (Toronto: McGraw-Hill).

2. William C. Pyle, Director of Human Resource Accounting Research at the University of Michigan, was responsible for originating and directing development of the first human resource accounting system in industry in conjunction with the R. G. Barry Corporation.
3. See Human resource accounting, R. L. Woodruff, Jr., Vice President, Human Resources, the R. G. Barry Corporation, *Canadian Chartered Accountant* (Sept. 1970), pp. 156-161.
4. Paul A. Samuelson, *Economics: An Introductory Analysis* (Toronto: McGraw-Hill).
5. Seventh Annual Review of the Economic Council of Canada, "Patterns of Growth," Sept. 1970.
6. Partners in Development, Report of the Commission on International Development, Lester B. Pearson, Chairman (Ottawa: Prager, 1969).

22

EDP: An Organizational Question*

Jim Bohnsack

Computers probably have evoked more heated discussions about organizational considerations than any other inanimate devices. Two decades after the introduction of the "electronic marvel" into local government, administrators still are asking, "Where should the computer be placed organizationally?"

Not a few local governments have experienced serious disruption over the friction and in-fighting occasioned by differing philosophical theories concerning the answer to that question.

And it can make a difference in the results obtained in a specific local government—not necessarily as a result of where the computer is located and who operates it, but as a result of who plans how it is to be used and from what point of view.

Many believe the data-processing unit should remain in the finance department where it historically originated. Others contend such a unit should report "only to top management" since it is a "management tool." Still others—somewhat less vocal—contend it should be housed in the "general services" department along with printing presses, photocopiers, and microfilm cameras. Some

---

*Reprinted from *Governmental Finance,* vol. 8 (August 1977), pp. 4-10.

"user departments" still espouse the concept that they should have their own work—an idea destined to receive more vociferous support as organizations continue their attempts to classify and locate the position and role of minicomputers in the electronic scheme of things.

Those local government functional departments fortunate enough to receive federal assistance in both dollars and separate computer facility concepts—such as criminal justice—may be expected to be among those wanting their "own thing."

Why are there so many organizational concepts concerning electronic data processing? There are, of course, the usual human organizational struggles involving control and prestige with carefully structured concepts supporting individual and positional status. There are also the arguments for organizational placement motivated by the less discussed emotions of fear and fascination.

But perhaps we continue in failing to resolve the organizational question concerning the electronic data-processing (EDP) function because we have not yet been able to define what it is, what it should be doing, and, therefore, where it should be located.

Some individual units of government have resolved the issue to the satisfaction of local role players. But even in these locales, the question has a way of popping up again as new hardware and software innovations modify some people's perceptions.

Historically, of course, most EDP operations began in local government finance departments. As a matter of fact, most are still there and continue to influence other local governments evolving into the computer age to follow their organizational leads.

Back in the days when computer vendor representatives knew little about local government's potential computer uses and local government people knew little about computers, the trend was set. Computers handled numbers well; finance departments had numbers to be handled; therefore, finance departments needed computers.

Other users—planners, engineers, utilities, police—were identified, and the battle over "one computer or many" (and, therefore, one EDP staff or many) was joined. The finance departments had most of the ammunition. They had heavy influence over money matters and by then had an in-house monopoly on computer expertise.

Computers were considered to represent a heavy financial investment, and that fact, more than the arguments about centrally planned and implemented information systems, probably carried the debate for the proponents of centralization, and finance departments took over most computer operations.

Most, but not all. In many local governments police administrators were able to advance the argument that their information required privacy and confidential handling. This, along with funds for separate computers and program development coming down from the federal government, sufficed in some communities to keep the police or criminal justice functions out of the central computer.

Similar situations occurred in some localities where other functional areas were able to procure funding outside the scope of the general-operations budget. It is not always clear whether the deciding factor was the source of funds, the information issues such as privacy or merely internal relation considerations.

At any rate, the finance departments and the centralized computer proponents won in most jurisdictions.

But, the issue would not stay resolved.

Cost factors contributed heavily to early decisions to centralize the computer operation. Early applications and the reluctance of most top administrators to deal with such a technical operation led to placing the more or less centralized computer operation in the finance department.

A tendency to approach the computer as a processing machine on an application-by-application basis caused it to be perceived as a service function. Staff surrounding the computer then often were organized as a division located within the finance department and functioning as a centralized data-processing service group. This usually was organized as shown in Figure 1.

As the finance department progressed with implementation of its own applications on the computer, it became necessary to offer the service to other local government departments. This came about because potential uses of the computer were being identified in other than the financial area and because, as already seen, the cost of computers already had assured the prevalence of a centralized installation.

With more than one department using the computer, it became necessary to add the data control activity to the EDP organizational chart. Likewise, expand-

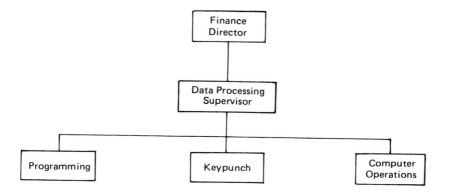

Figure 1 Organization of computer staff within finance department.

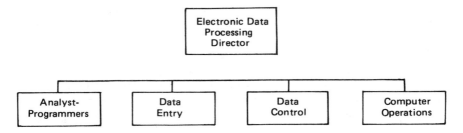

Figure 2 Modification of organization to serve additional departments.

ing media alternatives (cards, tapes, disks) and teleprocessing capabilities caused training of some programmers as analysts—people who analyzed the computer-related alternatives and designed the system to meet the user's requirements. These brought on EDP organizational modifications as shown in Figure 2.

These programmer-analysts, however, had as a major concern the design of the computerized system to meet user-expressed needs. They were not trained, nor expected, to redesign the user's functional system to utilize all the potential capabilities of the computer.

Two factors brought forth new discussions: (1) the emergence of proponents of the management information system (MIS) concept and the integrated system idea, and (2) expanded use of telecommunications—the use of computer-related equipment and computerized data at locations remote from the central processor.

Both factors would prove to be symptomatic of the types of developments which would continue to raise organizational, management, and operational questions concerning the computer, its technical support staff, and the "user-" and computer-related activities conducted in this department.

Related, although different, the MIS and integrated system concepts each had proponents who contended that such concepts could be implemented only under the auspices of the chief executive. The argument was—and is—that these kinds of programs would cross organizational lines and that priorities, scheduling, and equal treatment of departments could be achieved properly only with the authority of the city manager, mayor, or chief administrative officer.

Under both of these concepts, data would be collected from a number of organizational units and combined to form "new information" of use to managers at diverse levels in various organizational compartments. Certainly, top level management was to be a major beneficiary of the results of these approaches. While considered necessary, although somewhat mundane, computer products such as payroll checks, utility bills, and traffic citation listings were relegated to a lesser level of importance than was previously the case.

While this kind of thinking was evolving in the minds of those who conceived information system components and computerized applications, software and hardware developments were bringing the computer closer to the functional department users. Computer terminals were installed in user departments. These permitted user personnel to inquire of the computer's data base instead of requesting the data-processing department to produce run-out computer-produced listings of information. In a very limited and structured sense, the user was now a computer operator.

As software and procedures were developed to protect the central computer files from being destroyed through having the uninitiated non-EDP personnel act upon them, entry of data also was permitted from the terminals. Some users became their own keypunch and verification operators (although the new term was "data entry").

Further discussion was advanced as to whether these "data entry people" should report to EDP or to the user department head. Data-processing directors argued that all data entry personnel should be EDP department employees to protect the files and achieve the best scheduling of entries. User departments contended the entry tasks were not full-time jobs and that if the data entry people were user department personnel, they would then be available to user supervisors for assignment to other tasks when not entering data into the computer files.

Physical location usually won out. Many data-processing directors became mollified in losing the argument as they realized the new arrangement made users responsible for the accuracy of their own files. This helped eliminate a situation in which EDP directors felt they had been unjustly criticized for inaccurate data bases which actually resulted from original errors made by the user rather than EDP staff. If the user were now responsible for accuracy of data-as-entered into computer files, then the EDP department could only be responsible for the accuracy of computer operations and computer programming.

These somewhat decentralizing aspects of the organization of tasks and responsibilities involved in computer operations were given another boost as remote computer printers came into use. The printers allowed the user not only to enter data into the computer and make structured inquiries from the computer files, but also to run data-processing programs which resulted in hard-copy reports and listings. Printed out at the user site, these reports were the result of a process which became known as *remote* job entry and meant that for some applications the user was then free of dependence on the central EDP staff except for "run time schedules" and the development of computer programs.

Some remote job sites installed "intelligent terminals" which had the capability of storing limited data at the user location and of performing merges, sorts, and editing before the data were transmitted to the central computer. This could be interpreted as further decentralization of EDP tasks.

EDP directors and programmers have come to feel less threatened by these decentralizing aspects, feeling that EDP types still are designing and implementing both the user's systems and programs as well as the hardware and software involved in the teleprocessing network. The users, under this line of thought, only are performing certain operational chores mostly on a mundane, detail level of the EDP functional hierarchy. Analysis, design, configuration planning, and computer programs development still are in the hands of the EDP department.

Even that, however, is being approached by ever newer hardware and software development. Some minicomputers and related peripheral devices are decreasing in cost to a point that challenges centralization for the purpose of spreading hardware expenses among multiple users. Some operating system software and data-based management software is being developed with the idea that any user could be easily trained to successfully develop a computer program and operate the computer with little more difficulty than operating a photocopy machine.

This kind of development could challenge not only the centralized computer operations concept, but could erode the centralized analysis-programming staff which has prevailed nationally in units of local government.

While these technological developments have and will continue to impact the EDP centralized/decentralized organizational debate, the discussion is made more complex by the processing service vs. management tool argument.

In the service concept the EDP department is viewed as a response-oriented group. A functional department requests a particular application to be "put on the computer." Establishing what reports are desired, programmer-analysts design the data collection and input forms needed, format the reports, and prepare programming specifications. A programmer codes the instructions to the machine and the programs are tested, debugged, and implemented.

Although modern EDP groups also respond to requests for on-line applications which involve placing computer terminals in the user's location, most still are designed and implemented on an application-by-application basis.

The application approach to data processing was the initial concept under which computers were used. It was based largely on the concept that the computer could be economically used to process large volumes of data in a voluminous redundant operation. The concept was that large numbers of clerical personnel would thereby be replaced, thus justifying the cost of the computer and its operation.

Experience over the years, however, has shown local governments to have only a few such applications. Among these are utility billing, payroll, traffic/parking citations, assessment files, tax rolls, voter registration, and vehicle registration or licensing.

Other applications tended to be added to the computer's files just because the computer was there and not because there were any savings to offset the costs. It became popular to shrug off the demands for cost justification by explaining that the computer provided many intangible benefits such as faster information and more accurate information. No one could say what the dollar value of these benefits might be and, anyway, the late '60's and early '70's was not a time requiring as much financial justification as today's productivity-minded local governments might demand. It was a time for going to the moon, installing color television, and all sorts of new technologies. The computers made much of the technological change possible while riding to popular usage on the wave of such change.

In fact computers spread among units of local government so rapidly that there was little time to examine such a dull subject as organizational placement. Some discussion was held in a few jurisdictions and a few academicians raised questions but, for the most part, it was "follow-the-leader" with service-oriented, application-directed computer units located in finance departments.

Even as the profligation was occurring, however, technological innovations were raising new questions about organizational placement. New data base management software made it possible to (in effect) draw data from various files to make up new kinds of reports.

This helped spawn the idea of the integrated data base in which data from several departments could be stored in the same base and used for a multiplicity of purposes. How did this affect organizational considerations? Many finance departments were not prepared to cope with other department heads who did not want their data stored with anyone else's data. Nor were they prepared to mount analysis and design project teams that had to deal with several departments simultaneously in order to design and implement such bases.

The idea spread because it helped get back at the old cost-benefit question. If local government had only a few applications of sufficient volume to justify the cost of computerization, surely there must be savings through multiple uses of data and multiple users of a single data base. After all, the collection of data was, and is, the most expensive part of an information system—automated or manual.

Again, the push-organizationally—was to place the computers with the chief executive. This was the only authority strong enough to extract cooperation from all agencies who might be involved in the integrated data base. Organizationally, within the EDP function, the concept also gave rise to a new position— the data base coordinator.

From quite another front—that of noncomputer technicians—came support for the motion to place the EDP function with top management. This came from proponents of older concepts such as systems and procedures analysts, forms management personnel, industrial engineers, and work measurement analysts.

Brushed aside from their traditional pursuits of improving management and operations as computer advocates hailed the new improver, these analysts were beginning to understand what a computer could and could not do and just how it might fit in with their own tried and proven techniques.

From this marriage of ideas came the idea of designing a new information system with the computer seen as one tool, forms design and management as another, procedures and methods analysis as a third tool, and logical physical alignment of work station yet another tool.

This obviously required staffs of management analysts as well as computer analysts and raised the question about these functions being in the same department and whether it should be the finance department or the chief administrator's office.

Management analysts and budget analysts, already brought together in the formation of local offices of management and budget modeled on federal lines, also raised questions about computer analysts being located in another organizational unit.

After all, these different types of analysts were "doing their thing" in the same functional departments. It soon became apparent that what one did, the other might undo. At the least, more coordination was clearly needed and there needed to be some thought of achieving it by placing all the analysts in the same organizational unit.

While these thoughts were becoming more widespread, EDP traditional staffs were ill equipped to enter into the conversation because of their necessary concentration on changing computer technologies and configurations.

Some of the more detailed levels of EDP duties already were being somewhat decentralized as more varied uses of remote terminals located in user departments were being implemented. Users were beginning to do some of their own data entry, inquiries, and even job submissions. Some report dissemination was occurring through terminals and remote printers also located in user departments.

Other sharp learning curves in terms of new operating system software and new telecommunications software requirements also were taking place. Management too, however, was involved in learning and making decisions about these new technologies, so organizational changes remained relatively few and slow.

Now, local governments have more experience in how these areas of expertise interface with each other and with using departments. The ad hoc advisory committees, instituted in many instances to give users representation in data-processing decisions, often prove to be too slow and burdensome. Administrators are moving back toward cost justification and productivity considerations. In short, organizational placement of EDP is up for discussion again in many jurisdictions.

To add to the complexity, as noted previously, inexpensive, flexible, easily programmed minicomputers are challenging even the EDP centralization decision.

This time we have the experience to realize that there is not just one function in the EDP area or, perhaps more to the point, that there are more functions than electronic data processing in a local government information system. We know there is a difference in planning a system, designing a system, and operating a system. We know that organizational placement should not be decided by considering just the equipment and where it is located.

Considering the impact on the cost and benefits to a local government, it is not as important to decide where the equipment is located and operated as it is to decide who is planning and designing how it will be utilized and who is establishing priorities, both for development and for operations.

The "who?" is an important question since results tend to take on the character of the organizational level to which the function is assigned.

In short, it is not just the electronic equipment which dictates where it should be placed. Rather, the determining factor is the use to which it is put. If an operations-based information system is desired, it should be placed at the operational department level. If a more comprehensive system addressing overall management and jurisdictional goals is desired, the function should be placed on that level. If only portions of the system lending themselves to computerization are to be considered, place the matter in the hands of computer analysts and programmers. If broader concerns of productivity, such as those resulting from comprehensive, hybrid analysis and design are needed, this calls for other types of people with broader technological and jurisdictional knowledge.

If the top layer of administration wants its own goals and priorities to be addressed, then that level of management should become involved.

It is an irony of information systems in local government that the "systems concept," the idea of having several areas of expertise look at a problem for a conjoint solution, is seldom used.

Perhaps the idea of organizing on the Office of Management and Budget concept or the concentration of analytic talent in a single department would bring better or more acceptable solutions. Such a department could include budget analysts, management analysts, computer analysts, and operations research personnel (see Figure 3).

Organizational theory holds that one of the factors to be considered in structuring an organization is the focusing of resources to achieve desired results. This can be followed in areas of multiple disciplines as well as single areas of expertise, and it certainly is applicable when planning, organizing, and utilizing the EDP function.

The key to the suggested organization chart is to systemate as you automate.

Many local government information systems grew up over a period of time with pieces being added or modified to meet demands of the moment. Sometimes little thought was given to how these changes might affect other parts of the system. The result was that personnel in the detail levels of the organization made adjustments so that the system would continue to work.

Most of these people had little knowledge of the techniques or technologies available to make these operational adjustments more efficient or more effective. Besides, they—like most others—were busy with their operational jobs.

The result, in most cases, was a poorly designed system with which the organization has continued to live.

With the advent of the computer, some of these poorly designed systems

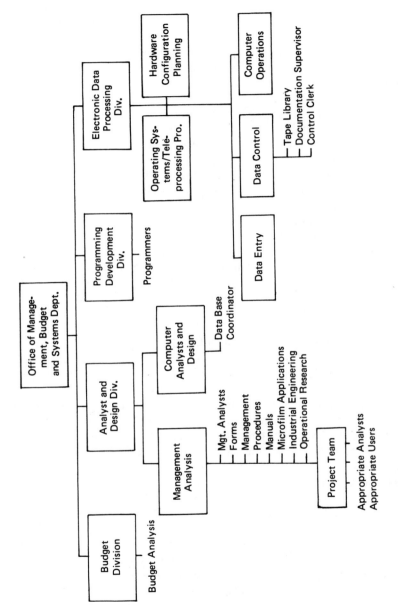

Figure 3   The Office of Management and Budget concept: concentration of analytic talent in one department.

were automated. This often meant the computerized version also was inefficient and certainly not as effective as it might be.

In addition, there was the tendency to regard the computer as only a processing tool. Many established the data processing as a service function just as they had the reproduction.

Further confusion resulted when the computer personnel began to be referred to as "systems people." Certainly, a few of them had any training as information systems or operational systems analysts. They were mostly computer systems analysts.

In this confusion of terms, information systems as a concept covering all information produced and circulated in a given chain of events or activities became lost. Many came to regard the computer system as the information system. This was fragmented thinking.

The computer is only one technology which may be used in an information system and the *processing* of data is only one of the steps in an information system.

Focusing the analytic capability of a local government unit in projects aimed at accompanying or preceding automation is an attempt to analyze the whole system and determine the needs for a computer—and other technologies—before the sometimes long and expensive work of computerization begins.

With some things already running on the computer and with the computer's teleprocessing network reaching into the very heart of departmental operations, the need to analyze and design information systems on a comprehensive basis with detailed consideration of the resulting impact on operational and management systems is even more implicit.

Automation does not remove the necessity for the aged techniques of systems and procedures, industrial engineering, forms design and management, nor the newer techniques of operations research and microfilm technologies. Rather, the cost and time spent on developing computerized processes heighten the need for more careful analysis in the operational areas and more thorough design considerations concerning ascertaining the natural parameters of a given system, how the individual parts affect each other, and how the whole system works in the organization.

As Les Matthias, international systems man even before the proliferation of computers, has often written, "Systemate before you automate."

23

MAKING SENSE OF NONBUSINESS ACCOUNTING *

Robert N. Anthony

After a first course in accounting, students have a pretty good idea of the story
that is told by a balance sheet and an income statement. Their knowledge deepens
from additional study and from using financial statements, either in the company
in which they work or as analysts, investors, or lenders interested in other companies. They learn that business financial statements are constructed according
to a common framework. Those of General Motors are sufficiently similar to
those of a drugstore that a business person can make sense out of either. They
know the importance of the bottom line on the income statement and what it
tells about the success of a given company.

When those accustomed to business financial statements try to read the
financial statements of a nonbusiness organization, however, they find themselves in a different world. Instead of a report on the entity as a whole, they
find fragmented data, presented in columns on a single statement, or in a succes-
sion of separate statements, each of which deals with a piece of the organization.

*Reprinted by permission of the Harvard Business Review. Making Sense of Nonbusi-
ness Accounting by Robert N. Anthony, vol. 58 (May-June 1980), pp. 83-93. Copyright ©
1980 by the President and Fellows of Harvard College. All rights reserved.

They find such terms as "interfund transfers" that have no counterpart in business accounting and that seem to be similar to, but not the same as, revenues or expenditures. They serarch in vain for a "bottom line"—that is, an indication of the financial performance of the organization as a whole.

Those who become involved in the nonbusiness world—as managers, taxpayers, members of governing boards or legislatures, or as prospective bondholders or other lenders—must learn a new accounting language. This task is in some respects more difficult than learning a foreign lenguage because in this second world, although many numbers may be identified by familiar labels, the labels have different meanings from those to which they are accustomed. Because about a third of the economic activity in the United States is conducted by nonbusiness organizations, a proportion that is increasing, this problem is by no means trivial.

Its seriousness is highlighted by the financial problems of New York City, or Cleveland, and of many other, smaller municipalities. Readers of the financial statements of these municipalities generally did not even know there was a financial problem until a few months before the cities were unable to pay their bills. With understandable financial statements, the plight would have been discovered much sooner. In New York, for example, it turned out that the city was counting as operating revenues the proceeds of bond issues that presumably were made to finance its capital budget, and even in 1978 it had to rely on $577 million of such financing to continue operation. Bond proceeds are not revenues by any sensible definition.

My thesis is that the existence of these two worlds of accounting is unnecessary. With one major exception, the financial statements of a nonbusiness organization can be constructed according to the same principles that apply to business financial statements, and these financial statements can be just as understandable to the reader.

NONBUSINESS ACCOUNTING PRACTICES

Until the 1920s, nonbusiness accounting was approximately the same as business accounting (although both were fairly crude compared with today's business accounting). In the 1920s, nonbusiness organizations, particularly municipalities, became enamored of the concept that is now called fund accounting, and this led to the schism that persists today.

Five different versions of fund accounting are set forth in official publications of the American Institute of Certified Public Accountants and are reflected in manuals of the organizations involved, which include state and municipal governments, voluntary health and welfare organizations, colleges and universities, hospitals, and all other nonprofit organizations. The principles for hospitals are fairly close to those of business accounting; those for state and municipal governments are the most different; and the others fall between these extremes.

These accounting principles represent the best current practices for the organizations to which they apply, but not all organizations, by any means, adhere to them. A large majority of municipalities, for example, continue to keep their books on what is essentially a cash basis—that is, they record the cash receipts and cash disbursements for each fund and stop there.

I shall discuss the reasons why fund accounting is said to be necessary, but first I want to show, by referring to the 1978 financial statements of the city of Boston, that the difference between business and nonbusiness accounting practices is substantial. These financial statements are of special significance because they are the first statements that Boston has prepared in accordance with generally accepted accounting principles in its 346-year history and the first to be audited by independent public accountants. Their publication represents a tremendous achievement by James V. Young, deputy mayor, and by Coopers & Lybrand, the auditors.

In examining a set of financial statements, the typical reader turns first to the report of operating performance during the year. (The balance sheet, which lists assets and liabilities at the end of the year, is of secondary importance.) Table 1 shows the page from these statements that is closest to the operating statement of a business. It is not, and does not purport to be, an actual operating statement. It is a mixture of what in business would be called an operating statement and a funds flow statement.

The first remarkable thing about this report is its complexity. Even the largest industrial company presents its income statement in a single column of numbers that starts with revenues and ends with net income. This one has five separate columns, with many subtotals and many strange terms. What does it tell us about Boston's financial performance in 1978?

The headline of the *Wall Street Journal* story on this report read,"Financial Health of City Seen Improving." The impression of improvement was derived from the bottom section of the first column of Table 1. The last number, a deficit in the general fund equity of $9.4 million as of June 30, 1979, was less than the $22.6 million deficit as of June 30, 1977, and this does indicate an improvement.

If one looks a little higher in that column, however, one notes that there was a "deficiency of sources over uses of financial resources" of $13.5 million in 1978. How can the equity have increased when there was a $13.5 million "deficiency" for the year? The answer is found in the next to the last item, the $26.7 million of "net transfers to general long-term obligation group of accounts." This item represents liabilities incurred during the year that will not be paid in the relatively near future, principally pension payments. On the grounds that current taxpayers do not have to pay for them, these long-term obligations are not counted as general fund liabilities in municipal accounting. In business accounting systems a liability is a liability; the fact that it is not payable in the near future is irrelevant. So from the first column we should get the impres-

Table 1 All Governmental Funds of City of Boston—Statements of Sources and Uses of Financial Resources and Changes in Fund Equity (for year ended June 30, 1978)

	General fund	Special revenue funds	Debt service funds	Capital projects funds	Combined total (memorandum only)
Sources of financial resources					
Local					
Real and personal property taxes	$421,500,994				$421,500,994
Motor vehicle excise taxes	10,528,744				10,528,744
Payments in lieu of taxes	647,639				647,639
Licenses and permits	3,409,456				3,409,456
Fines and forfeits	8,076,151				8,076,151
Rents	3,848,690				3,848,690
Interest	1,845,675	$ 274,749	$ 164,705		2,285,129
Departmental and miscellaneous	12,300,279		171,806	$ 100,000	12,572,085
Total local	462,157,628	274,749	336,511	100,000	462,868,888
Intergovernmental					
Federal	103,988,582	140,436,559		890,945	141,327,504
State		11,257,699	17,946,637	49,762	133,242,680
Boston Water and Sewer Commission			2,092,734		2,092,734
Total intergovernmental	103,988,582	151,694,258	20,039,371	940,707	276,662,918
Other					
Interfund transfers	1,500,000		45,772,071	280,000	47,552,071
Proceeds of general obligation bonds				65,101,318	65,101,318
Total other	1,500,000		45,772,071	65,381,318	112,653,389
Total sources	567,646,210	151,969,007	66,147,953	66,422,025	852,185,195
Uses of financial resources					
Current					
City					
General government	28,632,691	341,431			28,974,122
Public safety	84,386,179	20,791,320			105,177,499

Inspection	1,797,740				1,797,740
Public works	35,253,379	811,082			36,064,461
Health and Hospitals' Enterprise Fund operating assistance subsidy	22,825,213	12,910,105			35,735,318
Veterans' services	3,094,293				3,094,293
Libraries	9,191,972	1,567,600			10,759,572
Parks and recreation	8,488,844	483,960			8,972,804
Community development	745,748	30,515,166			31,260,914
Human services	268,495	40,413,767			40,682,262
Miscellaneous	210,271				210,274
Schools	174,615,959	32,480,004			207,095,963
County	32,041,824	23,569			32,065,393
Retirement costs	66,546,546				66,546,546
Other employee benefits	20,937,377				20,937,377
Judgments and claims	6,547,725				6,547,725
Metropolitan District Commission and Massachusetts Bay Transportation Authority charges	38,531,874				38,531,874
Capital outlays	3,427,109	8,949,372		51,062,548	63,439,029
Debt service					
Principal retirement			37,730,000		37,730,000
Interest	1,117,966		32,544,206	154,000	33,816,172
Interfund transfers	42,420,413	1,500,000			43,920,413
Total uses	581,081,621	150,737,376	70,274,206	51,216,548	853,359,751
Excess (deficiency) of sources over uses of financial resources	(13,435,411)	1,181,631	(4,126,253)	15,205,477	(1,174,556)
Fund equity, July 1, 1977, as previously reported	54,419,500	74,569,161	11,553,907	(8,654,950)	131,887,618
Restatements	(77,055,042)	(50,985,332)	30,273,736	(12,483,227)	(110,249,865)
As restated	(22,635,542)	23,583,829	41,827,643	(21,138,177)	21,637,753
Net transfers to general long-term obligation group of accounts	26,663,150				26,663,150
Fund equity, June 30, 1978	$ (9,407,803)	$ 24,765,460	$ 37,701,390	$ (5,932,700)	$ 47,126,347

Author's note: Original footnotes have not been reproduced.

sion that operations were $13.5 million in the red for the year. But what of
the other columns?

The last column, headed "combined total," should be the most informative
of all as to overall performance. But observe that the heading contains the caution "memorandum only." The caution is well advised because one of the other
columns is labeled "capital project funds." These funds have to do with the
financing and construction of capital assets and therefore are not related to 1978
operations.

The $15.2 million "excess" in this column is what makes the last column
come out to the small deficiency of $1.2 million, but this excess has nothing to
do with operations. It means essentially that the city raised more money for
capital projects in 1978, principally from selling bonds, than it spent for capital
projects in that year. This difference is no more favorable than would be the
case if a corporation sold bonds in one year and did not use all the proceeds in
that year.

The second column, "special revenue funds," is related to operations. In fact,
it is so closely related that there is little sense in setting out this column separately
from the general fund. Special revenues are those whose spending is restricted to
some specified purpose. As can be seen, they are almost entirely federal and state
grants for operating purposes, and they are spent for almost every program in the
city. Thus total spending for schools is not just the $174.6 million shown in the
first column, but it includes in addition the $32.5 million in the special revenue
column.

Other Peculiarities

Even the sum of the first two columns does not tell the whole story about Boston's
operations. Not shown in this table at all, but appearing in another statement, is a
report of what are called "enterprise funds." Enterprise funds are municipal activities that generate significant amounts of revenues. (A city can decide for itself what "significant" means.)

In Boston the operation of city hospitals is reported as an enterprise fund,
and this operation had a loss of $12.8 million in 1978 (in addition to the $35.7
million subsidy reported in Table 1). Such losses must eventually be borne by the
taxpayers, and profits on enterprise activities are available to finance other operations. They are an integral part of Boston's financial story.

The special revenue funds column indicates another difference between business accounting and municipal accounting. Note that the total revenues, $152
million, exceed the total uses, which are $151 million. Although the difference
in this case is small, an important principle is involved. In business, receipt of an
advance payment to perform a service is not counted as revenue until the service
has been performed. Until that time there is a liability to perform the service.

Municipalities count these payments as revenues as soon as they receive the funds. They disregard the fact that a liability has been created.

There are many other peculiarities of nonbusiness accounting. For example, the principles governing the reporting of enterprise funds are substantially different from those for other funds; depreciation is reported in the former but not in the latter.

This brief analysis of the two different worlds is sufficient to make these points:

1. In nonbusiness financial statements, there is no "bottom line" that shows the overall result of operations. The audit guide, *Audits of Colleges and Universities,* is unequivocal about this: "It [the statement corresponding to Table 1] does not purport to present the results of operations. . . ."

2. Reports of operations are fragmented by the division into funds. Amounts for several funds must be combined to arrive at total spending for operating programs. Reports of operating performance are not separated from reports of capital transactions.

3. Some accounting numbers do not report the economic realities of the transactions. In addition to the revenue and expenditure items that one would expect to find in a report of operations, there are items labeled "transfers," which are neither revenues nor expenditures, some having economic significance and some representing merely movements from one artificial pot to another with no effect on the entity as a whole.

RATIONALE FOR TWO WORLDS

Two reasons have been advanced and continue to be advanced for the existence of this second world of accounting. First, nonbusiness organizations, by definition, do not exist to earn a profit and it is therefore argued that they should not use business accounting principles, which are focused on the measurement of profitability. Second, managers of nonbusiness organizations must adhere to restrictions on spending—either legal, such as those set forth in the approved budget of a governmental unit, or other limitations specified by donors or grantors— and it is argued that the purpose of accounting should therefore be to ensure compliance with these restrictions.

In my opinion, although both the absence of a profit objective and the need for fiscal compliance are characteristics of nonbusiness organizations, neither is a sufficient reason for the differences in accounting that currently exist.

Profit Measure

By definition, nonprofit organizations (which is another name for nonbusiness organizations) do not exist for the purpose of earning a profit. Their basic purpose is to provide services—health care in a hospital, education in a school, public safety, and a variety of other services in a municipality. Their success should be measured by how much service they provide with the resources available. However, there is no way of measuring the quantity of services provided in most nonprofit organizations. We can measure the number of students who graduate but not the amount of education that they took away with them; we can count the number of patient days in a hospital, but we cannot express in numerical terms the adequacy of the care each patient received; we can measure the amount spent for public safety, but there is no good way of knowing whether the amount was well spent.

In a business, revenues are a good (albeit not perfect) measure of the amounts of goods and services that the organization provided. In a nonbusiness organization, there is no corresponding measure, except to the limited extent that the organization earns revenues from the sale of its services. It follows that the operating statement of a nonbusiness organization cannot have the same meaning as the operating statement of a business. In a business, the bottom line—the difference between revenues and expenses—measures success in achieving objectives; in a nonbusiness organization, the bottom line cannot have this meaning.

It can, however, have a highly significant meaning of its own. Expenses in a nonbusiness organization are essentially the same as those in a business; in both cases, they represent the resources used in an accounting period, i.e., the material, labor, and other services consumed in that period. Thus the difference in the meaning of the operating statement relates solely to revenues.

In nonbusiness organizations, revenues do measure (or, at least, can measure with proper accounting principles) the amount of resources provided for operations in an accounting period. These resources may come from the sale of services, contributions for operating purposes, membership dues, taxation, government grants, or elsewhere. Thus the difference between revenues and expenses measures whether the organization "lived within its means"—whether its spending for operations was no more than its revenues. Although it does not focus on profitability, this measurement does have an important meaning.

The idea of "operating capital maintenance" unites these two meanings of the operating statement. A business maintains its capital through operations if its revenues for a period exceed its expenses for the period by an amount that provides a satisfactory return to its equity shareholders. A nonbusiness organization has no equity owners and therefore no equivalent need to earn a return on equity, at least as a general rule. (If an organization accumulates equity in order to finance working capital requirements or to provide for expansion or replacement of assets and if this equity could be used for other purposes, the organization does need to earn a return on this equity to maintain its capital. Some cost reimbursement formulas, especially for health care, are defective because they do not allow for this requirement.) A nonbusiness organization maintains its capital through operations if it breaks even, i.e., if its revenues at least equal its expenses.

Thus a business and a nonbusiness operating statement can convey the same message: the extent to which the organization has maintained its capital through operations. Maintenance of capital is the most important single piece of information about nonbusiness operations. It is also important for a business, but in a business the bottom line conveys an additional message—how well the organization attained its objective of earning profits.

A nonbusiness operating statement can also convey important additional information on how much was spent for various services—instruction, research, and athletics in a university, public safety, roads, parks and recreation, and welfare in a municipality. The amounts spent for each program do not represent the quantity of services provided, but they do indicate relative magnitudes of effort.

In summary, a business operating statement measures revenues, expenses, and the difference between them; a nonbusiness organization's operating statement should also report that information, even though the meaning of the bottom line is not the same.

Fiscal Compliance

Another argument often heard for having two separate worlds of accounting is that nonbusiness organizations must comply with restrictions on their spending and that accounting must therefore report the degree of compliance. There are two things wrong with this argument.

First, spending limits are not peculiar to nonbusiness organizations. Businesses must comply with restrictions on spending when they produce goods or services under cost-type contracts, when they must adhere to requirements of regulatory agencies, when they receive advance payments (which may range from a one-year magazine subscription to a multimillion-dollar construction contract), and for a variety of other reasons.

The second defect in the argument is that fiscal compliance can be reported in ways other than the separate reports for the various funds that are intended to reflect these restrictions. Keeping track of restrictions is important, but a business accomplishes this by appropriate internal accounting controls. The amounts do not show up on the financial statements, except to the extent that there are liabilities for work not yet performed.

It is a responsibility of the auditors to determine whether the restrictions have been complied with. When there is noncompliance, the auditors should call attention to it in their report; otherwise, there is no need to "prove" this by a funds statement that shows that revenues available for a given purpose were as much as the expenses incurred for that purpose.

PROBLEMS PECULIAR TO NONBUSINESS ORGANIZATIONS

Does the foregoing mean that business accounting and nonbusiness accounting should be identical? It does not. There is one significant difference between a business and a nonbusiness organization that has accounting implications. Other than capital provided by investors, a business obtains its financial resources from the sale of goods and services. Nonbusiness organizations also obtain resources for current operations from sales (e.g., tuition in colleges, fees in hospitals), from taxes, and from contributions made for operating purposes.

A nonbusiness organization, however, has one type of resource inflow that has no counterpart in business. This is contributed capital. Many organizations receive funds for endowment, and the essential nature of such funds is that the principal must be maintained intact, leaving only the earnings on this principal available for operating purposes.

An organization may receive contributions of art objects that are intended for display and that do not help to finance operating activities, or it may finance a new building by a capital fund drive. The construction of roads, public buildings, and other infrastructures in a municipality may be financed by grants from the state or the federal government. Transactions of this type occur only rarely in a business, which ordinarily finances its new capital assets from revenues; even if construction funds are acquired by borrowing, the debt must be paid off from future revenues.

Any organization that receives contributed capital has an accounting problem because contributed capital that is intended to benefit future periods must be separated from revenues, which, by definition, relate to operations of the current period. If a college has revenues in a given year of $9.9 million and expenses of $10 million, the receipt of a $2 million bequest for its endowment does not mean that its operating margin for the current year has been changed from a $100,000 deficit to a $1.9 million surplus. The income from the investment of the $2 million will be available to help finance operations in future years, but the principal will never be used to finance operations.

Depreciation is a related problem. If an organization obtains funds for capital assets from grants or contributions, should it charge depreciation on these assets as an operating expense? Annual charges for depreciation are such that over the life of an asset they equal the cost of that asset. If revenues are not large enough to equal this charge plus other expenses, the investment in plant has not been recovered. When capital assets are contributed, however, there is no need to recover the cost from revenues because the organization did not use its own resources in acquiring the assets. Some people argue that contributed assets should nevertheless be depreciated in order to report the full cost of services rendered during the period. Others believe that a depreciation charge is unnecessary.

I do not attempt here to resolve the depreciation controversy. My point is that this is one of the few accounting problems peculiar to nonbusiness accounting. The separation between revenues and capital contributions is a problem, but one that is easily solved with existing principles. Minor difficulties arise about the treatment of certain revenue transactions, such as those from taxes and operating contributions, but these can be solved within the basic concept of revenue recognition. And that completes the list of differences between business and nonbusiness accounting problems.

COMBINING THE TWO WORLDS

With a few modifications, it is possible to prepare the financial statements of nonbusiness organizations according to the same standards that apply to business organizations. Fund accounting, as such, is not needed except to the extent that it is a convenient way of making the essential separation between operating transactions and capital transactions just described. Aspects of fund accounting are useful as internal control devices, but they need not govern the format or content of the financial statements. The following section describes what these statements should contain.

Operating Statement

In a nonbusiness organization, the operating statement (a better name than "income statement" because a nonbusiness organization does not exist for the purpose of generating income) should have the same content as a business income statement. For an accounting period, it should report revenues, expenses, gains, and losses, and it should have a bottom line showing the net effect of these operating inflows and outflows. "Operating margin," rather than "net income," is a good term for this bottom line.

The Financial Accounting Standards Board (FASB), which is the body currently responsible for setting all financial accounting standards, should develop standards for the measurement of revenues from taxation, contributions, grants, membership dues, and similar sources peculiar to nonbusiness organizations. The concepts governing these transactions, however, are the same as those for measuring sales revenue, namely, the organization should report revenue in the period to which it applies and at an amount that is likely to be realized.

Revenues, which relate to operations in an accounting period, must be separated from resource inflows, which are intended for capital purposes. Accountants have wrestled for many years with the problem of distinguishing between capital and revenue transactions. Some aspects are clear-cut; e.g., legally restricted bequests to endowment are capital transactions, not revenues. In other cases, the legal facts do not give the answer, and a standard is needed to guide the accountant in making the proper distinction.

There is also the problem of deciding how much of the earnings of an endowment fund are to be counted as revenues of a period. Some people advocate the "total return concept"; others suggest a treatment similar to that for the income from marketable securities in a business. A standard is needed to resolve this difference of opinion or to permit either alternative.

With respect to expenses, there is only one problem peculiar to nonbusiness organizations—depreciation. The problem has two facets, one relating to depreciable assets that have been or will be paid for from operating resources and the other relating to assets that are derived from capital contributions.

With respect to assets that are financed from operating sources (either accumulated operating capital or debt that must be repaid from future revenues), a charge for the use of these assets should be reported as an expense. As mentioned earlier, there are advocates of a depreciation charge, calculated in the conventional way.

There are others, however, who point out that when operating assets are financed entirely by borrowing, as is often the case in municipal buildings and equipment, college dormitories, and hospital facilities, the portion of the annual debt service charge that represents principal repayment may be a satisfactory approximation of depreciation. In these circumstances, the use of the principal component of the debt service charge in lieu of depreciation may provide both a sufficiently reliable number and a number that is easier to understand than conventional depreciation. A standard is required to resolve this question.

With respect to contributed depreciable assets, the question is whether a sufficiently useful purpose is served by depreciating these assets at all. Again, a standard is needed. Existing standards that should apply to all organizations can govern accounting for sales revenue, for expenses other than depreciation, and for operating gains and losses.

Balance Sheets

As already noted, we must make a clear distinction between operating transactions and capital transactions. Although there are various ways of presenting balance sheet information to make this distinction, I think the simplest and easiest to understand is by means of separate balance sheets—one for operating capital and one for contributed capital.

Operating equity, mechanically, is the sum of the operating margins that have been recorded since the organization's inception (with a few adjustments beyond the scope of this overview). It corresponds to retained earnings on a business balance sheet. Assets on the operating balance sheet would be those related to operations, including the capital assets that were financed by operating revenues or that will be so financed as future revenues are used to pay off bonded debt incurred to acquire these assets.

A second balance sheet would report contributed capital, i.e., the aggregate of resource inflows intended for capital purposes rather than for operating purposes. It might be desirable to have two such balance sheets or to divide this balance sheet into two sections—one for the contributed capital related to endowment and the other for the contributed capital related to plant and other nonmonetary assets. Each of these balance sheets would report the assets and liabilities associated with a given type of equity. If assets on the contributed balance sheet are not depreciated, they would remain at cost until they are disposed of.

Thus, if there were three balance sheets, there would be three types of cash reported separately for the entity—one for operating cash, another for endowment cash that is temporarily not invested, and the third for cash held to pay invoices for contributed plant assets being constructed or purchased.

Funds Flow Statements

Associated with each balance sheet should be a funds flow statement (technically, a "statement of changes in financial position") reporting the sources and uses of funds during an accounting period for each of the three types of capital. The principles governing the content and format of these statements would be exactly the same as those now given in Accounting Principles Board *Opinion No. 19* for businesses.

In a municipality, a budgeted funds flow statement for operations might well be more important than the operating statement as a tool for arriving at the amount that must be raised by taxation in the coming year. The funds flow statements for contributed capital would give all necessary information about the sources of new contributions and about changes in the assets in which these contributions were invested.

Sample Financial Statements

A set of financial statements prepared according to the principles outlined is given in the accompanying exhibits. Although they are for a municipality, to provide a contrast with the city of Boston statement in Table 1, the general ideas apply to any nonprofit organization. Details of format and terminology are, of course, matters of personal preference.

The operating statement in Table 2 reports the expenses of providing each program service, the revenue directly attributable to that service, and the difference, which is the net cost that must be financed from general revenues (or the amount contributed to the municipality, as in the case of municipal services). Expenses include depreciation or its equivalent in the form of repayment of debt principal, as indicated in note 1. In the example, general revenues exceeded these net costs by $5.25 million, which indicates that the municipality's operations were financially sound.

Table 2 Sample Municipality–Operating Statement for Year Ended June 30, 1979 (in $ thousands)

General revenues		
Taxes		$40,800
Licenses and permits		400
Interest and rentals		1,800
Endowment revenue		50
Other revenues		1,000
Total general revenue		44,050
Programs (note 1)	Expenses	Revenues
Schools	$23,400	$ 1,700
Public safety	7,300	200
Municipal services	8,000	8,600
Social services	1,600	600

Health and hospitals	4,500	4,100	400
Parks and recreation	3,800	300	3,500
Libraries and museums	2,300	200	2,100
General government	3,900	300	3,600
Total programs	$54,800	$16,000	$38,800
Operating margin			$ 5,250

Note 1: Current amortization incorporated in expenses includes the portion of principal repayment from total debt and depreciation as below:

Programs	Repayment of principal	Interest	Total debt service	Depreciation	Total fixed charges
Public safety	$1,900	$ 500	$2,400	—	$2,400
Municipal services	1,500	900	2,400	1,400	3,800
Other assets	—	—	—	1,600	1,600
Total	$3,400	$1,400	$4,800	$3,000	$7,800

Table 3 Sample Municipality—Balance Sheet, Contributed
Capital as of June 30 (in $ thousands)

Monetary capital Assets	1979	1978
Cash	$ 40	$ 20
Securities	1,000	500
Total assets	$ 1,040	$ 520
Equity		
Contributed monetary equity	1,040	520

Nonmonetary capital Assets		
Cash and marketable securities	$ 500	$ 300
Museum collections	1,400	1,400
Property, plant, and equipment at cost		
Public safety	10,300	10,300
Roads and bridges	24,600	24,600
Parks and recreation	3,000	3,600
Libraries and museums	1,200	1,200
Other	7,300	7,300
	46,400	47,000
Rehabilitation of public housing	400	—
Plant under construction	300	—
Total assets	$49,000	$48,700

Liabilities and equity		
Accounts payable	$ 100	$ 100
Contributed nonmonetary equity	48,900	48,600
Total liabilities and equity	$49,000	$48,700

Table 3 is the contributed capital section of the balance sheet (the operating section is entirely conventional and is omitted to conserve space). Assets, liabilities and equity for monetary capital are reported separately from those for nonmonetary capital. Assets are reported at cost with no provision for depreciation. As explained earlier, depreciation on plant financed by capital contributions is a controversial question; an argument can be made for recognizing it.

Table 4 is the statement of changes in financial position, which explains changes in balance sheet amounts that have occurred during the year. Endowment

Table 4 Sample Municipality—Statement of Changes in Financial Position, Contributed Capital Section for Year Ended June 30, 1979

Monetary capital Sources	
Endowment income	$100
Additional endowment	470
Total	570
Uses	
Endowment revenues	50
Investment in securities	500
Total	550
Increase in cash	$ 20
Nonmonetary capital Sources	
Proceeds of insurance loss	$500
Government grant	400
Total	900
Uses	
Rehabilitation of public housing	400
Plant under construction	300
Total	700
Increase in cash and marketable securities	$200

revenues were derived by using the "total return concept." The Boston statement in Table 1 is essentially an amalgam of Tables 2 and 4. Separation of these two types of financial flows gives a much clearer picture, I believe, than mixing them together in a single statement.

Accounting Entity

One additional standard, or set of standards, is needed to define the accounting entity for which reports are prepared. What exactly is meant by the "city of Boston?" Definition of a consolidated business entity is governed principally by the proportion of equity that a parent company owns in each subsidiary. Because nonbusiness organizations do not issue equity securities, this definition does not fit them. Alternative definitions developed through the same general approach should be formulated.

SUMMARY

Nonbusiness organizations differ from business organizations in that their objective is something other than earning a profit. Both, however, must maintain their capital through operations if they are to continue as sound organizations. An operating statement, prepared according to a common set of standards, reports how well any organization has maintained its capital through operations.

Although nonbusiness organizations must comply with certain restrictions on spending, they are not alone in this respect. Many businesses have restrictions on spending. These require appropriate internal controls but need not shape the format or content of the financial statements. Attestation by the auditor that the restrictions have been complied with, or disclosure of the nature of noncompliance, is adequate.

Nonbusiness capital contributions must be excluded from revenues on the operating statement and must be disclosed separately on the balance sheet and funds flow statement. Whether the plant acquired with these contributions should be depreciated is a problem to be resolved. With the exception of these capital contributions, nonbusiness accounting should be essentially the same as business accounting.

24

ADVANTAGES OF FUND ACCOUNTING IN "NONPROFITS"*

Regina E. Herzlinger
H. David Sherman

ANSWERING THE CRITICS

Because of the complexity of the accounting statements, many accounting professionals have argued for aggregation of the several funds into two, restricted and unrestricted, and for cessation of budgetary and encumbrance accounting. Some critics of fund accounting would go even further and aggregate into one fund—were it not for legal requirements that justify differentiating between these two basic categories. (The law requires restricted funds to be separated from unrestricted funds in the books of account.)

Whatever the merits of simplification, clearly it must be achieved at the cost of fuller information. By reducing the number of interfund transfers reported, aggregation would limit the disclosure of policies that reveal the financial management philosophy. Moreover, combining activities of the restricted current fund and the endowment fund would obscure the difference between operating capital and permanent capital.

---

*Reprinted by permission of the Harvard Business Review. Excerpts from "Advantages of fund accounting in 'non-profits'" by Regina E. Herzlinger and H. David Sherman, vol. 58 (May-June 1980), pp. 94-105. Copyright © 1980 by the President and Fellows of Harvard College. All rights reserved. References have been renumbered.

Another recommendation, already accepted for hospital fund accounting, calls for merger of the plant fund with the unrestricted funds, except for certain replacement reserves that are legally required by bond covenants. It is not clear, however, that plant funds are unrestricted. (Hospitals have adopted this reporting primarily because third party insurance reimbursements are based on the operating costs of their unrestricted funds.)

The arguments for aggregation rest on the notion that all the detail in financial statements confuses the users and aggregation would make the data more accessible to them.[1] The obvious question is: Who are the users? One accountant has proposed the "grandmother test" to see whether the financial statement of the particular nonprofit organization is understood by a grandmother of average intelligence.[2] But none of the hundreds of researchers studying the problem has yet shown that a significant percentage of users are grandmothers or, for that matter, fit any other generalization. While many potential user groups can be listed, no one has documented the relative importance of each use to which they put financial statements.[3]

While one can applaud the sentiment that information should be accessible to all, proponents of the grandmother test or other fund-accounting-made-simple schemes fail to acknowledge that all communication is based on the assumption that the recipients understand the language. Philosophers assume that their readers can account, i.e., they are educated in this discipline. That necessary condition is not fulfilled by many corporate executives, let alone by the grandmothers of the world.[4] While that fact is regrettable, it will not be changed by oversimplification of accountants' reports.

Those arguing for aggregation also assume that users will find it easier to understand two funds than four funds, i.e., the human mind can process the information in two columns of numbers but it will become short-circuited when confronted with four columns. A substantial body of literature, ranging from Alvin Toffler's *Future Shock* to articles by accounting theorists, supports the argument that when ingestion of information reaches a certain point, an "overload" blocks further processing of data.[5]

No one, however, has conclusively located the point, and extensive research so far has turned up contradictory evidence.[6] A test of the effect of aggregating municipal financial statements yielded inconclusive results.[7] In fact, surveys of many users of the financial statements of nonprofits indicate that they want *more* information, not less.[8] While surveys are unreliable predictors of behavior in real situations, these results buttress the rationale for greater disaggregation rather than aggregation.

IN DEFENSE OF BUDGETARY ACCOUNTING

The argument for the removal of budgetary accounting rests in part on a similar assumption—that the presentation of a budget and recognition of encumbrances and other future items are too complicated for the mythical user to decipher. But surveys of users of financial statements indicate that they want *more* information about budgeted events.[9] Security analysts have been agitating for more forward-looking data in corporate annual reports, including data on capital expenditures, construction plans, and future financing.

Nonprofit enterprises have a more basic need for this kind of budgetary information. Profit is an inappropriate measure for these organizations. Existing to benefit society as a whole or particular groups in it (students, the sick, the needy), they are by definition *not* for profit. The appropriate measure of their performance is the level of benefits achieved, not revenues. But the ability to measure that level is obviously quite limited. Although our society clearly profits from education of our children, it is impossible to put an objective value on that education. So, such benefits are not included in the accounting statements of nonprofit organizations.

The revenues and expenses spelled out in financial statements are incomplete measures of performance. For example, the large negative fund balance in the consolidated balance sheet of the U.S. government represents, in part, an investment in future social benefits. The investments made to achieve these benefits should be counted as assets and expensed as the benefits manifest themselves. But because of our inability to measure benefits, the government expenses the investments and puts no corresponding asset on the balance sheet.

The resulting financial statements must be interpreted differently from corporate statements. A deficit in a nonprofit enterprise may mean that it has invested in activities benefiting future generations. The nonprofit organization tries to make a match; the generation that gets the benefits also pays for them through future tax payments. The deficit is not necessarily a signal of failure or a cause for concern, as it is in a business.

For nonprofit organizations, therefore, traditional corporate reporting is almost meaningless. How, then, should their performance be measured? By comparing actual performance with that intended or budgeted. In the case of private nonprofits, the reporting format is structured to provide performance measurement information showing the extent to which management complied with the wishes of the board; in the case of government organizations, the format measures performance in executing the budgetary mandate of the appointed and elected officials who represent the public. The funds represent external restrictions on the use of resources, while the budget represents legislatively mandated restrictions on the distribution of monies.

IMPROVEMENT OF PROCEDURES

In urging the universal adoption of certain nonprofit accounting practices, we do not mean to praise the state of the art as a whole; in both theory and practice it leaves much to be desired. Little theory lies behind accounting for nonprofits, particularly government organizations. The nomenclature is peculiar and inconsistent, and some fundamental issues, such as the recognition of depreciation, valuation of gifts in kind (like art and books), and the standardization of reporting by municipalities, remain to be resolved.

The *practice* of accounting in nonbusiness enterprises is even less admirable. For example, a recent survey found that of a group of 100 cities studied, 70 percent had qualified opinions for at least some funds due to noncompliance with generally accepted accounting principles or inadequate disclosure, or both.[10] These results are far better than those obtained in a 1975 survey; it found that 93.8 percent of the municipalities were not even audited.[11]

There is still considerable room for improvement. Many hospitals, voluntary organizations, and educational institutions need better information systems to generate accounting data in a form that allows them to improve control of receivables and program costs and to coordinate these data with nonaccounting data.

Furthermore, their financial statements should be more accessible to users and potential users in order to promote the kind of accountability that corporations have to their shareholders. Because nonprofit organizations enjoy tax-exempt status, all taxpayers should have the right to examine their financial statements and compare their financial performances with their objectives and accomplishments.

PURPOSEFUL COMPLEXITY

Fund accounting was developed to present fairly the financial transactions unique to nonprofit organizations. The problem of the complexity of their accounting statements should be resolved not by simplification but by better education of users about the meaning and purpose of the components of a fund accounting statement and by greater accessibility to these statements.

The weaknesses of nonprofit accounting would be more fruitfully addressed by resolving problems in nomenclature and quality of accounting information than by converting fund accounting to the simpler (but increasingly complex) for-profit standards.

Finally, nonprofit accounting offers numerous insights into financial management and planning that are not readily available in business accounting:

- Accounting for accruals and encumbrances is useful for tracking the availability of resources for specified purposes.
- Accounting for budgeted vs. actual events offers a useful measure of how well management has carried out its plans.
- Segregation of fund balances into mandatory and discretionary components indicates that emphasis placed on various organizational objectives and on future vs. current financial mobility.

- Separation of capital and operating transactions, coupled with disclosure of the funds available or required for plant addition or replacement and the amount of liquid assets at hand for this purpose, permits comparison of the available resources designated for capital additions with the expected demand for such resources.

The need for this sort of information has been endlessly examined in business accounting. Fund accounting provides a good example of how this need can be met.

NOTES

1. See, for example, Price Waterhouse & Co.'s position paper, 1975.
2. Malvern J. Gross, How to make your financial reports easy to understand, *Association Management,* Sept. 1973, p. 65.
3. See Arie Y. Lewin and Hames H. Scheiner, *Requiring Municipal Performance Reporting: An Analysis Based upon Users' Needs* (Durham, N.C.: Graduate School of Business Administration, Duke University, May 1977). K. Fred Skousen, Jay M. Smith, and Leon W. Woodfield, *User Needs: An Empirical Study of College and University Financial Reporting* (Washington, D.C.: NACUBO, 1975).
4. See Vincent C. Brenner, Are annual reports being read? *National Public Accountant,* Nov. 1971, p. 16.
5. See, for instance, Lawrence Revsine, Data expansion and conceptual structure, *Accounting Review,* Oct. 1970, p. 704. Henry Miller, Environmental complexity and financial reports, *Accounting Review,* Jan. 1972, p. 31.
6. See Harold M. Schroeder, Michael J. Driver, and Siegfried Streufert, *Human Information Processes* (New York: Holt, Rinehart & Winston, 1967).
7. James M. Patton, An experimental investigation of some effects of consolidating municipal financial reports, *Accounting Review,* April 1978, p. 402.
8. The Council of State Governments, State and local government user survey. Unpublished study, 1970. Lexington, Ky., Touche Ross & Co. and the First National Bank of Boston, *Urban Fiscal Stress: A Comparative Analysis of 66 U. S. Cities* (New York: Touche Ross & Co., 1979).
9. John H. Engstrom, User views of budget information. Unpublished survey, Athens, Ga., University of Georgia School of Accounting, 1977.
10. Ernst and Whinney, *How Cities Can Improve Their Financial Reporting* (Cleveland: Ernst & Whinney, 1979).
11. John E. Peterson, Robert W. Doty, Ronald W. Forbes, and Donald D. Bourque, Searching for standards: Disclosure in the municipal securities market, *Duke Law Journal,* Vol. 6, 1976, p. 1188.

INDEX